IN THE SHADOW OF THE PAST:
PSYCHOLOGY
PORTRAYS THE SEXES

PATH IN PSYCHOLOGY

Published in Cooperation with Publications for the
Advancement of Theory and History in Psychology
  (PATH)

Series Editors:
David Bakan, York University
John Broughton, Teachers College, Columbia Univer-
  sity
Howard Gruber, Rutgers University
Miriam Lewin, Manhattanville College
Robert Rieber, John Jay College, CUNY, and Columbia
  University

In the Shadow of the Past: Psychology Portrays the Sexes

A SOCIAL AND INTELLECTUAL HISTORY

Miriam Lewin, editor

New York   Columbia University Press   1984

The quotation from *My Father Bertrand Russell,* by Katharine Russell Tait, which appears in article 6 is copyright © 1975 by Katharine Russell. Used by permission of Curtis Brown, Ltd.

Library of Congress Cataloging in Publication Data
Main entry under title:

In the shadow of the past: Psychology portrays the Sexes

    (Publications for the advancement of theory and history in psychology;   )
    Includes bibliographies and index.
    1. Psychology—Philosophy—History—Addresses, essays, lectures.   2. Sex Role—History—Addresses, essays, lectures.   3. Mother and child—History—Addresses, essays, lectures. I. Lewin, Miriam, 1931—   . II. Series. [DNLM: 1. Psychology—History. 2. Sex—History. 3. Identification (Psychology)—History. BF 692.2 P974]
BF38.P785 1983   155.3'09   83-10072
ISBN 0-231-05302-9 (cloth)
ISBN 0-231-05303-7 (paper)

Columbia University Press
New York   Guildford, Surrey

Clothbound editions of Columbia University Press books are Smyth-sewn and printed on permanent and durable acid-free paper.

Contents

Preface   vii

1. The Power of the Past: History and the
   Psychology of Women
   Barbara J. Harris   1

2. Freud's Heritage: Fathers and Daughters
   in German Literature (1750–1850)
   Gabriele Wickert   26

3. The Victorians, the Psychologists, and
   Psychic Birth Control
   Miriam Lewin   39

4. Leta Hollingworth: Toward a Sexless Intelligence
   Rosalind Rosenberg   77

5. Not Quite New Worlds: Psychologists' Conceptions
   of the Ideal Family in the Twenties
   J. G Morawski   97

6. "Give Me a Dozen Healthy Infants": John B. Watson's
   Popular Advice on Childrearing, Women, and the Family
   Ben Harris   126

7. "Rather Worse Than Folly?" Psychology Measures
   Femininity and Masculinity, 1: From Terman and Miles
   to the Guilfords
   Miriam Lewin   155

8. Psychology Measures Femininity and Masculinity, 2:
   From "13 Gay Men" to the Instrumental-
   Expressive Distinction
   Miriam Lewin   179

9. The Theory of Male Sex Role Identity: Its Rise and Fall,
   1936 to the Present
   Joseph H. Pleck   205

10. Mother: Social Sculptor and Trustee of the Faith
    Susan Contratto   226

11. "To Pet, Coddle, and 'Do For' ": Caretaking
    and the Concept of Maternal Instinct
    Stephanie A. Shields   256

12. Metatheoretical Influences on Conceptions of
    Human Development
    Kenneth J. Gergen and Suzanne Benack   274

13. The Study of Employed Mothers Over Half a Century
    Lois Wladis Hoffman   295

    Index   321

Preface

This is an excellent moment in history to take a fresh look at how psychologists have seen women and men, children and the family. Psychologists will agree that no thinker can be divorced from the intellectual currents of the day, which are themselves intimately linked to the major social, economic, and political issues of the time. But how, specifically, the young science of psychology was shaped and patterned by the social and intellectual currents of the nineteenth and twentieth centuries is virtually never discussed during the education of a psychologist, except in the form of origin myths. That is most unfortunate. It leaves us unable to recognize those basic assumptions that depend on now-outmoded scientific, economic, and social theories. Thus we cannot rid our discipline of a sluggish mass of ideas that impede development.

The two quotations on the second half title page, from James and Köhler, explain our purpose. This book explores the "apparently innocent suppositions" about women and men that have caused "astonishing havoc" within psychology and often among the public as well. There is a wealth of exciting and innovative recent scholarship in many disciplines, much of it feminist.

Therefore, one of our objectives is to bring psychologists in touch with advances in other fields that they have missed.

In the first article, historian Barbara Harris does a masterful job of integrating what is now known of the history of social relations between women and men over a vast time period. Gabriele Wickert, whose field is German literature, brings us a new understanding of Freud—no small accomplishment when dealing with a man already so thoroughly discussed. My article 3 sets the intellectual and social scene for the development of psychology in the nineteenth century in terms of four major currents in Victorian thought. These Victorian concepts are prime examples of detrimental "hidden presuppositions." Historian Rosalind Rosenberg shows us how critically important pioneer women graduate students and psychologists such as Leta Hollingworth were to the questioning of long-accepted beliefs about female inferiority that occurred early in the twentieth century.

Our other contributors are all psychologists. In articles 5 and 6, J. G. Morawski and Ben Harris reveal what some of psychology's most illustrious father figures thought about how women and men should relate to each other and to their children. Who can forget J. B. Watson's pithy but disastrous advice that each child should have 260 sets of foster parents in rotation, so that no one would know their own kin? Watson strongly opposed the showing of affection: "Remember that mother love is a dangerous instrument . . . which may inflict a never healing wound, make infancy unhappy, adolescence a nightmare . . . [and] wreck your adult son or daughter's vocational future and marital happiness" (1928:87, 127). Since then, too little rather than too much love has become the source of all evil, but Maternal Determinism is still an article of faith in psychology.

The next articles, by myself and by Joseph Pleck, on the history of MF tests and the male sex role identity paradigm, look at the sometimes hilarious and sometimes appalling efforts of psychologists to grapple with those two mysteries, femininity and masculinity. (I have found that audiences invariably burst out laughing at presentations of how psychologists have measured masculinity-femininity.) We think these selections demolish the existing paradigms of femininity and masculinity. Susan Contratto and Stephanie Shields, in articles 10 and 11, take a closer look at the Mystification of Motherhood and its ugly underside, Mother

Blaming. Mystification can be recognized by reliance on what the pioneer psychologist Helen Thompson Wooley (1910) would have called "sentimental rot and drivel" as a substitute for empirical connections between cause and effect and by the marked absence of adequate data. Its partner, Mother Blaming, is the tendency to hold mothers responsible for whatever goes wrong in human functioning, the family, and society. Mother Blaming has been the all-time favorite indoor sport of psychologists and of mental health professionals in general. It did not start yesterday. A few brave souls have objected. In 1916 Dr. Dorothy Mendenhall wrote: "The literature of child psychology is so muddled and contains so much twaddle that the average American mother should be warned against it."

Kenneth J. Gergen and Suzanne Benack demonstrate the intimate links between our dominant behaviorist metapsychology, which denies voluntary choice to child or adult, and Mother Blaming, the "early impact" assumption, etc. Finally, Lois Wladis Hoffman describes the history of the study of working mothers, to which she herself was a major contributor.

I wish to thank Howard Gruber, David Bakan, John Broughton, and Robert Rieber for their assistance.

If, after reading this book, you question some of the hidden presuppositions you took for granted, we shall be well satisfied.

Miriam Lewin

References

Mendenhall, Dorothy. 1916. Cited by Nancy Potishman Weiss, 1977. "Mother, the Invention of Necessity: Dr. Benjamin Spock's *Baby and Child Care." American Quarterly* (Winter) 29(5), n.26.

Wooley, Helen Thompson. 1910. "A Review of the Recent Literature on the Psychology of Sex." *Psychological Bulletin* 7:340. Cited by Stephanie Shields. 1975. "Functionalism, Darwinism and the Psychology of Women." *American Psychologist* 30:739.

Watson, John B. 1928. *Psychological Care of Infant and Child.* New York: Norton. Cited by Weiss, 1977, n.23.

The quotation from Köhler is cited in George Hartman. 1935. *Gestalt Psychology.* New York: Ronald Press, p. 295.

IN THE SHADOW OF THE PAST:
PSYCHOLOGY
PORTRAYS THE SEXES

It is astonishing what havoc is wrought in psychology by admitting at the outset apparently innocent suppositions that nevertheless contain a flaw.
William James 1890. *Principles of Psychology,* 1:224.

Psychologists in general ought to know that the main task of a new generation is to discover the *hidden* presuppositions of their fathers. It is these hidden presuppositions which usually have the most general and far-reaching effect, and this precisely because no one is aware of them at the time they are operative.
Wolfgang Köhler 1931. "Some Notes on Gestalt Psychology," *International Forum* 1:16–20.

1 The Power of the Past

History and the Psychology of Women

BARBARA J. HARRIS

I n 1933 Sigmund Freud closed his final essay on female psychology with the confession that he considered women a mystery. "If you want to know more about femininity, enquire from your own experiences of life, or turn to the poets, or wait until science can give you deeper and more coherent information" (Freud 1961: v. 22:135). Ever since, psychologists working both inside and outside the psychoanalytic tradition have responded to Freud's challenge and tried to construct a more nearly complete and satisfactory psychology of women. One of the major purposes of this book is to avoid Freud's error and to study both female behavior and the discipline concerned with it in their proper historical contexts.

The immediate historical background for understanding the psychology of contemporary American women is the nineteenth-century cult of true womanhood (Welter 1966:151–74). The cult of true womanhood defined female nature as pious, pure, domestic, and submissive and supported an economic, social, and cultural division of labor appropriate to its conception of femininity.

Although assumptions about female nature and women's actual roles have changed enormously in this country in the last hundred years, the basic debate about woman's proper sphere still takes place in terms of the issues and conflicts first articulated more than a century ago. Furthermore, because psychology emerged as a discipline in the second half of the nineteenth century, psychological theories about female personality and capabilities incorporated many of the assumptions of the cult of true womanhood. Psychology thus underscored and extended the influence of nineteenth-century ideas about women.

Despite its enormous impact, the cult of true womanhood did not completely displace far older traditions of female inferiority. Most Victorian Americans were as convinced as their medieval and renaissance forebears that women were physically and intellectually inferior to men and that this inferiority justified female subordination in the domestic and public spheres. The pervasive Western tradition of female inferiority is thus as much a part of the ideological inheritance of contemporary American women as the cult of true womanhood. Both traditions, as well as the complex interaction between them, have to be explored in order to understand the historical forces shaping female psychology.

The strength and persistence in American society of the beliefs that women are inferior, that work should be divided along gender lines, and that some form of gender hierarchy is natural and desirable can be understood only by viewing these convictions in the context of human history as a whole. For the fact is that the subordination of women is a universal or near universal condition (Rosaldo 1980:393).

The social division of labor by sex is as pervasive as male dominance and seems both to grow out of and to support the gender hierarchy. Lévi-Strauss has suggested that the purpose of the division of labor by sex is "to insure the union of men and women by making the smallest viable economic unit contain at least one man and one woman" (Rubin 1975:178). If Lévi-Strauss is correct, it is not surprising that the division of labor by sex is virtually universal, while the particular tasks assigned to males and females respectively vary enormously from one society to another. The issue is not so much what men and women do specifically but simply that they not do the same things. In practice, of course, tasks are not randomly distributed between men and women. Certain functions are assigned to females in virtually all societies, particularly the care of young children and food preparation (Rosaldo 1974:17–25; Ortner 1974:76–80; Sacks 1979:129, 133, 145).

Sherry Ortner and Michelle Rosaldo have explicitly tied this division of labor to the universal subordination of women. According to Rosaldo, the dichotomy between male and female roles creates a structural opposition between the "domestic" and "public" spheres (Rosaldo 1974:23–24; Ortner 1974:71–72). "The opposition does not *determine* cultural stereotypes or asymmetries in the evaluations of the sexes, but rather underlies them, to support a very general (and, for women, often demeaning) identification of women with domestic life and of men with public life" (Rosaldo 1974:23–24). Ortner sees women's roles in caring for young children and preparing food as a major factor in the symbolic association of the female with nature, an association that plays a major role in defining women as inferior.

The universality of the gender hierarchy has itself become a powerful force for maintaining the subordination of women. Advocates of the status quo cite anthropology and history over and over to prove that male domination is inevitable, desirable, and a biological necessity. They trace the division of male and female roles and the related subordination of women to biological differences, particularly because of the close connection between the physiological functions of childbearing and lactation and the social function of caring for young children, rather than to "social relationships in concrete (and changeable) societies" (Rosaldo 1980:393). Both Ortner and Rosaldo have warned their readers against reaching this conclusion and point out that both gender and the gender hierarchy are social — and therefore mutable — facts (Ortner 1974:71; Rosaldo 1974:22).

Despite the universality of the gender hierarchy, there are societies where relations between the sexes are far more egalitarian and the division of labor along gender lines far more flexible than the Western norm (Barstow 1978:8–9; Draper 1975:77–109; Sacks 1979; Leacock 1977:11–35). These societies grant women considerable autonomy, power, and prestige. They are significant because they underscore the enormous range in women's roles and status and the wide variation in the intensity of female subordination in human societies.

To twentieth-century American women, what is most notable about the societies described as egalitarian is their profound difference from any that exist in the West. These egalitarian cultures were based on hunting and gathering or agricultural economies with communal or kin ownership of the means of production (Brown 1975:246; Draper 1975; Sacks 1979:112–15, 130–31, 154). Western societies, on the other hand, have been characterized historically by private ownership of the means of production, the development of a class structure, and the emergence of an organized state—all factors that contribute to the subordination of women (Ortner 1978:19–36; Sacks 1979). Western divisions of labor by sex are relatively rigid and contribute to a pronounced gender hierarchy, which is accentuated by an explicit ideology of female inferiority.

Christianity, with deep roots in the patriarchal philosophy and religion of the Judaic and classical worlds, has played a key role in justifying the subordination of women. From St. Paul through the early Church Fathers and St. Thomas Aquinas, the seminal Christian thinkers asserted that Eve's sin proved women were morally inferior to men and should be subject to them. They particularly emphasized the danger women posed to men as sexual tempters and the consequent necessity of confining women to the home and channeling their sexuality into childbearing.

St. Paul: "The head of the woman is the man. . . . For the man is not of the woman: but the woman of the man. Neither was the man created for the woman: but the woman for the man." "Let your women keep silence in the churches: for it is not permitted unto them to speak." "I suffer not a woman to teach, nor to usurp authority over the man. . . . For Adam was first formed, then Eve. And Adam was not deceived, but the woman being deceived was in the transgression. Notwithstanding she shall be saved in childbearing. . . ." "Wives, submit yourselves unto your own husbands, as unto the Lord. For the husband is the head of the wife" (O'Faolain and Martines 1973:128–29).

Chrysostom: "The woman taught once, and ruined all. On this account . . . let her not teach." "God hath given her no small consolation, that of childbearing. . . . By these means women will have no small reward on their account, because they have trained up wrestlers for the service of Christ" (*Ibid.*, p. 129).

St. Augustine: "The woman together with her own husband is the image of God . . . but when she is referred to separately in her quality of helpmate, which regards the woman herself alone, there is not the image of God; but as regards the man alone, he is the image of God as fully and completely as when the woman too is joined with him" (*Ibid.*, p. 130).

Tertullian: "And so a veil must be drawn over a beauty so dangerous as to have brought scandal into heaven itself. . . ." "Wear rags and mourning, weep and show an Eve plunged in penance, trying to expiate by her contrite appearance the disgrace of that first crime and the shame of having brought ruin to humanity. In pain shall you bring forth children, woman, and you shall turn to your husband and he shall rule over you. And do you not know that you are Eve? God's sentence hangs still over all your sex and His punishment weights down upon you. You are the devil's gateway" (*Ibid.*, 132).

St. Thomas Aquinas: "As regards the individual nature, woman is defective and misbegotten, for the active power in the male seed tends to the production of a perfect likeness according to the masculine sex; while the production of woman comes from defect in the active power, or from some material indisposition, or even from some external influence. . . ." "For the good of order would have been wanting in the human family if some were not governed by others wiser than themselves. So by such a kind of subjection woman is naturally subject to man, because in man the discernment of reason predominates" (Bell 1973:122).

Philosophers and scientists buttressed the view that women were inferior by depicting them as defective or incomplete men. Aristotle, whose philosophy dominated Western thought until the scientific revolution, wrote, "The female, in fact, is female on account of inability of a sort . . . we should look upon the female state as being as it were a deformity, though one which occurs in the ordinary course of nature" (Bell 1973:18). Even after the development of modern science and the more egalitarian natural philosophy of the Enlightenment in the seventeenth and eighteenth centuries, the conviction that women were imperfect men persisted. The two most influential scientists of the nineteenth century, Charles Darwin and Sigmund Freud, perpetuated this notion. Darwin believed women were less highly evolved than men:

with women the powers of intuition, of rapid perception, and perhaps of imitation, are more strongly marked than in man; but some, at least, of these faculties are characteristic of the lower races, and therefore of a past and lower state of civilization. . . . The chief distinction in the intellectual powers of the two sexes is shown by man's attaining to a higher eminence, in whatever he takes up, than can woman . . . although men do not now fight for their wives, and this form of selection has passed away, yet, during manhood, they generally undergo a severe struggle in order to maintain themselves and their families; and this will tend to keep up or even increase their mental powers, and, as a consequence, the present inequality between the sexes (Darwin 1967:873–75).

Freud's entire account of women's psychic development depended on his arbitrary definition of them as human beings without penises. As Margaret Mead has cogently pointed out, he might just as accurately have defined women as human beings with wombs (Mead 1979:56). According to Freud, this defect made women passive, narcissistic, and masochistic and inhibited the development of their superegos or consciences. Their relatively weak libido or sex drive (itself rooted in penis envy) and their lesser capacity for sublimation explained women's intellectual inferiority and negligible contribution to civilization (Freud 1961: v. 19, 248–58; v. 21, 225–43; v. 22, 112–35).

Although Western thought remained overwhelmingly misogynist before the era of the Enlightenment and French Revolution, there were periodic challenges to the view that women were inferior to men and more prone to evil. Boccaccio published *De Claris Mulieribus* (*Concerning Famous Women*), containing the biographies of 104 outstanding women, between 1360 and 1374. It was the first such collection in Western literature. In 1399 Christine de Pisan, a woman of Italian birth who lived at the French court, started the first literary quarrel in French history by writing a poem that attacked the misogyny of the second part of *Le Roman de la Rose*. Later, she wrote *The City of Women* to justify her sex. Christine drew on history to fill an imaginary city with women rulers, female scientists and inventors, virtuous women, and female saints.

Once Christine de Pisan had opened the subject, the debate about women remained a perennial theme in European literature. During the Italian Renaissance, one of the most famous presentations of the debate appeared in Book 3 of Castiglione's *Book of the Courtier* in a discussion between Guiliano d'Medici and Gasparo Pallavicino. Although Castiglione did not indicate his position openly, his sympathies seem to be with d'Medici, who was defending women. In England, the sixteenth and seventeenth centuries saw the publication of scores of books and pamphlets attacking and defending the female sex. The *querelle des femmes* occupied French writers in the same period. In the sixteenth century the debate in France focused on women's moral worth; in the seventeenth century on the social influence they exercised through their participation and leadership in the salons (Lougee 1976:3). None of these debates were resolved or succeeded in destroying the traditional arguments of Western misogyny. However, they did break the virtual unanimity about female nature that had previously characterized European thought.

The belief in women's intellectual inferiority and the actual division of labor between the sexes worked together to justify the exclusion of females from the formal educational structure until well into the nineteenth century. European universities founded in the middle ages educated men for professions closed to the opposite sex. Cathedral and grammar schools prepared boys for entrance into the universities.

In the early middle ages, convents were often important intellectual and educational centers. Double monasteries headed by women, which became great religious houses, were founded in Anglo-Saxon England at Whitby, Thanet, Ely, Barking, and Wimbourne. One of the most important of the abbesses of these institutions, Hilda of Whitby (d. 680), was the patron of the poet Caedmon. Gandersheim, a convent founded in Germany around 852, became a major literary center by the tenth century. A nun at Gandersheim, Hrotswitha (d. 1002), wrote the first plays in Western literature since the collapse of Rome. Hrotswitha, who knew Latin and was well educated in classical literature and philosophy, modeled her plays after the Roman playwright Terence. Another German nun, Hildegarde of Bingen (1098–1178), was a major figure in the intellectual life of her era. Her books on secular subjects included two major treatises on medicine and a description of nature called *Liber Divinorum Operum.*

By the twelfth century, however, female monasticism was entering a long period of decline. Abbesses ceased to be among the most learned or influential religious figures of their age, and standards in convent schools deteriorated significantly. The reasons for this unfortunate change were complex. The Gregorian reforms of the eleventh and twelfth centuries emphasized the monastic duty of reciting the liturgy and the intercessory value of monastic masses. Since only men could perform these functions, the monastic orders founded in connection with the reform movement, the Cluniacs and Cistercians, excluded women and tended to be very misogynist. The reformers' insistence on clerical celibacy also reduced women's influence in the church by reawakening suspicion of female sexuality and encouraging popular hostility toward the double monasteries that had played such an important role in the spiritual life of the early Middle Ages. The Gregorian reforms also undermined the role of lay patronage within the church, which severely reduced the religious influence of aristocratic women as a class. These were the women who had founded and headed the great early medieval convents. Finally, the center of intellectual life in the West was shifting from monasteries to the universities in the twelfth and thirteenth centuries.

From this period convents increasingly functioned as little more than fashionable boarding schools for upper class girls (Stock 1978:23–24; Power 1975:80–82; McMahon 1947:139–45). Particularly serious was the disappearance of Latin from their curricula, which meant that fewer and fewer women could read the language of serious medieval scholarship. Heloise (twelfth century), Marie de France (thirteenth century), and Christine de Pisan (fourteenth-fifteenth century), all of whom had mastered Latin, were rare exceptions among their sex. Much more typical was Margaret Beaufort (1441?–1509), one of the great patrons of education in late medieval England, who complained that "in her youth she had not given to her the understanding of Latin" (Fisher 1906:16).

The situation improved little in the early modern period. In Catholic countries, the impulse of the Counter-Reformation frequently led to the foundation of teaching orders like the Ursulines in France and Italy, but their standards of secular education were not very high. When Louis XIV's second wife, Mme. de Maintenon, reformed the Maison Royale de Saint-Louis at St. Cyr, which became the model for women's education in eighteenth-century France, her educational program placed much more emphasis on piety and training in the domestic arts than on book learning or intellectual achievement. The curriculum consciously excluded humanist, classical studies and embodied Mme. de Maintenon's conviction that too much reading was dangerous for women.

The situation was not much better across the Channel in

Protestant England. There the few girls' schools beyond the elementary level emphasized fashionable accomplishments such as fancy needlework, French, music, and dancing. In 1694 Mary Astell proposed that a college be established to educate single women. Her goal, however, was to create "pious and prudent Ladies," not female "walking libraries" (Kinnaird 1979:64–65). Three years later Daniel Defoe included a plan for a female college in his *Essay Upon Projects*. His limited conception of what would constitute an improvement shows how poor most women's education was. Defoe's curriculum included reading, music, dancing, French, Italian, and the art of conversation.

The lack of adequate schools did not entirely deprive women of higher education. As Mary Beard pointed out, to measure women's education by the availability of formal institutions to teach them is to distort their history seriously (Beard 1969:59–60; Beard 1944:A-9, box 2, folder 29). Between the twelfth and nineteenth centuries the most advanced female education took place in the home under the aegis of parents and tutors. Many of the women who achieved the highest reaches of learning were largely self-taught.

During the high Middle Ages, aristocratic women like Eleanor of Aquitaine and Marie de Champagne were among the most important patrons of literature. In the thirteenth century, Marie de France knew Latin well enough to contemplate a career as a translator and was a leading author of Arthurian romances. Indeed, some historians believe that because learning was unnecessary to achieve the masculine ideal of the knight, even bare literacy was more common among women than men in the feudal classes (Beard 1931:129; Putnam 1910:119–20; Langdon-Davis 1927:151; McNamara and Wemple 1977:10). Medieval cookbooks and books on herbal medicine certainly assumed that aristocratic women could read.

During the Renaissance, exceptional women all over Europe received first-rate humanist educations. Unlike their medieval predecessors, these women did learn Latin and occasionally Greek. Exclusion from the universities was not as great a disadvantage as during the Middle Ages, since the conservatism of the universities meant that the new learning flourished outside their walls. Most of the learned women of the Renaissance came from royal or aristocratic families. Women such as Cecilia and Elizabetta Gonzago, Isabella d'Este, Elizabeth I of England, Lady Jane Grey, and Marguerite of Navarre studied with the leading humanists of the day. Their courts became centers of learning, while they personally functioned as important patrons of both literature and the arts. A few women from more modest backgrounds, such as Olympia Morato of Ferrara, Louise Labé of Lyons, and Margaret More of England, also scaled the heights of Renaissance learning.

It is difficult to account for the appearance of the highly educated Renaissance woman. In its own way, humanist education was as professionally oriented as medieval education in the schools of medicine, law, and theology. Humanists used their knowledge of the classics to earn a living as teachers, civil servants, secretaries, writers, and rhetoricians and claimed that humanist studies would make all men better citizens. This orientation toward the public and professional spheres necessarily excluded women.

At the same time, however, the humanists did believe that on an individual level women would benefit from studying the classics. They particularly emphasized the value of the humanist curriculum in teaching ethics but also noted that women who knew the classics would be more urbane, cultivated, and entertaining wives. Furthermore, since aristocratic women played an important role as patrons of literature and art, the humanists had a professional interest in winning them over to the new learning.

Leonardo Bruni's essay on female education, written in the form of a letter to Baptista di Montrefelto, illustrates the way in which Italian humanists created a program that neatly balanced their commitment to give women a classical education with their ideas about the female social role. Bruni had no doubt that women were capable of mastering Latin and thought they should be given the opportunity to do so. He recommended a wide variety of pagan and Christian authors as suitable reading in that language, particularly emphasizing religious and moral works. For practical reasons, he thought women should also study elementary arithmetic, geometry, and astrology. Among the wide range of studies that "conduce to the profitable enjoyment of life," he singled out poetry, history, and oratory. The only subject in the humanist curriculum he considered totally inappropriate for females was rhetoric, a discipline specifically designed to equip the individual for action in the public sphere.

In the centuries following the Renaissance, roughly from 1550 to the outbreak of the French Revolution, somewhat contradictory trends affected the higher education of women outside the institutional structure. On one hand, the coming of the Reformation and Counter-Reformation increased suspicion of secular learning, particularly in the case of women, whose moral frailties were once again highlighted. In England, for example, fathers were much more reluctant to teach their daughters Latin in the seventeenth century than in the sixteenth. There was also much more suspicion of the learned lady. Margaret Cavendish, Duchess of Newcastle, probably the most erudite woman in seventeenth-century England, was popularly known as "mad Madge" (Goulianos 1974:55). The learned lady was a stock figure of ridicule in Restoration drama, while in the eighteenth century the term "bluestocking" was used to deprecate women with intellectual aspirations. In France, Molière's *Les Femmes Savantes* reflected a similar hostility toward women with intellectual pretensions. Although the development of the salon provided women with an important role in the French literary world, it did not foster their intellectual achievement. The women who ran the salons were more skilled as hostesses and conversationalists than as thinkers. The gatherings in their homes stimulated the pens of the men they entertained rather than their own.

Despite the reaction against the Renaissance ideal of the learned lady, there were highly educated, intellectual women in seventeenth- and eighteenth-century Europe. In England, for example, Katherine Philips, Anne Finch (Countess of Winchelsea), Elizabeth Elstob, Lady Mary Wortley Montagu, Anne Killigrew, and Catherine Macauley come to mind. This period also saw the appearance of the first professional female author, Aphra Behn. Significantly, women increasingly published arguments for improved female education. Among the most important were Mary Astell's *Serious Proposal* (1694), Bathsua Makin's *An Essay to Revive the Antient Education of Gentlewomen* (1673), Catherine Macaulay's *Letters on Education* (1790), and Mary Wollstonecraft's *Vindication of the Rights of Women* (1792). During this same period the first woman received a doctorate from a European university; Elena Cornaro received her Ph.D. from the University of Padua in 1678.

The pattern of exclusion and discrimination that characterized women's education in traditional Western societies derived from the convergence of an ideology of female inferiority and a rigid division of labor by sex that closed the professions to women. Limited educational opportunities simultaneously reflected and reinforced female subordination. Although exceptional women from the Middle Ages on surmounted the obstacles to acquiring first-rate educations and demonstrated their intellectual capabilities, women as a group were severely disadvantaged, with far higher illiteracy rates than men. The statistics for colonial New England, which conformed to European attitudes and practices in the area of female education, illustrate the size of the literacy gap between the sexes. In the seventeenth century, about half of the men and a third of the women could sign their names; by the late eighteenth century, the figure for men had risen to 80 percent, while that for women stagnated at 40 to 45 percent (Cott 1977:102–3). The gap was not closed until around 1830, the cumulative result of improvements in female education that began around 1790 (Kerber 1980:190–93).

Like the educational structure, the law in Western society both reflected and reinforced women's subordinate status. Although the law varied from one country or region to another and from one period to another, it invariably embodied the assumption that women were inferior to men and should be subject to them. The legal system most relevant to the historical experience of American women was, of course, the English common law, which was established in the colonies and formed the basis of the American legal system after independence. That women were deprived of political rights and any role in the courts goes without saying. Inheritance laws favored males by preferring sons to daughters and husbands to wives, although female heirs did receive preference over males more distantly related to the deceased.

What was far more important in most women's lives was the common law doctrine that a husband and wife were one and that one was the husband. In essence wives ceased to exist as separate persons before the law. They had no power to own or dispose of property (whether acquired before or after marriage), to control their earnings, to make contracts, to make wills, or to exercise custody rights over their children. Oddly enough, in a society that considered marriage the ultimate goal of all female lives, single women retained these rights because they escaped the status of femme couvert. To make matters even worse for wives, there was almost no way of securing a divorce in the United States until the reforms of the 1830s and 1840s or in England until the Divorce Act of 1857 (O'Neill 1973:20–22; Kerber 1980: ch. 6). The overall effect was to make St. Paul's view of the proper relationship between husbands and wives the law: "For the husband is the head of the wife, even as Christ is the head of the church" (Ephesians 5:22–23).

In *Woman as Force in History,* Mary Beard suggested that equity mitigated women's disabilities under the common law long before the reforms of the mid-nineteenth century (Beard 1962; ch. 6). According to Beard, the equity courts enforced trust funds and prenuptial agreements or marriage settlements, which gave wives control of their property. In fact, Beard greatly overestimated the significance of these equitable remedies in either England or America (Carroll 1976:26; Degler 1974:68–69; Salmon 1979, ch. 4; Kerber 1980: 141–42; Norton 1980:47; Gampel 1981). Most women were not aware that such legal devices existed. Furthermore, they needed the consent and cooperation of their fathers or guardians and future husbands to take advantage of them. In practice only a relatively small number of legally sophisticated, affluent families created trusts to protect their daughters, while the conservative and narrow rulings of the equity courts frequently undermined the effectiveness of the small number of trusts executed.

The doctrine of female inferiority reflected in the educational and legal systems of the traditional West rested on a well-defined, gender-based, division of labor that played a primary role in subjecting women. A separation between the public and private domains marked one of the major divisions between female and male functions, although the specific activities performed in the respective areas varied over time and from place to place. In addition, men and women performed different tasks within the private sphere, the primary location of the economy until the Industrial Revolution.

After the collapse of the Roman Empire, there was a long period when the distinction between the public and private domains ceased to exist. During this period, the early Middle Ages, many functions that we normally think of as public—for instance, collecting taxes or administering justice—were thought of as property rights attached to land and were exercised in the interest of the owner. Since the legal customs of the Germanic tribes who controlled Europe allowed women to inherit, own, and manage land, upper-class women could exercise a considerable amount of power and influence. The development of feudalism, which connected land ownership to the performance of military service; the accompanying constriction of female rights of inheritance; and the reemergence of the public sphere in the form of feudal monarchy converged to change the situation to women's disadvantage. From the twelfth century until the feminist agitation of the nineteenth, the expansion of the public domain and the growth of the state worked in tandem to reduce female power even in the ruling classes (McNamara and Wemple 1977:111–15). Thus, the history of the West illustrates a number of generalizations that appear frequently in the anthropological literature, particularly the connection between the development of the state and the public sphere on one hand and the accentuation of male dominance and female subordination on the other.

Except for international trade and finance, the Western economy was centered in the home until the Industrial Revolution. Most people worked as members of a family in small-scale units that combined the functions of production, consumption, and reproduction. The family economy required the labor and cooperation of men and women because a gender-based division of labor was the rule. Under normal circumstances males and females did not perform the same tasks (Tilly and Scott 1978:43–51). The location of the workplace in or near the home meant that wives could combine their work easily with childcare and such traditional female domestic tasks as cooking and baking.

Beginning with Alice Clark's classic study, many historians have argued that women's crucial role in the family economy gave them considerable power and authority in their households (Clark 1968; Tilly and Scott 1978: introduction & ch. 3; Lerner 1976). In their view, the Industrial Revolution, which separated women from their productive role by taking work out of the home, caused a major deterioration in women's status. Although industrialization certainly weakened women's position by increasing their economic dependence, an overly positive picture of female status in preindustrial society is inaccurate. Studies such as Olwen Hufton's (1975) and Mary Beth Norton's (1980) illuminate the complex reasons why women were not able to translate their economic contribution to the family into power, authority, or personal autonomy (Hufton 1975).

Central to the female situation was the near universal assumption that women were inferior to men and the accompanying institutionalization of their secondary status. Furthermore, the constant reiteration in religious and political doctrine that the husband was the divinely appointed head of the household and that the wife's chief virtue was obedience to his will influenced the behavior and self-perceptions of both sexes (Norton 1980:61–65). Within the family economy, for instance, wives were invariably seen as their husband's assistants, however important their contribution to the household (Tilly and Scott 1978:48). The lack of legal or political rights and negligible educations also encouraged female dependence. Moreover, because women were considered inferior, their labor was not valued as highly as men's, even though it was crucial to the survival of the family. Employers everywhere paid males two or three times as much as females (Tilly and Scott 1978:31, 45; Hufton 1975:13). Single women rarely earned enough to be self-supporting (Tilly and Scott 1978:31; Hufton 1975:2; Norton 1980:41–42). Finally, the burden of childbearing in a precontraceptive age increased female dependence immeasurably. Pregnancy and childbirth often impaired women's health and ability to work. Even more important, the presence of children reduced women's power vis-à-vis their husbands because they ultimately felt a greater responsibility for the children's survival, as Hufton shows in her poignant discussion of the "economy of expedients" among the poor in eighteenth-century France (Hufton 1975:19–22).

Preindustrial or traditional Western society was therefore a clear illustration of a complex human culture that subordinated women. Female subjection was reflected in the gender-based division of labor, the exclusion of women from the public or political realm, the educational and legal systems, and the doctrine of female inferiority. At the same time, exceptional women from the Middle Ages on showed over and over how wrong conventional estimates of female capabilities and achievements were, while women's role in the family and economy made them as important as men in the survival and growth of Western culture.

Women's position became even more complex and difficult

to generalize about after the Industrial Revolution. From the female point of view the major effect of industrialization was to separate the workplace from the home. This created a new contradiction in women's lives by making it difficult or impossible for them to combine their roles as mothers with their roles as producers. In addition, since the development of factories first affected the textile industry, industrialization had a major impact on single women, who had made their largest contribution to the family economy by spinning.

Women's response to the movement of work out of the home varied with their age, marital status, and class. During the nineteenth century, native-born, white American wives rarely entered the labor force unless their financial circumstances were desperate. The first generation of factory workers was made up of young single women from farms in stagnating or declining rural areas. Beginning with the Irish in the 1840s, successive groups of immigrants displaced them in the mills. Middle-class single women who sought employment turned, not to the factories, but to the expanding profession of teaching and, in the last decades of the nineteenth century, to sales, clerical, and social work. Native-born, white wives did not enter the labor force in large numbers until after 1900, with the real breakthrough postponed until the second World War and subsequent decades. Among immigrants and blacks, poverty forced wives to seek paid employment in large numbers at a much earlier period. Even so, many immigrant groups preferred sending their children to work rather than their wives and mothers, even if this meant curtailing their offspring's education.

Although the Industrial Revolution gradually changed the place where women worked, it had little effect on one of the most fundamental characteristics of any society characterized by male dominance: a gender-based division of labor. The American labor force is overwhelmingly segregated by sex, with the vast majority of women doing "women's work" alongside other women. In 1980, just under 50 percent of the female labor force worked as salespersons, clerical workers, beauticians, and waitresses. More than half of all female professional and technical workers were teachers and nurses (*Spokeswoman* 1980:6). Childrearing and housework are still predominately female responsibilities.

Consistent with women's lower status, female workers earn

significantly less than men, another continuity with the preindustrial economy. In 1980 the average woman in full-time employment earned 59 percent of that earned by the average man, a statistic that has been remarkably (and dishearteningly) static since 1910 (*Spokeswoman* 1980:6). The Equal Pay Act of 1963 has made little difference thus far.

The competitive capitalism of the Industrial Revolution and the separation of the home from the workplace affected attitudes toward women in complex and even contradictory ways. By the middle of the nineteenth century, three distinct views of female nature and women's proper social roles were competing for public approval. The belief in female inferiority continued to find defenders, even among influential thinkers and scientists, such as Darwin and Freud. This position gained enormous strength from its long history and served as the rationale for those who openly favored the retention of the gender hierarchy.

Much more central to nineteenth-century thought, however, was the view of women known as the cult of true womanhood. This set of ideas directly reflected the impact of the Industrial Revolution on female lives. At its base was the distinction between the home and the economy and the association of women with the former and of men with the latter. The dichotomy between the male and female spheres extended to their respective natures. Women were virtuous, passionless, passive, weak, submissive, self-sacrificing, and intuitive; men were inclined to vice, lusty, strong, domineering, self-assertive, rational, and objective. Women's reproductive functions, particularly their menstrual cycles, placed them closer to nature than men and endowed them with relatively weak intellects, the human faculty considered to be the most highly evolved and, therefore, furthest from the natural (Welter 1976:71–72).

The function of the home was to provide a haven from the materialistic, competitive, and ruthless environment of early industrial capitalism. In an enclosed world free of vice and conflict, virtuous women would heal the physical and spiritual wounds their husbands sustained in the marketplace. Clean, orderly, cheerful homes and attentive, obedient wives would encourage men to repress their vicious instincts and resist the temptations of bar and brothel. Such a home would also shelter women from the dangers of the world and preserve their ignorance of ugly political, economic, and social realities. With an astounding inconsistency, the Victorians assumed that only complete innocence would prevent the irreversible fall of the morally superior sex. Above all, women fulfilled their ultimate destiny as mothers in the home. On their success in raising virtuous, Christian children depended the whole future of civilization.

The cult of true womanhood appealed to the American middle classes because it provided women with important new functions and sources of self-respect at a time when industrialization was eroding their traditional economic roles. In a culture where wealth was the measure of social power and prestige, middle-class women were being deprived of direct access to money by the movement of production from the home, a situation that made them increasingly powerless as more and more goods and services were exchanged on the market. Middle-class and upper class women were reduced to consuming and displaying their husbands' wealth, a function that underscored their economic dependence. In this context the cult of true womanhood provided an escape by denigrating male economic activity as unethical and elevating women as the moral saviors of society. Furthermore, the cult of true womanhood emphasized women's unique importance by focusing on their role as mothers. The home presided over by the virtuous wife and mother stood out as a symbol of stability in a nation where rapid demographic, economic, and political change was creating enormous personal and social insecurity.

The cult of true womanhood contained both traditional and new elements. It supported the age-old authority of the husband and father as head of the household, insisting that wifely obedience was consistent with women's submissive, self-abnegating nature. It also perpetuated the belief in female intellectual inferiority. On the other hand, the assertion that women were morally superior to men turned the image of the female as Eve completely upside down. This view of female nature was closely related to the new emphasis on the centrality of woman's role as mother.

During the preindustrial era, women spent relatively little time and energy raising children. Despite the high birthrate, their primary commitment was to their responsibilities in the family economy (Tilly and Scott 1978:58–59; Aries 1962). Among the poor and working classes, the wife's contribution was necessary to provide the family with the barest subsistence, and among artisans and retail merchants, to ensure the success of the family business. Even among the wealthy classes, wives were too busy managing large households and participating in the social activities of the elite to devote themselves to their offspring. The practice of boarding infants with wetnurses for long periods shows how unimportant the young were to the family unit. Upper class parents employed wetnurses primarily for their own convenience; artisans and workers to allow the mother to continue as a full-time worker. Moreover, the educational system encouraged children of all classes to leave home between the ages of ten and fifteen (Harris 1978:51–53). High infant and child mortality rates and large families combined with these economic conditions to discourage parents from making a heavy emotional commitment or investment of time in their children.

Economic and religious developments combined to change these patterns in the seventeenth and eighteenth centuries. The growth of an upwardly mobile commercial bourgeoisie led to the gradual exclusion of wives from business and domestic production. The transformation of bourgeoise from helpmates into ladies removed the economic obstacle to the expansion of women's role as mother (George 1973:152–77; Hill 1962: ch. 14). In the same period positive ideological pressures in this direction were growing. Both the Reformation and Counter-Reformation had created a strong demand among influential religious and educational groups for the moral purification and discipline of society. In England and the colonies, the Puritans voiced this demand. They considered the family an essential unit in their program for the regeneration of society (Morgan 1966). In this context childrearing became more and more important; only those reared properly would grow into godly adults. As the young moved toward the center of the family, the role of adults as parents expanded proportionately. Although in theory parents shared responsibility for their children, the withdrawal of bourgeoise from the economy meant that in practice mothers rather than fathers assumed the growing burden of childrearing.

The separation of the home from the workplace during the Industrial Revolution simply accentuated and encouraged a process already under way in both England and the colonies.

The belief that women were morally superior to men provided the ideological justification for giving women responsibility for the moral education of the young. Since bourgeoise culture tended to equate virtue with sexual innocence and the confinement of all erotic activity to marriage, the new view of women primarily involved a transformation of ideas about female sexuality. The image of Eve as the archetypal female gave way to the passionless and passive heroine of the late eighteenth-century novel: Clarissa, Pamela, Evelina.

The new female stereotype grew out of the Puritan insistence on confining sexuality to marriage and eliminating the kind of tolerance of sin in this area characteristic of traditional Catholic culture. Above all, the Puritans called for an end to the double standard. To facilitate achieving their goal, they advocated marriage for love and encouraged parents to follow their children's inclinations when they arranged matches. In practice, the Puritans learned that it was much more difficult to force men than women to be sexually virtuous. Puritans were particularly sensitive to the complacent vice of aristocratic males—a product of their reaction to the openly libertine courts of James I and Charles II, their hostility to Cavalier culture during the era of the Civil War, and their resentment of the sexual threat upper class men posed to the virtue of their own wives and daughters. While male sexuality loomed larger and larger as a threat to private and public morality, women appeared increasingly as their innocent, passionless victims or saviors, as Richardson's novels, *Clarissa* and *Pamela*, demonstrate. The best remedy for male vice was marriage to a virtuous woman, who would inspire her husband to confine his erotic impulses to proper channels. The virtuous wife was also, of course, preeminently suited for the exalted role of motherhood (Watt 1957; ch. 5).

Nineteenth-century industrial society gave birth to egalitarian feminism, as well as to the cult of true womanhood. Where the cult of true womanhood built its view of women's proper role on a sharp dichotomy between male and female nature, feminism asserted that the sexes were essentially equal and alike except for the specific area of reproduction. They completely rejected the misogynist tradition of female inferiority. Feminists demanded an end to the gender hierarchy and the social division of labor by sex. The Seneca Falls Declaration of 1848 is the most compelling statement of this kind of feminism. This document, which paraphrases the Declaration of Independence, makes clear the ideo-logical roots of egalitarian feminism in the Enlightenment and American revolutionary tradition.

While Enlightenment political theory provided the philo-sophical framework for feminists, their fundamental grievance was about the effect of the Industrial Revolution on women. They would not accept the loss of power, reduced range of activities, and di-minished self-esteem that resulted when women were relegated to a domestic sphere stripped of its economic functions. Their solution to the problems that industrialization posed for women was to demand equality in every area of society. Their program posed a radical challenge to proponents of the cult of true wom-anhood, as well as to defenders of female inferiority.

The ferment and reform of the 1830s and 1840s provided the immediate catalyst for the emergence of a feminist move-ment. A number of the changes of these decades underscored women's inferior status and sharpened their sense of grievance. The spread of public elementary education and first-rate female seminaries ended illiteracy among white females but at the same time increased the anger and frustration of those who wanted to go on from these schools to colleges and the learned professions. Female teachers in the public schools experienced their lower sta-tus in a particularly bitter way when they discovered they were paid a third to a half of that paid their male colleagues (Harris 1978:79–80). The extension of the vote to virtually all white males showed the predominance of gender over other social categories and represented a relative decline in the position of females as a group. Most important, work in the radical abolitionist movement awakened women to the parallel between their status vis-à-vis men and the status of slaves vis-à-vis their owners. The number of women who became feminists after active work as abolitionists is impressive; abolitionism was truly the seedbed of the early wom-en's movement.

Egalitarian feminist ideology was never as popular as the cult of true womanhood. By the last quarter of the nineteenth cen-tury feminists tacitly admitted the limited appeal of their view of female nature by exploiting the doctrine of the morally superior woman and mother. They pointed out the absurdity of excluding the sex recognized for its virtue from the political process. They also argued that the extension of women's concerns as mothers and housekeepers to the public sphere would create an irresistible force against corruption and vice and in favor of reforms to solve the massive problems created by urban slums, deplorable working conditions in factories and sweatshops, and large-scale immigration. The new ideological emphasis broadened the appeal of certain aspects of the woman's rights program but at the same time necessitated a retreat from the demand for change in areas (for example, divorce and the relations between husbands and wives) where feminist ideology was incompatible with the cult of true womanhood (Kraditor 1971; Leach 1980:part 1, ch. 5).

Whatever the theoretical basis fo their argument, feminists had only a limited success. They unquestionably played a role in opening higher education and the professions to women and in the passage of legal reforms, beginning with the Married Women's Property Acts of the antebellum period. After 70 years of arduous and expensive campaigning, they succeeded in winning the vote. Nonetheless, neither the first nor the second woman's movement succeeded in fundamentally changing the gender hierarchy or sexual division of labor in the United States. Few employed women hold well-paid, prestigious positions. Most work for low wages in female sectors of the economy. Women's economic weakness perpetuates their powerlessness in their personal relations with men, the family, and the political arena.

On an ideological level, the three views of female nature and women's proper sphere discussed here still compete for popular support and the influence to shape public policy. The relative weakness of feminism stems from the fact that the cult of true womanhood appears to be the traditional, and therefore presumptively correct, view of women, while the long history and near universality of female subordination and the sexual division of labor encourage support for the gender hierarchy. Ideological confusion, the persistent contradiction between women's secondary status and our egalitarian political heritage, and the long history of female subordination all influence the way contemporary American women act, think, and feel and the way experts conceptualize these matters. The psychology of women is thus, like everything else in human society, a product of the past.

References

Aries, Philippe. 1962. *Centuries of Childhood: A Social History of Family Life.* New York: Vintage.

Barstow, Anne. 1978. "The Uses of Archaelogy for Women's History: James Mellaart's Work on the Neolithic Goddess at Catal Huyuk." *Feminist Studies* (October) 4(3):7–18.

Beard, Mary. 1931. *On Understanding Women.* New York: Longmans.

——1944. Letter to W. K. Jordan June 10. Schlesinger Library. Mary R. Beard Papers. A-9, box 2, folder 29.

—— 1962. *Woman as Force in History.* New York: Collier.

—— 1969. *America Through Women's Eyes.* New York: Greenwood.

Bell, Susan G. 1973. *Women: From the Greeks to the French Revolution.* Stanford: Stanford University Press.

Bridenthal, Renate and Claudia Koonz, eds. 1977. *Becoming Visible: Women in European History.* Boston: Houghton Mifflin.

Brown, Judith K. 1975. "Iroquois Women: An Ethnohistoric Note." In Reiter, *q.v.,* pp. 235–51.

Carroll, Berenice A. 1976. "Mary Beard's Woman As Force in History: A Critique." In Carroll, *Liberating Women's History,* pp. 26–41. Urbana: University of Illinois Press.

Clark, Alice. 1968. *Working Life of Women in the Seventeenth Century.* New York: Augustus M. Kelley.

Cott, Nancy F. 1977. *The Bonds of Womanhood.* New Haven: Yale University Press.

Darwin, Charles. 1967. *The Descent of Man.* New York: Modern Library.

Degler, Carl N. 1974. "*Woman as Force in History* by Mary R. Beard." *Daedalus* (Winter) 103(1):67–73.

Draper, Patricia. 1975. "!Kung Women: Contrasts in Sexual Egalitarianism in Foraging and Sedentary Contexts." In Reiter, *q.v.,* pp. 77–109.

Fisher, John. 1906. *A Mornynge Remembrance, Had at the Moneth Mynde of Margaret, Countess of Rychemonde.* London: Essex House.

Freud, Sigmund. 1961. *The Standard Edition of the Complete Psychological Works of Sigmund Freud,* v. 19, 248–58; v. 21, 225–43; v. 22, 112–35. London: Hogarth Press.

Gampel, Gwen. 1981. "The Planter's Wife Revisited: The Legal Status of 17th Century Maryland Married Women." Paper delivered at Fifth Berkshire Conference on the History of Women. June 1981. Vassar College.

George, Margaret. 1973. "From 'Goodwife' to 'Mistress': The Transformation of the Female in Bourgeois Culture." *Science and Society* (Summer) 37:152–77.

Goulianos, Joan. 1974. *By a Woman Writt.* Baltimore: Penguin.

Harris, Barbara. 1978. *Beyond Her Sphere.* Westport, Conn.: Greenwood.

Hill, Christopher. 1962. "Clarissa Harlowe and Her Times." In *Puritanism and Revolution.* London: Mercury, ch. 14.

Hufton, Olwen. 1975. "Women and the Family Economy in Eighteenth Century France." *French Historical Studies* (Spring) 19(1):1–22.

Kerber, Linda. 1980. *Women of the Republic, Intellect and Ideology in Revolutionary America.* Chapel Hill, N.C.: University of North Carolina.

Kinnaird, Joan. 1979. "Mary Astell and the Conservative Contribution to English Feminism." *The Journal of British Studies* (Fall) 19(1):53–75.

Kraditor, Aileen. 1968. *Up From the Pedestal.* Chicago: Quadrangle.

—— 1971. *The Ideas of the Suffrage Movement, 1890–1920.* New York: Doubleday.

Langdon-Davies, John. 1927. *A Short History of Women.* New York: Blue Ribbon.

Leach, William. 1980. *True Love and Perfect Union, The Feminist Reform of Sex and Society.* New York: Basic Books.

Leacock, Eleanor. 1977. "Women in Egalitarian Societies." In Bridenthal and Koonz, *q.v.,* pp. 11–35.

Lerner, Gerda. 1976. "The Lady and the Mill Girl: Changes in the Status of Women in the Age of Jackson." In Jean Friedman and William Shade, eds. *Our American Sisters: Women in American Life and Thought,* 2nd ed., pp. 120–32. Boston: Allyn and Bacon.

Lougee, Carolyn. 1976. *Le Paradis des Femmes: Women, Salons and Social Stratification in Seventeenth-Century France.* Princeton: Princeton University Press.

McMahon, Clara. 1947. *Education in Fifteenth-Century England.* Baltimore: Johns Hopkins Press.

McNamara, Jo Ann and Suzanne Wemple. 1977. "Sanctity and Power: The Dual Pursuit of Medieval Women." In Bridenthal and Koonz, *q.v.,* pp. 90–118.

Mead, Margaret. 1979. "On Freud's View of Female Psychology." In Junaita H. Williams, ed. *Psychology of Women: Selected Readings,* pp. 53–61. New York: Norton.

Morgan, Edmund. 1966. *The Puritan Family: Religion and Domestic Relations in Seventeenth-Century New England.* New York: Harper & Row.

Norton, Mary Beth. 1980. *Liberty's Daughters.* Boston: Little, Brown.

O'Faolain, Julia and Lauro Martines. 1973. *Not in God's Image.* New York: Harper Torchbook.

O'Neill, William. 1973. *Divorce in the Progressive Era.* New York: New Viewpoints.

Ortner, Sherry. 1974. "Is Female to Male as Nature Is to Culture?" In Rosaldo and Lamphere, *q.v.,* pp. 67–88.

—— 1978. "The Virgin and the State." *Feminist Studies* (October) 4(3):19–36.

Power, Eileen. 1975. *Medieval Women.* New York: Cambridge.

Putnam, Emily. 1910. *The Lady.* New York: Putnam.

Reiter, Rayna R., ed. *Toward an Anthropology of Women.* New York: Monthly Review Press.

Rosaldo, Michelle. 1974. "Woman Culture and Society." In Rosaldo and Lamphere, *q.v.,* pp. 17–24.

—— 1980. "The Use and Abuse of Anthropology: Reflections on Feminism and Cross-Cultural Understanding." *Signs* (Spring) 5(3):389–417.

Rubin, Gayle. 1975. "The Traffic in Women: Notes on the 'Political Economy' of Sex." In Reiter, *q.v.,* pp. 157–211.

Sacks, Karen. 1979. *Sisters and Wives, The Past and Future of Sexual Equality.* Westport, Conn.: Greenwood.

Salmon, Marylynn. 1979. "Equality or Submersion? Femme Couvert Status in Early Pennsylvania." In Carol Berkin and Mary Beth Norton, eds., *Women of America: A History,* ch. 4. Boston: Houghton Mifflin.

Spokeswoman. 1980 (October) 10(10):6.

Stock, Phyllis. 1978. *Better Than Rubies, A History of Women's Education.* New York: Putnam.

Tilly, Louise and Joan Scott. 1978. *Women, Work, and Family.* New York: Holt, Rinehart and Winston.

Watt, Ian. 1957. *Rise of the Novel.* Berkeley, Calif.: University of California.

Welter, Barbara. 1966. "The Cult of True Womanhood." *American Quarterly* (Summer) 18(2), pt. 1:151–74.

—— 1976. *Dimity Convictions.* Athens, Ohio: Ohio University Press.

2 Freud's Heritage

Fathers and Daughters in German Literature (1750–1850)

GABRIELE WICKERT

Sigmund Freud is generally credited with our century's most significant breakthroughs in conceptions of human sexuality. From a modern vantage point, however, we can see that many of his views were influenced, unconsciously as well as consciously, by a longstanding German middle-class tradition. Particularly Freud's views of masculinity and femininity, the Oedipus complex, and the relation of daughters to their fathers are cast very much in the mold of past centuries, especially the eighteenth and nineteenth centuries in Germany. In this article I describe and illustrate some aspects of Freud's indebtedness to this traditional perception of sexual roles by drawing on examples from eighteenth-century German literature and society.

The Position of Women in the German Enlightenment

The eighteenth-century in Germany was the century of the Enlightenment. This movement was carried by the middle class, which developed its own set of values in clear opposition to the courtly values of the past. One of the most distinctive features of this new middle class was its attitude toward the feminine. At least at first, the basically egalitarian stance of the European Enlightenment movement included the goal of equality between the sexes. In France and England this movement culminated in public manifestos, as for example with the "Declaration of Women's Rights" of the French feminist Olympe de Gouges in 1791, or a year later, Mary Wollstonecraft's "A Vindication of the Rights of Women." In Germany, however, no such action occurred. Although the Enlightenment otherwise emphasized the commonality of human experience and deemphasized particular distinctions, in Germany this tendency was not carried over into the realm of the sexes.

On the one hand, the German middle class tended to put women on a pedestal and granted them a much larger role in culture and education than they had previously. On the other hand, a policy of "different but equal," which did little to improve actual conditions for women, continued to prevail. The new female type of the "learned woman," briefly accepted and celebrated, for example, in the life and career of Anna Maria Schürmann (1607–78), was soon relinquished in favor of an entirely different one: that of the sweet, innocent, and intellectually limited homebody (Bovenschen 1979:84–91).

By the middle of the century, with very few exceptions, sweet and passive women dominate in literature. This is certainly the tendency of the "weinerliche Komödie" (the German version of the "comedie larmoyante"), which had become popularized in Germany by C. F. Gellert. But even in the satirical comedies of the Saxon school this is true. By 1745, Louise Adelgunde Gottsched, wife of the early Enlightenment theoretician, is already satirizing (among other things) "unnatural" scholarly interests in a woman in her play *Die Pietisterei im Fischbeinrocke* (*Pietism in Hoopskirts*).

Political Realities and the Self-Image of the German Middle Class

The reasons for the eighteenth-century German middle-class preference for the sweet homebody as a literary ideal are social and historical. The regressive political and economic situation of the German states, which were disjointed and largely feudal in structure, precluded the successful ripening of real political power for the emerging middle class. The German middle class remained politically and economically powerless, while its counterparts in England and France were building a very real power (Bruford 1935).

Germany had never developed into a centralized nation-state, as the other major powers had, but was divided into countless territories and petty dukedoms, each of which was ruled more or less absolutely by a not always enlightened monarch, backed by an aristocratic bureaucracy. The very nature of its antiquated political structures made general political reforms that would have been to the advantage of the middle class impossible to carry out in the German empire. In fact there was never a successful middle-class revolution in Germany. What one revolution achieved in France would have had to be reenacted nearly 300 times over in the disjointed German territories. In the area of public life, the German middle class acquiesced to passivity and as a result it developed a basically "feminine" view of itself.

This political impotence of the middle class was, however, offset by an intensified working out of spiritual values. Since the area of public life was completely controlled by the ruling aristocracy, the hamstrung German middle class retreated into an inner realm of moral excellence and artistic achievement. There were significant accomplishments in art, literature, and philosophy, but the "real" world of the corrupt aristocracy was consciously rejected. The middle-class Enlightenment philosopher Emmanuel Kant (1724–1804) exemplifies the tendency of his class to set up absolute standards of morality with his insistence on a "moral imperative." These standards made any involvement in the necessarily imperfect world of political action appear questionable.

The German middle class strictly separated the inner world, where pure thought and feeling resided, from the outer world of deceptive appearances. It retreated into the inner world. The realm of morality became identified with private conscience and personal relationships, in particular with the family. The family became the haven of refuge from a corrupt outer world, and the private, domestic sphere was made absolute as the realm of true humanity: "das rein Menschliche." Thus an enforced passivity and helplessness were elevated into virtues for a whole class; they became its ideological self-rationalization.

To express and represent this self-concept, a particular image of virtuous human frailty was needed. It was found in the virginal maiden, the female in her role not as mature woman, wife, and mother, but as dependent daughter. By the second half of the eighteenth-century this image of womanhood prevailed and exerted a powerful emotional impact on contemporary readers. They empathized with her sweetness and her vulnerability. These qualities were celebrated in the archetypal situation of the passive and domestically oriented young girl threatened by the sexual advances of an aristocratic public figure. An important influence here was Richardson, whose novels *Pamela* and *Clarissa* (1742, 1748) profoundly appealed to middle-class German taste and had long-lasting literary reverberations. There, as well as in the many German works influenced by him, the loss of feminine innocence, specifically the loss of virginity, is the ultimate evil, equivalent to original sin (Petriconi 1953). In German works the devilish seducer of pious bourgeois maidenhood is always a member of the aristocracy.

The sweet, submissive, but necessarily threatened heroine is particularly memorable in Lessing's *Miss Sara Sampson* (1755) and in Sophie de la Roche's *Fräulein von Sternheim* (1771). The latter illustrates the power of these middle-class ideals to cross class lines, since Sophie de la Roche came from a patrician family and had married into the nobility. In both examples, as well as in countless popular and trivial others, passivity and vulnerability are the heroine's central attributes. These qualities are often delineated even more sharply by the presence of an entirely different female type who functions as a foil: the aggressive and sexually wanton courtesan figure.

The feminine figure in fiction was idealized to the point of beatification. She became the carrier for the bourgeois sense of self. However, the actual role of women in eighteenth-century society did not improve noticeably. Wulf Köpke (1979:96) claims that feminine emancipation in eighteenth-century Germany meant breaking away from bondage to the father. He is thereby referring to the legal, emotional, and moral guardianship exercised by the father over his daughter and transferred by him to her husband at the time of her marriage, an act ensuring that the woman remained in a perpetual state of dependence.

Female emancipation from this kind of bondage was rarely achieved. In her book *Die imaginierte Weiblichkeit* (*The Imagined Feminine*), Silvia Bovenschen (1979) convincingly demonstrates that the idealized feminine heroine in eighteenth- and early nineteenth-century German literature was an exclusively fictional creation of male authors. The fact is that women dominated in literature only, while remaining subservient and without historical dimension at home (pp. 19–24). Bovenschen adds that the apparent feminization of literature at this time represents at best an enlargement of the male author's emotional repertoire. Men were allowed to indulge in feelings that had previously been associated exclusively with women. It did not involve surmounting sexually determined limitations for the women (p. 162).

The middle-class German family in the eighteenth and nineteenth centuries continued to be highly patriarchal. It is most significant that less than 100 years before Freud's time there was serious philosophical debate on whether women had souls! Women did not obtain the same legal rights over their children as their husbands until well into the twentieth century. In the eighteenth and nineteenth centuries, although the image of the feminine was celebrated in art, the male continued to exercise near-feudal privileges over the women in his household, including the ultimate privilege of disposing of the innocence (virginity) of his daughter. During the second half of the eighteenth-century in Germany, there is abundant literary evidence of the father's emotional coercion of his dependent daughter. The father in literature is fixed upon his daughter: he makes her the emblem of male bourgeois helplessness vis-à-vis the aristocratic power structure. The relationship of the father toward his daughter is necessarily ambiguous, unhealthily mixing paternal idolatry with disdain and exposing thereby the father's ambivalent attitude toward his own helplessness. In the father-daughter relationship patriarchal power and aggression are affirmed. Masculine dominance is maintained at the same time that feminine passivity is aesthetically glorified.

The Father-Daughter Fixation
in Lessing's "Emilia Galotti"

It is now time to illustrate this rather murky state of affairs with an example or two from literature. While any number of examples might have been used, Gotthold Ephraim Lessing's drama *Emilia Galotti* (1772) is the most interesting. Not only is the father-daughter fixation particularly pronounced, but also Lessing seems to be more conscious of what is going on than is the case with writers of lesser genius. An innovative thinker in many ways, Lessing is the most important writer of the German Enlightenment. His stance of tolerant humanism and his incisive psychological insights represent an important link to the later Classicism of Goethe, the highpoint of German literary achievement.

Lessing's source for *Emilia Galotti* is Roman history as recounted by Livius. Livius tells of an upright Roman republican who saves his daughter, Virginia, from the sexual advances of the despot Appius Claudius by stabbing her to death. In the Latin version this is a political drama: the sacrifice of the daughter incites the Roman populace to rebellion and reassertion of its republican rights. In Lessing's German treatment the political purpose is no longer dominant. Lessing himself dubbed his play "eine bürgerliche Virginia" (a middle-class Virginia). The main emphasis of Lessing's play is not politics but personality. The two camps, middle-class morality and courtly corruption, are clearly drawn, but they do not culminate in political action. In a sense, Lessing's play investigates the reasons why the same circumstances in eighteenth-century Germany (though disguised as Italy of an undefinable period by Lessing) did not produce Roman results.

The shift in perspective between the two treatments is highly significant — away from the public sector into the inner world of character. The two most important characters — both representative of the dominant direction of middle-class morality — are the father, Odoardo, and his daughter, Emilia. Interpretations of this play have varied considerably over the years, depending upon the interpretation of Odoardo and of the nature of his relationship with Emilia. Some earlier critics falsely assumed that Lessing intended to glorify the middle-class position represented by Odoardo and Emilia. On the contrary, it is greatly to Lessing's credit that he was able to pierce the veneer of middle-class idealism and expose the problematic psychological ambiguities it covered.

Like Livius' Virginia, Emilia is an innocent and sheltered girl who, when confronted with the advances of a powerful monarch, begs her father to save her by killing her. It would be senseless to question the unconscious motivation behind the daughter's willingness to die at her father's hand in Livius' account, since Livius is not concerned with psychology but with politics. For Lessing, however, the inner dimension is the central concern. All the characters in his drama are masterfully depicted in their own psychological density. Each has a distinct private identity, while nevertheless retaining a representative character and suggesting a certain type. Emilia, for example, belongs to a recognizable type: the beautiful but virtuous middle-class maiden who is pursued with lust by a corrupt member of the aristocracy, here the playboy prince Hettore Gonzaga. Lessing has individualized her by giving her an additional psychological dimension. Though Emilia is pure and has been raised according to the strict middle-class value system, Lessing injects an element of uncertainty into her profile. This uncertainty reveals the existence of a struggle within her to live up to the ideal of static inviolability in which she has been cast. It is Emilia's father, Odoardo, who has concerned himself with the upbringing of his daughter and who constantly worries about possible threats to her virtue. It is his vision of her that Emilia attempts to live up to. Completely his creation, she has totally incorporated the world of the authoritarian father.

Interestingly enough, Odoardo is rather unsympathetically depicted, especially when contrasted with other fathers in Lessing's work, who tend to be overwhelmingly positive figures. There is an inhuman coldness in his stoic adherence to absolute moral standards. Equally questionable is the upbringing he has given his daughter, an upbringing so repressive that it has rendered her incapable of dealing with the realities of an imperfect outside world. Lessing suggests there is an unhealthy symbiosis of dominance and submission in this father fixation. However, he also opens up the wider psychological and sociological perspective of that fixation. Odoardo makes Emilia into a feminine version of himself. She represents the externalized "feminine" passivity that has been forced on this archetypal representative of middle-class morality by the nature of eighteenth-century Germany political realities but that has been rationalized by him into an ultimate virtue. In Odoardo's value system, the real world of political action is necessarily corrupt, and so he retreats from it. Instead of remaining at court to advise the impressionable and vacillating young prince, he leaves the field open for an unscrupulous adviser like Marinelli, who encourages the prince in his illicit desires and sets the trap for Emilia. Odoardo's retreat reaffirms the passive ("feminine") stance that middle-class conceptions of morality had come to identify with itself.

For Odoardo, his passively virtuous but threatened daughter becomes the symbolic representative of that stance. Odoardo thus continues the established middle-class practice of defining itself—and therefore its emblematic representative, the woman—as a victim and glorifying that victimhood as the only guarantee of true virtue. Both Odoardo and his daughter assume that Emilia's death is truly tragic—that it is necessary to affirm certain supraindividual values. In our century critics have often noted how unconvincing and unsatisfying the "tragic necessity" of Emilia's death is. There is a persistent sense of helplessness in Odoardo's and Emilia's predicament, and helplessness can never be truly satisfying, even when necessity idealizes it and fashions it into a virtue.

Odoardo's ambivalence toward himself is manifested in his ambivalence toward his daughter. He both cherishes her as the best part of himself and feels aggression toward her as the outer manifestation of his own helplessness. Emilia for her part is in an equally equivocal bind. After having been abducted to the prince's palace, she is forced to entertain the horrifying thought that she may in fact be unconsciously attracted to the prince, to his very real power, and to the life of carefree sensual pleasure he offers her. For Emilia, merely entertaining such possibilities is tantamount to a betrayal of her father that, given the identification between them, threatens her very identity. In asking Odoardo to "save" her by killing her, she not only avoids an identity crisis but also reestablishes the Oedipal bond, as Frederick Wyatt has recognized (1971:32). In accepting his daughter's invitation to be her executioner, Odoardo relates to her with the combination of aggression and tenderness that had informed their relationship from the start.

Later treatments of the Oedipal bond, for example, in

Schiller's play *Kabale und Liebe* (*Intrigue and Love*, 1786), do not exhibit the same level of insight into the male middle-class psyche. Lessing's depiction of Odoardo reveals a surprising awareness of the hidden psychological realities—one that was never really surpassed. The literary movement that ended the Enlightenment, the German Classicism of Goethe and Schiller, continued to perpetuate a traditional view of women but one that did not illuminate the problematic nature of that womanhood. Unlike most of the literary generation that he subsequently dwarfed, Goethe does not dwell on father figures. The father-daughter conflict is conspicuously absent in his work. Though women are very important in Goethe's thought, they do not function as representatives of male middle-class helplessness. Building upon feminine ideals of the Enlightenment, but devoid of the father-daughter configuration, Goethe elevates women to a cosmically symbolic function in his principle of the "eternal feminine." "Eternal Womanhood leads us on high" are the culminating words of Goethe's *Faust*. Here both the innocent Gretchen and the beauteous and worldly Helen of Troy represent the natural holistic goodness toward which the erring male principle, Faust, dimly strives. In German Classicism the prevailing notion of woman was an ahistorically static pole reminding the struggling male of eternal, natural laws. The "sweet young thing" recurs in Goethe's work as a particularly apt representative of the wholeness of unspoiled nature.

After Goethe, as the bourgeoisie became more established over the course of the nineteenth century, there was ever less awareness of the deeper significance of an idealization of the female type. By about 1830 the central position of this type of heroine had declined in serious literature, but she continued to hold unrivaled sway in trivial literature for the rest of the century. She even crops up intermittently in serious works, notably in the recurring figure of the "süsses Mädel" in the literature of Freud's own Vienna (see, for example, the works of Arthur Schnitzler).

Freud's Conception of the Feminine
and his Patriarchal Orientation

Perhaps the most striking difference between Freud's conception of women and that which prevailed around 1800 in Germany is his lack of idealization of the feminine. This tendency toward un-romantic objectivity may seem to be inherent in the scientific attitude, but a glance at other scientists of Freud's circle will suffice to illustrate that this is not necessarily the case. Freud's contemporary and colleague Fritz Wettels, for example, insisted on a romantic glorification of the feminine principle that, while drawing on many sources, is very mindful of Goethe. The fact that Freud himself utterly rejected this view of the feminine is a potentially progressive aspect. It probably accounts for the absence in his work of the idea of women as essentially "whole" beings in contradistinction to the striving incompleteness of the male. His description of the female psyche—most comprehensively presented in his lecture on "The Psychology of Women"—stresses the greater problems in psychic adjustment weighing upon the female and is hardly an idealizing portrait.

Freud's ability to divorce himself from previously established tendencies to romanticize the feminine might have paved the way for an entirely new view of women. However, it was not coupled with a divorce from the paternalistic orientation that had originally spawned such views, and Freud was therefore destined to repeat the mistakes of the past. Although he declined to idealize the essential nature of women, he continued to expound an essentially male point of view. Viola Klein (1946:83) claims that "in generalizing the masculine type and making it a universal norm Freud went further than anyone else." The male stands firmly in the center of Freud's investigations and the female is interpreted only in relation to the male. She is the "other" whose anatomical deficiencies give rise to far-reaching cultural ones.

Freud's work also perpetuates the stereotype of the male as the essentially active (sadistic) being and the female as the essentially passive (masochistic) being. Intellectual ambition in a woman is subsequently written off as a "masculinity complex." Freud presents women as deviant from the human norm (i.e., the male) and thus as unknowable, an enigma to be wondered at and feared. "You are the riddle," he says in his lecture on the psychology of women (1962:145). Here too Freud is walking on well-trodden ground. The mystique of the unfathomable feminine, while actually dating back to the myth of the earth mother, had been reactivated in Germany by Goethe's elevation of women to a cosmic principle and by his preference for presenting them as creatures with an especially direct link to positive natural forces.

Freud's Female Oedipal Complex

A particularly important aspect of Freud's interpretation of the feminine is his explanation of the libidinal inevitability of the female attachment to the father. While admitting the unresearched importance of an earlier attachment to the mother, Freud focuses upon the unavoidable father fixation as the decisive sexual phenomenon for the little girl. While the boy's oedipal stage of attraction to the mother is fraught with anxiety (fear of castration by the vengeful father), the girl "enters the Oedipal situation, as though it were a haven of refuge" (Freud 1962:166). The oedipal relationship is so satisfying that "the girl remains in it for an indefinite period; she only abandons it late in life, and then incompletely" (Freud 1962:166).

In this account of the sexual bond between the dominant father and the passive, receptive daughter, Freud is operating with conceptualizations from the past. We have already seen how often German fiction and drama of the later eighteenth and early nineteenth centuries deals with the father-daughter fixation. Nowhere before in fact is the literary treatment of problems between fathers and daughters so emotionally charged and so recurrent as in the literature produced by the German middle class around 1800. We have seen, however, that the image of the idealized virginal daughter and her problematic relationship with her moralistic father grew out of a specific set of sociohistorical circumstances. Through such images the politically impotent middle class was trying to work out feelings of ambiguity about its own helplessness vis-à-vis the aristocracy.

By Freud's time, nearly a hundred years later, the situation of the middle class had, of course, changed. It had become dominant in the economic realm and indirectly also in the political one, but it was now in a sense boxed in on two fronts. On the one hand the elevated social "tone" continued to be set by the aristocracy (this was particularly true in Austria), while the challenge of the lower working classes to the economic hegemony of the bourgeoisie was becoming an increasing threat. The German middle class of the late nineteenth century seems to have a defensive sense of insecurity in common with the middle class of the eighteenth century. This insecurity may have encouraged the perpetuation of patriarchal attitudes.

While Freud rejected the poetic mystification of the feminine common to the later eighteenth century, he did inherit and accept its patriarchal orientation, which evolved under him into a kind of "phallocentricity." Devoid of its poetic superstructure, the father-daughter fixation became in his hands a matter of anatomical determinism that has a direct bearing on cultural distinctions between the sexes. Freud no longer acknowledges the male's interest in arranging the sexual dominance-dependence structure for the male's advantage, as Lessing had made it visible at least momentarily. Early in his career Freud believed that fathers might play an active role in creating the bonds of sexual dependence with their daughters. Later, however, by completely rejecting the notion of an actual seduction and by focusing on psychic phenomena as the basis of the disturbance, Freud relocated the seat of neurosis within the daughter. Freud sees the female as anatomically, thus fundamentally, deficient—though he claims that it is she who necessarily experiences herself as incomplete, deficient in comparison with the phallus-bearing male. Her all-determining penis envy supposedly arises out of her primary experience of castration which causes her to reject her mother and attach herself to her father in a more or less permanent oedipal fixation.

Freud rigidified the dynamic tensions of earlier poetic depictions into the "objective facts" of science. Devoid of the corrective potential of incongruity—the incongruity of patriarchal superiority coupled with an idealization of the feminine—Freud's description of the female oedipal complex relieves the male of responsibility for this state of affairs. He backs away from the problem of who is primarily interested in sexual bonding and the father-daughter fixation. Whereas German literature a century before had at least suggested the importance of the patriarchal father in this connection, Freud claims it is exclusively the woman who hopes to recover in the father the penis she has lost. His biased male point of view prevented him from recognizing the importance of the father in initiating and encouraging this bond as compensation for his helplessness in the real world. In this sense, German literary treatments of father-daughter relationships in the eighteenth century, particularly in Lessing's *Emilia Galotti,* reflect the hope for a reevaluation of sexual roles that was subsequently lost and that Freud himself was unable to make good. Freud did his part to perpetuate the curious ambiguity of "feminine" middle-class values (introspection, cultural concerns, private morality) coupled with a patriarchal power structure. Psychoanalysis represents a further turning away from political action in the public (male) sphere to the inner (female) sphere of self-examination — the only middle-class arena where true virtue may successfully be sought. Freud accepted and continued the established conventions of the German middle class, without in any important way breaking out of the sexual stereotyping it had established more than a hundred years before his time.

References

Bovenschen, Silvia. 1979. *Die imaginierte Weiblichkeit. Exemplarische Untersuchungen zu kulturgeschichtlichen und literarischen Präsentationsformen des Weiblichen.* Frankfurt a.M.: Suhrkamp.
Bruford, W. H. 1935. *Germany in the Eighteenth Century. The Social Background of the Literary Revival.* Cambridge, England.
Freud, Sigmund. 1962. *The Psychology of Women. New Introductory Lectures on Psycho-Analysis,* No. 33. London: Hogarth Press.
Klein, Viola. 1946. *The Feminine Character. History of an Ideology.* London:Routledge & Kegan Paul Ltd.
Köpke, Wulf. 1979. "Die emanzipierte Frau in der Goethezeit." In Wolfgang Paulssen, ed. *Die Frau als Heldin und Autorin.* Bern/München: Francke Verlag.
Mitchell, Juliet. 1974. *Psychoanalysis and Feminism.* New York: Pantheon Books.
Petriconi, Helmuth. 1953. *Die Verführte Unschuld. Bermerkungen über ein literarisches Thema.* Hamburg.
Wyatt, Frederick. 1971. "Das Psychologische in der Literatur." In Wolfgang Paulsen, ed. *Psychologie in der Literaturwissenschaft.* Heidelberg: Lothar Stiehm Verlag.

3 The Victorians, the Psychologists, and Psychic Birth Control

MIRIAM LEWIN

When psychology developed during the nineteenth century, it was especially influenced by four important concepts in its understanding of the nature of women and of men: Darwinian evolution, Newtonian Conservation of Force, Victorian sex-role ideology, and a component of Victorian life I call the system of Psychic Birth Control. The ideology of Psychic Birth Control and Victorian sex-roles, explained and defended in the vocabulary of Darwinian evolution and of Conservation of Force, were the building blocks for nineteenth-century psychology.

As it developed, psychology itself eventually became a social influence. By giving the stamp of scientific and scholarly approval to Victorian ideas, psychology prolonged their lifespan. Today's psychological ideas about women and men are impossible to understand unless we trace their origins in the conditions of nineteenth-century life. I set the stage by a preliminary glance at the status and social position of women and men in the nineteenth century.

The Position of the Sexes
in the Nineteenth Century

Historical Antecedents

The patriarchal nuclear family and the nation-state rose together in the seventeenth century, two powers that divided the
dwindling strength of feudalism. Schooling for men increased
substantially, but European women were virtually excluded from
even primary education throughout the seventeenth century. Their
lives, little changed from the Middle Ages, included marriage at
12, 13, or 14 and functional illiteracy. According to Aries, even
many women of the aristocracy could barely sound out written
words with difficulty. They were "unable to pronounce what they
read . . . even more at fault with their spelling, and in shaping
and joining letters of the alphabet when writing" (Aries 1962:332;
see Barbara Harris, article 1).

The modern family, an adult woman and man, dwelling
alone together with their children in a bounded, private dwelling
space, which did not exist in the Middle Ages, had developed in
Europe by the eighteenth century (Janeway 1971). At that time
secondary education and an extension of childhood were instituted for middle-class and upper class European boys, setting
them apart from poor boys and from girls. Aries believes that
schooling is so critical to the development of "man's nature" that
the extension of education brought about a fundamental change
in postmedieval history and in "human" nature. But for a long
time women did not participate fully in that change. A new "wom-
en's nature" could not develop until, with much struggle, women
did receive schooling.

In the eighteenth century the inferiority of women to men
was not seriously questioned. For example, the eighteenth-century Italian art historian G. B. Passeri wrote:

Women have never been lacking in intellect, and it is well known that when
they are instructed in some subject, they are capable of mastering what they
are taught. Nevertheless, it is true that the Lord did not endow them properly
with the faculty of judgment and this he did in order to keep them restrained
within the boundaries of obedience to men, to establish men as supreme and
superior, so that with this lack women would be more docile, more amenable
to suggestion (quoted in Glueck 1977:54).

This quotation illustrates some characteristics of eighteenth-century male thought: (1) the belief in the inferiority of women is confident and secure; (2) the desirability of restraining women "within the boundaries of obedience to men" is unquestioned; and (3) the continued success of that restraint is assured, for it is ordained by divine plan.

This frank, unabashed, and unembarrassed assertion of male dominance gradually became defensive in the nineteenth century, although male supremacy remained the predominant ideology. In England, Mary Wollstonecraft published her "Vindication of the Rights of Women" in 1792. She was inspired by the American Revolution of 1776 and the French Revolution of 1789, as well as by the fact that her alcoholic, physically abusive father did not support his wife and daughters. (Her sister was a tutor in the Darwin family.)

Sex Roles in Victorian America

The separation of the public, male sphere of work for cash from the private, female sphere of the home resulted from the Industrial Revolution and urbanization, which took work out of the home for the first time in history (see Barbara Harris, Chapter 1). Women's more prestigous and economic functions at home were reduced. Education moved out into the schools, health care into the hospitals; food, clothing, and other necessities were produced elsewhere. Many trades and the professions, once loosely regulated and thus possibly accessible for women, were strictly closed to them. These changes had their positive aspects, but what remained at home for women to do was an endless round of isolated, repetitive, activities—earning no cash—of low status, with one (relative) exception: child care. It is understandable that a compensatory ideology glorifying and mystifying motherhood developed early in the nineteenth century. "The hand that rocks the cradle rules the world" (see Contratto, Chapter 10).

This ideology was adopted wholeheartedly by psychologists late in the century, especially by child psychologists, whose needs to justify their new endeavor, the scientific study of children, were somewhat parallel to the needs of mothers to find meaning in their newly narrowed sphere. There was also an attempt to upgrade the new Science of Home Economics, although housework was never successfully raised to the status of child rearing.

The new industrial technology made it possible for the entire country to aspire to become middle class, if not immediately then in the next generation. Urged on by society, many men internalized a passionate desire to "succeed" and accepted the belief that the individual should be blamed for "failure." Under these conditions, men badly needed a home, a "haven in a heartless world," preferably one occupied by a wife who found joy in total devotion to her husband (Lasch 1977; Zaretsky 1976).

The Doctrine of the Two Spheres

As a result the distinctions between the sexes were emphasized significantly more in the nineteenth than in the eighteenth century. By 1840 this extreme differentiation of the sexes found ideological expression in the Doctrine of the Two Spheres: the male sphere and the female sphere. The place of women was further defined by the Cult of True Womanhood (Welter 1978).

The nineteenth century (like our own) was a period of struggle between doctrines of equality (of the races, of the sexes, of social classes, of ethnic groups) and doctrines of hierarchy and inequality. Although the Cult of True Womanhood reached full growth around 1840, its basic premises are already apparent in the views of the founders of the Young Ladies Academy of Philadelphia, which opened in 1789. The Academy, a private school, was the first American high school open to women to offer instruction in grammar, arithmetic, geography, and oratory. It drew a national, if small, clientele. The founders of the Young Ladies Academy held these beliefs:

1. The cultivation of reason in a woman was controversial and had to be defended. One of the founders, Dr. Benjamin Rush, told the young ladies in 1787 that it was up to them to demonstrate "that the cultivation of reason in woman is alike friendly to the order of nature and to private as well as public happiness" (Gordon 1979). Here Rush raises an issue that was later assigned to psychologists to settle one way or the other.

2. Women are naturally submissive. According to a second trustee, they are by nature "perfectly inoffensive, courteous, and obliging to all." They should cultivate "habits of obedience."

3. Women have a natural affinity for religion.

4. Women have a natural superiority in spiritual and moral behavior. They were created to enable men to support the "vicissitudes and misfortunes" of the world. Trustee John Swanwick said, "Like the guardian angels of our sex, they will gradually lead us to those celestial realms from which we (men) have been exiled" (Gordon 1979:74).

5. Women must confine their activities entirely within their families, and not venture into the world outside the home. A young valedictorian at the Academy apologized for speaking in public at graduation.. She acknowledged that she would never speak publicly again in her lifetime.

Some of the young women had other ideas. Salutatorian Priscilla Mason offered a vision of a society in which women were active in the Church, at the Bar, and in the Senate. She thought that only man's power, not woman's lack of talent, stood in the way. This high school graduate was hopeful, in 1793, that change would come soon (Gordon 1979).

The Cult of True Womanhood reached its greatest strength between 1820 and 1860. The True Woman had four cardinal virtues: piety, purity, submissiveness, and domesticity (Welter 1978). Women were passive, conscious of dependency, and grateful for support. "True feminine genius" said Sara Jane Clark in 1846 (writing modestly under a pseudonym) "is ever timid, doubtful, and clingingly dependent; a perpetual childhood" (Welter 1978:319). But there was more to the Victorian woman.

Moral Superiority of Women:
a Doctrine Unique to America

The True Woman was not, however, simply submissive and obedient to man. An extremely significant innovation distinguishes nineteenth-century Americans' beliefs from those held in earlier periods.

The new and remarkable American conviction was that women were morally superior to men. Alexis de Tocqueville observed it on his visit to America in 1830. Young girls, he said, are taught to survey the "great scene of the world" with a "firm and calm gaze," viewing vices and dangers clearly "without illusion," "full of reliance on their own strength." In a democracy, "as it is neither possible nor desirable to keep a young woman in perpetual and complete ignorance, they (the Americans) hasten to give her a precocious knowledge on all subjects." The result was "to make cold and virtuous women instead of affectionate wives and agreeable companions to man" (de Tocqueville 1835:209–11).

In contrast to the freedom of the young girl from parental control, once married, the wife has irrevocably lost her independence. Much "abnegation" is required of her, and "a constant sacrifice of her pleasures to her duties, which is seldom demanded of her in Europe" (de Tocqueville 1835:212). He describes the submission of the pioneer wife, ripped from a New England town, isolated in the wilderness with her husband and children:

her features are drawn in, her eye mild and melancholy; her whole physiognomy bears marks of religious resignation, a deep quiet of all passions, and some sort of natural and tranquil firmness . . . without fearing, without braving. Her children cluster about her, full of health, turbulence, and energy. . . . one might imagine that the life she has given them has exhausted her own, and still she does not regret what they have cost her. . . . The house . . . has one chamber . . . a hundred steps beyond it the primeval forest spreads (de Tocqueville 1835:383–84).

In "How the Americans Understand the Equality of Sexes," de Tocqueville explains that Americans certainly do not believe in full equality:

by attempting to make one sex equal to the other, both are degraded, and from so preposterous a medley of the works of nature, nothing could ever result but weak men and disorderly women (de Tocqueville 1835:222).

(Significantly, he did not concern himself with the problems that weak women and disorderly men might create.) Instead, Americans have taken the "great principle of political economy which governs the manufacturers of our age," the *division of labor,* and applied it to the sexes. In no other country are the two pathways kept so carefully distinct. American women submit to the authority of their husbands: they "boast to bend themselves to the yoke, not to shake it off. Such at least, is the feeling expressed by the most virtuous of their sex; the others are silent . . ." (de Tocqueville 1835:223).

Nevertheless, women have a moral authority in America

which is lacking elsewhere: "in Europe a certain degree of contempt lurks even in the flattery which men lavish upon women; although a European frequently affects to be the slave of a woman, it may be seen that he never sincerely thinks her his equal." In the United States men seldom compliment women but daily show "esteem," "confidence," or "profound respect."

The Seneca Falls "Declaration of Sentiments and Resolutions" of 1848 was the first major American document to demand equal rights for women. Elizabeth Cady Stanton and Lucretia Mott included the following significant passage:

Resolved, that inasmuch as man, while claiming for himself intellectual superiority, does accord to woman moral superiority, it is preeminently his duty to encourage her to speak and teach (Mott and Stanton, in Hecht et al. 1973:65).

The belief in the moral superiority of women was found to a lesser degree in England. See, for example, the widely read English essay of 1850 "Woman's Mission" (Peters 1975). The author of "Woman's Mission" claims that nothing that women truly disapprove of with their souls can live. If only the wife and mother tries hard enough, her sons and husband must be moral. If they are not, the blame is hers.

The passage reveals the venerable age of the belief that if husbands and sons fail to be moral (or, as psychologists would say today, well adjusted and normal) the fault lies with the wife and mother. This 1850 belief was adopted by psychologists. It remains a truism within child development, personality theory, and psychopathology. Mother blaming has a long history (see Contratto, Chapter 10).

Peters, discussing midcentury England, sees

a fundamental Victorian dichotomy; the coarse brutal male who gouges and hacks his way out in the world; the gentle, spiritual angel who guards the moral decencies and refinements of the home. The dichotomy was part fact, part myth. The middleclass Englishman was intent on wresting a fortune out of the new mills. . . . a brutal man, made callous in society by the new capitalism and in his home by unlimited power over wife and children. In defense the Victorian woman could only grasp the empty weapon of moral and spiritual superiority and try to convince herself and her master that it was loaded. To her credit she often succeeded (Peters 1975:305).

The continental belief in female superiority seems to have been weaker still. In German-speaking areas, the ideal of the "innocent" daughter carried some degree of moral superiority, but in practice real woman did not (see Wickert, Chapter 2).

The Advantages of Assigning Moral Superiority to Women. Given that power is rarely relinquished without good cause, we may ask why men in America, without conceding their superior political, legal, and economic status, found it plausible to believe in the moral superiority of women.

1. In America women were seen as the carriers of civilization, of culture, of the arts, of refinement. In Europe, in contrast, men represented Culture, while women represented Nature.

2. The moral superiority of women was closely linked to their asexuality. By defining women as (asexually) good and pure, and men as sexual beings, men could find some sexual satisfaction outside marriage. They could turn to prostitutes, servants, and slaves. Women could not. Prostitution increased significantly in the nineteenth century (Smith 1979). "Gentlemen's Guides" to houses of prostitution in the major American cities were published. Women's sense of their own moral superiority, which was acknowledged by the community, functioned to compensate them somewhat for their sexual frustrations.

3. Giving women moral superiority was a compromise and a bulwark against stronger claims. It was a halfway concession to granting women full equality. As such it appealed to conservative persons of both sexes who were threatened by the claim to full equality.

4. Weakness may be associated with morality. Because the relative legal, economic, and social power of husbands, fathers, and employers was great, they naturally provided the dramatic examples of cruelty and exploitation. Women, like poor workers, were morally superior partly by virtue of their lack of real power. Without real power it is hard to be an effective, large-scale sinner. The claim to moral superiority is traditionally the weapon of the weak.

5. Assigning moral superiority to women strengthened the mystique of motherhood. Teaching their children a moral code was one of the few ways women could legitimately exercise power. From the masculine point of view, assigning responsibility for the

moral training of children to women relieved men of this time-consuming and often stressful task. But American men were never totally excused from disciplining their children. Still the contrast between the feared European patriarchal father of Freud and Jung's day, whose children trembled at the sound of his footsteps, and the American father, who eventually became good old Pop, the bumbling, incompetent, mock-hero of a thousand sitcoms, is quite dramatic.

6. Assigning morality to women had another useful advantage: it left men free to practice vicarious morality and worry less about the ethical nature of their own activities. In a time of ruthless, unregulated, competitive business practices and the possibility of enormous wealth, or at least of a rise from one's parents' station in life, a lack of concern with the niceties of ethics could be helpful. In the Victorian economic climate, nice guys often finished last. Mark Twain advised satirically that the uneducated railroad worker would steal a few nails a day but that the ambitious young man who got a good education could steal a whole railroad! Some did. Men could practice vicarious morality through their wives, while wives practiced vicarious achievement through their husbands (or went without achievement).

When morality became inconvenient, there was always the comforting thought that it was, after all, meant for sissies. Morality was for "Miss Nancy," not for he-men. Once assigned to women, morality could safely be ridiculed. In the 1940s Erikson still found the American man to be closely identified with the rebellious son who, unlike his European counterpart, never identifies with the authoritarian father but remains forever jealous of his own freedom from responsibility. "Miss Nancy" could be the responsible one.

Once women were installed as the guardians of morality they naturally became the target of those who profited by immorality and who believed that it was in their own interest to keep women weak. Specifically, the liquor industry poured millions of dollars into the fight against suffrage in the belief that women would vote for prohibition. When prohibition was made law, many men, including some of the most respectable, were prepared to flout the law openly and eagerly, because it represented female, not male, morality. It was not their law. It was just a sissy law, to be obeyed by "mama's boys." The prohibition episode illustrates very well the dangers inherent in the Victorian solution of assigning morality to the weaker sex (Thompson 1970).

Of course, assigning moral superiority to women had its limitations. Around midcentury, legal journals still contained learned argument over "the rule of thumb." Under that rule a husband could legally beat his wife with a stick no thicker than his thumb to induce her compliance with his orders. Some jurists attacked the rule of thumb; others defended it (Bonsignore et al. 1974).

We will now temporarily leave the Doctrine of the Two Spheres and female moral superiority to see how Darwinian and Newtonian scientific principles enriched Victorian sex-role ideology.

The Impact of the Theory of Evolution
on Ideas About the Nature of Women and Men

What was decided among the prehistoric Protozoa cannot be annulled by an act of Parliament (Geddes and Thompson 1890/1899).

To understand how nineteenth-century men looked at women we must remember that the inferior position, status, abilities, and capacities of women were very much taken for granted. The activities of daily life, both large and small, confirmed this fact, a fact obvious even to children of three years (as Freud eventually discovered—he called it penis envy). Victorian ideology needed an authoritative intellectual foundation. Religious authority reluctantly conceded one beachhead after another to militant science. The belief in female inferiority, which had once rested more or less comfortably on selected misogynous teachings within Genesis, Aristotle, St. Paul, and others, now required a scientific base. That intellectual base became Darwinism, the most powerful idea of the mid-nineteenth century.

Because they were largely taken for granted in the eighteenth century, the nature and duties of the two sexes were rarely debated. In the nineteenth century both public and scholarly discourse on the place of women and men became substantial. Two powerful social forces clashed. Economic pressures and the male's psychological need to restrain women to limited activities at home came into conflict with an active feminist movement. Inspired by the ideas of the Enlightenment and by the restraints that were now tightly imposed, feminists tried to free women from ignorance and confinement. Darwin and his successors provided the conservative establishment with a powerful weapon with which to prove the biological inferiority of women. Darwinism prevailed among early social scientists. It defined the terms of the struggle (Rosenberg 1974, 1982).

The Development of Evolutionary Theories

The general idea of evolution was influential in the nineteenth century for some time before Charles Darwin developed it. Erasmus Darwin (Charles' grandfather), who worked for women's education, had proposed an earlier version of a theory of evolution, which he presented in the form of a long poem! His poem was originally well received in the social climate of the Enlightenment.

But after the terrific shock of the French Revolution in 1789, matters changed. Fearful Protestants, lacking a Pope as a source of absolute truth, emphasized a literal belief in the word of the Bible. When science challenged the rival authority of religion, crises were precipitated throughout the nineteenth century, similar in their violence to those now appearing in countries such as Iran, where the Ayatollah and the Mullah are pitted against that "Great Satan": Western scientific secular thought. Lamarck proposed a theory of evolution in 1809. Chambers published a theory of evolution anonymously in 1844, provoking the Reverend Mr. Sedgwick to horror:

It is our maxim that things must keep their proper places if they are to work together for any good. If our glorious maidens and matrons may not soil their fingers with the dirty knife of the anatomist, neither may they poison the springs of joyous thought and modest feeling, by listening to the seductions of this author . . . [who comes with] . . . the serpent coils of a false philosophy and asks them again to stretch out their hands and pluck forbidden fruit—to talk familiarly with him of things which cannot be so much as named without raising a blush upon a modest cheek (Hardin 1959; He means, to talk about the theory of evolution! 31).

Notice the reference to the sin of Eve, the appeal to women's obligation to be sexually repressed, and the premonition (quite accurate, as it turned out) that women, once exposed to education, would seek to leave their proper place and go to medical school.

Darwin's success in 1859 in demonstrating the validity of the theory of evolution had an overwhelming effect upon both social and scientific thought.

Superior and Inferior

Evolutionary theory appeared to provide impressive support for those who wanted to discriminate between better people and worse people. The unfortunate phrase "Survival of the Fittest" was borrowed from Spencer (Rosenberg 1974). It has been a source of liberal hand-wringing ever since (cf. Glasersfeld 1980). A better phrase would have been "differential reproduction."

The ancient idea of the Great Chain of Being, the hierarchy of superior and inferior forms, of development and progress along a predetermined Ladder of Perfection gained a new life. The concept now included a somber underside: brutal struggle, the elimination of the unfit, the need to keep lesser persons in their place. In the later part of the nineteenth century in England and in America, the theory of evolution was understood to mean, literally, that men, whites, Protestants, and Anglo-Saxons were more *evolved* and more fit (especially fit to rule) while others — women, blacks, Jews, Catholics, and immigrants — were less evolved, less fit, and inferior. At Oxford, Cecil Rhodes was inspired by evolutionary theory to recognize his divine mission to rule the less evolved South Africans.

Darwin himself, although relatively moderate compared to many who came after him in the later part of the nineteenth century, clearly described women's lesser abilities. The woman, Darwin believed, carefully selects her male mate. By virtue of this selection, over the generations men get stronger and handsomer and acquire other desirable characteristics. Men, more driven by lust, will mate with any woman who selects them. Thus they fail to improve the female breed by selecting their women thoughtfully.

Darwin's theory appears to reflect the thinking of a restrained English gentleman, eager to be selected but unwilling to impose himself upon a reluctant woman and certainly not given to the use of brutal force. In contrast, in Herbert Spencer, Darwin's contemporary, we glimpse a more aggressive temperament. Spencer assumed that women had no choice or power to select. Spencer argued that women's greater sensitivity to other's feelings, their empathic skills, had evolved through generations of dealing with those savage brutes, their men:

Women who betrayed the state of antagonism produced in them by ill-treatment were less likely to survive and leave offspring. . . . A woman who could, from a movement, a tone of voice, or an expression of face instantly detect in her savage husband the passion that was rising would be likely to escape dangers run into by a woman less skillful in interpreting the natural language of feeling (Spencer 1896/1910: 342–43).

Somehow the women turned out to be inferior either way, whether they did more or less of the selecting than their men.

The lesser metabolism of the female also causes her to vary less. Some evolutionists held a Lamarckian theory called pangenesis. By this theory, each sex acquired numerous characteristics, including environmentally induced traits, only from the parent of the same sex. Thus men's greater variability, combined with their broader contact with the world, led to their evolution, which they passed on to their sons. The women, who varied less to begin with, also experienced a less stimulating environment and passed on their inferior state to their daughters. (Note the concession that women did live in an unstimulating environment.) Not one to join in the more extreme misogyny of some of his contemporaries, Darwin believed that if women's environments were changed they would ultimately reach the same stage of evolution already achieved by men (Rosenberg 1974:7–15). Therefore he favored educating women who could then pass on these qualities to their daughters by heredity.

Darwin ranked intellectual abilities from *reason* (the highest) through *intuition,* to *instinct,* a lower trait. Women were better at the lower mental processes of *intuition* and *sensitivity,* men at the higher processes of *abstract reasoning* and *creativity* (Darwin 1871:596–98, 873–74, 446, cited by Rosenberg 1974). Unfortunately woman's chief claim to superiority, her greater moral and spiritual sensitivity and intuition, was thus undermined. By explaining the brain and its mental powers in biological terms Darwin reduced women's special strength to another form of inferiority. It was women's mental functions in particular that demonstrated the similarity between the mental faculties of human beings and those of the higher mammals (Darwin 1871:446, cited by Rosenberg 1974).

The implications of the new science were not lost on feminists. A few years after Darwin published on selection in relation to sex in 1871, the American feminist Antoinette Brown Blackwell (1875) published a critique accepting the theory of natural selection but objecting to the doctrine that women had failed to evolve, or that females were inadequate and incomplete males, or that females were inferior. However, except for a small group of avowed feminists, such as her sister-in-law Elizabeth Blackwell, the first American woman to obtain the M.D. degree, nobody listened. Evolutionary theorists did not get around to the question of the evolution of females again until the 1970s. (Hrdy 1981:12).

Ironically the theory of evolution—at first so upsetting to educated thought—rapidly became establishment doctrine among scientists and then became the ideology of political conservatism. The theory of evolution was used to argue against suffrage for women. Spencer, for example, contrasted primitive women, who were very strong, with civilized, evolved women, who were physically fragile. Anthropological expeditions, said Spencer, find that primitive women are stronger than men. "Women were made for labour: one of them can carry, or haul, as much as two men do" (Spencer 1876:75). Spencer added parenthetically that primitive women also "keep us warm at night." Now that women have evolved (but not so far as men), they are "prisoners of progress" who need to be protected at home (Duffin 1978).

Attacks on feminism and women's suffrage were couched in the language of evolution. In 1871 the *English Saturday Review* published an essay titled "The Probable Retrogression of Women." A biological retrogression of evolution would occur if "subordination in women were discouraged." Their "competition in masculine careers" would "barbarize our race." If the social conditions that "raised us from the condition of orang-outangs" [sic] are altered, a "relapse into savagery" can be expected (cited in Duffin 1978:84).

It was proposed that evolution requires of women that the

good of the individual woman be sacrificed for the good of the race (although that view contradicted the belief in individualistic struggle that was applied to men). This interesting argument appears to concede that under the conditions of Victorian life the development of the individual woman was sacrificed for the good of the boys she would rear. In their widely read *The Evolution of Sex*, Geddes and Thompson (1890/1899:267) nicely summed up the relationship between woman's suffrage and evolution: "What was decided among the prehistoric Protozoa cannot be annulled by an act of Parliament!"

The modern reader is astounded to discover that respected men (and later women) of science, not just ignorant popularizers, took the evolutionary argument for the inferiority of women very seriously. Many years were devoted to developing and challenging the Darwinian theory of female inferiority (Rosenberg 1982). Time-consuming labor was devoted to the gathering of enormous quantities of data, some of dreadful quality and some not, to prove and disprove these theses.

Link Between Social and Biological Science

By adopting Darwinism, in a way social science was only borrowing back its own creation. Darwin himself emphasized his debt to Malthus. Malthus' studies of economics, the "dismal science," taught him the truth of economist Ricardo's iron law of wages: as wages rose above subsistence, human fertility rose as well, increasing the labor supply and thus driving wages down to subsistence level again. Economist Adam Smith taught that the "invisible hand" of individual competitive self-interest regulated the laissez-faire economy for the good of all. Darwin "grafted Adam Smith upon nature" (Gould 1977a:100). The individual's competitive "self-interested" struggle to reproduce led to biological adaptation. The invisible hand was at work again.

Darwin was impressed by the French founder of positivist social psychology, Auguste Comte, as well as by the pioneer Belgian statistician Adolphe Quetelet, who had a great impact on Francis Galton, Darwin's cousin, and through Galton on other psychologists such as Karl Pearson. Like the great majority of men of his day, Galton accepted the inferiority of women. In fact, he believed that his own research had demonstrated that fact empirically (see Lewin, article 7; Rosenberg 1982). Galton's student Karl Pearson, who developed the Pearson correlation coefficient, originally shared his mentor's belief in female inferiority, but he had some doubts. In 1888 he published "The Woman Question" in *The Ethic of Free Thought*. (A second essay on women was published in 1894.) At that time he thought there might be an irreconcilable conflict between educating women and perpetuating the race, in which case, unfortunately, "the subjugation of women" would be required (Duffin 1978). Like Galton, Pearson believed that a high birth rate was of critical importance. Under the influence of the South African feminist Olive Schreiner, among others, he gradually shifted his views. In 1900 Pearson's assistant Alice Lee was already demonstrating that the skull capacity of several leading male scientists was less than that of some women students at Bedford College and was thus casting doubt on the evidence for female inferiority (Rosenberg 1982).

Comte was another social scientist who argued against female equality. In 1875 he explained that most women did not really want to be considered equal. Women would "suffer morally," they would not be able to tolerate the competition, and "affection between the sexes would be corrupted at its source." The last comment provides a poignant if unwitting glimpse of the nature of the relationships between men in the competitive Victorian milieu. Comte did consider women to be superior to men in "social feeling," a vital attribute (Robinson, 1982:41).

The link between social science and evolutionary theory was recognized at the time. Marx, that most critical of men, exempted Darwin from his general contempt for his contemporaries (Berlin 1948). Marx was delighted with evolutionary theory; he wrote to Engels in 1862:

It is splendid that Darwin again discovers among plants and animals his English society with its division of labour, competition, opening up of new markets, "inventions" and Malthusian "struggle for existence" (Bannister 1979:14).

In typical Victorian fashion — a fashion that persists today — Marx argued simultaneously that social forces act inevitably, impersonally, and mechanically and yet that active intervention and struggle (in his case, violent warfare) are essential to ensure that nature's deterministic laws are obeyed. Darwin himself was far too sophisticated to make such an argument, but several generations of post-Darwinians argued that the position and nature of women and men must be strictly enforced by authority, although they were already rigidly determined by biology.

John Stuart Mill, for one, pointed out the irony of this argument in 1867, in *The Subjugation of Women,* but to no immediate effect in either psychology or politics. How odd, said Mill, that those who consider marriage and motherhood to be woman's only natural states nevertheless act as though women would at once abandon those states if given the slightest opportunity to do so. Conservatives urge that the entire weight of society be used to compel women to marry and to mother, as though these were the last things women would ever do if left to their own choices. The same argument is often used today. President Nixon used it when he vetoed day-care legislation.

To summarize:

1. Darwin's biological ideas have been closely linked to the social sciences from their inception to the present.

2. Evolution was thought to involve not just change but also progress, that is, development to a higher, not just a different, level through struggle. Evolutionists today argue that we have no basis for claiming that evolution leads to better species, only that it leads to different species, each adapted to their local, temporary circumstances (Gould 1977a).

3. It appeared to follow that some people (of a given race, sex, nationality, or religion) are scientifically superior (more evolved) while others are inferior.

4. In understanding human nature, a doctrine of competitive biological determinism was substituted for the Enlightenment doctrines of Equality, Natural Rights, and the Harmony of Nature. This new world view, named Social Darwinism, proved to be so powerful intellectually that both feminists and traditionalists conducted their debate within its framework.

5. The Lamarckian theory that environmentally induced traits could be inherited, which Darwin believed, had a profound impact on Freud's thinking.

I return to the relationship between Darwinian thought and

psychology later. For now, I consider how Newtonian physics was grafted onto Darwinian biology to explain Victorian women and men to their own satisfaction.

Newton, Conservation of Force, and the Spermatic Economy

To develop his system of physics, Isaac Newton (1642–1727) made the momentous assumption that matter and energy (or force) are neither created nor destroyed but rather are endlessly converted from one form (such as heat or light) to another form. A fixed total quantity of matter and energy exist, which cannot be increased. This hypothesis is known as Conservation of Force.

Newton's concepts permeated academic thought in many disciplines. Both medicine and psychology drew on the concept of Conservation of Force. In America, in 1833, Arimiah Brigham, a doctor, explained that it was a fundamental law of living beings that when vital powers "are increased in one part, they are diminished in all the rest of the living economy" (Barker-Benfield 1978:375). Dr. Benjamin Rush held the same belief somewhat earlier. Notice the expression "the living economy." Many nineteenth-century economists believed in the Conservation of Wages or "wages pool" theory. This principle proposed that a society produces a fixed pool of money that can be spent on wages. The total devoted to wages cannot be increased. If wages in one sector are raised, then wages elsewhere must be reduced. The only way to pay Peter is by robbing Paul. The social impact of such a doctrine is obvious.

Although conservation of force had been established for the inanimate world, it was not clear in the early nineteenth century whether or not it applied to animals or to human beings. Johannes Müller (1801–58), an outstanding scientist who founded the first institute for experimental physiology, was a vitalist. That is, he believed that a nonmaterial vital or life force, inaccessible to scientific methods, existed in living organisms. Hermann Helmholtz (1821–94), a founder of psychology and perhaps Müller's most gifted student—among a very talented lot—was determined to overthrow the vitalist theory of his mentor. In a famous paper on Conservation of Force, which he published in 1847, Helmholtz introduced that concept into psychology and into physiology.

Helmholtz first electrified European science by proving that a measurable amount of time passed while a nerve impulse traveled from one end of the body of a frog to another site. He thus demonstrated that a nerve process closely related to mental life could be measured scientifically. He was also able to show that the energy used in the work performed by a frog was roughly equal to the energy contained in the food that the frog consumed, minus the energy required for the functioning of the frog's vital processes (Fancher 1979). Fechner (1801–87), another pioneer psychologist and the founder of psychophysics, also contributed to the application of Conservation of Force concepts in psychology. Among the other students at Müller's Institute were Brücke, who became Freud's teacher and mentor, and Virchow, who was later Karen Horney's professor. As we shall see, Freud accepted Conservation of Force as a fundamental assumption in his psychology. He gave the name libido to the sum of the vital force within each person.

The concept of Conservation of Force was also applied to Victorian sex-roles. To understand the objectives of the Victorians as they used Darwinian and Newtonian ideas, I now continue the study of the conditions of Victorian life.

Psychic Birth Control in Victorian America

The Problem: Why Was the Nineteenth Century the Period of Sexual Repression?

Everybody knows that the Victorians before Freud were exceptionally sexually repressed, and for once everybody is reasonably accurate. Historians agree that the nineteenth century was a time of unusual inhibition of sexuality (Cott 1978).

Modern readers are surprised to discover that eighteenth-century views of sexuality were far closer to our own ideas than were the beliefs of the nineteenth century. To learn something of eighteenth-century concepts of sexuality we may consult G. Archibold Douglas, one of the authors of a widely distributed sex manual of that time. He and a series of other writers used the pen name "Aristotle" to add a touch of prestige to their manuals. Sex was regarded as a healthy passion by these eighteenth-century "Aristotles," quite normal in both sexes. Virginity was "the boast and pride of the fair sex," but in due time women should be "honestly rid of it, for if kept too long, it loses much of its value, a stale virgin (if such a thing there be) being looked upon like an old almanac, out of date" (Douglas 1795, cited by Haller and Haller 1974:94). In direct contrast to nineteenth-century marriage manual authors, Douglas thought that sexual malfunctions might be caused by *lack* of sufficient sexual release. Douglas adds a comment on the merits of quality over quantity: "Women rather choose to have a thing done well, than have it done often." The ability to conceive was thought to depend directly on the sexual pleasure received. The clitoris was recognized as the organ that "both stirs up lust and gives delight in copulation, for without this, the fair sex neither desire mutual embraces, nor have pleasure in them, nor conceive by them" ("Aristotle" 1795, cited by Haller and Haller 1974). The clitoris had been identified by John Hunter (1728–93), a medical scientist, as the organ whose excitation led to orgasm (Haller and Haller 1974:93). Douglas erred in believing pleasure essential to conception, but in many ways he had an understanding of female sexuality in 1795 that was not recaptured for 171 years until Masters and Johnson published *Human Sexual Response* in 1966.

In the nineteenth century, sexuality fell upon hard times. By Freud's day the understanding of the functions of the clitoris and of female sexuality in general had been smothered by Victorian sexual ideology. It was claimed that women had no sexual feeling and that sexual desire was itself "inherently masculine."

That belief made it natural for Freud to claim that little girls went through a phallic-masculine phase. The discovery that a girl of three or four normally enjoys rubbing her clitoris was genuinely upsetting to Freud's Victorian sensibilities. He fully expected to be pilloried for saying so in print. Why was sex solely masculine? To answer this question it is helpful to look at the demographic revolution that occurred during the nineteenth century.

The Victorian Demographic Revolution in America

The Victorian era in America was a period of drastic decline in the number of children reared by the average couple. At the beginning of the nineteenth century, a healthy woman might bear thirteen to twenty-five children. According to Yans-MacLaughlin (1977), the *average* Italian immigrant woman in Buffalo around 1880 bore eleven children (cited by Ryan 1979:130). Between 1800 and 1900 the American birth rate fell from 50 per 1000 (of the general population) to 18.5 per 1000. To put it another way, whereas in 1800 the average white woman bore 7.04 children, in 1900 she bore 3.56 children (Harris 1978:54). (A similar pattern appeared in black families but starting at a later date.) Farm as well as urban families showed this decline (Easterlin 1978). The birthrate per family had been cut in half, the general birthrate more than half. (The sharp decline in the death rate due to major advances in public health made fewer children acceptable.) This quiet demographic revolution in the nineteenth century had the greatest importance for our lives today. But for this massive drop in the birthrate, America would now resemble India. How was it done?

The Solution: Psychic Birth Control

Family limitation in the nineteenth century was not accomplished primarily by mechanical birth control techniques. It was accomplished mostly by psychological means, which resulted in abstinence, a process I call "psychic birth control," by which I refer both to a behavior pattern and to a value system.

It is my thesis that a culture of sexual repression, combined with the American belief in the moral superiority of women, made possible a method of family limitation based on abstinence within marriage. It was an important aspect of Victorian society. Psychic birth control dominated Victorian views of men and women. The ideology of psychic birth control made it possible for married women to successfully insist upon abstinence for significant periods of time, sometimes for most of a lifetime.

The Voluntary Motherhood movement arose in the middle of the nineteenth century (Gordon 1974a, b). These reformers argued that sexual self-control and self-discipline, by which they meant abstinence and careful use of withdrawal, would make smaller but better families possible. At that time the belief that sexual restraint and sublimation were the price of civilization was not just a metaphor. Nor was it invented by Freud. It was a concrete statement of the facts as they appeared to many concerned persons. To have public education for all, to relieve grinding poverty, women and men must learn to control their sexual urges.

It was specifically the rejection of the woman's duty to have sex on demand with her husband—a duty written into law and confirmed by custom and tradition—that motivated a small group of more radical reformers who directly attacked the institution of marriage. What they meant by "Free Love" was a relationship in which a woman could have or could refuse to have sex with her spouse, depending upon her wishes and her desire for a child at the time. Reformers wrote about sexual abuse, that is, about husbands who demanded and obtained sex from their protesting and miserable wives and impregnated them against their will, if necessary by using painful force to induce obedience (Gordon 1974b:105–6). Daniel Scott Smith (1979) provides data to support the assumption that Victorian women exercised increased control over the number of children they bore, a practice he calls "domestic feminism." I believe that a critical component of Psychic Birth Control was the belief in the moral superiority of women, which gave women the legitimate right to say "no" to their own husbands, a right that had rarely, perhaps never, existed before in civilized societies and that is not yet acknowledged by all Americans.

Psychic Birth Control made possible the rise of the American middle class. (The function of a behavior refers to its consequences whereas causes initiate behavior.) Whatever the initial causes of the Victorian culture of Psychic Birth Control, it in fact functioned to permit movement into the middle class. Those who did limit the size of their families were more likely to rise into the middle class. Having "succeeded" they were in a good position to influence others.[1]

"Hold Still"

In the service of Psychic Birth Control female sexuality fell under scientific, moral, and theological assault. Once asexuality became the standard, women were specifically forbidden to take the initiative and were warned by doctors that if they moved during intercourse they would be infertile, or their husbands rendered impotent (Kern 1975:100).

Victorians could be quite explicit in their demand that female sexuality be quiet, passive, and motionless. In 1881 an English girls' academic high school, then five years old, held a cricket match. A local paper complained that the match was "very spirited": "We can only hope that when these muscular maidens come to be married no similar entry will have to be made in the chronicle of their connubial felicity" (Whitecut 1876, cited in Delamont and Duffin 1978:149).

By Freud's day activity was synonymous with masculinity, and passivity with femininity for many. By understanding Psychic Birth Control we can recognize the function of Victorian sexual beliefs that seem odd: that good women have no sexual needs, that there is so such thing as female orgasm, and that men need not concern themselves with satisfying women. (If men did, it would only interfere with the first two beliefs!) These beliefs lingered on. In an article published in 1950, Clara Thompson reported that a "well-known psychiatrist had told a group of students that in the female sexual life there is no orgasm"! (Thompson 1950/1973:60).

Why Was Psychic Birth Control Used Instead of Contraception?

Experts on the history of contraception, such as Reed (1978), Gordon (1974), and Noonan (1967) agree that almost all the major methods have been known since antiquity and were relatively effective. No true advance in birth control technology occurred for centuries until the development of the pill in the 1960s. We can therefore ask why contraception was not simply practiced directly in the nineteenth century, especially after the vulcanization of rubber in 1843 made the condom both cheaper and more reliable (Noonan 1967:469). Why did sexual repression decline only between 1890 and 1915 when, not by coincidence, psychoanalysis came into the picture? Why was family limitation not advocated openly by churches, academia, and science from 1800 on, since in fact its practice in some form was widespread and the human misery involved in the Victorian system of Psychic Birth Control was great? Could we have gone directly from the eighteenth century into the twentieth, psychologically speaking, and skipped over the era of sexual repression altogether? To this brash question, four answers may be tantatively offered.

1. *Religious tradition.* The Catholic tradition against contraception was maintained by a celibate clergy and was adopted by Protestants as well. Religion in America was not linked to an oppressive landed aristocracy that was deeply resented by a rising middle class, as it was in Europe. Psychic Birth Control, which was nothing if not highly moral, was more acceptable than the open or even private break with the teachings of religion required by the use of technological birth control.

2. *Competition between groups.* As immigration increased, the WASP descendants of the early English settlers in America became very worried that their country might be dominated by the new ethnic groups. By the later part of the nineteenth century a veritable panic over the declining Anglo-Saxon Protestant birthrate occurred in certain powerful establishment quarters. The Comstock laws, which made it a crime to provide either contraceptive information or devices, were passed in 1873 (Reed 1978). The Eugenics movement expressed one version of this fear. As it became obvious that it was the middle and upper class who were limiting family size most effectively, a Darwinian fear that the "best" elements were not reproducing developed.

The psychologist G. Stanley Hall was concerned that "race suicide" might result if more American women went to college—the fertility of the small number of college graduates was low. In 1886 he believed that the connection between education and low fertility was biological not social: excessive mental activity caused degeneration of the ovaries and the uterus. (John Dewey looked at the same data but disagreed about their significance.) Women were told that they shirked their duty to their "race" (i.e., cultural group) if they avoided motherhood (Rosenberg 1974:32). Family planning might help the individual family, but it appeared to be bad for the survival of the WASP community.

3. *Male fears of loss of status and prerogatives.* If the risk of pregnancy could be removed, then women might find it no harder than men to have lovers before or during marriage. Women might become as sexually experienced as men, as able to compare one man with another. Within marriage women might take the initiative. Male sexual prerogatives would have to be shared. Apparently the thought was not appealing to many men.

Those men whose own sense of potency had been significantly undermined by Victorian sexual inhibitions were perhaps particularly threatened by such changes. If Freud was right in believing that "castration anxiety" was universal these were a large category of men. The Doctrine of the Two Spheres functioned to increase male "castration anxiety" (i.e., the fear of femininity). By emphasizing the great difference between the sexes, as well as women's general inferiority, the dire nature of the man's potential fall into femininity was increased. Psychic Birth Control made sexuality itself dangerous (with wives) and disease ridden with prostitutes. (There is however, no record of medical castration of males actually being practiced to the extent that female castration and clitorectomy were carried out.)

4. *Female fear of contraception.* If sex without the fear of pregnancy were possible with women of their own social group, husbands, Victorian women feared, would stray (Gordon 1974b). Few women reported fears that they themselves would be tempted. Involvement with a woman of the husband's own background was a far more serious threat to the stability of the marriage than sex with a servant or a prostitute. Women understood that the Victorian division between Good women and Bad women prevented extramarital relationships from becoming permanent.

This was the Victorian "catch-22": abstinence and the sexual repression of women, required for effective Psychic Birth Control, stimulated the desire for extramarital sex in men; but contraceptives, which would make satisfying marital sex more possible, would also reduce the risk in extramarital sex and thus increase the risk of marital breakup. Today what Victorian women anticipated has come to pass. As contraceptive use becomes almost universal, divorce rates rise sharply. We keep the contraceptives and unhappily put up with the divorces—we feel we have no choice. They kept their marriages and put up with coldness, sexual frustration, and male infidelity—they felt they had no choice.

Reforming Capitalism: How Capitalism Contained the Seeds of Its Own Improvement

Family limitation not only broke the iron chain of Malthusian poverty; it also encouraged the reform of capitalism. When they liberated themselves from ceaseless childbearing and childrearing, women channeled their energies into effective social reform movements.

At one point a substantial percent of the graduates of women's colleges did not marry at all. Between 1865 and 1874 the proportion of ever-married women dropped to the lowest point it has ever reached in the United States. By 1915, 42 percent of the graduates of Eastern women's colleges were gainfully employed; 75 percent of female professionals were single in 1920 (Ryan 1979:142–43). Mothers of small families were especially likely to be social activists.

These educated women led the progressive movement to restrain and regulate capitalism. Because they had been reared to postpone immediate gratification, to discipline, self-denial, and struggle, they were effective long-term reformers. In that sense the capitalist emphasis on hard work, self-denial, and patience in waiting for rewards contained the seeds of its own reform. Unionization, integration of immigrants, studies of factory working conditions, and protective legislation were much indebted to these women reformers, who took women's moral superiority seriously and made constructive use of the mission they believed they had.

Femininism as a social reform movement collapsed only with "the return of the repressed," that is, with the rise in female sexuality and hedonism and with the general collapse of Victorian sex role ideology in 1918 after World War I.

The "Life Force" in Women Under Psychic Birth Control

Psychic Birth Control was given a scientific foundation by linking the doctrine of Conservation of Force to the service of Victorian sex-role ideology. It is a curious episode in the annals of science. Conservation of energy was applied to the individual on both the psychological and the physiological levels. The assumption was that a fixed pool of physiological-emotional energy exists. The human body is a closed system containing a limited quantity of this Life Force. Freud called it libido.

Life Force is used up by the functioning of a woman's reproductive system. If the vital force is drained off to the brain by intellectual activity, a host of ailments, including sterility or feeble infants, may result, according to Herbert Spencer and various American experts (Spencer 1880, cited in Smith-Rosenberg and Rosenberg 1973).

Women's intellectual deficiencies are due to the concentration of vital force in her reproductive organs. G. Stanley Hall, America's first Ph.D. in psychology, agreed with Spencer and added further refinements. Describing the adolescent girl, he explained:

Her sympathetic and ganglionic system is, relative to the cerebro-spinal, more dominant. Her whole soul, conscious and unconscious, is best conceived as a magnificent organ of heredity [i.e., reproduction] and to its laws all her psychic activities, if unperverted, are true (Hall 1904:561).

Freud and G. S. Hall saw eye to eye here. Hall invited Freud to give his first American presentation of psychoanalysis at Hall's university, Clark, in 1909. Through Freud, Erik Erikson echoed these ideas in his classic work *Childhood and Society* (1950). Although the vocabulary had been somewhat updated, Erikson, like Hall, believed that woman's whole soul (or psyche), especially her unconscious, is best conceived as a magnificent organ of reproduction. All her psychic activities are true to the laws of inner space. Following Rousseau, who was a severe misogynist in spite of his liberal views about (male) childrearing, and Helene Deutsch, Erikson agreed that men were males only part of the time but that a woman was never not-a-woman (Gordon 1974b:57; Erikson 1950). In recent years Erikson has modified these views in the light of feminist criticism.

Hall's strongly antifeminist influence was considerable (see Morawski, Chapter 5). Not only at Clark, but also at Wisconsin and Iowa, where Hall's students taught, conventional beliefs about sex differences were maintained (Rosenberg 1982). At Cornell, Titchener, the famous structural psychologist, held to the old ways. He explicitly excluded women from his newly founded Society for Experimental Psychology on the grounds that their admission would lower the status of the organization.

In sharp contrast to European psychologists, Hall, an American, did emphasize women's moral superiority. He explained that

she is at the top of the human curve from which the higher super-man of the future is to evolve, while man is phylogenetically by comparison a trifle senile, if not decadent.

Hall argued that women are not intellectually superior but that they are superior in their sensibilities, even though they are arrested on the evolutionary scale, as proved by their earlier maturation to puberty and thus their earlier fixation at a lower level (Hall 1904:561. See Morawski, Chapter 5). Thorndike, the famous inventor of the puzzle box for cats, also believed in women's moral superiority, which, in 1914, he attributed their maternal instinct (see Rosenberg 1982).

The Spermatic Economy of the Victorian Male

The concept of the "Spermatic Economy" (Barker-Benfield 1978) was the male counterpart to the Victorian belief in the asexual female. Again the Newtonian concept of Conservation of Force was called into play. For the man, the "spending" of vital powers (as sexual activity was called) diminished all other energies of the system. Given the limits to the Life Force, spending it on sex needlessly was wasting it. Sex drained Force from other activities, such as social mobility and economic achievement. The loss of sperm was equated with the loss of will power and of order. "Excessive" ejaculations could cause skin, lung, and brain disease, headaches, and nervousness. What was excessive? Once a month was recommended as the maximum frequency for sex for men (Haller and Haller 1974:97). Masturbation exhausted both the power of the sperm and the "living economy." A healthy male infant resulted from saving up sperm until it became rich.

The Victorians developed several related ideas as follows:

1. *Sublimation.* The concept of sublimation was based on conservation of vital force. The idea of sublimation assumes that the restriction of sexual activity saves specific quantities of Life Force that can then literally be translated into other valuable activities such as economic or cultural achievements. The idea was prevalent in educated nineteenth-century thought well before Freud used it (Barker-Benfield 1978).

2. *Masculine women.* Sexuality had become a masculine phenomenon. Once the sexual appetite had been defined as a male quality, it followed that the female who showed sexual interest must resemble a man. According to mid-nineteenth-century (male) gynecologists, she did (Barker-Benfield 1978).

3. *Sexuality as disease.* As female asexuality became normal, doctors came to see the presence of sexuality in women as a disease (Barker-Benfield 1978:383). Surgical removal of the cli-

toris to "cure" sexuality was first used in Berlin in 1858. It was used in London in 1882 by a future president of the Medical Society of London, to "cure" masturbation (Kern 1975:101–2). There was a sharp reaction against it in England. Clitorectomy to "cure" masturbation attracted considerable attention in France around the 1880s. It was used in the United States from at least 1867 to 1937 (Barker-Benfield 1978:388).

The Western practice of cauterization or partial or total removal of the clitoris never reached anything like the frequency that is still prevalent today in Muslim areas and in the Sudan. It is estimated that at least 30 million Muslim women living today have had clitorectomies performed on them, traditionally without any anesthesia, when the girl is four to six years old (Morgan and Steinem 1980; Saadawi, 1982). It is believed that clitorectomy (and in the Sudan, removal of the adjacent external genitals as well), makes Islamic women docile, fearful, sexually undemanding, and faithful, for the possibility of obtaining satisfaction outside (or inside) marriage has been largely removed.

4. *Sex and madness.* The necessity for establishing restraint, limits, and order upon unruly and dangerous sexuality, primarily in women and secondarily in men, was accompanied by the fear that sexuality was intimately linked to insanity. From masturbation to marital coitus, sexuality was thought to lead to madness. By the 1890s female castration (removal of the ovaries) as a treatment for neuroses and mental ailments was debated and practiced (Barker-Benfield 1978:389). When Charcot told Freud that mental illness always, always involves sexuality ("C'est toujours une chose sexuelle — toujours, toujours"), he drew on a belief system widely shared on both sides of the Atlantic.

How Widely Were These Sex Role Concepts Accepted?

Degler (1978) has located a number of experts more "reasonable," by our standards, than those quoted by Barker-Benfield. We need not make the implausible assumption that the entire educated population took the more extreme views literally to agree on a profound degree of sexual inhibition during that time.

Among lower class and immigrant groups the ideology of Psychic Birth Control and sexual repression was often lacking. Even in the 1920s and 1930s, among many low-income groups, Margaret Sanger found that women had no socially recognized right to refuse their husbands' sex no matter how destitute the family might be or how poor the health of the wife might be.

The Emotional Costs of Psychic Birth Control

In terms of personal unhappiness and suffering, the cost of the Victorian method of Psychic Birth Control through psychological repression was often great. Recall de Tocqueville's comment on the "cold, affectionless" wife.

Some women, frustrated under the Two Spheres doctrine by lives with little purpose or opportunity for the exercise of socially useful power, became domestic tyrants. Robert Benchley had these women in mind when he wrote of "aunt calling to aunt like mastodons bellowing across the primeval swamps." Japanese wives today are similarly constrained by a restrictive social code of female inferiority. They too are reputed to be tyrannical in the privacy of their homes.

The life of Charlotte Perkins Gilman, a foremost feminist theoretician (1898), is instructive. Charlotte's mother had married, adored her husband, had several babies in rapid succession, witnessed the death of one, and was told that she must not conceive again. Upon hearing that news, her husband, who came from an excellent upper class Boston family (the Beechers), deserted her and the children. Thereafter, he had only brief and occasional contacts with the children. Mrs. Perkins was forced to live with one relative after another, for she had no means of support for her family.

Charlotte's mother concluded that "love kills." She made a conscious effort not to show affection to her children and not to cuddle, hold, or pet them, so that as adults they could repress their affectionate feelings and would be spared her sufferings. Charlotte struggled for much of her life to overcome the effects of paternal abandonment and maternal depression. After many years Mrs. Perkins formally divorced Mr. Perkins. She was then treated as a social outcast. Psychic Birth Control could be a cruel system for both women and men.

Fragile Masculinity. Another cost of the system of Psychic Birth Control was the belief in the fragile nature of masculinity.

Victorian American ideology included the belief that masculinity is highly precarious. Enormous effort and energy are required, first to achieve masculinity and then to maintain it. There was little faith that masculinity might be an inborn trait that would develop in virtually any male infant of its own accord. It was not assumed that boys become men as naturally as acorns become oak trees. Why not? A culture might assume that life involves effort, or even tragedy, without assuming that masculinity is the focus of that struggle.

By dividing the sexes so sharply, adding a choice between being manly and being good, defending male superiority, and emphasizing female inferiority (the awful alternative to being manly), Victorians made the task of becoming a man doubtful. Then Victorian men felt even more threatened by women's strivings for equality. Men felt burdened by the moral, respectable, asexual Victorian woman they had helped to create. When a lower status group (women) presses with some modest success to raise their status, as occurred in the period 1865–1900, one must run very hard just to stay in place, that is, to maintain the original status gap. The belief in the fragile and precarious nature of masculinity was taken over by psychologists who took it for granted until very recently (Pleck 1980 and Chapter 9).

Sexual Frustration. There was also the price to be paid in terms of sexual needs. The nineteenth-century male was often sexually frustrated, with an equally frustrated wife who had even less opportunity for socially acceptable sexual satisfactions than he did. Loving sexuality as a means of soothing the frictions of marriage was undermined by the risks of unwanted pregnancy and poverty. It is not surprising that some unhappy mothers turned to "breaking the will" of their rebellious sons. Such behavior may be seen as a socially supported displacement of their anger against the system of Psychic Birth Control. The increased risk of contacting venereal disease was another cost of Psychic Birth Control— the risk to the prostitute, to the man, to the wife at home, and to children subsequently born blind or otherwise damaged—was real. No wonder sex appeared to be dangerous, dirty, and low to Victorians.

Neurosis. Finally there was the price of widespread neurosis. Functional (nonorganic) disorders seemed to increase markedly, especially among middle and upper class women (that is, those who practiced Psychic Birth Control) (Sicherman 1977).

Alice James, the sister of two famous brothers, William James the psychologist and Henry James the novelist, was one of the victims of neurosis. Their father may well have passed on a tendency to depression. He certainly provided an eccentric up-bringing. However, there is reason to believe that Alice was as able as her brothers. Hers is a tragic example of a life sacrificed to Victorian sex-role ideology and to the values demanded by Psychic Birth Control (Strouse 1980).

The Return of the Repressed: Decline of the Victorian System of Psychic Birth Control

In the later decades of the nineteenth century and the early decades of the twentieth century the system of Psychic Birth Control began to crumble as the repressed returned. Psychoanalysis appears from this vantage point as one of several social movements that assisted the population to leave behind a method of family limitation whose high cost became increasingly clear. Havelock Ellis preached a gospel of sensuality and gratification, although he himself suffered from various embarrassing sexual inhibitions. By 1904, Dr. T. Lockwood was even able to say a good word for male masturbation: "So dear hearer, if you find yourself [either sterile or impotent] blame no one for it but self-modesty and rare opportunities to cultivate the little pitiful appendage that now adorns the middle anterior portion of your anatomy" (Haller and Haller 1974:211).

The First World War severely damaged the rationalist-enlightenment faith in social reform, postponement of gratification, and self-denial. A frank hedonism seemed justified in such a brutal world. The era of the flapper had arrived. College women refused to sacrifice sex for good works. After extensive struggle, Margaret Sanger and other hardy pioneers opened birth control clinics. Contraceptives became available and widely used in America by about 1935, although the U.S. Government abandoned efforts to ban contraceptive shipments through the mail only in 1958 (Noonan 1967:487). The legacy of the Victorian era nevertheless lingered on, not least among psychologists.

A Final Note on Freud

Freud was born in 1856. Many of his beliefs about women, men, and neurosis were naturally the rather ordinary beliefs of an educated physician-scientist of his day. It is unreasonable to blame Freud for this, but it is essential to understand the context of his thought. Because of Freud's enormous contemporary impact, those of his ideas that depend on outmoded biological or other concepts have been lifted out of their historical context and treated as mysteries derived from the insights of a man of genius, all of which must be carefully preserved (e.g., Mitchell 1974). Many of the Freudian statements that are most baffling or offensive to modern sensibilities were banal when they were written. Other concepts that Freud expected his readers to find horribly disturbing are no longer upsetting—for example, the idea of infantile sexuality, that is, of childhood masturbation. The puzzling non sequiturs and the incomprehensible turns of thought in Freud's otherwise lucid writings are quickly clarified once we know his premises.

The modern student of Freud must remember at least four of Freud's Victorian assumptions. Freud, like Darwin, believed in the Lamarckian *inheritance of acquired characteristics:* the view that experiences and traits acquired during the lifetime of an organism could then be passed on to offspring by heredity. In the nineteenth century that was a plausible theory. We now know it is wrong. Freud combined that belief with the theory of *recapitulation:* that the young organism duplicates in its development the major historical stages of its kind. Thus the human child repeats in infancy and youth the stages whereby mankind rose from primitive levels to civilization. Recapitulation was expanded by Haeckel to include the "biogenic law" whereby unconscious memories, beliefs, and traits are inherited in Lamarckian fashion (Flanagan 1981; Gould 1977a, b; Sulloway 1979). For example, according to Freud, the little girl is smitten by a powerful and instantaneous envy of her brother's organ only because the sight evokes unconscious hereditary knowledge of "its organic significance for the propagation of the species" (Freud 1925:257, cited by Flanagan 1981).

Under the influence of his good friend Fliess, Freud also accepted a not uncommon belief in physical and *psychological bisexuality:* that the organism has the rudimentary characteristics of the other sex and has the psychologicat characteristics of the other sex to some degree as well. At the time embryology seemed to support the concept of bisexuality. Finally *the whole complex of ideas associated with Psychic Birth Control* inevitably had a major impact on Freud's work.

Here I can only briefly list some of the major Freudian theories that are dependent on these four principles according to Freud himself (Sulloway 1979; Gould 1977a, b; Flanagan 1981). They include the theory of psychosexual stages of development, the Oedipus complex, penis envy, and castration anxiety. Freud repeatedly says so:

The behavior of a neurotic child to his parents when under the influence of an Oedipus and castration complex . . . can only be understood phylogenetically, in relation to the experiences of earlier generations . . . the archaic heritage of mankind includes not only dispositions but also ideational contents, memory traces of the experiences of former generations (Freud 1939).

They also include the concepts of sublimation, of the libido, and of a phallic phase in girls that must be suppressed, as well as the beliefs that sublimation of sex is the price of civilization, that sexuality leads to neurosis, that women have an inferior sense of morality and justice (since Freud was not an American), that sexuality is necessarily masculine, that the clitoris is a masculine organ, that females are and must be passive (not take the initiative), that a woman must renounce her masculine clitoris, that there are two different kinds of female orgasms (a belief not invented by Freud: Sulloway 1979:185), that female sexuality and the female organs are inferior, that a successfully analyzed woman accepts her inferiority (Freud 1937:373), that the "undoubted" intellectual inferiority of women is due to "inhibition of thought necessitated by sexual repression" (Freud 1908:199), that sexual desire can be dammed up and sublimated into entirely different accomplishments like piano playing or architecture, and that childhood masturbation leads to neurosis. (Sulloway reports that Freud's relationship to his adolescent son Oliver was strained when Freud insisted that masturbation would harm him and must be stopped [Sulloway 1979:185].

Freud's concepts have been widely misunderstood by those

who do not accept their Victorian intellectual foundations and yet cling to these outmoded concepts. If Freud were alive today, would he continue to accept these concepts? I doubt it. It is time for psychologists to rid themselves of Victorian ideas. The thoughtless or ignorant use of psychological concepts that are comfortably familiar but that depend on outmoded theories and prevent innovative thought and progress must end.

Notes

1. I am indebted to Daniel Scott Smith (1979), Linda Gordon (1974a, b) and Carl Degler (1980:191), who helped me recognize the significant relationship between sexual repression and the demographic revolution that I call Psychic Birth Control.

However, none of the historians I have read emphasize the functional relationship between the ideology of sexual repression and the demographic transition as strongly as I have. None of them argue that it was sexual repression which made possible the demographic transition in America under the ideology of Psychic Birth Control.

I disagree with some of Degler's interpretations. Degler sees American women as struggling "against the family." He repeatedly makes the point that women's autonomy and self-awareness conflicted with "family values" of self-sacrifice, hierarchy, and putting others first. That is close, but that is not quite it. Women were and are not in conflict with "the family." They are at odds with men's values and men's roles in the family. Women's obligations would not leave them at a disadvantage compared to men in the outer world, if men shared equally in family obligations or applied women's values to themselves (whether or not that may be desirable for other reasons). By using a euphemism such as the "family value of hierarchy" when he means "male dominance," Degler sidesteps this issue and somewhat papers over the nature of the conflict.

References

Aries, Phillipe. 1962. *Centuries of Childhood. A Social History of Family Life.* New York: Knopf, p. 332.

Bannister, Robert. 1979. *Social Darwinism.* Philadelphia: Temple University Press.

Barker-Benfield, G. J. 1978. "The Spermatic Economy; a 19th-Century View of Sexuality." In M. Gordon (1978), *q.v.,* pp. 374–402.

Berlin, Isaiah. 1948. *Karl Marx.* London: Oxford University Press, ed. 2.

Bernard, Jessie. 1981. "The Good-Provider Role: Its Rise and Fall." *American Psychologist,* (January) 36(1):1–12.

Blackwell, Antoinette Brown. 1875. *The Sexes Throughout Nature.* New York: Putnam. Reprint, Westport, Conn: Hyperion Press, 1976. Cited by Hrdy (1981), *q.v.*

Bonsignore, John, E. Katsh, et al. 1974. *Before the Law.* Boston: Houghton Mifflin.

Boring, Edwin. 1930. "Gestalt Psychology and the Gestalt Movement." *American Journal of Psychology* 42:308–15.

Cott, Nancy. 1978. "Passionlessness: An Interpretation of Victorian Sexual Ideology, 1790–1850." *Signs* (Winter) 4(2):219–36.

Darwin, Charles. 1871. *The Descent of Man and Selection in Relation to Sex.* London: no publisher cited.

Degler, Carl N. 1978. "What Ought To Be and What Was: Women's Sexuality in the Nineteenth Century." In M. Gordon (1978), *q.v.,* pp. 403–25.

—— 1980. *At Odds: Women and the Family in America from the Revolution to the Present.* New York: Oxford University Press.

Delamont, Sara and Lorna Duffin. 1978. *The 19th Century Woman.* New York: Barnes and Noble.

Douglas, G. Archibald. 1795. "Aristotle's Complete Master-Piece in Three Parts, Displaying the Secrets of Nature in the Generation of Man." Cited by Haller and Haller (1974), *q.v.*

Duffin, Lorna. 1978. "Prisoners of Progress: Women and Evolution." In Delamont and Duffin (1978), *q.v.,* pp. 57–91.

Easterlin, L. "Factors in the Decline of Farm Fertility in the United States." In M. Gordon (1978), *q.v.,* pp. 533–45.

Erikson, Erik. 1950. *Childhood and Society.* New York: Norton.

Fancher, Raymond. 1979. *Pioneers in Psychology.* New York: Norton.

Flanagan, Owen. 1981. "The Freud-Lamarck Connection: The Philosophical Foundations of the Penis Envy Hypothesis." Paper delivered at the Cheiron Annual Meeting, River Falls, Wisconsin (June 10–13).

Freud, Sigmund. 1908. " 'Civilized' Sexual Morality and Modern Nervous Illness." *Standard Edition of the Complete Psychological Works of Sigmund Freud.* London: Hogarth Press, 9:179–204.

—— 1925. "Some Psychical Consequences of the Anatomical Distinction Between the Sexes." In *Standard Edition, q.v.,* 19:243–58.

—— 1937. "Analysis Terminable and Interminable." In *Standard Edition, q.v.,* 23:211–53.

—— 1939. Cited in Musto, David. 1980. "Continuity Across Generations: The Adams Family Myth." In Mel Albin, ed. *New Directions in Psychohistory.* Lexington Mass: Heath, pp. 117–33.

Geddes, Patrick and Arthur Thompson. 1890/1899. *The Evolution of Sex.* London: Walter Scott. Cited by Duffin (1978), *q.v.,* p. 63.

Gilman, Charlotte Perkins. 1898. *Women and Economics.* Boston. Cited by Rosenberg (1974), *q.v.,* pp. 41, 60, 133, 195, vii.

Glasersfeld, Ernest von. 1980. "Adaptation and Viability." *American Psychologist* (Nov.) 35:970–74.

Glueck, Grace. 1977. "The Woman as Artist: Rediscovering 400 Years of Masterworks." *New York Times* (Sept. 25), section 6, p. 54.

Gordon, Ann D. 1979. "The Young Ladies Academy of Philadelphia." In Carol Ruth Berkin and Mary Beth Norton, eds. *Women of American History,* pp. 68–91. Boston: Houghton Mifflin.

Gordon, Linda. 1974a. "Voluntary Motherhood." In Mary Hartman and Lois Banner, eds. *Clio's Consciousness Raised,* pp. 54–71. New York: Harper and Row.

—— 1974b. *Woman's Body, Woman's Right*. New York: Penguin.

Gordon, Michael. 1978. *The American Family in Social-Historical Perspective*, ed. 2. New York: St. Martin's Press.

Gould, Stephen Jay. 1977a. *Ever Since Darwin*. New York: Norton.

—— 1977b. *Ontogeny and Phylogeny*. Cambridge, Mass: Harvard University Press.

Hall, Stanley G. 1904. *Adolescence, vol. 2*, New York: no publisher. Cited by Rosenberg (1974), *q.v.*, p. 27.

Haller, John and Robin Haller. 1974. *The Physician and Sexuality in Victorian America*. Urbana, Ill.: University of Illinois Press.

Hardin, Garrett. 1959. *Nature and Man's Fate*. New York: Holt, Rinehart, Winston.

Hecht, Marie, J. D. Berbrich, S. A. Healey, and C. M. Cooper. 1973. *The Women, Yes*. New York: Holt Rinehart Winston.

Harris, Barbera, 1978. *Beyond Her Sphere: Women and the Professions in American History*. Westport, Conn: Greenwood Press.

Hrdy, Sarah Blaffer. 1981. *The Woman That Never Evolved*. Cambridge, Mass: Harvard University Press.

Janeway, Elizabeth. 1971. *Man's World, Woman's Place*. New York: Dell.

Kern, Stephen. 1975. *Anatomy and Destiny*. Indianapolis: Bobbs Merrill.

Lasch, C. 1977. *A Haven in a Heartless World*. New York: Basic Books.

Mitchell, Juliet. 1974. *Psychoanalysis and Feminism*. New York: Random House.

Morgan, Robin and G. Steinem. 1980. "The International Crime of Genital Mutilation." *Ms*. (March).

Mott, L. and Stanton, E. C. 1848. "Declaration of Sentiments and Resolutions." In M. Hecht et al., eds. (1973), *q.v.*

Noonan, John T., Jr. 1967. *Contraception*. New York: Mentor-Omega.

Peters, Margot. 1975. *Unquiet Soul, a Bibliography of Charlotte Bronte*. Garden City, New York: Doubleday, p. 305; "Women's Mission." *Westminster Review* (Jan. 1850), pp. 181–96.

Pleck, Joseph. 1980. *The Myth of Masculinity*. Cambridge, Mass.: MIT Press.

Reed, James. 1978. *From Private Vice to Public Virtue*. New York: Basic Books.

Robinson, Daniel. 1982. *Toward a Science of Human Nature*. New York: Columbia University Press.

Rosenberg, Rosalind Lee. 1974. "The Dissent from Darwin, 1890–1930: The New View of Women Among American Social Scientists." #75-6915 University Microfilms, 300 N. Zeeb Rd., Ann Arbor, Mich. 48106.

—— 1982. *Beyond Separate Spheres: Intellectual Origins of Modern Feminism*. New Haven, Conn.: Yale University Press.

Ryan, Mary P. 1979. *Womanhood in America*, ed. 2. New York: New Viewpoints Press.

Saadawi, Nawal El. 1982. *The Hidden Face of Eve: Women in the Arab World*. Boston: Beacon Press.

Schweber, Silvan. "The Origin of *The Origin* revisited." *Journal of the History of Biology, vol. 10*, (no further data given). Cited by Gould, S. J., 1979. "Darwin's Middle Road." *Natural History* (Dec. 27–31) 88(10).

Sicherman, Barbara. 1977. "The Uses of Diagnosis: Doctors, Patients, and Neurasthenia." *Journal of the History of Medicine* 32(1):35–54.

Smith, Daniel Scott. 1979. "Family Limitation, Sexual Control and Domestic Feminism in Victorian America. In Nancy Cott and Elizabeth Pleck, eds. *A Heritage of Her Own,* pp. 222–45. Originally in *Feminist Studies* (Winter–Spring, 1973) 1:40–57.

Smith-Rosenberg, Carroll and Charles Rosenberg. 1973. "The Female Animal: Medical and Biological Views of Woman and Her Role in 19th Century America." *The Journal of American History,* (Sept.) 9(2):340–43.

Spencer, Herbert. 1876. *Principles of Sociology.* London: Williams and Norgate, *vol. 1.*

—— 1896/1910. *Principles of Sociology,* 3 vol. New York. Cited by Haller and Haller (1974), *q.v.,* p. 64.

Strouse, Jean. 1980. *Alice James: A Biography.* Boston: Houghton-Mifflin.

Sulloway, Frank J. 1979. *Freud: Biologist of the Mind.* New York: Basic Books.

Thompson, Clara. 1950. "Some Effects of the Derogatory Attitude Toward Female Sexuality." In Jean Baker Miller, ed. *Psychoanalysis and Women.* Baltimore: Penguin. 1973.

Thompson, Mary Lou. 1970. *Voices of the New Feminism.* Boston: Beacon Press.

Tocqueville, Alexis de. 1835/1945. Edited by Phillips Bradley. *Democracy in America, vol. 2,* chapters 8–13. See especially chapters 9, 10, and 12, and appendix U, 383–84. New York: Vintage.

Welter, Barbara. 1978. "The Cult of True Womanhood: 1820–1860." In M. Gordon, (1978), *q.v.,* pp. 313–33.

Whitecut, Janet. 1876. *Edgbaston High School, 1876–1976.* Birmingham, England: privately printed, p. 43. Cited in Delamont and Duffin (1978), *q.v.,* p. 749.

Yans-MacLaughlin, Virginia. 1977. *Family and Community: Italian Immigrants in Buffalo, 1880–1930.* Ithaca, New York, p. 105. Cornell University Press.

Zaretsky, Eli. 1976. *Capitalism, The Family, and Personal Life.* New York: Harper & Row.

4 Leta Hollingworth

Toward a Sexless Intelligence

ROSALIND ROSENBERG

EDITOR'S NOTE *This article on the work of the early psychologist Leta Hollingworth and her contemporaries is an excerpt from chapter 4 of Rosalind Rosenberg's* Beyond Separate Spheres *(1982). Before this section Rosenberg describes another pioneer woman psychologist, Helen Thompson, who entered the new, half-built University of Chicago after she graduated at the head of her high school class in 1893. Chicago's President Harper, backed by ample funds and high aspirations, had recruited John Dewey, George Herbert Mead, James Angell, and James Tufts—all then under age 35—to his philosophy department. As was customary, it included psychology. Rosenberg traces the fascinating and unique circumstances that made that psychology department the most receptive in the country to challenging the traditional view of the sexes. One source of the unusual departmental climate were the highly able, college graduate, feminist women who married Dewey, Mead, and Angell. (Angell's father, once president of the University of Michigan was also a staunch defender of women in higher education against the more conservative beliefs of the Eastern colleges). Gradually these faculty changed their thinking about women.*

    After a brilliant undergraduate career Helen Thompson con-

tinued toward her Ph.D. at Chicago, where she conducted the first major study of the mental differences between women and men. Her review of the existing literature demonstrated the marked inconsistencies, contradictions, and lack of data behind the conventional wisdom on sex differences (such as men's alleged active vs. women's quiescent metabolism —and hence intellect). In 1900 she conducted the first experimental laboratory study of sex differences in mental traits for her summa cum laude dissertation. Breaking new ground, she used measures of information, associations, emotional reactions, motor skills, and sensory abilities. (At the time sensory and motor measures were believed to directly reflect intelligence and mental traits.) Unlike most psychologists of her day, she carefully matched her sets of male and female subjects on background variables. She graphed her data distributions instead of using only the usual simple averages. She discovered both wide individual variations and the remarkable similarity of the two sexes, relative to what had been expected. She was the first to discover the difference between the sexes in the handling of spatial materials (puzzles), which is the focus of so much current interest. Her book The Mental Traits of Sex *(1903) stressed environmental determinants, as well as the basic similarities of the sexes. Her work was important in undermining biological determinism and inspired other women in more traditional psychology departments to further challenge the old views. Unfortunately after her marriage and the birth of two daughters, Helen Thompson Woolley was not able to obtain another academic post in Cincinnati, where the family settled, but she remained very active in social reform and suffrage work and made important contributions to the field of child development.*

The psychologist most influenced by the graduate work of Helen Thompson Woolley was Leta Stetter Hollingworth, who began graduate work in psychology at Columbia in 1911. At that time, Columbia's psychology department, under the direction of James McKeen Cattell, led the country in the study of individual differences and gave the best training available in statistics, testing, and experimental procedures. But Columbia was much slower than Chicago to welcome women graduate students, and Columbia's psychologists were singularly unsympathetic to feminist ideas. Leta Hollingworth might never have studied sex differences there had she not been married to Henry Hollingworth, a Cattell student teaching at Barnard, who, in contrast to his Columbia colleagues, was an outspoken defender of feminism. Henry's encouragement made it possible for Leta to raise questions to which the rest of the Columbia faculty was initially hostile.

After Woolley's work, psychologists were less ready to emphasize the differences between the male and female mind than they had been before, but, especially among the builders of the new departments of psychology, there remained the firm conviction that at the upper ranges of intelligence and creativity women were less well represented due to their lesser variability. The leaders of psychology believed further that women were less reliable than men, due to their periodic incapacity while menstruating, and less suited to the rigors of graduate training, due to their instinctive preference for motherhood. These were the beliefs that Hollingworth devoted her early career in psychology to challenging.

From Nebraska to New York

When the Hollingworths married in 1908, Henry had not yet finished his graduate training. The couple had met at the University of Nebraska two years earlier, and Leta had stayed behind to teach high school until Henry finished at Columbia. But they had tired of waiting and had decided they could live on the income that Leta could earn as a teacher in New York. What they did not realize, but soon discovered, was that New York barred married women from teaching. After four years of college preparation and two years of teaching experience, the new Mrs. Hollingworth found herself reduced to making a home in a small, dark New York apartment on the limited resources of some meager savings (H. Hollingworth 1943).

In the time left over from housework, cooking, dressmaking, mending, washing, and ironing, she tried writing and took a few literature courses at Columbia, but her stories did not sell, and her classes, she declared, were full of "dry bones." Through her husband she developed an interest in psychology and applied for fellowships to pursue full-time graduate study but with no success. Henry Hollingworth later recalled his young wife's sense of despair:

Almost always she effectually stifled her own eager longing for intellectual activity like that of her husband. Day after day, and many long evenings, she led her solitary life in the meagerly furnished quarters, while he was away at regular duties or seizing on this and that opportunity to earn a few dollars on the side, by lectures, tutoring and assorted odd jobs. . . . There were occasional periods of discouragement; once in a while she would unexpectedly and for no apparent cause burst into tears. These slips from her customary determined and courageous procedure she could hardly explain then, even to herself. Later she was able to make it clear that it was because she could hardly bear, with her own good mind and professional training and experience, not to be able to contribute to the joint welfare more than the simple manual activities that occupied her (1943:98–100).

In 1909 Henry Hollingworth completed the work for his Ph.D. and received an appointment as instructor in psychology and logic at Barnard College. With his new income he decided to finance his wife's graduate work in educational psychology at Columbia and Teachers College. For most academic couples the commencement of a steady income signaled the start of childbearing, but the Hollingworths remained childless. Leta Hollingworth clearly enjoyed children and spent much of her career working with them; perhaps she would have liked having some of her own but discovered she could not. On the other hand, her own frontier childhood had been a singularly miserable one—"There's no place like home—Thank God!" she once quipped, remembering her mother's early death in childbirth and her father's bitter fighting with his second wife. Leta Hollingworth saw no romance in motherhood and publicly condemned the social pressures that forced most women to become mothers. Perhaps she chose to remain childless, believing that the financial and professional constraints on her life were too great to allow for motherhood (1916a).

Women at Columbia

Few women had braved the struggle for a Columbia doctoral degree in psychology before Leta Stetter Hollingworth began graduate work in 1911. Twenty years before, in 1891, the Columbia trustees had modified their long-time opposition to female graduate education by delegating to the individual graduate faculties the power to enroll women as auditors. Even so slight a relaxation of traditional standards outraged the Faculty of Political Science, which voted to exclude women from all of its classes. The Faculty of Philosophy, however, which offered work in psychology, took a more sanguine view of female visitors and agreed to extend women auditing privileges upon the consent of individual instructors. Under this provision Margaret Floy Washburn visited in James McKeen Cattell's laboratory in 1891 and 1892. Realizing that she would never be able to work for a degree, however, she left after a year for Cornell to pursue regular graduate study. Barnard, which opened as an undergraduate college in 1889, offered limited graduate work with the help of a few moonlighting Columbia professors, but not until 1898, when Teachers College became part of Columbia and began offering graduate work in educational psychology, and 1900, when Barnard surrendered all graduate instruction to Columbia, did women become regular students in Columbia's graduate degree programs (Rosenberg 1982:86).

By 1906 women comprised half of the student body in the Faculty of Philosophy and one-third in all of the faculties, including pure science and political science, where women were still barred from some classes. This feminine enthusiasm for graduate education caused some concern among the faculty and administration. As Dean of Philosophy Edward Perry noted in his annual report to the president, "The great increase in the number of women has naturally brought with it some problems of administration, the solution of which has not been easy. Certain subjects are almost entirely incapable of satisfactory treatment before a mixed audience." Though Dean Perry did not specify which courses posed this difficulty, he explained that the problem had been solved by teaching the offending courses twice, once for women and again for men. Whatever the difficulties, he recognized that women were there to stay.

As has been often pointed out, the unusually large proportion of women graduate students at Columbia is due to our situation in a huge city, where women are in a large majority among the teachers in the schools. Many of these women have both the time and the ambition for self-improvement by attendance upon university courses (Columbia 1906:132).

About 150 women a year were enrolling in advanced philosophy, psychology, and anthropology courses by 1906. Only two, however, had earned the Ph.D. Though many women could pay the $30 to $45 per course on an occasional basis, few could devote themselves to full-time study at a cost of at least $600 a year for tuition and living expenses. Columbia offered twelve University fellowships each year, valued at $650, but none was open to women, and of the thirty-two scholarships offered to cover the $150 tuition, women could apply for only four. (Rosenberg 1982:87).

Added to the financial pressure faced by would-be women doctoral candidates was the more subtle, but equally powerful weight of prejudice. Columbia's faculty and administration had little confidence in women's scholarly abilities. "In most cases the women make good students, and some of the best we have had in the School of Philosophy have been women," Dean Perry conceded, "but on the whole, I think, a smaller proportion of them than of the men are capable, either by natural endowment or opportunity, of undertaking really advanced or original work, and the proportion of them who reach the doctorate is almost pathetically small." With the exception of Henry Hollingworth, the frontiersman from the coeducational University of Nebraska, none of the psychology faculty had ever studied with either an undergraduate or graduate woman, and their wives filled very traditional roles, centered around rural homes from which their academic husbands made lengthy commutes to Columbia (Rosenberg 1982:88).

Long after Edward Clarke raised the specter of race suicide, psychology chairman James McKeen Cattell was warning of its threat in the pages of the *Popular Science Monthly.* In 1909 Cattell observed,

Girls are injured more than boys by school life; they take it more seriously, and at certain times and at a certain age are far more subject to harm. It is probably not an exaggeration to say that to the average cost of each girl's education through high school must be added one unborn child.

It was bad enough, Cattell believed, for women to be educated, but the great curse to modern society came from allowing them to be teachers.

When spinsters can support themselves with more physical comforts and larger leisure than they would as wives; when married women may prefer the money they can earn and the excitement they can find in outside employment to the bearing and rearing of children; when they can conveniently leave their husbands should it so suit their fancy—the conditions are clearly unfavorable to marriage and the family. . . . There are in the United States about 400,000 women employed as teachers, and the numbers are continuously increasing. . . . This vast horde of female teachers in the United States tends to subvert both the school and the family (1909:91–92).

The younger faculty tended to be somewhat more temperate in their views about the evils of educating women, but even they voiced doubts about female intellectual capacity. In his 1906 article, "Sex in Education," Edward Thorndike, a student of Cattell's and the man Cattell designated for an opening in educational psychology at Teachers College, recommended against the advanced training of women because of the well-established fact, known since Darwin, that women were less variable than men and therefore less likely to have the necessary ability to succeed in advanced work. "Not only the probability and the desirability of marriage and the training of children as an essential feature of women's careers, but also the restriction of women to the mediocre grades of ability and achievement should be reckoned with by our educational systems," he wrote, "postgraduate instruction, to which women are flocking in large numbers is, at least in the higher reaches, a far more remunerative investment in the case of men" (1906:213).

Like Cattell, Thorndike thought it unwise to encourage women to pursue graduate work, but he saw a certain utility in having a few women working at the doctoral level. In 1902 he hired Naomi Norsworthy, Columbia's first woman graduate student in psychology, to assist him at Teachers College. As he informed his former Harvard Professor William James, "You will be glad to know that I have for next year and thereafter an instructor to take off a great deal of the burden of my work, so that I shall be able to give myself up almost entirely to graduate courses and the direction of research" (Joncich 1968:221).

The difference between Cattell's generation and Thorndike's can be seen in Thorndike's argument with Cattell six years later when Thorndike wanted to make Norsworthy an assistant professor. Cattell adamantly opposed promoting a woman to a professorial rank, but Thorndike argued with him that Teachers College had special needs that women could best meet.

If you were in full acquaintance with our situation and with her work, I think you would include it in a wider point of view. Teachers College is in part a graduate school and in part a professional school. The most gifted people for training teachers in certain lines (e.g. elementary methods, kindergarten, domestic art) are at present and will for a long time be women. . . . Dr. Norsworthy is beyond any question enormously successful in training teachers. . . . I would be sacrificing the interests of Teachers College to do anything that helped withhold from her the promotion that a man equally competent would be sure to have had (Thorndike 1908).

Thorndike won Norsworthy her promotion by persuading his superiors that the employment of a woman at Teachers College would not undermine the conventional view of womanhood to which most academics subscribed. But Norsworthy's example and the example of women who followed her modified this conventional view considerably.

The Experimental Perspective

Though Columbia gave no more than grudging support to its women students and faculty and adhered to a conservative view of women's potential, its psychological researchers manifested an aggressive skepticism in their experimental work that threatened that very conservatism. Thorndike, in particular, achieved notoriety for the enthusiasm with which he tore into established psychological doctrine. As psychologist Lewis Terman later recalled, "He seemed to me shockingly lacking in a decent respect for the opinions of mankind!" (1936:319).

Between 1900 and 1910 Columbia became an important center of the growing attack on armchair, evolutionary thinking, as a new generation of psychologists completed their doctorates and began looking with a jaundiced eye at the current understanding of the human and animal mind. Less encumbered with the religious and philosophical baggage of the past than were their mentors, Edward Thorndike, Robert Woodworth, Clark Wissler, and others practiced what their teachers often only preached—a rigorous, experimental examination of human behavior. For all of their prejudices against women they slowly put together the skeptical elements of a psychological system that could accommodate a very different view of feminine behavior from the one their own biases allowed.

As they devised ever more carefully controlled experiments, they developed a special scorn for those fathers of modern science like Lester Frank Ward and G. Stanley Hall, who indulged in romantic speculations about the origins of human society and intelligence. In 1898 Edward Thorndike articulated that scorn in his doctoral thesis on animal intelligence. Evolutionists believed that the mental likeness between animals and human beings could be demonstrated by the reasoning powers displayed by animals and the instinctive behavior exhibited by human beings, but Thorndike argued that animals were neither so intelligent nor so instinctive in their behavior as most evolutionists assumed (1898:109).

Thorndike studied animal intelligence with the help of a slotted cage in which he built a door that opened by pulling a string. He placed a hungry dog, cat, or monkey in the cage and set some food outside as a reward for getting out. Leaving the animal to its own devices, he observed its behavior until it succeeded in opening the door. The animals Thorndike studied gave no sign of trying to reason their way out, nor did they show any instinctive understanding of how to open the door. Instead, they clawed all over the box until, by accident, they struck on the right technique. Gradually, through subsequent trials, and much additional flailing, they reduced the time it took to get out. Blind trial and error, Thorndike concluded, not reasoning or instinct, explained their behavior. Increasingly skeptical of both instinct and reasoning in animals, he began to look more critically at behavior assumed to be either instinctive or rational in human beings. Much of the activity that psychologists casually labeled instinctive, e.g., the "instinct of self-preservation," could be better explained, he decided, as a simple reaction to a particular experience, e.g., "eating to get rid of hunger." On the other hand, much of human learning, conventionally attributed to conscious reflection, stemmed, he believed, from the same kind of trial and error displayed by animals in his box. Neither animals nor human beings, he concluded, relied as heavily on either instinct or ratiocination as most social theorists assumed (1898:38–46, 105–109; 1913:14).

Thorndike's colleague Clark Wissler added fuel to the anti-evolutionary fire with his ill-fated attempt to correlate lower mental activity with intelligence in his 1901 doctoral thesis. Further work at Columbia confirmed Wissler's finding that no direct connection existed between morphology and ideas and that Cattell's initial faith in the possibility of constructing tests of intelligence based on simple motor tests would have to be abandoned. By 1909 Thorndike could report that sensory discrimination had little to do with general intelligence.

The present results [demonstrate] that the efficiency of a man's equipment for the specifically human task of managing ideas is only loosely correlated with the efficiency of the simpler sensori-motor apparatus which he possesses in common with other species (1909:367).

Faith in the body's power to control the mind waned further as psychologists examined the problem of mental fatigue. One of the basic assumptions of Spencerian psychology, as well as the critical foundation of Edward Clarke's condemnation of advanced education for women, was the belief that the mind and body formed a closed energy system. When demands on that energy grew too heavy, psychologists and psychiatrists believed, the body broke down and nervous disease ensued. Trying to test this basic assumption, researchers conducted dozens of experiments on the mental effects of fatigue. As Columbia's Robert Woodworth told a group of psychiatrists in 1906, these experiments showed that the brain was not so susceptible to fatigue as had long been thought. The tiredness that overcame subjects engaged in prolonged mental labor was "a sensory or emotional affair, a feeling of fatigue not a true fatigue in the sense of incapacity." When experimenters urged subjects to resist the desire to stop work and to "determine to stick to it for a while longer," the subject usually found that his brain was "still in good working order, that the feeling of fatigue" had passed away. Very often, in fact, the subject found that his best work was "done after rather than before the time his feelings told him he was played out." Attitude, Woodworth and his colleagues came to believe, played a more important role in intellectual accomplishment than physical endurance did. Along with the work being done on animal intelligence, human instinct, and the correlation of mental traits, studies of fatigue prompted a few male researchers to question the popular belief that a unique female physiology gave rise to a unique female intelligence (Rosenberg 1982:93).

In 1906 the New York *Independent* sponsored a debate on the issue of female intelligence between members of the old guard and the new. Lester Frank Ward, representing the liberal wing of the traditional evolutionary theorists, opened the discussion with a recapitulation of his theory of sexual divergence. This divergence, he argued, which had begun with the lowly protozoa and had steadily increased with evolutionary development, could be arrested, or even reversed, if only men would begin choosing their mates for qualities of intelligence and strength rather than for qualities of delicacy and vacuity as they had in the past. G. Stanley Hall, representing the more conservative evolutionists, accepted Ward's evolutionary premise but ridiculed his Lamarckian faith that feminine characteristics had been acquired and could be eradicated. No such mortal interference in evolutionary development as Ward envisioned, Hall charged, could obviate the biological trend toward ever greater sexual differentiation (1906).

Edmund Wilson, a young Columbia cytologist who had just discovered the chromosomal basis of sex determination, and psychologist Clark Wissler castigated Ward and Hall alike for their speculative evolutionism. Wilson objected particularly to Ward's anthropomorphic description of the origins of sexual differentiation in which he assumed that lowly organisms discriminated among sexual contenders in the same way that human beings did. How could Ward seriously argue, Wilson wondered, that "males when no more than 'shapeless masses' or 'mere sperm-sacs' engaged in a rivalry to be selected, and that females of animals at so low a stage of development had the wit to 'select the best and reject the inferior' from their misbegotten progeny." While Wilson, the cytologist, questioned the anthropomorphic imposition of esthetic standards on physiological activity, Wissler, the psychologist and ethnologist, challenged the imposition of physiological laws on human intelligence. "It is curious," Wissler wrote,

that it has always seemed necessary to carry the theory of evolution up through morphology into the psychic life of animals and men and finally into those human practices that are designated conventional. While there is doubtless some connection between the fundamental elements of psychic life and physiological function, the direct connection between the details of ideas and such function is not clear (1906:664).

Wilson and Wissler believed that their research cast doubt on some of the popular beliefs about the nature of womanhood, but they did not pursue this doubt. Their chief interest lay in their research, not in public debates over the social implications of their research. Not until scientists began training women as researchers did the revolutionary implications of some of these experiments for the understanding of woman's nature become evident.

Periodicity, Variation, and Maternal Instinct

Henry Hollingworth introduced his wife to experimental psychology by asking her to assist him on an experiment of the effect of caffeine on mental and motor abilities. One of the precautions he took in his "zeal to control all of the possible variables," as he later recalled, "was to have the women subjects record the occurrences of the menses, during the six weeks experimental period." When the results of the experiment were reported, Leta Hollingworth noticed that no mention was made of the influence of menstruation on the work of the women subjects. Out of curiosity she studied the data herself and found no evidence that the women's performances had varied with their menstrual periods as her husband had feared they might (H. Hollingworth 1943:114–15; Shields 1975).

Though Henry Hollingworth saw no special importance in this nonfinding, Leta Hollingworth found it highly significant. No dogma about women's nature enjoyed wider acceptance among doctors and psychologists, from Edward Clarke to Havelock Ellis, than the idea that women suffered periodic incapacity from menstruation. In fact, some did not limit their allegations of women's disability to the menstrual period itself. Ellis, for instance, believed:

Menstruation is not an isolated phenomenon. It is but the outward manifestation of the climax of a monthly physiological cycle, which influences

throughout the month the whole of a woman's physical and psychical organism (L. Hollingworth 1914a:1).

Whatever one thought of women's mental abilities, one could still
argue that the debilitating effect of the menses and the deranging
influence of the physiological cycle associated with it justified separate male and female spheres of activity, and many argued just
that.
    Incensed by charges of menstrual-related disability, Leta
Hollingworth chose to study the effect of women's menstrual cycle
on their motor and mental abilities for her doctoral research. From
among the students at Teachers College, where she was studying
with Edward Thorndike, she recruited twenty-three women and two
men to serve as subjects for her study. She told no one of the
experiment's purpose but asked each subject to give a daily report of any physical complaints or unusual events and asked the
women to record the occurrence of their menses. The subjects
ranged in age from 20 to 40 years and had worked or were working in a variety of professional occupations (teaching, nursing,
administration, etc.) in addition to studying at the college. Eight
of the volunteers took the battery of mental and motor tests daily
for three months, while the remaining seventeen were examined
only every third day for a month (1914a:11–14, 86–87).
    When she had tabulated data, Hollingworth looked in vain
for evidence of a cyclical pattern in her subjects' test results. In
two instances women suffered pain on the first day of menstruation and these two women fell off in their performance on the
"naming of opposites test," but in no other test could any cycle
be seen in any of the tests administered. "The present study by
no means covers all phases of the question of the mental and
motor abilities of women during menstruation," she conceded,
but on the other hand, nothing in the test results provided any
evidence for the widespread belief that women suffered periodic
incapacity in their physical and intellectual abilities (1914a:57, 92–
95).
    Hollingworth attributed the "striking disparity" between re-
ceived wisdom on this subject and her empirical findings to the
bias of most authorities. Prejudice against the uterus, that ultimate and most compelling symbol of feminine divergence from

the male type, and belief in its disturbing power had simply been passed from author to author without critical analysis. Furthermore, she observed, the belief that the uterus incapacitated women from normal work in the male world had originated in reports from male physicians.

It should be obvious to the least critical mind that normal women do not come under the care and observation of physicians. To investigate the matter experimentally has been somewhat difficult, because until recently all investigators were men, and the taboo put upon the phenomenon by men and women alike rendered it a more or less unapproachable subject for experiment by men who were not physicians (1914a:95).

The only woman doctor to study menstruation systematically, since Mary Putnam Jacobi examined Clarke's charge that menstruating women needed rest, was Clelia Duel Mosher, whose results, published in 1911, added support to Hollingworth's conclusions. Mosher began her study of menstruation as a graduate student in physiology at Stanford in 1894 and continued it, first, at Johns Hopkins Medical School and then back at Stanford, where she became the physician for the women students. In the course of her experiments Mosher examined the menstrual periods of 400 women over 3,350 menstrual cycles. Like Hollingworth, she faulted earlier studies, observing that they had been unsystematic and based on single interviews with a limited number of women. Even Jacobi's study had been flawed by its reliance on a mailed questionnaire. Most studies suffered further by being conducted by men, with whom women could not be frank. Mosher, by contrast, conducted a longitudinal survey. Each woman kept a diary throughout each month, while Mosher conducted frequent interviews and had "an intimate knowledge of the conditions under which the women were living and working." Throughout the study she kept records of respiration, blood count, and blood pressure. When patients reported physical complaints, she tried to determine whether the symptoms were caused by the menstrual function or simply associated with it, as she believed was usually the case (1911).

Mosher attributed most complaints to constricting dress, inactivity, poor diet, constipation, and the standard assumption that discomfort, if not pain, was inevitable.

The effect upon the mind of constantly anticipated misery can scarcely be measured. Imagine what would be the effect on the function of digestion if every child were taught to refer to it as a sick time! After each meal every sensation would be exaggerated and nervous dread would presently result in a real condition of nervous indigestion, a functional disturbance (1911:10).

A climate of opinion rooted in superstition, together with poor diet and dress, produced most disability, Mosher believed.

Mosher's finding that periodic incapacity was not the inevitable byproduct of womanhood but rather the remediable effect of poor habits and a morbid attitude reinforced Hollingworth's own conclusions. The general good health and confidence of her Teachers College subjects and their steady performances on her battery of psychological tests suggested that the idea of periodic incapacity had been grossly overstated. As Thorndike, Woodworth, and others were finding in their studies of fatigue, the mind enjoyed a certain independence from the body. A person's attitude appeared to be at least as important as his or her supply of nervous energy in determining mental performance. Neither Hollingworth nor any other contemporary researcher advocated returning to Descartes's mind-body dualism; they all accepted the post-Darwinian belief that the mind was rooted in physical structure and physiological forces. They increasingly doubted, however, that the link between the body and the mind was as simple and predictable as Darwin's early followers had thought. Clearly the mind was far more complicated and far more susceptible to outside forces than had been suspected.

While Hollingworth was completing her course work and research, she learned of a temporary, part-time job as a mental tester at the Clearing House for Mental Defectives, run by the City of New York. Few testers had been trained by 1913, and Hollingworth saw this part-time job as an opening wedge to a full-time professional career. Indeed, the temporary, part-time job quickly became a full-time job as the work of mental testing expanded in the next two years, and in 1914 Hollingworth filled New York's first civil service position in psychology. By 1916, when she completed her Ph.D., she was offered the job as chief of psychology at Bellevue Hospital (H. Hollingworth 1943:101–4).

In its early days clinical psychology dealt predominantly with retarded children, and Hollingworth typically saw children referred to her by the courts, various charitable agencies, and school authorities. Most of these children were boys, as any psychologist at the time would have expected. Ever since Darwin, scientists had believed that men were more variable than women and that one should expect to find a disproportionate number of idiots among them. As Hollingworth's advisor Edward Thorndike reported in his 1914 treatise on experimental psychology, "It is well known that very marked intellectual weakness is commoner amongst men than amongst women. Two times as many men as women will be found in asylums for idiots and imbeciles" (1914:189).

Hollingworth noticed something about the population at her clinic, however, that no one had ever observed before: the preponderance of males resulted from the disproportionate number of boys under sixteen years of age. In speculating on the reason for this curious fact she suggested that social influences might be responsible. First, she noted, "boys, because they are less restricted, come more often into conflict with the law than do girls, and are thus scrutinized and referred more often by the courts." Second, "the subjective notion as to what constitutes intelligent behavior is different in the case of girls from what it is in the case of boys."

A female with a mental age of six years has as good a chance to survive inconspicuously in the educational, social, and economic milieu of New York City as a male of a mental age of ten years.

When women were finally brought to mental institutions for commitment, it was usually because they had lost their dependent status, through the death of a husband for instance, or because of illness, if the woman was a prostitute. "There seems to be no occupation which supports feebleminded men as well as housework and prostitution support feebleminded women," Hollingworth ruefully observed. (1922:44, 46, 53, 55; L. Hollingworth 1914b; L. Hollingworth and Schlapp 1914).

The apparent preponderance of male retardates provided evidence for only one side of the variability position, of course. The greater incidence of male genius contributed the most compelling evidence of greater male variability. As James McKeen Cattell wrote in his study of eminent men,

I have spoken throughout of eminent men as we lack in English words including both men and women, but as a matter of fact women do not have an important place on the list. They have in all 32 representatives in the thousand. . . . Women depart less from the normal than men—a fact that usually holds throughout the animals series (1903:375).

Edward Thorndike agreed, "Eminence in and leadership of the world's affairs of whatever sort will inevitably belong oftener to men. They will oftener deserve it" (1914:188).

Cattell and Thorndike's statistics did not sway Hollingworth, however. If social factors could explain the underrepresentation of women among mental defectives, those same factors, she believed, could account for women's limited showing among those who had achieved eminence. Research that she conducted at the New York Infirmary for Women and Children reinforced her belief that females were just as variable as males. Reviewing measurements made at birth on 20,000 infants, she concluded that the variation in the female measurements matched the variation in male measurements. Given the growing doubts about the correlation of physical measurements with intelligence, Hollingworth's study of neonatal measurements provided less than overwhelming evidence of women's potential for genius, but it certainly undercut the contrary claim that women were innately mediocre. Before psychologists explained women's lesser eminence by reference to their alleged lesser variability, Hollingworth advised, they should consider first,

the established, obvious, inescapable fact that women bear and rear children, and that this has always meant and still means that nearly 100 per cent of their energy is expended in the performance and supervision of domestic and allied tasks, a field where eminence is impossible (L. Hollingworth and Montague 1914:335–70, 528).

Only when psychologists had exhausted women's domestic responsibilities as an explanation for their lesser eminence, she argued, should they "pass on to the question of comparative variability, or of differences in intellect or instinct."

The typical psychologist's reference to "maternal instinct" always represented the last word in the argument over sex differences. (see Shields, this volume) Whatever women's physical strength or intellectual capacity, maternal instinct precluded them from achievement. Curiously, Thorndike continued to believe in maternal instinct long after he had discarded as too vague and mentalistic such instincts as that of self-preservation. As he wrote in 1914,

The maternal instinct . . . is the chief source of woman's superiorities in the moral life. The virtues in which she excels are not so much due to either any general moral superiority or any set of special moral talents as to her original impulses to relieve, comfort and console (p. 27).

Hollingworth objected heatedly to this description of female character "in the absence of all scientific data" on the subject. Anyone who claimed to be a scientist should, at the very least, "guard against accepting as an established fact about human nature a doctrine that we might expect to find in use as a means of social control." Though Thorndike urged his students to "exhaust first the influence of the known physical differences and second the influence of instinct" before resorting to speculations about "the hypothetical cause of differences in purely intellectual caliber," Hollingworth insisted that physical differences and alleged instincts provided the least reliable measure of intellectual differences she could think of (1916b:238–39; 1916c; 1918).

Experimental psychologists resorted to a double standard of scientific proof, Hollingworth contended. In most of their work they condemned anthropomorphic thinking and the careless definition of instincts. In addition, they insisted that researchers should subject the assumptions that dominated psychological work to the most searching criticisms. When studying sex differences, however, they wore blinders, and when reporting their results they lapsed into conventional platitudes. The restricted vision of the male researchers who examined sex differences confirmed Hollingworth's conviction that women should train themselves for work in experimental psychology.

Thus in time, may be written a psychology of women based on truth, not opinion; on precise not on anecdotal evidence; on accurate data rather than on remnants of magic. Thus may scientific light be cast upon the question so widely discussed at present and for several decades past,—whether women may at last contribute their best intellectual effort toward human progress, or, whether it will be expedient for them to remain in the future as they have in the past, the matrix from which proceed the dynamic agents of society (1914a:99).

EDITOR'S NOTE *Between 1910 and 1918 Hollingworth and Helen Thompson Woolley prepared influential reviews of the literature on sex differences for the* Psychological Bulletin. *The greater male variability hypothesis was discredited. When it became clear that girls consistently tested somewhat higher than boys, the topic of sex differences in I.Q. was quietly dropped. But women still found it extraordinarily difficult to obtain professional positions in psychology. "Only the untimely death of Naomi Norsworthy opened a place on the faculty at Teachers College for Leta Hollingworth in 1916" (Rosenberg 1982:110). Hollingworth was unable to obtain financial support or grants. Her husband wrote: "No one will ever know what she might have accomplished for human welfare . . . if some of the sponsorship freely poured out on many a scholarly dullard had been made available for her own projects" (1943:100).*

Rosenberg concludes that women psychologists not only forced their male colleagues to live up to their critical scientific ideals when it came to sex differences but also had a major impact on the shift to environmentalism in psychology. To doubt the biological basis for feminine differences was "to loosen seriously the keystone from the arch of biological determinism." It was feminist challenges that forced psychologists to grapple seriously with the issue of group classification and, eventually, to come to doubt race differences as well.

References

Cattell, James McKeen. 1903. "A Statistical Study of Eminent Men." *Popular Science Monthly* (February) 62:359–77.

—— 1909. "The School and the Family." *Popular Science Monthly* (January) 74:84–95.

Columbia University. 1906. *Annual Reports of the President and Treasurer to the Trustees,* June 30.

Hall, G. Stanley. 1906. "The Feminist in Science." New York *Independent,* March 22, 661–62.

Hollingworth, Henry. 1943. *Leta Stetter Hollingworth.* Lincoln, Nebraska: University of Nebraska Press.

Hollingworth, Leta. 1914a. *Functional Periodicity: An Experimental Study of the Mental and Motor Abilities of Women During Menstruation.* New York: Teachers College, Columbia University.

—— 1914b. "The Frequency of Amentia as Related to Sex." *Medical Record,* October 25, pp. 1–14.

—— 1916a. "Social Devices for Impelling Women To Bear and Rear Children." *American Journal of Sociology* (July) 22:19–29.

—— 1916b. "The Vocational Aptitudes of Women." In H. L. Hollingworth. *Vocational Psychology,* pp. 222–43. New York: Appleton.

—— 1916c. "Sex Differences in Mental Traits." *Psychological Bulletin* (October) 13:377–85.

—— 1918. "Comparison of the Sexes in Mental Traits." *Psychological Bulletin* (December) 25:427–32.

—— 1922. "Differential Action Upon the Sexes of Forces Which Tend To Segregate the Feebleminded." *Journal of Abnormal Psychology and Social Psychology* 17 (April–June):35–57.

Hollingworth, Leta and Helen Montague. 1914. "The Comparative Variability of the Sexes at Birth." *American Journal of Sociology* (November) 20:335–70.

Hollingworth, Leta and Max Schlapp. 1914. "An Economic and Social Study of Feebleminded Women." *Medical Record* (June 6):1–15.

Joncich, Geraldine. 1968. *The Sane Positivist: A Biography of Edward L. Thorndike.* Middletown, Conn.: Wesleyan University Press, pp. 193–212.

Mosher, Clelia Duel. 1911. "Functional Periodicity in Women and Some Modifying Factors." *California Journal of Medicine* (January–February):1–21.

Rosenberg, Rosalind. 1982. *Beyond Separate Spheres: Intellectual Origins of Modern Feminism.* New Haven: Yale University Press.

Shields, Stephanie. 1975. "Ms. Pilgrim's Progress: The Contributions of Leta Stetter Hollingworth to the Psychology of Women." *American Psychologist* (July) 30:739–54.

Terman, Lewis M. 1936. "Autobiography." In Carl Murchison, ed. *History of Psychology in Autobiography,* II:297–332.

Thorndike, Edward L. 1898. "Animal Intelligence: An Experimental Study of the Associative Processes in Animals." *Psychological Review Monograph Supplement,* no. 8, June.

—— 1906. "Sex in Education." *Bookman* 23 (April):211–14.

—— 1913. *Educational Psychology,* vol. 1. *The Original Nature of Man.* New York: Teachers College, Columbia University.

—— 1914. *Educational Psychology,* vol. 3. *Mental Work and Fatigue and Individual Differences and Their Causes.* New York: Teachers College, Columbia University.

Thorndike, E. L. to J. M. Cattell. 1908. Cattell Papers. Library of Congress, Washington, D.C., November 17.

Thorndike, Edward L. et al. 1909. "The Relation of Accuracy in Sensory Discrimination to General Intelligence." *American Journal of Psychology* 20 (July) 364–69.

Woolley, Helen Bradford Thompson. 1903. *The Mental Traits of Sex: An Experimental Investigation of the Normal Mind in Men and Women.* Chicago: University of Chicago Press.

5 Not Quite New Worlds

Psychologists' Conceptions of the Ideal Family in the Twenties

J. G. MORAWSKI

At one point in B. F. Skinner's *Walden Two*, Frazer names the essential impediment to social progress: "No one can seriously doubt that a well-managed community will get along successfully as an economic unit. A child could prove it. The real problems are psychological" (1976:73). The psychological problems specifically pertain to social relations—those between men and women and between adults and children. As a psychologist, Skinner is not a specialist in the family, children, or the social psychology of gender relations, yet he has seriously contemplated the psychological problems of social life. Even several decades before Skinner presented his fictional plan for social amelioration, other psychologists drew up blueprints for social relations in an improved society. Some of them adopted the utopian genre; others did not do so explicitly. Despite theoretical differences, psychologists of the 1920s agreed with the Arcadian idea that attaining a harmonious and controlled society depended on healthy relations between men, women, and children.

These shared interests in normative social relations situated within a stable society raise questions about psychologists' involvements in such matters. Today little is known about earlier theories of the appropriate relations between men, women, and children. Conventional histories of psychology offer no accounts, for they mainly document the growth of grand theories and methodological techniques. Such histories rarely even discuss the subfields—developmental and social psychology—that typically dealt with human relations.

Among the prescriptions for social relations between women, men, and children are three utopian schemes written in the 1920s by G. Stanley Hall, William McDougall, and John B. Watson. Although clearly fictional creations, these works mirror much of their authors' psychological thought. The utopias constitute an illustrative introduction to theoretical presuppositions or normative ideals about gender, sex differences, and the family. But what is probably most intriguing about the utopian fictions is their similar, commonly held perspectives on social relations in American society. Hall, McDougall, and Watson shared beliefs about the urgent social problems in America and their respective resolutions. Furthermore, their conceptions were highly consistent with nonfictional analyses made by themselves and other experimental psychologists who also expressed concerns about the proper place of women, men, and children in an orderly society. Their scientific commitment to value neutrality did not seem to inhibit advocacy of particular social ideals, and the nature of their prescriptions suggests that they originated at least in part outside the professional confines of experimental psychology.

A thorough examination of these professional attitudes toward women, men, and children actually requires both social and intellectual histories. The ambitions of this article are somewhat more modest. They are simply to recount and compare some of the normative prescriptions made by psychologists during the decade and to show precisely how psychologists merged these prescriptions with the development of scientific theories. The task of bracketing such prescriptions is undertaken first by showing how several *utopian* conceptions of social relations resemble *professional* ones, and second by tracing the popularity of these conceptions. Given that in the twentieth century psychology was developed as an objective science, it is also necessary to try to understand how these normative interests in social conditions could be justified as legitimate projects of the scientific psychologist. The first section, then, describes several utopian visions about improved relations between women, men, and children, while the next section explores more closely the justifications offered for such professional involvement in remedying social relations. The concluding section is given to a more detailed examination of how these social prescriptions fitted with the emerging psychology of the decade, particularly with a behaviorist stance stressing social control and individual adjustment to the environment.

Before proceeding it is important to indicate what I do not attempt. Although the work of certain individuals—especially the three utopist-psychologists and Floyd Allport—is emphasized, minimal attention is given to biographical elements. This mindful neglect results partly from a prior need to understand the broader social and intellectual climate in which professional thinking about men, women, and children took form. As Harris (this volume) has noted, a substantial reliance on biography does not answer important questions about the social significance of psychologists' writings. Biographical explanations frequently suggest a certain uniqueness of ideas (and sometimes even an excuse for them) and may obscure how these ideas were shared among individuals. Intellectual thought such as treatises on the proper relations between women and men not only is an individual achievement (or foible) but also is rooted in a complex framework and sustained by an equally complex network of intellectual, political, and social influences.

In addition to the relative abeyance of biography, an important question is raised here but not answered. Although correspondences between psychological theory and the broader social context are illuminated, there is little detailed information about the actual social conditions against which psychologists were reacting. For instance, it remains to be determined what, if anything, psychologists were referring to when they spoke of family crises and what effect, if any, their work had on the dynamics or structure of social life in America. This question requires study of the actual social relations in that decade, including divorce rates, juvenile delinquency, and domestic and work patterns of men and women; it essentially proposes tasks for extensive studies in social history.

Utopias and Psychology

Scientists, including those studying psychology, have not neglected utopian thinking.[1] Around the turn of the century a number of psychologically oriented scientists exploited the utopian genre for disciplinary causes. Gabriel Tarde, a French social scientist whose work influenced many early American social psychologists, illustrated his social-psychological laws in a fanciful utopia (1905). In his theoretical undertakings Tarde had established laws based on social processes of imitation, invention, and genius and later employed them in a story about surviving the sun's extinction in an underground society. Francis Galton, a cousin of Charles Darwin and an investigator of human evolution, situated his science in a utopia about a world designed according to tenets of evolution.[2] Galton's utopia enacted eugenic principles whereby the fittest individuals, once tested with the latest devices for measuring mental and physical traits, were permitted to breed only with similarly superior stocks; lesser individuals either bred among themselves or remained childless. About the same time Havelock Ellis (1900), the noted sexologist, published a story of a future and perfected society where all science was known and yet metaphysics and aesthetics superseded science in directing everyday life. The works of Hall, McDougall, and Watson go further in that the authors were professional psychologists, figures of some authority, who argued for the importance of a science that had matured—for it had achieved recognition and a considerable degree of respect.

G. Stanley Hall and Atlantis

G. Stanley Hall (1844–1924) has been remembered for his role in the founding of American experimental psychology: he organized the first psychological journal, the first American psychological association, the first Wundtian laboratory in America, and the only visit of Sigmund Freud to America. He also has received acknowledgment as a versatile psychologist who promoted genetic psychology, an interest in psychoanalysis, and the use of the questionnaire method.

Omitted from most historical accounts are Hall's comprehensive view of human evolution and his proposals for improving humanity. One such proposal is contained in a utopia, "The Fall of Atlantis," which he wrote late in his career (1920a). The story of a perfected civilization, the lost Atlantis, purportedly was narrated by a cultural anthropologist who visited the city's remains in 2000 A.D. and learned that it was once the center of civilization, hosting a culture that had evolved far beyond the contemporary vision of progress. Atlantis symbolized human perfection in every detail: its language was the most flexible expression of the human psyche, medicine had excelled to the state of a philosophic science, the political structure integrated all known codes of justice, and education served every stage of life. Its citizens had realized a social consciousness or "mansoul" by subordinating individual to social desires and embracing the evolutionary unity of all nature. The fall of Atlantis was a gradual degeneration initiated by the rise of individualism and by transformations in the physical environment. Social institutions decayed as communal practices were abandoned in pursuits of individual interests (thus physicians began to practice for personal profit). Simultaneously the island-state was slowly engulfed by water.

During the flowering of Atlantis, science was lauded as a predominant achievement that brought such remarkable discoveries as the chemical synthesis of diamonds and gold and the generation of life from crystals. Its elevated status was derived from the belief that research was the highest expression of human improvement. And of all scientific endeavors, psychology was the most precious manifestation of this belief, for it dealt directly with human abilities. Psychology had been emancipated from metaphysics and physiology and "had become a culminating academic theme, the only one which all desired and which it was felt needful to know. It was genetic, comparative, clinical, and strove chiefly to give self-knowledge and self-control" (pp. 57–58). Researchers of this new synthetic psychology were exonerated from many social duties, supported for their work, and "regarded as the light and hope of the state" (p. 56). Psychology was instrumental in perfecting the social order, and the psychologist occupied a revered social role consonant with the discipline's unique responsibilities.

The relevance of psychology was apparent throughout Atlantean society, from the design of jurisprudence to education. Even the teachers of religion, the "heartformers," practiced a "higher psychology of the folksoul" (p. 80). It was these psychological applications that informed conduct between children and adults as well as between men and women. Childrearing or "learning" had become a domain in which the Atlanteans performed above all races. After their eugenic fitness and prenatal care were ensured, children were given the utmost attention during their first four years. Atlanteans believed—"even more than do our Freudians" (p. 46)—that these years were seminal ones for the growth of temperament, character, and disposition. Thus, all possible efforts were made to apply the pleasure-pain principle and minimize repressive tendencies. Experimental studies had determined that the early years be given to free play, dancing, storytelling, and music. At the age of six or seven, children were sent to the country to experience nature, and at the age of eight or ten they would begin a more conventional education in reading and writing. At puberty children began four to eight years of occupational or professional training, and during this period education was "more or less" segregated by sex "as the normal tastes and prospective spheres of each were differentiated" (p. 54). By "more or less" it was meant that all education was available to both sexes "although it was very early found that there was a great and natural difference in the fields to which each was drawn, as well as in the kind and strength of interest and the most effective methods" (p. 103). Throughout this educational regimen children were observed, measured, and tested by trained researchers.

The account of family relations was given almost entirely to describing the activities of women. Atlantean women were the pillar of psychological and moral order. As a mother, a woman "not only swayed man . . . but had in a sense fashioned him by molding his very diathesis in the first few years of life during which character is plastic" (p. 100). As a wife and citizen, her "naïve intuitions were, in a word, regarded as almost the sole and only guide given to man to direct and impel him upward in the path of progress" (p. 109). These expectations for women were implied in the Atlanteans' theory of evolution: women, by nature, were more representative of the race and of its moral development (pp. 99–100). Being exceptional in physical and moral strength, Atlantean women still bore healthy children at age sixty. The reverence for childbearing was such that every mother displayed a star on her breast for each child she bore. The moral and intuitional superiority of women earned them substantial leisure time, and independently of their spouses they were permitted to hold property, which consisted of special houses for social events and the care of the ill. The leisure time granted to women was successful because "the ambition of nearly everyone was to be a good mother, and to this end most were willing and eager to subordinate every other" (p. 102). Women were also responsible for governing public and private morals, as well as childcare, and in their old age, for dispensing advice to men.

Relationships between men and women, especially in marriage, were primarily determined according to women's special obligations and privileges. The high esteem granted to the family and childrearing meant that individuals who refrained from marriage were given additional duties and taxed for their socially reprehensible position. Relationships were prized not for their romance but for their lifelong efforts at mutual adjustment. Although the daily life, dress, and obligations of men are not as precisely described in the text as they are for women, it is clear that men's behavior was determined significantly by the roles of women. For instance, men tried to earn "badges" symbolizing their membership in women's houses, and to obtain the badges they had to undergo court procedures to judge their moral stature.

The utopian formula for the conduct of women, men, and children is apparent in many of Hall's professional writings. His interpretation of evolutionary theory is fundamental to nearly all of his psychology, beginning with *Adolescence* (Hall 1904a). The model holds that human evolution is primarily of consciousness and is progressing toward a permanent racial form; that is, toward a consciousness of the race or a folksoul (1899, 1940a). It includes two additional constitutive premises: that evolution of the race is repeated in the life of the individual—the idea of recapitulation—(1904a, see Ross 1972) and that evolution occurs not only at the level of the individual and the race but also in all human aggregates from the family to political institutions (1907, 1909). Given human knowledge of evolution, Hall believed that we must protect its patterns. This commitment to guarding evolution underscores his involvement in social reforms because they aided progress (1905, 1907, 1908, 1923b) and his criticisms of individualism and the purported "cult of the self" because human beings should be concerned primarily with survival of the *race* and not the *individual* (1923b).

This evolutionary model informed Hall's work on childrearing and pedagogy, and he regarded children as the key to our racial future. His writings on the child study movement often bore the motto that the child "controls the future" (1910:504). In accordance with recapitulation theory, childrearing should serve that particular stage of racial evolution that corresponds to the particular stage of the child's development. Hall argued that educational research has tended to focus almost solely on the intellectual stages of this development and that the home environment and the mother's involvement were requisite to optimal child care because the early years of life represented stages of emotional and physical maturation (1902, 1904b, 1905). This belief was augmented by acceptance of the Freudian notion that emotional and instinctual energies take priority over intellectual abilities (1913, 1914, 1915).

The argument for sex-segregated education and for domesticity and motherhood in women's lives also corresponds with Hall's evolutionary model. First, Hall held that progress entailed emergence of both greater differences between the sexes as well as closer proximity of the racial type to that of the adolescent (1903a, 1906a, b, 1919a). Women were closer to the child type and hence more representative of the racial type: "woman is more generic than man, nearer to, and a better representative of, the race, more liable to be injured by specialization. . . . She is more intuitive, less discursive, has a far richer emotional life. If man is a political, she is a religious, animal; more conservative, less radical" (1904a:538–39, 1905). Women were especially suited as mothers and moral teachers because they exemplified exalted racial objectives such as intuition and emotional sensitivity and because, with the child, the woman "shares more divinity than does the far more highly specialized and narrowed organism of the man" (1905:27). Hall was so convinced of the permanence of such traits that he believed that the trends of working and childless women were temporary (1903b), and he even saw the flappers of the 1920s as protecting these revered characteristics under "superficial" guises (1922a). Even a decade before the flappers made their appearance, Hall suggested that women's evolutionary position and emotional superiority might make the twentieth century "the century of woman" (1913:791).

These demands for the recognition of women's special characteristics and the related proposals for educational and family reforms gained urgency when Hall observed deterioration in American society (1921, 1922b, 1923a, b). He gradually became horrified by degeneration in the youth, politics, science, and family life. In a 1922 popular article he listed various intellectuals who had recognized impending disasters, and he advised that "Both individual and group selfishness (nationalism) must be transcended, and nothing less than a new dispensation of service and a new enthusiasm for humanity must be instituted" (1922b:840). Hall even saw psychology as a victim of these social diseases, yet he also continued to believe in the discipline's great potential to restore social health and revitalize progress (1919b, 1920b, 1923a).

William McDougall and Eugenia

William McDougall (1871–1948) was British by birth, but his career as a psychologist was spent equally in Britain and the United States. He has been credited with anticipating the behaviorist trend later promulgated by Watson, and his research in purposive psychology and instincts has earned him recognition as the progenitor of the hormic school of psychology (emphasizing goal orientation in behavior). Despite these kudos, little attention has been given to his published works on social psychology, evolution, and the psychology of politics and social ethics.

One of those neglected publications, "The Island of Eugenia," proposes a utopian society founded on eugenic principles (1921).[3] Eugenia is described as the plan of an academic scientist who, after thirty years of study, shared his scheme with an old college friend who had become an affluent philanthropist. The plan transpires through a dialogue between scientist and philanthropist, between the "Seer" and the "Practical Man." Eugenia would be devoted to the propagation of "superior strains" recruited on the basis of family history, intellectual abilities, and moral qualifications. Candidates for citizenship would be selected for superb phenotypic characteristics, which supposedly represent exceptional genotypic traits. The selected breeders eventually could reenter society either to raise genetic fitness through intermarriage or to apply their superior intelligence to social and political improvement.

Just as the design of Eugenia required the knowledge possessed by the scientific "Seer," so the maintenance of the island depended on science. The protagonist, a scientist of nature and society, drafted the plans precisely because of a belief in the efficacy of science and a conviction that other reform measures, those endorsed by Carnegie and Rockefeller, were merely "social plasters" (pp. 5–6). The primary institutions in Eugenia would be the universities, where research would flourish. Scientific studies would center on the science of Eugenia's founding, psychology (particularly its relation to eugenic issues). The extensive concern with human conditions and not social structure followed from the belief that "forms of organization matter little; the all important thing is the quality of the matter to be organized, the quality of the human beings that are the stuff of our nations and societies" (p. 7). Psychology would therefore be precedent: "the science of man will for the first time receive adequate recognition, that is to say, it will dominate the scene. To it all other sciences will be duly subordinated" (pp. 24–25).

The utopian essay merely sketches an ideal form of childrearing and family life yet clearly indicated that Eugenians would practice a "cult of the family" (p. 9). With a reverence for progeny, the family would be so important that for the citizens, "early marriage and the production of many children is their greatest privilege, at once their highest duty and their best guarantee of happiness" (p. 13). Family size would be of five to ten children, work schedules would be adjusted according to family needs, and failure to marry or bear children would seriously jeopardize one's position in the community. In keeping with the high esteem for family life is the special care taken in childrearing: education would take place in the homes and schools, where, given biological soundness, every child would "be fitted to attain eminence in some walk of life and to render great services to his fellow-men" (p. 16).

The emphasis on prolific reproduction and proper childrearing carried implications for the lives of Eugenian women. Contrary to the common expectation that educated women would avoid domesticity, McDougall claimed that refusal to bear children would come only from those women "in whom the maternal instinct is weak or who fail to absorb the ideals of Eugenia" (p. 14). Women would be reared in a moral atmosphere that valued motherhood and a community of women, or "gentlewomen," would ensure that no individual woman would be unduly burdened with domestic work. Less is revealed about the duties of the Eugenian men. Although producing a family would be a prerequisite to sound citizenship, occupational qualifications and social service would also be valued. Little else is said directly about men and the relations between men and women except on the question of monogamy. McDougall believed that knowledge of human nature had revealed that males were polygamous while females were monogamous; however, for the happiness of women and the survival of the family, Eugenian men would suppress their polygamous tendencies.

These utopian propositions about the family and roles of women and men relate to many of McDougall's professional writings, particularly to those outlining his unique conception of psychology. Although thoroughly committed to an empirical, behavioral, and specifically an experimental psychology, McDougall rejected a mechanistic model of human action in favor of a teleological or purposive one (1912, 1923b, 1928a). His teleological position implied that all human behavior was oriented to some goal; that is, humans possess a tendency to strive toward certain ends (1908).

McDougall studied human dispositions in terms of their innate or hereditary bases. This interest culminated in the evolutionary proposal that mind evolved and that these evolving mental dispositions were inherited (1923a, 1925, 1928b). In turn, the proposal guided two of his pet projects: promotion of eugenic measures and of psychological research on urgent social problems. Just as his evolutionary theory of mental dispositions supported suggestions for eugenics, so it directed his prescriptions for psychology. Assuming that mind evolved in a purposive manner, McDougall defined science as a product of mind whose purpose is the acquisition of useful knowledge (1929, 1934b, 1938).

From this perspective the priority of the science of psychology becomes evident, for scientists would benefit from the knowledge of purposiveness and mind that is attainable through psychological studies (1934b, 1937). Psychology was the means to control of all social life, for it could "render our knowledge of human nature more exact and more systematic, in order that we may control ourselves more wisely and influence our fellow-men more effectively" (1923a:1).

Understanding McDougall's directives for the lives of women, men, and children also requires knowledge of his conviction that society was deteriorating. He frequently outlined degenerative trends in social and political affairs and attributed them to a decline in genetic qualities and to a slippage in character and morals. Of the latter concern, there is perhaps no clearer example than his assertion that "Our present tendency is towards a world of gaudily attired neurotics and maniacs housed in barracks where they will pass the time between crises and disasters pleasantly enough, pressing innumerable buttons to set in automatic action the inane products of jazz and movie factories" (1931:69). Symptoms of degeneration included a rise in the "waster mind" or the individual's interest in sensuality over moral reason, which had been initiated by escalating materialism, the dropping genetic fitness, and the impact of Freudian notions of pansexualism (1936; see also 1921; 1927a, b, c; 1931).

Given these problems, McDougall proposed social regneration and eventual racial progress through eugenics (1920, 1921, 1926, 1931) and related family reforms (1907, 1933). With the purported need to revive traditional moral values, the family was held as fundamental to developing sound characters (1927a, 1931). Protection of the family, societal reforms in morality (1923a, 1926, 1934a), and reinstitution of early moral training over "generations would finally result in the birth of children who spontaneously, without precept and without example, react with passionate anger to all injustices and cruelty" (1934b:207). Since scientific knowledge of instincts and sentiments was thought to be necessary to establishing sound moral reforms, McDougall called for purposive psychologists who "shall make themselves the saviours of our collapsing civilization" (1936:viii).

John B. Watson and the Hopes of Behaviorism

John B. Watson (1878–1958) is noted for his zealotry and his role as a proponent of what became for a time the foremost orientation in psychology. He is also credited with persuasively defending the study of behavior over that of consciousness or introspection and for promoting the use of objective methods, the recognition of environmental influences on behavior, and the practical application of psychological research. Of the last, conventional histories do little more than mention his dedication to practical psychology.

Among Watson's interests in the practical applications of psychology that have not received attention is a utopian vision based on behaviorist principles. Originally titled, "The Behaviorist's Utopia," the manuscript was published as a magazine article titled, "Should a Child Have More Than One Mother?" (1929b).[4] Watson envisioned a thoroughly behavioristic country with "units" of 260 husbands and wives (and a few extras who serve as "spare" husbands and wives). Each husband and wife pair, aided by a "scientifically trained assistant," cares for three children, although they never know the identity of their biological children. Offspring rotate among the parent pairs, spending four weeks at each home, and at the age of twenty, "his 260th mother and father pat him on the head and send him out to earn his living unaided" (p. 33). Eschewing religion, politics, philosophy, history, and tradition, Utopia's citizens seek only "behaviorist happiness" and do so "by experimentation." Utopia contains both social innovations and traditions; for instance, Watson decreed that the country would be monogamous or "at any rate, I want to see monogamy tried" (p. 32).

In Watson's utopia the common measures for social order are replaced entirely by behavioral science. A cardinal feature of this system is the "behaviorist physicians" whose medical education is supplemented by training in behaviorism so they can "guard the community on the psychological side just as they guard it on the medical side. There also is preventive psychology in Utopia just as there is preventive medicine" (p. 34). The behavioral scientists do not alter the social and moral standards, precisely because the standards are identical with those of the science: both are behavioristic and thoroughly divorced from religion, politics, and philosophy. The morals of Utopia are of "behavioristic happiness," and the duties of the behaviorist physicians correspond to these morals. Elimination of the unfit through infanticide, retraining of the behaviorally maladjusted, and the practice of "preventive psychology" by conditioning constitute the scientific techniques for realizing social controls and sound personalities.

Behaviorist principles structure child care, and mothers are assisted in these crucial tasks by the behaviorist physicians. From birth onward the child inhabits an environment designed for conditioning special attributes. Each child has a separate room, and all houses have "a large common playroom well supplied with windows of quartz glass," as well as extensive yards with tall fences (p. 32). The aim of early training is to condition independence and an absorption in activity. The first attribute is initially encouraged by concealing information about the child's biological parents and is maintained by such techniques as equipping homes "with a periscope so that the parents can glance now and then at the child without being seen. The child learns to do his stuff without having to have notice" (p. 34). Schools in Utopia continue the training of independence and absorption, and in higher education children acquire the social ideals of Utopia through sex-segregated programs. Vocational or professional training commences at the age of sixteen when, segregated by sex, males learn medicine, science, or manufacturing while females learn to manage homes, handle men, perfect sex techniques, and rear children.

In Utopian culture women are trained in what they should and should not do. For instance, it was believed that the mother's overexpression of love leads to dysfunctional dependency in the child, and accordingly, Utopian family life consists of anonymous and continually rotating parents. Women remain in the home, for "There are no women in industry as such. They are not needed there. They are needed in the home. They are happy there" (p. 34). Dedicated domesticity also ensures that women do not compete with men yet still exhibit unique qualities. They are obliged to be graceful, strong, and beautiful, and large or ill-favored women are not allowed to breed. Despite their attractiveness, women overcome their narcissist tendencies at twenty-eight "—almost coincidentally with the appearance of the first wrinkle" (p. 34). Finally, women are specially trained to relate to men: they learn about handling their engagement, remaining interesting and desirable, and mastering the "technique of sex." With all these skills, Utopian women "are busy and happy from morning to night" (p. 35).

Relations between men and women are especially important, and in fact, mating is the only strong attachment permitted among individuals. Except for the requirement of physical attractiveness, little is said of the men's performance in these relationships. Some emphasis is given to the occupational and professional abilities of the men who are experienced and versatile such that "Anyone of them could start naked into the woods of Africa and conquer his environment." (p. 33).

Concerns about improving marriage and childrearing are common fare in Watson's psychology and popular writings, and to him, the concerns related directly to his program for psychology. Watson's noted behaviorist decree asserts the failure of American psychology to become a science and advises that the study of *behavior* would remedy the problems (1913b). Watson initiated a model for studying behavior—from the study of its origins (1913a, 1917, 1919, 1920b) to the laws governing its acquisition by the individual (1916, 1920a, 1927a, 1928a; Watson and Rayner 1920). Although he conducted little research, he grew convinced that nearly all behaviors were the product of learning, most of which occurred during the first three or four years of life (1919, 1924, 1928b, d, e; Watson and Watson 1921). Assured of such behavioral laws, Watson often ruminated on the social consequences of controlling behavior. In fact, he described the *aim* of research to be the discovery of human adjustments to stimuli and stated that "My final reason for this is to learn general and particular methods by which I may control behavior" (1913b:168). Thus, psychological research would ultimately yield knowledge for physicians, educators, jurors, and businessmen (1924, 1928a, d).

These aspirations for applying psychology support Watson's concerns about the relationship between women, men, and children; of all the social maladies he scrutinized, those of male and female relationships caused him the greatest worry. Watson believed that sexuality was a major problem in contemporary marriages, but women were creating others. Not only were young single women teasing older married men, but married women were abandoning all efforts to remain attractive (1929a). These conditions were worsened by the decrement in the economic and biological reinforcements for marriage and the failure of many women who embarked on careers (1927b, 1929a). The plight of modern marriage augmented childrearing problems; conventional family practices were responsible for creating lazy, dependent, unhappy, and neurotic children (Watson 1924, 1928a; Watson and Watson 1921).

Solutions to these problems could not be made through traditional modes of social reform, because society tried to adjust individuals through "round-about, hit-and-miss methods" (1917:330). But behavior psychology would generate means for control and adjustment by the superior methods of science, making it possible for "every boy and girl by the age of fourteen to know his own organism and its reactions. . . . I think this would lead the organism to be behavioristically self-correcting—just as now the body unaided . . . heals its own wounds" (1928c:113). Although Watson held that everyone could practice these experimental methods of control to achieve individual happiness, marital bliss, and social order, he recognized the need for a new type of specialist. He suggested that either psychologists or physicians would become the new "analysts" whose behaviorist training would allow them to condition, uncondition, and recondition patients (1924, 1928d). While these were conjectures about the future, Watson was certain that, for the present, "analysis based upon behaviorist principles is here to stay and is a necessary profession in society—to be placed upon a par with internal medicine and surgery" (1924:297).

Shared Ideals and the Question of Theory and Value

Hall, McDougall, and Watson held several divergent views on the ideal state. For Hall, utopia resulted from an evolutionary process that moved toward realizing social consciousness. McDougall's utopia would serve as a propaedeutic against world disaster by upgrading biological and consequently social life throughout the world. Watson envisioned utopia as a behavioral training ground for social order and individual happiness, as well as a model community upon which others could be patterned. These imagined worlds varied in the specific plans for attaining psychological perfection: by enlightened education for social harmony, by eugenic breeding for superior traits, or by conditioning appropriate behaviors from infancy onward.

The variations are understandable in terms of the well-known differences between the psychological theories of the authors. It is the similarities among the three utopias that require further explanation, most notably the ideals set for the lives and relationships of women, men, and children. All three writers stressed the necessity of scientific child-care practices both in the home and educational system. They endorsed monogamy and the nuclear family as imperative to moral and social well-being. The role of women was described in terms of their domestic and moral obligations, and the brief descriptions given to men's lives emphasized the importance of occupational competence. Finally, all three authors imagined some type of psychological expert who employed superior knowledge to monitor the social order.

The similarities in these utopias and the revealed symmetries between the authors' utopias and their psychological writings help us to identify certain shared ideals or metatheoretical prescriptions. However, they do not indicate the reasons why psychologists concerned themselves with the stability of social systems. Why, at this particular time, did many psychologists apparently accept responsibility for the welfare of society? And why did they decide that the problems were reducible to those of interpersonal or familial dynamics? The first question is essentially one of professional image and can be approached only through a broader view of the professional ethos and ethics of the early twentieth century. The latter question necessitates an examination of detail rather than breadth and is addressed through analysis of one psychologist's theory of social life.

Psychologists as Experts on Life

During the twenties psychology became a frequent subject of humor. Magazines and newspapers hosted articles on intelligence tests for bank managers and marine biologists (Leacock 1924), on tunes like "Yes, we have no mentalities" (Birnbaum 1964), and on the difficulties encountered when asking a cop to excuse one's traffic violations because personal will and responsibility were illusions (Estabrooks 1928). Probably never before had psychology been targeted for such jest, and while these lighthearted invectives are a telling indicator of the public appeal of psychology, they also smack of cynicism. Even psychologists themselves remarked on an acquired arrogance of their discipline, and many would have agreed with fellow psychologist Joseph Jastrow that psychology had been captivated by "the lure of the footlights and the glare of the headlights" (1928:134).

While amusing in their own right, these commentaries illuminate a stage that had been set for psychology and the multiple roles in which the profession had been cast. Some of these roles had roots in twentieth-century American reformism, beginning as early as the progressive period (1900–1917) and reappearing in the reconstruction spirit of post-World War I. Although the war is typically interpreted as a marker for the end of a reform era, viewing postwar disillusionment as its terminus obscures half of what Morton White (1957) has labeled the "double effect" of the war: a renewed optimism regarding reform fuelled by the putative success of professionals in the war effort. In addition to these contributions of the new specialists with social scientific techniques, there was an escalated apprehensiveness concerning the high level of immigration and the problems associated with immigrants' lives in America, as well as fears about the rising standard of living, higher divorce rates, liberalized sexual conduct, and the psychological health of individuals, be they businessmen, children, laborers, or housewives (for one perspective on these social concerns, see Report of the President's Committee 1933).

The progressives had asserted the eventual necessity for scientific guidance in social and political change (Haber 1964; McGraw 1974; Wiebe 1967), and the war made many of these a reality (Dupree 1957; Kaplan 1956; Tobey 1971; Yerkes 1920). The use of scientific techniques implemented by scientific experts became a common theme of many American intellectuals. In planning reconstruction, social critics such as Walter Lippmann (1922) and John Dewey (1922) revealed a certain loss of faith in citizen participation and, alternatively, placed greater responsibility for social change on the shoulders of an intellectual, specifically a scientific, elite. Scientists would provide leadership by "interposing some form of expertness between the private citizen and the vast environment in which he is entangled" (Lippmann 1922:368).

Lippmann's text reflects another important shift in reform policies in stipulating the essential part that social scientists, especially psychologists, would have in bettering American society (1922:374). For these writers, progress depended on social control and adjustment of individuals, and such measures obviously required knowledge about human action. The social scientist, as social engineer, seemed to be the "savior" (Kaplan 1956). These critics shared Schiller's idea that "a pragmatically efficient Psychology might actually invert the miracle of Circe, and really transform the Yahoo into a man" (1924:64).

Many psychologists held similar expectations for the social benefits of psychology. Their belief in the social relevance of psychological knowledge to social betterment emerged in efforts to promote applied psychology and to develop theories that suggested procedures for modifying society (Danziger 1979; O'Donnell 1979; Samelson 1979; Sokal 1980, 1981). Many psychologists expressed firm convictions that psychology was essential to a better society, and like other intellectuals, they viewed the psychologist as an indispensable expert for building an orderly and adjusted social world.

Most of the theories stipulating social improvement contain three claims: that democracy could be improved by maintaining social order and by adjusting the individual to society; that psychology occupied a unique status among the sciences as the only means of attaining such ends; and that the psychologist had a special responsibility as an expert in these tasks. Psychological researchers agreed that "social problems" such as family organization, civics, and sex life all required psychological expertise (Allport 1924; Bogardus 1924; Cattell 1927, 1930; Dunlap 1920, 1928; Terman 1922a, b; Judd 1926). Probably no psychologist's pronouncements on these matters carried more fervor than James McKeen Cattell's:

Psychology, not less than other sciences, perhaps more than any one of them, is concerned with problems of human welfare. The nation, the family, schools, churches, courts, prisons, armies, navies—these are all institutions which aim by emotional and rule of thumb methods to alter individuals and to control their behavior. When we have knowledge and understanding concerning institutions and individuals and learn how to apply knowledge and understanding for their betterment, it will be the product of a science of psychology (1929:345).

For Joseph Jastrow and others the obligation was a special one that implored the psychologist to "join the small remnant of creative and progressive thinkers who can see even this bewildering world soundly and see it whole. Such is part of the psychologist's responsibility" (1928:436). Hall, McDougall, and Watson belong on this list of involved psychologists, for their utopias, as well as other writings, elucidate psychologists' ultimate contribution to a better world.

Controlling and Adjusting Social Life

The confident expositions of psychology were not without specific theories for guiding everyday life. The social-psychological theories frequently dictated the appropriate forms of social control, order, and individual adjustments, particularly as they regarded family relations. For instance, applied psychology textbooks published between 1925 and 1933 generally claimed that adjustment and control of individuals provide the means to an orderly society and personal fulfillment (Napoli 1980). Theories of social work reflected similar ideas in a shift from emphasizing the environment to individual mental processes and their control (Lubove 1965). In psychologically oriented texts, social structures rarely received critical examination; rather, researchers concentrated on altering individual behavior in accordance with the existing structure of the school, the home, or the workplace.

The research of one psychologist, Floyd Allport, exemplifies these values and associated remedies for social life. Allport's *Social Psychology* is especially pertinent for it views social adjustment from a behaviorist perspective and represents a transition from relatively informal, intuitive theories of social action to more scientific, objective, and experimental ones. Allport's decision to examine social adjustments was defended in his stating that "Orderly social life necessitates a certain degree of subordination of individuals to one another and to the regulated institutions of society. Without such control unity and coordination would be impossible" (1924:391). Social control would serve family life, industry, and politics—a democratic social order—such that "a nice balance of socialization and adjustment is therefore required within the individual." (p. 427).

The terms "social order" and "adjustment" only vaguely construe the optimal social life that Allport and other psychologists envisioned; they receive more precise definition in his theory of social psychology. Allport postulated that individuals acquire behaviors through stimulus-response processes of learning such that "social behavior" becomes any response of an individual that is evoked by another individual. Allport defined any conflicts between these social behaviors and the demands of individual behavior as "the problem of adjustment between the individual and society" (p. 338). Resolution of these conflicts is essential to social order and harmony for "Wholesome expression of the vital activities in each individual must work hand in hand with the socialization of his behavior for the sake of others" (p. 427). For the truly moral person, "the right is identical with the welfare of all, not with the desire of his particular faction" (p. 429).

Successful conflict resolution relates to adjustment and happiness through the family system, because the family provides the primary source of individual well-being and is the institution that prepares one for social life. It is the bulwark of society and the mode for socialization, a chief element in social control processes. Just as socialization in childhood is an essential prophylactic for social conflict, so problems in adulthood result from social adjustment failures. While admitting that sex differences are "more probably due" to learning, Allport believed that marital disharmony and, ultimately, family breakdown are the failure to adjust the differences between husband and wife (especially in sexual relations). Therefore, in addition to providing socialization, the family ensures its own future stability by modeling the appropriate arrangements between the sexes (pp. 348–49).

Allport's conceptions were similar to those of concurrent theorists who proposed that the family is the primary mechanism for preparing an individual to adjust to social demands (see Angell 1929; Elmer 1932; Jastrow 1928; Krueger and Reckless 1931; Ruetner and Runner 1931). With Allport, these psychologists, sociologists, and social psychologists shared several other assumptions. They concurred that the family is universal and that its most natural form is the nuclear family, and when describing the socialization of children within the family, they emphasized the role of the mother. Consequently, failures in socialization were typically interpreted as failures of mothers. These assumptions intimate an implicit preference for studying only adult relationships between men and women that concerned the nuclear family.

There was also considerable consensus that the American family was in a state of crisis and that without some intervention it faced serious trauma and possibly collapse. Since the family was thought to form the bulwark of society, the consequences would be enormous. Whether a theorist stressed internal psychological or external social and economic causes of family crisis, psychological expertise was believed necessary to restore healthy and orderly family relations. In one study reporting that only 96 of 200 married men and women were happy, the authors suggested that "Some of us feel that if we were permitted to train the management, fewer of the exploring children would get hurt, and more of them would find the happiness they are looking for" (Hamilton and MacGowan 1928:287).

The Vicissitudes of Historical Reflection

Like the three utopist psychologists, Allport and his contemporaries detected problems in American culture, urged their remediation by adjusting individuals to the appropriate social order, and identified the nuclear family as central to these modifications. Psychologists were seen as crucial figures for administering remedial treatments, and in their pronouncements on social life and social controls, psychologists themselves exemplified some of the intellectual sentiments about the necessity of expertise in post-World War I reform. Their works, fiction and nonfiction, stipulated systems for bettering relations between men, women, and children.

The present study has attempted to better understand psychologists' thinking about women, men, and children during a brief period in America's past. The parallels found between these psychological treatises and reform ideals broaden our understanding of the apparently sudden rise in theories of social relations; in psychologists' concern about marriage, childrearing, and the family; and in proposals on psychology's responsibility in upgrading American social life. They permit us to see the connectedness of intellectual and social thought such that, for instance, Watson's pleas to remedy social disasters with behavioral controls can be seen not simply as anomalous actions of an eccentric but as one of many attempts to use psychology for social progress. The history of psychology, then, must extend beyond internal and intellectual accounts of events in order to make sense of psychology's intellectual accomplishments and its social impact.

The use of history to better understand and evaluate theories of the family, childrearing, and close relations has been advocated by both historians and psychologists (Gadlin 1978; Mechling 1975; Rothman 1971; Sears 1975; Skolnick 1975; Takanishi 1978; Vincent 1951). It is generally agreed that such studies punctuate the assumptions and social values that circumscribe psychological theories. However, such historical reflection has yet to be linked directly with examinations of contemporary research. There is considerable evidence that current theorizing on the family and close relationships belies any serious reflection on normative assumptions or values. For instance, research continues to tender debatable predictions about the imminent demise of the nuclear family (Uzoka 1979), and family therapists persist in a fairly uncritical use of traditional Freudian models of the family (see Hamilton 1981). Studies indicating a correlation between marriage and depression in women have spawned controversies over their implications for clinical practice and family stability such that some suggest protecting the family at the cost of the women's well-being (Gove 1980a, b; Johnson 1980). Similarly, the androgyny theories that were originally posited to correct value biases in sex-role research are themselves vulnerable to criticism for their implicit values: the current androgyny model assumes that the healthy individual is independent, self-sufficient, motivated by situational demands, and retains a stable gender profile through the adult years (Morawski 1982; Sampson 1977).

Within psychology the relation of values to theory is a far from resolved issue. Historical inquiry may not settle these quandaries but offers both an instrument and vocabulary with which they can be negotiated. As such, historical study is one mode from which we can initiate critical examination of our science. The requests for such reflection come from various theoretical contingents, yet they nevertheless concur that, in neglecting implicit values and beliefs, psychology has persisted in presenting borrowed images, models of not quite perfect worlds (Argyris 1975; Buss

1975, 1977; Israel 1972; Moscovici 1972; Samelson 1980; Sampson 1977, 1978; Sarason 1981; Shotter 1975). Critical thinking, whether initiated through historical reflection or some other method, enables us to identify what psychological images of human nature are actually perpetuated and marketed and to contemplate what images are ultimately possible.

Notes

1. An extended analysis of scientists (particularly psychologists) and utopias appears in J. Morawski, "Psychology and Ideal Societies: The Utopias of Hall, McDougall, Munsterberg, and Watson," (Ph.D. dissertation, Carleton University, Ottawa, 1979), chapters 2 and 3.

2. Galton's utopia, *Kantsaywhere,* never appeared in print, although he tried to publish it before his death. In settling Galton's estate, his niece destroyed those sections of the manuscript that she found scandalous (primarily for its content on sexual matters). The remainder was forwarded to Karl Pearson, who published it in his biography of Galton (Pearson 1914–38).

3. In introducing "The Island of Eugenia," McDougall (1921) claimed that he actually designed it some twenty years earlier.

4. The unpublished version of Watson's utopia is slightly longer and somewhat more adamant about enforcing behaviorist principles. I thank Cedric Larson for presenting me with a copy of the unpublished work.

References

Allport, Floyd H. 1924. *Social Psychology.* Boston: Houghton Mifflin.
Angell, J. R. 1929. Yale's Institute of Human Relations. *Yale Alumni Weekly,* April 19, 889–91.
Argyris, C. 1975. "Dangers in Applying Results from Experimental Psychology." *American Psychologist* 30:469–85.
Birnbaum, L. 1964. "Behaviorism: John Broadus Watson and American Social Thought, 1913–1933." Ph.D. dissertation, University of California, Berkeley.
Bogardus, E. S. 1924. *Fundamentals of Social Psychology.* New York: Century.
Buss, A. R. 1975. "The Emerging Field of the Sociology of Psychological Knowledge." *American Psychologist* 30:988–1002.
—— 1977. "In Defense of a Critical-Presentist Historiography: The Fact-Theory Relationship and Marx's Epistemology." *Journal of the History of the Behavioral Sciences* 13:252–66.
Cattell, J. M. 1927. "The Contribution of Science to the Welfare of the Nation: Science, the Declaration, Democracy." *Scientific Monthly* 24:203–5.
—— 1929. "Psychology in America." *Science* 70:335–47.
—— 1930. "The Usefulness of Psychology." *Science* 72:284–87.

Danziger, K. 1979. "The Social Origins of Modern Psychology." In A. R. Buss, ed. *Psychology in Social Context.* New York: Irvington, pp 27–46.

Dewey, J. 1922. *Human Nature and Conduct.* New York: Henry Holt.

Dunlap, K. 1920. "Social Need for Scientific Psychology." *Scientific Monthly* 11:502–17.

—— 1928. "The Applications of Psychology to Social Problems." In C. Murchison, ed. *Psychologies of 1925,* pp. 353–79. Worcester: Clark University Press.

Dupree, A. H. 1957. *Science in the Federal Government, a History of Policies and Activities in 1940.* Cambridge, Mass.: Harvard University Press.

Ellis, H. 1900. *The Nineteenth Century: A Dialogue in Utopia.* London: Grant Richards.

Elmer, M. C. 1932. *Family Adjustment and Social Change.* New York: Ray Young and Richard R. Smith.

Estabrooks, G. H. 1928. "Go Tell It to a Traffic Cop." *Harpers* 157:277–79.

Gadlin, H. 1978. "Child Discipline and the Pursuit of Self: An Historical Interpretation." *Advances in Child Development and Behavior* 12:231–65. New York: Academic Press.

Gove, W. R. 1980a. "Mental Illness and Psychiatric Treatment Among Women." *Psychology of Women Quarterly* 4:345–62.

—— 1980b. "Mental Illness and Psychiatric Treatment Among Women: A Rejoinder to Johnson." *Psychology of Women Quarterly* 4:372–76.

Haber, S. 1964. *Efficiency and Uplift: Scientific Management in the Progressive Era, 1890–1920.* Chicago: University of Chicago Press.

Hall, G. S. 1899. "Philosophy." In *Decennial Celebration: Clark University.* Worcester, Mass.: Clark University Press.

—— 1902. "Some Social Aspects of Education." *Pedagogical Seminary* 9:81–91.

—— 1903a. "Co-education in the High School." *Proceedings of the National Education Association,* pp. 446–60.

—— 1903b. "Marriage and Fecundity of College Men and Women." *Pedagogical Seminary* 10:275–314.

—— 1904a. *Adolescence: Its Psychology and Its Relations to Physiology, Anthropology, Sociology, Sex, Crime, Religion and Education* (2 vol.). New York: Appleton.

—— 1904b. "Co-Education." *Proceedings of the National Education Association,* pp. 538–42.

—— 1905. "New Ideals of Motherhood Suggested by Child Study." *Report of the National Congress of Mothers,* pp. 14–27. Washington, D. C.

—— 1906a. "Co-education in the High School." *Proceedings of the National Education Association,* pp. 446–60.

—— 1906b. "The Question of Co-education." *The Munsey.*

—— 1907. "Some Dangers in Our Educational System and How To Meet Them." *New England Magazine* 41:667–75.

—— 1908. "Recent Advances in Child Study." *Pedagogical Seminary* 15:353–57.

—— 1909. "The Budding Girl and the Boy in His Teens." *Southern California Teachers Association.* Redlands, Calif.: Review Press.

—— 1910. "The National Child Welfare Conference: Its Work and Its Relations to Child Study." *Pedagogical Seminary* 17:497–504.

—— 1913. "The Feelings and Their Education." *Friends' Intelligencer* 70:771–72, 787–91.

—— 1914. "Recent Progress in Child Study." *Child Welfare Magazine* 8:212–16.

—— 1915. "Child Training." *The Woman's World* 5:31–32.

—— 1919a. "Points of Difference Between Men and Women, Inherent and Acquired." *Proceedings of the International Conference of Women Physicians* 4:90 –99.

—— 1919b. "The Viewpoint of the Psychologist as to Courses of Study Which Will Meet the Future Demands of a Democracy." *Pedagogical Seminary* 26:90–99.

—— 1920a. "The Fall of Atlantis." In *Recreations of a Psychologist.* New York: Appleton.

—— 1920b. "Psychology and Industry." *Pedagogical Seminary* 27:281–93.

—— 1921. "The Message of the Zeitgeist." *Scientific Monthly* 13:105–16.

—— 1922a. "Flapper Americana Novissima." *Atlantic Monthly* 129:771–80.

—— 1922b. "Salvaging Civilization." *Century Magazine* 104:830–40.

—— 1923a. "The Gospel of Magnanimity." *Pedagogical Seminary* 30:252–63.

—— 1923b. *Life and Confessions of a Psychologist.* New York: Appleton.

Hamilton, G. V. and K. MacGowan. 1928. "Marriage and Love Affairs." *Harpers* 157:277–87.

Hamilton, V. 1981. "Something for Your Entire Family." *The New York Review of Books* 28:23–28.

Israel, J. 1972. "Stipulations and Construction in the Social Sciences. In J. Israel and H. Tajfel, eds. *The Context of Social Psychology: A Critical Assessment.* London: Academic Press.

Jastrow, J. 1928. "Lo, the psychologist!" in M. L. Reymert, ed. *Feelings and Emotions: The Wittenburg Symposium.* Worcester, Mass.: Clark University Press.

Johnson, M. 1980. "Mental Illness and Psychiatric Treatment Among Women: A Response." *Psychology of Women Quarterly* 4:363–71.

Judd, C. H. 1926. *The Psychology of Social Institutions.* New York: Macmillan.

Kaplan, S. 1956. "Social Engineers as Saviors: Effects of World War I on Some American Liberals." *Journal of the History of Ideas* 17:347–69.

Krueger, E. T. and W. C. Reckless. 1931. *Social Psychology.* New York: Yongmans, Green.

Leacock, S. 1924. "A Manual for the New Mentality." *Harper's* 148:472–80.

Lippmann, W. 1922. *Public Opinion.* New York: Macmillan.

Lubove, R. 1965. *The Professional Altruist: The Emergency of Social Work as a Career, 1880–1930.* Cambridge, Mass.: Harvard University Press.

McDougall, W. 1907. "A Practicable Eugenic Suggestion." *Sociological Papers* 3:55–80.

—— 1908. *Introduction to Social Psychology.* London: Methuen.

—— 1910. "Instinct and Intelligence." *British Journal of Psychology* 3:250–66.

—— 1912. *Psychology: The Study of Behavior.* London: Oxford University Press.

—— 1920. *The Group Mind: A Sketch of the Principles of Collective Psychology, With Some Attempt To Apply Them to the Interpretation of National Life and Character.* New York: Putnam.

—— 1921. "The Island of Eugenia," in *National Welfare and National Decay.* London: Methuen.

—— 1923a. *Outline of Psychology.* New York: Scribner's.

—— 1923b. "Purposive or Mechanical Psychology." *Psychological Review* 30:273–88.

—— 1925. "Mental Evolution." In *Evolution in the Light of Modern Knowledge: A Collective Work.* London: Blackie and Son.

—— 1926. *The American Nation: Its Problems and Psychology.* London: George Allen and Unwin.

—— 1927a. *Character and the Conduct of Life.* London: Methuen.

—— 1927b. *Janus: The Conquest of War, A Psychological Inquiry.* New York: Dutton.

—— 1927c. "Our Neglect of Psychology." *The Edinburgh Review* 245:299–312.

—— 1928a. "Men or Robots? I, Men or Robots? II." In C. Murchison, ed. *Psychologies of 1925,* pp. 273–92, 293–308. Worcester, Mass.: Clark University Press.

—— 1928b. "Was Darwin wrong?" *The Forum* 79:244–53.

—— 1929. *Modern Materialism and Emergent Evolution.* New York: Van Nostrand.

—— 1931. *World Chaos: The Responsibility of Science.* London: Kegan Paul, Trench, Trubner and Co.

—— 1933. "Family Allowances as a Eugenic Measure." *Character and Personality* 2:99–116.

—— 1934a. *Religion and the Sciences of Life, with Other Essays on Allied Topics.* London: Methuen.

—— 1934b. *The Frontiers of Psychology.* Cambridge: Cambridge University Press.

—— 1936. *Psycho-analysis and Social Psychology.* London: Methuen.

—— 1937. "Philosophy and the Social Science." In R. B. Cattell, J. Cohen, and R. M. W. Travers, eds. *Human Affairs.* London: Macmillan.

—— 1938. *The Riddle of Life: A Survey of Theories.* London: Methuen.

McGraw, T. K. 1974. "The Progressive Legacy." In L. L. Gould, ed. *The Progressive Era.* Syracuse: Syracuse University Press.

Mechling, J. 1975. "Advice to Historians on Advice to Mothers." *Journal of Social History* 9:44–63.

Morawski, J. G. 1982. "On Thinking About History as Social Psychology." *Personality and Social Psychology Bulletin* 8:393–401.

Moscovici, S. 1972. "Society and Theory in Social Psychology." In J. Israel and H. Tajfel, eds. *The Context of Social Psychology: A Critical Assessment.* New York: Academic Press.

Napoli, D. S. 1980. *The Architects of Adjustment: The History of the Psychological Profession in the United States.* Port Washington, N.Y.: National University Publications.

O'Donnell, J. M. 1979. "The 'Crisis of Experimentalism' in the Twenties: E. G. Boring and His Uses of Historiography." *American Psychologist* 34:289–95.

Pearson, K. 1914–1938. *The Life Letters and Labours of Francis Galton.* Cambridge, England: Cambridge University Press.

Report of the President's Committee. 1933. *Recent Social Trends.* New York: McGraw-Hill.

Ross, D. 1972. *G. Stanley Hall: The Psychologist as Prophet.* Chicago: University Press.

Rothman, D. J. 1971. "Documents in Search of a Historian: Toward a History of Childhood and Youth in America." *Journal of Interdisciplinary History* 2:367–77.

Ruetner, E. B. and J. R. Runner. 1931. *The Family.* New York: McGraw-Hill.

Samelson, F. 1979. "Putting Psychology on the Map: Ideology and Intelligence Testing." In A. R. Buss, ed. *Psychology in Social Context.* New York: Irvington.

Samelson, F. 1980. "J. B. Watson's Little Albert, Cyril Burt's Twins, and the Need for a Critical Science." *American Psychologist* 35:619–25.

Sampson, E. E. 1977. "Psychology and the American Ideal." *Journal of Personality and Social Psychology* 35:767–82.

—— 1978. "Scientific Paradigms and Social Values: Wanted—a Scientific Revolution." *Journal of Personality and Social Psychology* 36:1332–43.

Sarason, S. 1981. *Psychology Misdirected.* New York: The Free Press.

Schiller, F. C. S. 1924. *Tantalus, or the Future of Man.* London: Kegal Paul, Trench, Trubner.

Sears, R. R. 1974. "Your Ancients Revisited: A History of Child Development." In E. M. Hetherington, ed. *Review of Child Development Research.* Chicago: University of Chicago Press.

Shotter, J. 1975. *Images of Man in Psychological Research.* London: Methuen.

Skinner, B. F. 1948/1976. *Walden Two* (revised). New York: Macmillan.

Skolnick, A. 1975. "The Family Revised: Themes in Recent Social Science Research. *Journal of Interdisciplinary History* 4:703–19.

Sokal, M. M. 1980. James McKeen Cattell and American Psychology in the 1920's." In J. Brozek, ed. *Explorations in the History of American Psychology.* Lewisburg, Pa.: Bucknell University Press.

—— 1981. "The Origins of the Psychological Corporation." *Journal of the History of the Behavioral Sciences* 17:54–67.

Takanishi, R. 1978. "Childhood as a Social Issue. Historical Roots of Contemporary Child Advocacy Movement." *Journal of Social Issues* 34:8–28.

Tarde, G. 1905. Gabriel Tarde, *Underground Man,* trans. by Cloudesley Brereton. Westport, Conn.: Hyperion Press.

Terman, L. M. 1922a. "The Control of Propaganda as a Psychological Problem." *Scientific Monthly* 14:234–52.

—— 1922b. "The Psychological Determinist, or Democracy and the I.Q." *Journal of Educational Research* 6:57–62.

Tobey, R. C. 1971. *The American Ideology of National Sciences, 1919–1930.* Pittsburgh: University of Pittsburgh Press.

Uzoka, A. F. 1979. "The Myth of the Nuclear Family: Historical Background and Clinical Implications." *American Psychologist* 34:1095–1106.

Vincent, C. 1951. "Trends in Infant Care Ideas." *Child Development* 22:199–203.

Watson, J. B. 1913a. "Image and Affection in Behavior." *Journal of Philosophy, Psychology and Scientific Methods* 10:421–28.

—— 1913b. "Psychology as the Behaviorist Views It. *Psychological Review* 10:158–77.

—— 1916. "The Place of the Conditioned-Reflex in Psychology." *Psychological Review* 23:89–116.

—— 1917. "An Attempted Formulation of the Scope of Behavior Psychology." *Psychology Review* 24:89–116.

—— 1919. *Psychology from the Standpoint of a Behaviorist.* Philadelphia: Lippincott.

—— 1920a. "Is Thinking Merely the Action of Language Mechanisms?" *British Journal of Psychology* 11:87–104.

—— 1920b. "Practical and Theoretical Problems in Instinct and Habits." In H. S. Jennings, J. B. Watson, A. Meyer, and W. I. Thomas, eds. *Suggestions of Modern Science Concerning Education*. New York: Macmillan.

—— 1924. *Behaviorism*. New York: Norton.

—— 1927a. "The Place of Kinaesthetic, Visceral and Laryngeal Organization in Thinking." *Psychological Review* 34:339–48.

—— 1927b. "The Weakness of Women." *Nation* 125:9–10.

—— 1928a. "Recent Experiments on How We Lose and Change Our Emotional Equipment." In C. Murchison, ed. *Psychologies of 1925*. Worcester, Mass.: Clark University Press.

—— 1928c. "The Unconscious of the Behaviorist." In E. S. Drummer, ed. *The Unconscious: A Symposium*. New York: Knopf.

—— 1928d. *The Ways of Behaviorism*. New York: Harper.

—— 1928e. "What the Nursery Has To Say About Instincts." In C. Murchison, ed. *Psychologist of 1925*. Worchester, Mass.: Clark University Press.

—— 1929a. "Men Won't Marry Fifty Years from Now." *Cosmopolitan* 86:71, 104, 106.

—— 1929b. "Should a Child Have More Than One Mother?" *Liberty Magazine*, pp. 31–35.

Watson, J. B. and R. Rayner. 1920. "Conditional Emotional Reactions." *Journal of Experimental Psychology* 3:1–14.

Watson, J. B. and R. R. Watson. 1921. "Studies in Infant Psychology." *Scientific Monthly* 13:493–515.

Watson, J. B. (with R. R. Watson). 1928b. *Psychological Care of the Infant and Child*. New York: Norton.

White, M. 1957. *Social Thought in America: The Revolt Against Formalism*. Boston: Beacon Press.

Wiebe, R. 1967. *The Search for Order, 1877–1920*. New York: Hill and Wang.

Yerkes, R. M., ed. 1920. *The New World of Science, Its Development During the War*. New York: Century.

6 "Give Me a Dozen Healthy Infants..."

John B. Watson's Popular Advice on Childrearing, Women, and the Family

BEN HARRIS

I n *My Father Bertrand Russell,* Katherine Russell Tait describes her father's approach to the problem of his young son's fears:

My father was a philosopher and theoretician. He loved to take a complex problem, reduce it to simple components, then show how the parts could be reassembled. . . . He tackled the education of his children in this way. . . . If he had had full-time care of us, he might have been less confident.

Or if he had paid a little more attention to the theories of Freud and less to those of the American behaviorist John B. Watson. . . .

In order to be the "splendid human beings" our parents hoped for, [my brother] John and I had need of great courage, to be instilled in us by the moral training of our early childhood. Our parents hoped, in fact, to do much more than give us the old-fashioned kind of courage, which was based on concealment of fear; they hoped to train us to feel no fear at all. . . .

Although my father never went so far as to replicate Watson's conditioning of Albert using us, it was with the same dispassionate scientific attitude that he set out to observe [and remove] John's childish anxieties. Reading his account much later, I was belatedly thankful that I had been too young to participate fully in the experiment (Tait 1975:63–64).[1]

In 1923, when Bertrand Russell was first becoming concerned about his son's fears, John B. Watson was well on the way to becoming the best known psychological expert on childhood in the United States. Although he had been forced to leave the academic world a few years earlier, Watson's general psychological theory had become a major force in academic psychology, and within the field of child psychology his theory of emotional development had been cited as one that "should be known by any one who wishes to understand the behavior of the child" (Mitchell 1919:306; see also Samelson 1981).

To the general public, Watson became known in the 1920s through his lecturing, his many articles in magazines such as *Harper's* and *McCall's,* and through books such as his best-selling *Psychological Care of Infant and Child.* In these popular forums, Watson's message was both unorthodox in content and dramatic in style; it is best exemplified by his often-repeated story of how he experimentally induced a severe animal phobia in a young infant named "Albert" (Harris 1979). The cumulative effect of such stories, of Watson's public exposure, and of the controversy surrounding his theories was significant. It was such that by the end of the decade, millions had heard about the new, behavioristic view of childrearing, marriage, and family life.[2] Regardless of whether the public completely believed these popularized concepts of Watson, his writings were soon required reading for the middle classes—rivaling psychoanalysis as the popular psychology of the moment.

In what follows, I examine John Watson's views of women, children, and the family. My overall goal is to identify the social context in which Watson operated as the quintessential expert. This social context, I argue, was a significant determinant of the form taken by Watson's writings, perhaps more significant than the content of behaviorist theory.

In support of this argument I first review a representative sample of Watson's popular writing on the child, women, and the family. Then I analyze what I consider to be one of its most significant features: its relationship to the changing social values and ideology of the 1920s. My intent is to illuminate some of the implicit cultural messages contained in popular behaviorism that have been neglected by even the most recent studies of Watson and his work (Cohen 1979; Ehrenreich and English 1978; Herrnstein 1969; Lomax, Kagan, and Rosenkrantz 1978).[3]

Watson's Advice on Childrearing

As a popular author, John B. Watson was most productive in the years 1926–30, during which he wrote two books and more than two dozen articles. In this written material, Watson addressed three subjects of wide popular interest: the development and control of children's behavior (what I call "childrearing") and the related topics of family life and women's role in the family. Watson's views on childrearing are best summarized in an article he wrote for *Cosmopolitan*, "What About Your Child?" (Watson 1928b); his views on women and the family are best summarized in two provocative essays, "Men Won't Marry Fifty Years from Now" and "After the Family—What?" (Watson 1927a; 1930).

In "What About Your Child?" Watson opened his discussion of child development with the question of the relationship between social change and childrearing practices. He asked rhetorically, "Does society want to go on forever making the next generation more and more like the old?" Assuming that the progressive *Cosmopolitan* reader would answer "no," Watson asserted that new, behavioral childrearing techniques are needed to nurture "almost a new race, . . . in which every individual might have, except for essentials, a different personality" (1928b:76).

Following this promise of exchanging old personalities for new, Watson began an explanation of his basic behaviorist doctrine. This consisted of, first, an extreme environmentalistic view of human psychology. For example, Watson asserted that social forces, such as parents, could completely shape a child's behavior and "emotional organization" (although most parents fail to do so and thus allow the general culture to determine their children's habits). Using the process of classical conditioning as a basic explanatory mechanism, Watson then added developmental determinism to his environmentalist theme. The result was the familiar Watsonian doctrine of the "utter mutability of children 'from birth to four [years],' during which time a child can be made or broken for all time" (1928b:108).

To illustrate these principles in operation, Watson's *Cosmopolitan* article described the apparently successful conditioning of the infant Albert to fear small animals by presenting various animals at the same time that a frightening noise was sounded (Watson and Rayner 1920). Reference to this case study was followed by Watson's conditioning-related explanations for the acquired nature of children's loves, hates, habits of cleanliness, and even their right- or left-handedness. Finally, Watson spelled out two major implications of his psychological theory. First, that parents bear the responsibility either for smothering their child and producing a spoiled, fearful adult or for developing a future Washington, Lincoln, or Shakespeare. Second, Watson suggested that the danger of parental mistakes is so high that society should consider abolishing the family and turning all childrearing responsibilities to women professionally trained as behavioristic infant caretakers.

Watson's Assessment of Women and the Family

Throughout his writing on childrearing and child development, Watson often mentioned parents' role in raising maladapted and fearful children (Watson 1928a; 1928b, 1930). In doing so he usually portrayed mothers as homebound, underworked, and sexually frustrated, transferring their pent-up energies to the smothering of their children—particularly little boys. "Mother love," Watson wrote in *McCall's*, "is a dangerous instrument" (Watson 1928a).

In addition to making such references to parents' effects on their children, Watson also focused directly on the family itself, discussing its internal dynamics and its changing nature. Watson was characteristically brash and irreverent in this writing, attacking the family under the guise of offering expert advice about its flaws and about some possible corrective measures.

According to Watson, there were a number of major weaknesses that were destroying the family in what he termed a bloodless revolution. First was the physiological and social inequality of those husbands and wives who were over thirty years old. In Watson's view, women lose their sexual attractiveness by age thirty, while men reach their physical and social prime between the ages of thirty and forty-five. As a result, married men are dissatisfied with their (same age) wives and are hunted by aggressive, attractive younger women who are knowledgeable in what Watson termed "the seductive arts." Related to this problem was another difficulty of married life: lack of sexual training and hence sexual maladjustment in 80 percent of all marriages. To Watson, these dissatisfactions and maladjustments, in turn, were exacerbated by the hypocrisy and inflexibility of medical and religious authorities, resulting in chronic jealousy and emotional frustrations (Watson 1927a).

In Watson's diagnosis of the family's terminal illness, two final problems were the role of children in the family and women's increasing independence. As he saw it, unhappy families produced spoiled, dependent children with parent-fixations, which in turn put more stress on the family unit. This was made worse by the declining economic interdependence of husbands and wives, which Watson said had traditionally kept many marriages intact (Watson 1927a).

All told, there were a dozen or so ways in which the modern era had become an inhospitable environment for the ideal, middle-class family. Although this might have been cause for alarm among sentimentalists, Watson's only acknowledged reaction was that of scientific interest. He noted,

All I can say is that I am thankful that I am neither a priest nor a moralist who has to uphold a non-changing mores. . . . I thank my everlasting chromosomes . . . that I do not have to pass judgment upon my fellow man. I have only to understand him (Watson 1929b:xviii).

The Behaviorist's Remedies and Predictions

For Watson, his success in understanding the marriage problems of his fellow humans allowed him to offer some possible solutions to the continued worsening of family relations. As with Watson's other writing on the family, these bits of behaviorist advice were as much illustrations of their author's behaviorist ideology and social acumen as they were realistic proposals for social intervention. In implicit recognition of this, Watson's writing included not only forecasts of developing alternatives to the family but also a behaviorist utopia in which family relations would be scientifically engineered for optimum results, thus preserving monogamy and eventually resulting in the withering away of the state apparatus! (Watson 1929a; see also Morawski, this volume).

On a nonutopian level, Watson said that, short of instituting severe economic sanctions or the experimental conditioning of men to be faithful to their spouses, society would have to develop alternatives to traditional family functions on a trial-and-error basis. He saw this already occurring in young adults' sexual experimentation and praised their rebelliousness and sophistication. Looking ahead, he forecast that the future would see monogamous marriages replaced by temporary, nonbinding relationships. Although temporary in purpose, these pairings might actually be longer lasting than many marriages in the 1920s. This would occur, Watson reasoned, as social and scientific changes reduced the forces destructive to heterosexual fidelity. For example, as infants were increasingly raised by professional caretakers, they would no longer be subject to the parent-fixations that developed into feelings of jealousy and rebelliousness between spouses. Also, young people's anticipated demands for better contraceptives and for instruction in sexual technique would eventually be met by the medical profession, resulting in more sexually compatible relationships. Finally, Watson hoped that future couples would no longer be subject to governmental interventions (e.g., propaganda about race suicide and birth rates) or to the hypocritical pronouncements of priests, lawyers, and physicians. Free of such interference, monogamous relationships would again attain social stability (Watson 1930).

Analyzing Watson's Popular Writing

What are some possible interpretations of these pronouncements about women, children, and the family? Of what significance is this behavioristic advice of Watson's? It is significant, first, because of its subject matter and, second, because of its psychological content. That is, Watson had a unique theory of human social behavior, and he applied this theory to a set of topics with considerable cultural importance (e.g., children, the family). In addition to its content and subject matter, Watson's writing is also noteworthy because Watson wrote it—because of its relation to Watson himself. That is, beyond the significance of Watson's expert advice was the significance of the advice's having come from a self-proclaimed, highly successful expert.

In what follows I do not attempt to analyze Watson's popular writing as a whole. Rather, I divide his message into the three components: first, *the objects of study* that Watson selected (e.g., the family, children); second, the *theoretical content* of Watson's writing (e.g., his theory of psychology); and third, the *social philosophy* contained in Watson's advice (e.g., the assumptions about society and science).

The Behaviorist's Subject Matter

In 1916, Watson announced that he was changing the subject matter of his research from animals such as rats and monkeys to human infants. This was quickly reflected in his laboratory work, and together with the related topics of women and the family, the subject of infants and children soon became the focus of much of Watson's popular writings and lectures (Harris 1980b).

Considering the content of early behaviorist theory, the study of young children was very sensible. Watson was interested in both hereditary and environmental determinants of behavior, particularly in the relative roles of unconditioned and conditioned reflexes. Given these interests and his goal of developing a human psychology, it made sense for Watson to catalogue infant reflexes and their modification by early conditioning. Also, as Watson's view of heredity and environment became more dichotomous and environmentalistic, his work with very young infants allowed him to evoke the image of the newborn as a completely mutable, behaviorally innocent "untrained ball of protoplasm" (Watson 1928b:108).

In addition to its theoretical importance for Watson's psychology, the child had a professional and social significance that made it an attractive topic for both research and writing. Stated simply, the first three decades of the twentieth century saw America discover the child. In the institutional sphere this was reflected in the formation of agencies like the U.S. Children's Bureau and of events like the White House Conference on the Health and Welfare of the Child. It was reflected in the establishment of foundations like the Laura Spellman Rockefeller Fund; in the growth of groups like the PTA, the Child Study Association of America, and the International Kindergarten Union; and in the formation of university-based child study centers and laboratories (Schlossman 1976). On an ideological level, the child became a symbol of the racial aspirations of eugenecists and other progressivists, as expressed in the motto: "the future of the race marches forward on the feet of little children" ("Parents . . ." 1926).

Concurrent with this discovery of the child, women and the family also became topics of widespread popular discussion. One reason for this was the economic importance of women's primary identification with the home and the child (Ehrenreich and English 1978; Blair 1919; Gale 1919). More generally, however, the 1910s and 1920s were a time in which changed demographics of middle-class family life produced a heightened consciousness about both women and the child.

Compared to the mid- to late-nineteenth century, the middle-class family of John Watson's era contained significantly fewer children, who were more likely to survive into adulthood. Married couples of this era also waited longer after marriage before having their first child and were more likely to be divorced than were couples in previous decades (Fass 1977; O'Neill 1967). Added to these changed demographics was an increase in the social agencies and institutions serving both children and the family. The results of this were marriages that were more conjugal, more child centered, and in which issues of sexuality, women's rights, and relations with the larger social order became increasingly salient.

Watson's success as an expert on children and the family is in large part due to his speaking to these issues and concerns. In an era of changing sexual and gender-related standards Watson peppered his discussions of childrearing with references to the frustrations of married women and the effects of these on the family. In a time when more young women were looking beyond the home and beginning to assert their independence, he acknowledged their social skill and free spirit and then advised them to rely on experts for guidance in the difficult task of infant care (Watson 1927a, 1929a, 1927b; Contratto, this volume).

The guidance that Watson offered to such young women was often quite similar to accepted child care procedures, now rationalized by a new psychological theory and applied to the relatively new phenomenon of the conjugal, child-centered family. For example, with housewives portrayed as having more free time and with the decline in the middle-class birth rate, the relation of individual male children to their mothers became a frequently discussed issue. Watson was able to capitalize on this by decrying the effects of too much mothering (which he called "smothering") and by providing a solution that was much simpler than the one supplied by competing Freudian writings on childhood.[4]

Although Watson's recommended prohibition on intrafamilial affection may seem unnatural by today's standards, its emphasis on the individual's emotions was part of a larger protest by Watson against the excesses of progressivist state intervention. His timing in this was excellent, since his writings on marriage and family took advantage of the anticollectivist feelings of those disillusioned by overly eager attempts at social reform. At the same time that he sounded this antiprogressivist theme, Watson used the topic of the child to affirm the psychological supremacy of the individual and the individual's emotions. This took the form of an objection to the attempted homogenization of children by schools, and warnings about the dependency created by overprotective homes.[5]

As Watson himself noted, advice on rearing independent, psychologically healthy children was the psychological equivalent of Holt's *The Care and Feeding of Children*. In an analogous manner to Holt's and to earlier infant hygiene campaigns, Watson urged parents to save their children from the vagaries of their environment and not to accept a certain incidence of failure as "natural." Rather, he urged that each child be considered as an individual, whose chances of medical and psychological survival were high enough to warrant sustained parental attention. Thus Watson took advantage of popular mistrust of uncontrolled and impersonal sources of socialization, proposing that the behavioristically informed family could eventually replace the kindergarten, the school, the clinic, and the court.

Behaviorist Theory

Watsonian behaviorism was distinctive not only because of its *subject matter* (children, women, and the family) but also because of its theoretical content. Here, the significance of Watson's *psychological theory* is explored through an analysis of two of its central characteristics: environmentalism and developmentalism.

Watsonian psychological theory was, first of all, *environmentalist* in its insistence on the primacy of physical and social stimuli as the determinants of human behavior. According to Watson, changes in behavior occur by conditioning, whose mechanism is the association of new environmental stimuli with old. Since Watson hypothesized only a handful of inherited patterns of behavior, almost every human response was based on the experiencing of environmental, theoretically public events. Similarly, if any changes were to be made in a person's behavior, it would necessarily occur by the alteration of the person's stimulus environment. Thus the environment was presented as the major source of good and evil.

The second noteworthy characteristic of Watson's psychology was its *developmentalism*. This consisted of not just a focus on children as subjects but also on emphasis on the role of early experience in determining lifelong patterns of behavior. Although Watson discussed the possibility of reconditioning adults to remove maladaptive habits, his popular writing explicitly described the third or fourth year of life as the age when the individual's behavioral patterns were more or less permanently determined. As has already been mentioned, this placed Watson in agreement with popular psychoanalysis on the profound effects of early childhood experience.

Some Determinants. As with most psychological theories, much of the character of Watson's behaviorism can be explained in terms of disciplinary and personal factors (Herrnstein 1969; Burnham 1968; Creelan 1974, 1975). At the same time, there is reason to look beyond these factors to the cultural fit of certain implicit messages in behaviorism and to suggest a general, social determination for some of Watson's theorizing.

As evidence that Watson's writing carried strong implicit messages, consider Alix Kates Shulman's semiautobiographical description of a young woman's reaction to reading Watson in the 1940s:

In a strange scientific book from my father's shelves, *Behaviorism*, by the famous Dr. John Watson, I had discovered certain indispensable facts. *Personality*," said Watson in italics, "*is but the end product of our habit systems. . . . The situation we are in dominates us always and releases one or another of these all powerful habit systems.*"

If our situation dominates us, I would have to get out of my deadening situation. If personality is a result of habit, I would have to start forming the right habits. I would shun the rat race and prepare for college. I would practice raising an eyebrow, perfect my seductive glance, and cultivate a crooked smile. I would get top grades and harden myself.

There was another, even more remarkable, passage in [Watson's] book. "Between fifteen and eighteen, reported Dr. Watson, . . . "a female changes from a child to a woman. . . . After thirty, personality changes very slowly. . . . If you have an adequate picture of the average individual at 30 you will have it with few changes for the rest of that individual's life—as most lives already are lived. A quacking, gossiping, neighbor-spying, disaster-enjoying woman of 30 will be, unless a miracle happens, the same at 40 and still the same at 60."

I no longer believed in miracles. I would have to take matters into my own hands. How foolish the others were to expect that all they had to do was sit around and wait for their prince to come along, all the time developing God-knows-what ruinous habit patterns! I copied the entire passage into my notebook. "Don't believe everything you read," my father had warned, but I believed. The passage, with its time schedule, seemed to have been written expressly for me (1972:76–77).

In this account, Shulman expresses well one of the major cultural attractions of Watson's writings: its combination of cynicism and ameliorism. As part of his early-influence doctrine, Watson held out the promise of both personal gain and social betterment as a result of an improved psychological environment. This was expressed in his often-quoted boast that he could shape and channel an infant into any career and in his complaint that social progress is being held back by parents' failure to properly raise their children (Watson 1928b). It was also implied by his statements that the only "weakness of women (who seek careers) is that they have never been trained to work like men" and that "[the racial inferiority of Blacks] is a completely unproven [doctrine].

The negro has never been given a chance to develop" (Watson 1927c:234, 1927d:10).

In understanding these assertions by Watson (i.e., of the primacy of environment and habit), it is important to recognize that their author was not confronting his audience with a completely new or original doctrine. A similar message had, for example, been promoted by reformers such as Henry Beecher in the Protestant church beginning in the early nineteenth century. There, it took the form of the assertion that good works and the training of the will were more important than inherent sinfulness in determining an individual's damnation or redemption. As this position gained support in both religious and secular circles, it helped create significant changes in social attitudes toward children and childrearing. As a result, parents in the nineteenth and early twentieth centuries were exposed to childrearing literature that, long before Watson, emphasized the environmental, social determinants of the individual's character.[6]

Added to this moral antihereditarianism was the psychological concept of habit, popularized by William James and others in the nineteenth century and then adopted by Watson as a central element of behavioral theory. Although Watson eventually developed his own specific meaning for "habit," based on classical conditioning theory, most of Watson's readers probably understood this concept in the broader terms of popular philosophy. They knew that habits, once formed, could be difficult to change, that one could pick up bad habits from one's peers (the social environment), and that one's character could be described as a cumulation of all one's habits—both good and bad. To this extent, they knew the basic messages of Watsonian behaviorism without ever needing to understand Pavlovian theory, the difference between motor and autonomic conditioning, or Watson's less familiar doctrines such as his analysis of cognition as subvocal speech.

What was new in Watson's version of this basically Protestant view of humanity was its partial contradiction by the principle that an individual's character became more or less fixed by the end of early childhood. This meant that on the level of social philosophy, the potentially unbridled ameliorism of Watson's environmentalist views was kept in check by his equally strong doctrine of developmental determination. After all, one could not be too much of a cultural optimist if one accepted Watson's belief that environmental improvements would take at least a generation to create real behavioral changes. Also, if one took seriously Watson's emphasis on the evils of uninformed parenting, one would have to expect that significant cultural change would have to await basic changes in the family—something much farther into the future than one generation's time.

Given popular disenchantment with reformist optimism after the First World War, the popularity of Watson's combination of cynicism and ameliorism is not surprising. Rather than predicting a suddenly better life through institutional and environmental changes, Watson mostly stressed the need to avoid further deterioration of one's emotional state or one's family relations. This would be done not by massive social intervention (e.g., intelligence testing and sterilization), but by individual families' attention to the psychological climate in their homes. Moreover, said Watson, he was not concerned whether his advice on such matters proved either ineffective or revolutionary in its results.

This perspective, I assert, was quite different from that of the muckrakers, prohibitionists, international interventionists, and others in the progressive era. Moreover, it was not an accidental difference; it was due to Watson's self-proclaimed status as not only a champion of behaviorism but also a new type of social reformer: the dispassionate, experimental social scientist.

The Behaviorist Himself

In talking directly to the public, John Watson was doing more than just promoting his behaviorist theory as the best approach for understanding certain topics, e.g., women and the family. He was simultaneously promoting himself as a prototype of the new social scientist: an unsentimental, objective, masculine expert who was willing to place his experimental skills and experience at the service of society.

Although it was not an acknowledged topic of study, the image of the behaviorist as scientific expert was always a part of Watson's popular message. This was due, first, to the central role of the behaviorist's expertise in Watson's proposed remedies for social and psychological problems. Also, the supposed objectivity and social utility of the Watsonian as expert was an implicit corollary to behaviorism's principles that psychology should be a science of behavioral control through objective experimental study. Viewed in this way, Watson's popularity in the 1920s and 1930s reflected public acceptance of his role as scientist and as social control agent as much as it signified their belief in behavioral theory.

As Experimentalist and Expert. To Watson, the behaviorist was first of all an experimentalist and expert consultant. He was experimental because of his strictly empiricist approach to both biological and social phenomena and expert because he was willing to provide authoritative advice to those less knowledgeable. As an example of these qualities in operation, consider the relationship of the behaviorist to his client, "the mother," as portrayed in the first chapter of *Psychological Care of Infant and Child.* First, Watson wrote of mothers' discovery that they need expert help:

Mothers [are beginning] to ask themselves the question, "Am I not almost wholly responsible for the way my child grows up? Isn't it just possible that almost nothing is given in heredity and that practically the whole course of development of the child is due to the way I raise it?" When [a mother] first faces this thought, she shies away from it as being too horrible. She would rather load this burden upon heredity, upon the Divine shoulder other than her own. Once she faces it, accepts it and begins to stagger under the load, she asks herself the question, "What shall I do? If I am responsible for what this tiny being is to become, where shall I find the light to guide my footsteps?" (Watson 1928c;15, 16).

Then, Watson explained the only way in which the mother's "load" could be lifted:

No one today knows enough to raise a child. The world would be considerably better off if we were to stop having children for twenty years (except those reared for experimental purposes) and were then to start again with enough facts to do the job with some degree of skill and accuracy. Parenthood, instead of being an instinctive art, is a science, the details of which must be worked out by patient laboratory methods (1928c:12–13).

In saying this, Watson was describing the qualities of the behaviorist in a thoroughly modern manner: by itemizing the needs and inadequacies of the consumer of behaviorism. The consumer, Watson wrote, needs to understand the child scientifically but is too sentimental and too busy to objectively and reliably observe the child.[7] What is needed is an experimentalist who can dispassionately study the child and then explain its workings to the interest parent.

In describing the behaviorist as such a dispassionate expert, Watson was doing more than exposing his own view of psychology's proper method (that it should be observational) or his own preferred style of interpersonal behavior (unemotional). He was expressing the middle classes' distrust of moralistic reformers and their growing interest in supposedly objective scientists in the post-First World War period.

The first of these themes, distrust of moralists, was a reaction against the moral direction that was so obvious in progressivist reform campaigns. To distinguish himself from such reformers, Watson often issued disclaimers:

The behaviorist hastens to admit that he has no "ideals" for bringing up children. He does not know how the ideal child should be brought up. The standards imposed by present society are not his standards (1928c:184).

The behaviorist, who is only an observer, is not grieving or worrying about [sexual experimentation], nor is he trying to reform anybody or anything (1928b:77).

As a substitute for the moralist meddler, Watson offered the objective experimentalist:

The behaviorists . . . believe in the objective re-examination of millions of age-old social customs and habits. . . .

Who started this business of monogamy anyway? Who said that man should have one wife, and woman one husband, and that the relationship should endure for life. This is an age of science (1927a:104).

It must be understood at the outset, though, that psychology at present has little to do with the setting of social standards of action and nothing to do with moral standards (Watson 1917:329).

. . . the behaviorist advocates the early building of appropriate common sense negative reactions by the method of gently rapping the fingers or hand or other bodily part when the undesirable act is taking place, *but as an objective experimental procedure*—never as punishment (Watson 1928c:64).

This image of the behaviorist as an ultraempiricist was not just a reaction against moralism; it was also an expression of middle-class faith in "basic science," in natural social evolution, and in the scientific management of human behavior. The first of these faiths, faith in basic science, was related to the belief of many that scientists' proper role in the First World War was to help the Allies make the world safe for democracy. This was best done, many thought, by having researchers from the academic world apply their theoretical knowledge to urgent problems of the day (e.g., the vocational assessment of soldiers for the Army).

The second of the faiths that Watson expressed was a faith in cultural evolution. This can be seen most clearly in his writings on heterosexual relations, which contain an imaginary history of how economic forces and sexual preferences acted to create the institution of monogamous marriage. In Watson's hands, this history of marriage was then combined with a Darwinist ideology to suggest that the then-current social tensions over marriage were simply signs of continued adaptation to changing economic conditions. According to this view, family ills were a product of recent social changes (e.g., women's increased leisure time) and could be corrected through behaviorally designed changes in childrearing (Watson 1927a, 1930).

The underlying message was that social structures and norms eventually change to fit larger economic and technological changes, unless disturbed by social and political bungling. The behaviorists' role, then, "as an evolutionist . . . [was] to understand; not to praise, or blame or lead us into righteousness" (Mitchell 1936:xix).

Although Watson did not attempt to lead anyone into righteousness, his predictions and admonitions reflected his biases in favor of individualism and social productivity. As an expert, however, Watson made these biases seem like the obvious needs of a modern society. In doing so, Watson played a role similar to that of the efficiency experts and "scientific managers" who had captured the nation's attention in the 1910s. Like Frederick Taylor and Frank Gilbreth, Watson was willing to apply methods of science and technology to all social institutions and to turn any of them — including the home — into a factory or business (Braverman 1975; F. Gilbreth 1912; Gilbreth and Carey 1948; Kelley 1923; Leupp 1911; Purrington 1918). Just as Taylor attacked the supposedly nonproductive social norms of the factory (i.e., union work rules), Watson attacked the superstititions and maladaptive norms of family life that were supposedly contributing to the production of emotionally inefficient offspring. And just as Taylorism was insensitive to the human cost of increased productivity, Watson's "experimental" approach to childrearing included little consideration of the long-term effects on both mother and child.[8]

In addition to these similarities in the social philosophies of scientific management and early behaviorism, Taylorism and Watsonianism also shared an elitist distrust of popular democracy. As Samuel Haber has described in his study of the rise of Taylorism as a social movement, scientific management provided an attractive solution to the dilemma of how elite reformers could fulfill popular demands for the egalitarianism and democracy that were promised in much of progressivist ideology (Haber 1964). They could do both, by forecasting equal *economic* gains to all from scientific management's efficiency-increasing reforms, while at the same time they demanded *political* obedience to the rule of the expert consultant, his stopwatch, and his calculations of "the one best way to do work" (L. Gilbreth 1926).

Using similar logic as the Taylorites, Watson was able to rationalize his role as self-appointed arbiter of childrearing practices. This was said to be justifiable, first, because the widespread application of Watson's methods would benefit all of society. The second justification for such an elitist role was as follows: because the systematic, scientific observation of infants each minute of the day was the only valid source of child development knowledge, mothers throughout history must have been ignorant of the proper way to raise children. Now, however, Watson and other experts were finally amassing the data necessary to understand the child; thus it is reasonable that they be given a position of leadership in the movement toward professional parenthood.

In this way Watson was able to subvert the idea that mothers should collectively control childrearing resources, such as child care facilities and scientific consultants. That would not be wise, the behaviorist implied, since mothers were chiefly a source of superstition and inefficient parenting strategies. What was needed instead was someone with enough scientific capital to buy a controlling interest (intellectually speaking) in the new business of bringing up children correctly.

As Agent of Social Control. In addition to promoting his theoretical expertise and pragmatic experimentalism, John Watson took on the role of social control agent at the service of the state. Although this aspect of Watson's persona has received little attention in this essay, it has been a frequent emphasis of recent writing on Watson and early behaviorism. For example, David Bakan has described Watson's "vaulting urge toward the mastery of other human beings," associating it with "the growth of urban industrial life . . . in the late 19th and early 20th centuries." Thus, Bakan explains, "In the new world of the city, 'change of behavior' [the behaviorist's definition of 'learning'] was a critical phenomenon; for 'adjustment' in the world of the city continuously called for change in behavior" (Bakan 1966:13, 14). As described by Ehrenreich and English, Watson stressed "that the child could be trained to behave like a machine, or at least to fit into a world requiring machinelike regularity and discipline . . . the problem in child raising was simply to program the little machines to fit into the larger industrial world" (Ehrenreich and English 1978:184). Finally, Dana Bramel has identified the one "over-all orientation" of Watsonianism as "the drive to control the behavior of people so as to achieve some kind of perfected society" (Bramel 1978:17).

Although these accounts describe a theme that does play a prominent role in Watson's work, his overall message seems to be more complex than a simple promise of social control. At the same time that Watson was describing the behaviorist's job as "moulding," "adjusting," and "shaping" various "human instruments" (Watson 1927e:74) he was also protesting the effects of the conformist, institution-laden environment of the 1920s on the individual. Thus, Watson complained:

The hold that all this political and religious organized ballyhoo gets upon the timid, fearful, unthinking individual . . . is nigh all-powerful. The individual loses his identity. He cannot buck it—he cannot escape —he is brought up in the schools or churches of this and that doctrine until he has ceased to struggle to escape. . . .

A child coming to adulthood in an American family is so wrapped up in layers of obsolete social, religious and political bandages that one must look upon him almost as a kind of living mummy, so restrained and restricted are the limits of his behavior. . . .

Throughout high school and college he is forced to fit into molds that have been carved out for him for ages. He must learn Latin, Philosophy,

Ancient History, Geometry, Algebra, Trigonometry, in spite of the fact that such disciplines, except for the training of specialists, are utterly out of line with the human needs of the day" (Watson 1930:61, 62, 64).

The Behaviorist's Conflicting Roles

How could John Watson be both a prototype of the scientist as social control agent and also a vocal opponent of the rising tide of institutionally created social conformity and homogenization? How could Watson both complain that social change was not occurring at a rapid enough rate and also develop a new psychology that stressed how completely the individual's behavior was determined by his or her current social environment, ridiculing the notion of internal forces working toward developmental change? In order to resolve these conflicting aspects of Watson's popular message, it is necessary to recognize that message's expression of the conflicting relationship of the middle classes to the social institutions of modern urban life: the family, the school, the charities, and the urban political machine. Stated simply, this conflict was between a middle-class desire to survive as an individual and these institutions' function as collectivizing, homogenizing agents.

Consider, for example, the urban middle-class family of Watson's era. As this family was becoming more conjugal and more democratic, its members' loyalties were becoming more contradictory. As a member of such a family, one's emotional and economic life was not under one's own control; feelings of even the "head of the family" could become enmeshed in a collective system of loves, hates, needs for dependency, dominance, and so forth. Thus, there was plenty of reason for an unsentimental individualist such as Watson to protest against the family's stifling effects and to demand its dissolution. At the same time, however, the support of a family was increasingly necessary (even for Watson) in an increasingly professionalized and "business-like" (profit-oriented) urban society. In other words, while the business world of the 1920s made men like Watson need a family to which one could come home, it also increasingly demanded that one sacrifice all traditions and loyalties, including those represented by the family. No wonder Watson both urged the family's reform and predicted its abandonment. No wonder his writing often seemed to proclaim: "The family is dead! Long live the family!"

Similarly conflicting feelings were expressed by Watson in relation to other institutions of the new urban environment, such as schools, courts, and the political machine. For example, compulsory general education was a necessary part of the cultural assimilation of immigrant populations, and some form of higher education was necessary if industry was to find the increasing numbers of managers and skilled technicians it needed. At the same time, however, compulsory education meant that everyone learned certain predetermined subjects (rather than each individual's pursuing selected topics), and since business trends were often unpredictable, higher education had to be general rather than trade oriented. This went against the middle-class hope that everyone could be engaged in education for work that was personally fitted to their interests; yet it was a necessary feature of the postwar economic boom, which Watson called the "new era of opportunity" (Watson 1928b:108).

Similar tensions characterized the middle classes' relation to the courts, the charities, and urban political institutions. Individuals of Watson's social class felt that they needed the courts to protect them from lawless forces in the city (i.e., criminals, unscrupulous businessmen) and the charities to protect the less fortunate from the city's effects. Yet the courts based their decisions on general class interests rather than on individuals' needs, and the charities were, by design, equally undemocratic. Like these institutions, the city's political machine offered the individual certain rewards and benefits, but only when he was willing to surrender some individual freedom (i.e., free choice at the polls).

As we have seen, Watson compared such sacrifices of individuality with the practice of swaddling babies — the only innately enraging act according to behaviorist theory. Yet at the same time, he could not call for the abolition of the functions of the courts, of Tammany Hall, or of charitable foundations. That was because such institutions were the source of Watson's authority as an expert. On a general level, experts such as Watson needed a social reform/welfare system to help promote the idea of professionally directed amelioration. On a specific level, the last year of Watson's own academic research was made possible by an orphanage (the source of infants such as little Albert), a clinic (where

Watson moved his work in 1916), and a foundation (which helped finance the research of Watson's final student, Mary Cover Jones) (Jones 1924; Watson 1928b).

The Behaviorist at Work:
Watson's Separate Spheres Doctrine

In his popular writing, Watson did not simply acknowledge these conflicting social needs (social control versus personal freedom). He also offered a resolution of this dilemma and of his own conflicting roles as both social control agent and protector of individual differences. In doing so, he promised "to help the home, the school, the church, [and] society to bring up a socialized but individual human product," while restoring each person's right to "the pursuit of happiness which our Constitution so kindly affords" (Watson 1926a:729).

For Watson, the mechanism for resolving the conflict between social and individual needs was a version of the doctrine of separate spheres. That is, Watson first asserted that everyone deserved a happy, fulfilling life, with happiness defined as "[the] complete absorption [of an individual] in activity" (Watson 1929a:35). Then, in both subtle and sometimes not so subtle terms, Watson explained that different social groups (i.e., men, women, the elite, and the masses) would find their fulfillment through separate spheres of activity within the home and the factory.

The most obvious example of this doctrine is found in Watson's description of the social lives of men and women in the behaviorist utopia (Watson 1929a). In this carefully designed society, men's happiness in the world of work would be guaranteed by having them, as boys, "try out several industries, and make a selection of the vocation that they are to follow in later life" (Watson 1929a:35). For women, Watson also promised happiness and freedom:

The young women of Utopia feel and act as freely as the men. They have a high respect for the art and science of being a woman.

These benefits would, however, necessitate special training:

At the age of sixteen the training of girls becomes different from that of boys. . . . Girls learn domestic science, cooking, dietetics. They have special instructions in the art of interesting and handling men. They are given instructions in the art and technique of being engaged. They spend a great deal of time learning the technique of sex. . . . They are busy and happy from morning till night. It is during these ages that they begin in earnest the study of dancing, of the use of cosmetics, of how to stay thin, of how to be successful hostesses and to put on the intellectual attainments that go into the making of a beautiful, graceful, wise woman (1929a:35).

Here one can see the irony of Watson's promise (in *Psychological Care . . .*) to elevate motherhood to a profession, and his complaint (in "The Weakness of Women") that women have never been given a chance to pursue their own careers. While saying this, his underlying belief was that the only proper career for women was as wife and mother and that even motherhood should not be practiced until women's "narcissism disappears . . . around the twenty-eighth year—almost coincidentally with the appearance of the first wrinkle" (Watson 1929a:34). Before then, Watson saw women's job as that of pleasant sexual companion for their husbands.

In addition to sex, the other dimension along which Watson divided his social world was that of general social standing. Although not as obvious as Watson's recommended confinement of women to the home, the idea of separate spheres for an elite and for the masses is an equally important method by which Watson resolved the conflicting roles of behaviorist as enforcer versus liberator.

This was done, first, by Watson's assertion that the best possible world would be one in which the dominant ideology is that of science and where "there are no churches and no clergymen . . . and incidentally no philosophy." In the place of courts and prisons, Watson proposed, there would be clinics staffed by behaviorally trained physicians who "take the whole care of the whole individual, . . . unconditioning" and then reconditioning anyone who "shows signs of conduct deviation." The power of these medical specialists would be such that "If [someone] becomes hopelessly insane or incurably diseased, if idiots and feebleminded children appear, the physicians do not hesitate to put them to death" (Watson 1929a:34).

Applied to the nonutopian world of Watson's era, this techn-ocratic vision was one method by which Watson hoped to reduce his readers' possible concerns about the growth of institutions of social control. Watson did so by asserting that scientific training would produce a pragmatic, managerial elite that would structure the social environment for the satisfaction of all. If that meant imposing different fates on the elite and the masses, such an im-position would be made in the name of science, rather than on behalf of some hereditarian aristocracy.

That Watson did envision different fates for different social classes can be seen most clearly in his article, "What About Your Child?" In it, Watson complains that "since our environment is rapidly becoming uniform everyone is growing up almost like everybody else" (Watson 1928b:77). Although this may sound like the grumbling of a pure individualist, a careful reading shows it to be more of an elitist's lament. What most concerned Watson was the failure of certain men from good backgrounds to make a prominent place for themselves in society. Thus, Watson reminds his readers that "there are still plenty of potential George Wash-ingtons, Lincolns, Napoleons and Shakespeares as there ever were." After all, he says, "geniuses like other people are made — not born . . . that is our behavior is created . . . by our parents (and others)." "It is the sharp sudden change in the environment plus the very definite situation he happens to be placed in at the moment of the environmental change that gives a man his chance for sudden eminence"[9] (Watson 1928b:77).

For the purpose of my argument, the crucial feature of this philosophy is its ability to be interpreted differently for different classes. For the middle classes, it provided scientific support for the feeling that traditional religious, family, and social standards were stifling to progress but that, in a free marketplace, popu-lated by nonfearful people, one's position could be improved by a combination of hard work and "lucky breaks" (e.g., personal influence, outside capital).

At the same time, Watson's philosophy could be applied to the majority of the working class and poor, who were not gifted with technical training, lucky breaks, or mothers who read Wat-son's books. In this sphere, Watson's complaints of the stifling effects of school and other institutions were not appropriate. After all, working mothers didn't have the time to overindulge their children, so there was no reason to remind them that "the pioneers of our industries were not reared like hothouse plants" (Genn 1928:440). Also, the masses did not have the enriched early experience that Watson implied was necessary to be either a captain of industry or even a skilled professional; thus there was not a wide variety of interesting jobs from which working-class young men were being kept by useless schooling.

Although this may seem like an overly interpretive reading of behaviorist childrearing advice, Watson's own views were quite straightforward on the question of separate spheres for different social classes. For example, when he was once asked how behaviorism could hope to change the daily life of an entire society, Watson replied that his plans were not for "people who live in the slums." He explained, "I only mean them [to be] for the cultured. . . . These are the only sort of people who will assimilate my ideas and be guided by them" (Oaks 1929:10).

Thus, Watson's appeals for the raising of independent, fearless children were aimed at the middle and upper classes. Calls for better moulding of the individual to the environment, by contrast, were aimed at the working class and urban poor. For these latter groups, behaviorism was one more technique for better fitting the worker to his job, rather than vice versa. That such different messages could be found in behaviorist doctrine was a key to Watson's success as a social philosopher of both freedom and adjustment. More freedom was promised by Watson to his fellow professionals and to his businessman clients; more adjustment was to be the fate of women, of workers, and of most children — the true subject matter of behaviorist science.

Notes

1. This reference and the subsequent reference to Alix Kates Shulman were called to my attention by Kerry W. Buckley.

2. As an example of Watson's impact, consider the report of a contemporary writer: "Whenever two or three young mothers are gathered together, the conversation will finally turn upon the modern theories of child training. Someone, then, is sure to ask, perhaps with strong antagonism in her voice, 'Have you read Dr. Watson's book on "Behaviorism and Child Training"?' " (Cosgrove 1929:36).

3. In focusing on the ideological content of Watson's advice, this essay is relatively unconcerned with social history and with psychohistorical analysis. That is,

it does not attempt to assess the direct, behavioral effects of Watsonian precepts on individual parents and children, or the cultural and generational effects of parents' using Watson's advice throughout the 1920s and 1930s.

One reason for this is the lack of clear evidence concerning the public's adoption of behaviorist techniques. On the one hand it is possible to find personal testimonies to Watson's influence, and secondary sources that assert that an entire generation of infants was raised according to Watsonian "strict schedules" (Goldsmith 1980; Russell 1926; Stendler 1950; Tait 1975; R. Watson 1930). On the other hand, there is a growing historical literature that questions whether childrearing advice has reliable, uniform effects on parents' behavior (e.g., Mechling 1975). Applied to Watson, this challenges the assumptions that (1) behaviorist advice changed the *attitudes* of parents toward childrearing practices and (2) parental attitudes (even if behaviorist) would have a strong relationship to parents' overall *behavior* toward their children.

A second reason for not dwelling on the actual effects of Watsonian advice is that such advice was often not different from already existing childrearing practices. On the question of strict scheduling of infant feeding and sleeping, for example, Watson was no more of a strict scheduler than the nationally prominent Mrs. West, whose infant care manual began recommending child care "by the clock" in 1914. Despite her assertion that "all babies need mothering and should have plenty of it," Mrs. West generally stressed the need for independent children, recommending (for example) that older children be taught to sit on the floor or in a crib and not make demands on their mother's time (West, 1914). Also, on the question of handling emotional outbursts, Mrs. West's basic advice was that crying babies should be checked for physical problems and then be left to cry themselves to sleep—a quite similar recommendation to that by Watson. Such advice, then, was not necessarily behavioristic; rather, it could be made consistent with a wide range of philosophical views, from Watsonianism to instinctivist, empathy-based "nursery ethics" (Winterburn 1895).

4. As an example of the perceived complexity of Freudian developmental theory, David Mitchell's reaction to one psychoanalytic article is: "one almost invariably wonders if a simpler explanation would not have been equally satisfactory" (1918:318). Also, on the topic of behaviorism vs. psychoanalysis, Watson himself acknowledged the agreement between some of his ideas and those of Freudian theory, praising the "wonderful and valuable work now being done by a limited group of analysts" (Watson 1926b:249). As evidence that some of Watson's own objections to psychoanalysis were due to its style (e.g., vocabulary, complexity) rather than to its effectiveness or social message, consider his recommendation to those interested in psychological self-improvement: "I think the best single thing to do is to take three or four of the simplest books of the psychoanalysts written by the best among them—and read and reread them carefully. But for heaven's sake don't get into the habit of talking psychoanlaytic jargon. Talking psychoanalysis to friends has gone out of style" (Watson 1932:9; see also Harris 1980a; Mahl 1978).

5. It is important to recognize the nineteenth-century origins of the concept of the child as a malleable organism, easily corrupted by its guardians. For example, in *The Mother's Role . . .* Kuhn explains how mid- to late-nineteenth-century emphasis on strict feeding schedules and letting children "cry it out" were a reaction against the earlier practice of overfeeding and drugging infants in order to keep them quiet. As a result of such domestic reforms, pre-Watsonian childrearing advice often con-

tained statements such as "[the mother] would not be guilty of pulling up the sprouting plant to see if it was growing; why carry her baby about in her arms or hold him in her lap when he can kick or crow so much more freely in his own bed" (Cowles 1919:70).

6. For example, in a medical advice column in the *Ladies Home Journal*, Dr. William Sadler stated:

> While certain dominant strains of the character are acquired by heredity, environment exerts by far the greatest influence upon the evolution of character. Environment is able even to modify and practically change numerous hereditary traits of character. While to a certain extent the laws of heredity are inexorable, and it will remain forever true that "the fathers have eaten sour grapes, and the children's teeth are set on edge," nevertheless there is another scripture which is equally true, which portrays the operation of the laws of environment and personal obedience, which declares that when men's thoughts and hearts are changed it shall no longer be said of them that "the fathers have eaten sour grapes, and the children's teeth are set on edge," but "every man that eateth the sour grape, his teeth shall be set on edge" (Sadler 1911:12).

Although based on a Lamarckian concept of heredity, this statement clearly expresses the degree to which early twentieth-century environmentalism was an optimistic blend of biological, social, and religious ideologies.

7. As described in Watson's writing, the mother sometimes seemed to be in a no-win situation. If she dared to observe her child regularly, Watson complained that "the children are not allowed to draw a breath unscrutinized" (1928c:12). However, if she left her child alone, then she could not fulfill the behaviorist's standards for a reliable gatherer of behavioral data. Either way, she needed expert guidance.

8. The analogy between the home and a laboratory or factory was more than metaphor and did not originate with Watson. In the 1920s there had been a widespread "household efficiency" movement that advocated the application of scientific management to the home. Such an application was most graphically presented in newsreel coverage of the Gilbreths' use of time-motion study principles in their own home.

9. Although Watson could have been referring here to his overcoming of his own poor, South Carolina heritage, he was speaking *to* the readership of *Cosmopolitan*. Thus his message was not primarily a reminder that *anyone* could become a millionaire but a discussion of the fate of the middle classes (e.g., college professors, small businessmen, physicians).

References

Bakan, David. 1966. "Behaviorism and American Urbanization." *Journal of the History of the Behavioral Sciences* 2:5–28.

Blair, Emily N. 1919. "What Are We Women Going To Do?" *Ladies Home Journal* (May) 36:47, 114.

Bramel, Dana. 1978. "The Resistable Rise (And Fall?) of Behaviorism—A Brief History." *Red Balloon* (Winter) 13:17–19.

Braverman, Harry. 1975. *Labor and Monopoly Capital.* New York: Monthly Review.

Burnham, John C. 1968. "On the Origins of Behaviorism." *Journal of the History of the Behavioral Sciences* 4:143–51.

Cohen, David. 1979. *J. B. Watson.* Boston: Routledge & Kegan Paul.

Cosgrove, Jessica G. 1929. "Behaviorism in Bringing Up Children." *Delineator* (May) 114:36–37.

Cowles, Edith C. 1919. "Begin Early To Form the Habits of Your Child." In U. S. Bureau of Education, ed. *Training Little Children.* Washington, D.C.: U.S. Government Printing Office.

Creelan, Paul. 1974. "Watsonian Behaviorism and the Calvinist Conscience." *Journal of the History of the Behavioral Sciences* 10:95–118.

—— 1975. "Religion, Language, and Sexuality in J. B. Watson." *Journal of Humanistic Psychology* (Fall) 15:55–78.

Ehrenreich, Barbara and Deirdre English. 1978. *For Her Own Good.* Garden City, New York: Anchor.

Fass, Paula S. 1977. *The Damned and the Beautiful: American Youth in the 1920's.* New York: Oxford University Press.

Gale, Zona. 1919. "Is Housework Pushing Down the Birth Rate?" *Ladies Home Journal* (May) 36:41.

Genn, Lillian G. 1928. "The Behaviorist Looks at Youth" *Independent Woman* (October) 7:439–40, 479.

Gilbreth, Frank B. 1912. "Scientific Management in the Household." *Journal of Home Economics* 4:438–47.

Gilbreth, Frank B., Jr. and Ernestine G. Carey. 1948. *Cheaper by the Dozen.* New York: Crowell.

Gilbreth, Lillian M. 1926. *The Quest of the One Best Way, A Sketch of the Life of Frank Bunker Gilbreth.* Chicago: Society of Industrial Engineers.

Goldsmith, Barbara. 1980. *Little Gloria . . . Happy at Last.* New York: Knopf.

Haber, Samuel. 1964. *Efficiency and Uplift: Scientific Management in the Progressive Era, 1890–1920.* Chicago: University of Chicago Press.

Harris, Ben. 1979. "Whatever Happened to Little Albert." *American Psychologist* 34:151–60.

—— 1980a. "The Social Context of Watsonian Behaviorism: John B. Watson's Use of Psychoanalytic Concepts." Paper presented at the annual meeting of the Southeastern Psychological Association, Washington, D.C.

—— 1980b. "John B. Watson as Film Producer and Developmental Psychologist." Paper presented at the annual meeting of the American Psychological Association, Montreal, Canada.

Hermstein, Richard J. 1969. "Behaviorism." In *Schools of Psychology*, David L. Krantz, ed. New York: Appleton Century Crofts.

Jones, Mary C. 1924. "The Elimination of Children's Fears." *Journal of Experimental Psychology* 7:383–90.

Kelley, Fred C. 1923. "Running a Home for Eleven Kids." *Colliers* (July 21) 72:14.

Kuhn, Anne L. 1947. *The Mother's Role in Childhood Education: New England Concepts 1830–1860.* New Haven, Conn.: Yale University Press.

Leupp, Francis E. 1911. "Scientific Management in the Family." *Outlook* (August 12):832–37.

Lomax, Elizabeth M. R., Jerome Kagan, and Barbara G. Rosenkrantz. 1978. *Science and Patterns of Child Care.* San Francisco: W. H. Freeman.

Mahl, George F. 1978. "The Views of John B. Watson About Psychoanalysis." Paper presented at the annual meeting of the Eastern Psychological Association, Washington, D.C.

Mayo, Elton. 1924. "Civilized Unreason." *Harper's Monthly* 148:527–35.

Mechling, Jay. 1975. "Advice to Historians on Advice to Mothers." *Journal of Social History* 9:44–63.

Mitchell, David. 1918. "Child Psychology." *Psychological Bulletin* 15:311–23.

—— 1919. "Child Psychology." *Psychological Bulletin* 16:299–315.

Mitchell, Wesley C. 1936. *What Veblen Taught.* New York: Viking.

Oaks, Gladys. 1929. "Take Children From Parents? A Tempest Over the Teacups." *New York World* (December 29), pp. 1, 10.

O'Neill, William L. 1967. *Divorce in the Progressive Era.* New Haven, Conn.: Yale University Press.

"Parents, We Are Here!" 1926. *Children* (October):1.

Purington, Edward E. 1918. "Personal Efficiency." *Independent* 94:86.

Russell, Bertrand A. W. 1926. *Education and the Good Life.* New York: Boni & Liveright.

Sadler, William S. 1911. "What Wears Thousands of Us Out." *Ladies Home Journal* (October) 28:12, 26, 77.

Samelson, Franz. 1981. "Struggle for Scientific Authority: The Reception of Watson's Behaviorism, 1913–1920." *Journal of the History of the Behavioral Sciences* 17:399–425.

Schlossman, Steven L. 1976. "Before Home Start: Notes Toward a History of Parent Education in America, 1897–1929." *Harvard Educational Review* 46:436–67.

Shulman, Alix K. 1972. *Memoirs of an Ex-Prom Queen.* New York: Knopf.

Sklar, Kathryn K. 1973. *Catherine Beecher.* New Haven, Conn.: Yale University Press.

Stendler, Celia B. 1950. "Psychological Aspects of Pediatrics." *Journal of Pediatrics* 36:122–34.

Tait, Katherine. 1975. *My Father Bertrand Russell.* New York: Harcourt Brace.

Watson, John B. 1917. "An Attempted Formulation of the Scope of Behavior Psychology." *Psychological Review* 24:329–52.

—— 1926a. "What Is Behaviorism?" *Harper's Monthly* 152:723–29.

—— 1926b. "Memory as the Behaviorist Sees It." *Harper's Monthly* 153:244–50.

—— 1927a. "Men Won't Marry Fifty Years From Now." *Cosmopolitan* (June) 86:71, 104, 106.

—— 1927b. "Can Psychology Help Me Rear My Child?" *McCall's* (September) 55:44, 72.

—— 1927c. "The Behaviorist Looks at Instincts." *Harper's Monthly* (July) 155:228–35.

—— 1927d. "The Weakness of Women." *Nation* (July 6) 125:9–10.

—— 1927e. "Are You Giving Your Child a Chance?" *McCall's* (October) 55:64,74.

—— 1928a. "A Good Child Just a Little Spoiled." *McCall's* (January) 56:50, 66.

—— 1928b. "What About Your Child?" *Cosmopolitan* (October) 85:76–77, 108–12.

—— 1928c. *Psychological Care of Infant and Child.* New York: Norton.

—— 1929a. "Should a Child Have More Than One Mother?" *Liberty* (June 29) 6:31–35.

—— 1929b. "Introduction," In G. B. Hamilton and Kenneth Macgowan, eds. *What is Wrong With Marriage?* New York: Albert and Charles Boni.

—— 1930. "After the Family What?" In V. G. Calverton and S. D. Schmalhausen, eds. *The New Generation.* New York: Macaulay.

—— 1932. *How To Grow a Personality.* Chicago: University of Chicago Press. [Psychology Series Lecture No. 12, National Broadcasting Company.]

Watson, John B. and Rosalie Rayner. 1920. "Conditioned Emotional Reactions." *Journal of Experimental Psychology* 3:1–14.

Watson, Rosalie R. 1930. "I Am the Mother of a Behaviorist's Sons." *Parents' Magazine* (Deecember):16–18, 67.

West, Mary Mills. 1914. *Infant Care.* Washington, D.C.: U.S. Government Printing Office. [U.S. Department of Labor. Children's Bureau, Publication No. 8.]

Winterburn, Florence Hill. 1895. *Nursery Ethics.* New York: Merriam.

7 "Rather Worse Than Folly?" Psychology Measures Femininity and Masculinity, 1

From Terman and Miles to the Guilfords

MIRIAM LEWIN

It may be objected, however, that the exactness of the test score, even apart from any question as to the soundness of its statistical presuppositions, is illusory, because it stands for an unanalyzed complex of Heaven-knows-what contributing elements; that the attempt to test . . . in our present state of ignorance of what these traits are, is rather worse than folly (Terman, APA Presidential Address, 1923).

The support of a 1979 summer stipend from the National Endowment for the Humanities for preliminary work on MF testing is gratefully acknowledged.

The story of psychologists' attempts to understand and to measure femininity and masculinity is a chronicle of failure. For 60 years psychologists have tried to quantify "MF," but without success (Constantanople 1973, Harrison 1975, Pleck 1975; Lewin 1982a, b). They failed, I believe, not because methodology for studying personality traits was in the early stages of its development—although it was (Lewin 1979)—but because adequate conceptions of femininity and masculinity were lacking. The failure was fundamentally conceptual, not technical. I argue here that we have still not overcome that basic conceptual confusion.

The Nineteenth Century:
Measuring Sex Differences

Before psychologists conducted studies of femininity and masculinity as such, they measured sex differences. In 1869, in "On the Real Differences in the Minds of Men and Women," McGrigor Allen wrote, "radical, natural, permanent distinctions in the mental and moral conformations" of the two sexes must exist (Allen 1869:cxcvi, cited in Duffin 1978:65). In 1874, in "The Mental Differences Between the Sexes," W. L. Distant argued that modern, domesticated women, like Mr. Darwin's domestic rabbits, were frailer and dumber than either their primitive ancestors or their contemporary mates. In 1884, Francis Galton opened his Anthropometric Laboratory in England. After testing 9,337 persons, he concluded that "women tend in all their capacities to be inferior to men" (Boring 1929:477). This conclusion was eventually challenged by two pioneer women psychologists, Helen Thompson Wooley (1903, 1910, 1914) and Leta Hollingworth (1914, 1916, 1922; see Rosenberg article 4).

In 1890 William James published his monumental classic *The Principles of Psychology,* which introduced a whole generation of American college men and a growing number of women to psychology. James proposes that the sexual instinct is opposed by the "anti-sexual instinct," which makes intimate contact with another person repulsive to us. In women this instinct takes the form of coyness. It must be "positively overcome" by wooing.

Women are also distinguished by the greater strength of

their parental instinct. (This theory remains popular among a few feminists, such as Alice Rossi.) James enthusiastically includes a long 1882 quotation on maternal instinct from the German scholar G. H. Schneider, who contemptuously portrays women before motherhood as vain, egotistic, irritable, and nervous. Women are, however, instantly transformed when they have a baby. They become totally selfless, no longer need sleep, function unconsciously and intuitively, find absolute delight in their hideous infants, are similar to animal mothers, and do not mind holding feces in their "naked hands." But "alas" unspoiled, naturally bred mothers are growing rarer (1890, 2:439–40). We see that the Mystification of Motherhood was already in full swing. Where Mystification rules, Mother Blaming, social scientists' favorite indoor sport, cannot be far behind.

The Calkins-Jastrow Controversy:
Masculine and Feminine Mental Traits.

Mary Whiton Calkins was one of William James' most distinguished students. James agreed to travel across Harvard Yard to Radcliffe to instruct females after Calkins was forbidden to attend lectures at Harvard (Furomoto 1979, Finison and Furomoto 1980). At one point Mary Calkins was James' only Radcliffe student, but he and she persevered. By 1895 she had completed all requirements for the Ph.D. in psychology. In spite of the fact that both William James and Hugo Munsterberg—then visiting at Harvard from Germany—recommended that she be awarded the Harvard doctorate, the Harvard Board of Overseers refused to grant the degree, and she never received it. James wrote her that being kept out was "enough to make dynamiters of you and all women" (Furomoto 1979:350). A later petition for Calkins signed by Yerkes, Woodworth, and Thorndike was also rejected. Calkins taught at Wellesley College soon after it was founded, invented the "method of paired associates" for the study of learning and memory, and became president of the American Psychological Association in 1905.

Joseph Jastrow, a former student of G. S. Hall and a well-known psychologist at the University of Wisconsin, conducted an empirical study of the "mental traits of masculinity and femininity" in 1891. He asked 25 men and 25 women to list 100 words as rapidly as possible. Jastrow found that women showed less variability than the men, a fact of great theoretical significance in evolutionary theory; because men varied more, they had evolved to a higher level than had women who were thus inferior. Also the women thought concretely, whereas the men thought abstractly.

Calkins, doubting the accuracy of these findings, decided to repeat the study at Wellesley. Her student Cordelia Nevers completely failed to replicate Jastrow's findings (Calkins 1895). The Wellesley women produced more abstract terms than either sex did at Wisconsin. They did not produce a preponderance of words related to what Jastrow called "the peculiar field of women's household instincts" (Calkins 1895:365–66). Stung, Jastrow wrote a lengthy reply, including the charge that the "words written at Wellesley seem to be less natural and unreflective" (Jastrow 1896:69).

When Jastrow objected, Calkins repeated her experiments, even permitting him to set seemingly incorrect standards for "abstract" words. Calkins felt that the second results vindicated her position. Jastrow held firmly to his own convictions. Calkins concluded that it is impossible to measure innate intellectual differences between the sexes that are uncontaminated by the effects of the environment, because "the differences in the training and tradition of men and women begin with the earliest months of infancy and continue through life" (1896:430).

The Paradigm Shifts From Sex Differences to Masculinity-Femininity.

As the belief in the intellectual inferiority of women gradually receded, psychologists turned their attention to noncognitive "mental traits of sex." "Sex differences" continued to attract attention, but "masculinity-femininity" became a new arena for research under the leadership of Lewis Terman, who set the style for all the MF tests developed between 1925 and 1949 (when the Franck test appeared). In many ways the tests of the 1970s and 1980 still follow in Terman's footsteps.

Terman and Miles Measure
Femininity and Masculinity:
What Went Wrong?

Lewis Terman was born in rural Indiana in 1877, the twelfth of fourteen children. He attended and later taught in one-room schools. From high school days onward he read widely in the great Victorians: Spencer, Darwin, Huxley, Haeckel, Havelock Ellis, Krafft-Ebing, Freud, James (surreptitiously—Terman's high school teacher disapproved of James) and G. Stanley Hall, with whom he did graduate work at Clark from 1903 to 1906 (Terman, 1936; Seagoe 1975). Hall, whose Monday seminar was one of the peak experiences of Terman's graduate study days, stressed recapitulation and the Lamarckian inheritance of acquired characteristics (see Lewin, article 8 and Morawski, article 5). Terman's doctoral dissertation (1906) was inspired by the work of Frances Galton, who had emphasized the importance of hereditary factors in intelligence. Most of these authors expounded the commonly accepted belief in the intellectual inferiority of women.

Terman made a major contribution to psychology by extensively revising Binet's intelligence test. His Stanford-Binet test remains one of the most widely used of all I.Q. tests today. During the First World War millions of men took the Army Alpha and the Army Beta (nonreaders) I.Q. tests, which Terman and his colleagues had designed. This event marked the birth of large-scale psychological testing.

Given his intellectual background, one might expect Terman to emphasize the innate or hereditary superiority of some people and the inferiority of others. At times he did overemphasize heredity. With hindsight we may call Terman's vehement rejection of the Iowa studies of Beth Wellman, Harold Skeels, and Marie Skodak one of the low points of Terman's career. Wellman, Skeels, and Skodak's classic research documented serious, apparently irreversible, declines in infant I.Q. that were traced to severely early social deprivation in orphanages. Terman argued heatedly (and, it turned out, incorrectly) that I.Q. was fixed by heredity and could not possibly react as Wellman and her colleagues claimed it did. It is to Terman's credit that over the course of his life he changed many of these ideas. In later years he said there was no evidence for innate racial inequality (Seagoe 1975).

In spite of Terman's strong hereditarian views about intelligence — views sometimes associated with ethnocentrism — on the personal level he objected to prejudice and he was politically liberal. His concern over sexism was reflected in a review by Terman of a biography of the pioneer woman psychologist Leta Hollingworth. Terman commented:

comparable productivity by a man would have led to the presidency of the American Psychological Association or even to membership in the National Academy of Sciences. . . . this opinion . . . is a reflection on the voting habits of male psychologists.

For the same reasons Terman resented his editor's decision to publish the material on Hollingworth in the *Journal of Applied Psychology* rather than in a more prestigious journal (February 1944, Terman Archives).

Once Terman was satisfied (by I.Q. data) that differences in intelligence between women and men were trivial or nonexistent, he concluded that the real mental differences between the sexes could best be identified by measuring femininity and masculinity. He was deeply convinced that there must be traits of mental masculinity and mental femininity. The MF topic was ripe for research. Before 1900 it had been feared that women admitted to higher education would be masculinized. After 1900 it was also feared that the "threat" posed by women's increased nondomestic activities, the decline of the American frontier, and the increase in male white-collar (that is "sissified") employment were emasculating men. Women finally obtained the vote. Terman began with high hopes that his MF test would become as magnificent a tool for human betterment as he believed his I.Q. test had proved to be. He planned to use the same techniques that had been so successful in measuring intelligence (see Pleck, article 9).

To assist him in this work he recruited Catherine Cox, later Catherine Cox Miles. Catherine Cox had been one of Terman's outstanding graduate students. Terman supervised her dissertation, which became the second volume of his series, *Genetic Studies of Genius* (1926). In 1926 her first postdoctoral employment was a full-time clinical position at a mental health facility in Cincinnati. (Dr. Mabel Fernald was a colleague.) An applied job in mental health was a typical career path for a woman at the time — it carried distinctly lower status than a university post.

Terman's student Mary Ann Bell did her Master's thesis "On Sex Differences in Non-intellectual Mental Traits" in 1926 (Seagoe 1975:209). On March 2, 1927, Terman wrote to Cox in Cincinnati "my masculinity-femininity study is getting to be about the most interesting thing I have ever tackled. . . . I recommended you for a position at Minnesota — but I suppose there is the old question whether a woman will be given a fair chance at it" (Terman Archives). Terman pointed out to Cox that returning to Stanford to work on the MF test would do far more to advance her career than applied work at the clinic would. He was delighted to hire Cox as a Research Associate for 1927–28. Terman reported on a preliminary study of MF in married couples in 1928, evoking some derogatory, mocking comments in the press, which perhaps reflected sex-role anxieties of the day (Terman Archives).

Together Terman and Miles created the 456 item Attitude Interest Analysis Survey (AIAS) (1936). It consists of multiple-choice items divided into seven subjects and comes in two forms, A or B. The majority of the criterion group who determined the statistical norms were youngsters in junior high and high school, as well as some in elementary school.

The AIAS was based on statistically typical sex differences. Numerous items were given to the youths. If the answers of the girls differed on the average from those of the boys, the item was retained with the answer choices identified as F, M, or neutral. Once items had been selected, then subjects received Femininity points for all F answers and Masculinity points for all M answers. The F score was subtracted from the M score to obtain a total MF score.

Subtests 1, Word Association, and 2, Ink Blot Associations, require the subject to select the "best" or "most natural" of the available responses to the stimulus. On test 3, Information, the girls received Masculinity points if they knew too much. To get Femininity points girls should believe that Goliath was killed by Cain, that the earth turns once on its axis in about 12 hours, that the tides are caused by ocean currents, that Belgium was an ally of Germany in the World War, that TNT, not FOB, is a shipping term, etc.

Terman and Miles considered test 4, Emotional and Ethical Attitudes, and test 5, Interests, to be their strongest, most reliable subtests. (Test 5 was weighted twice.) On test 4, subjects indicate how much emotion (from Very Much to None) is evoked by each of about 100 phrases referring to things that may arouse anger, fear, pity, or disgust or that are "acts of various degrees of Wickedness or Badness" (Terman and Miles 1936:494–98). (One of the fear stimuli is "Negroes"!) Girls consistently indicated stronger arousal. Girls were far more likely than boys to be angry at "Seeing a person treated unfairly because of his race," "Seeing an innocent man punished for another's crime," "Seeing someone laugh when a blind man runs into an obstacle," "Hearing your friends unjustly abused," "Seeing someone cheat in an examination," etc. (1936:391). Boys got angrier than girls at "Being disturbed when you want to work"; the average male felt "A Little" anger, the average female felt "None" (1936:494). The normative female apparently did not feel entitled to resent being interrupted at her work.

Given a forced choice, boys preferred to "Make Plans," girls, to "Carry Out Plans"; girls preferred to "Persuade Others," boys, to "Command Others." Boys preferred to "Work for Themselves", girls, to "Work under a Respected Superior"—but only a little. Boys preferred "Uninteresting work with a large income"—they were Good Providers. Girls preferred "Interesting work with a small income." Boys felt more strongly than girls about "Being a Bolshevik" and "Being an Atheist"—these were Decidedly Wicked (1936:498, 522, 523). Girls adhered faithfully to the cultural demand that they find dirty ears, smoking, bad manners, bad smells (of onions, cooked cabbage, or tobacco), words like "belly" or "guts," and the sight of dirty clothes disgusting. In other words, the girls knew just how little ladies should act. The boys knew that only sissies act like little gentlemen.

On test 5 you get Femininity points if you *Dislike* "People with loud voices," "Argumentative people," and "Baldheaded men," but if you *Like* "Very forgiving people," "Washing dishes," and "Being alone." You get Masculinity points if you *Dislike* "Tall women," "Mannish women," "Thin women," or "Women cleverer than you are" but *Like* "Being the butt of a joke." (Boys should be dominant but able to take it.)

Sex differences on test 6, Admired Persons and Opinions,

were "almost negligible" (1936:44). The boys, oddly enough, *Liked* Mussolini, Lenin, Bismarck, Jefferson Davis, and Oliver Cromwell and *Disliked* Thomas Jefferson and Abraham Lincoln, compared to the girls. That sounds as though the boys were members of the Future Traitors of America, but presumably they were just identifying with the aggressive rebel.

On test 7, called Introversion–Extroversion, you get Femininity points if you "Nearly always prefer for someone else to take the lead," are "Extremely careful about your manner of dress," "Are much embarrassed when you make a grammatical mistake," and "Often get cross over little things." You get Masculinity points if you believe you "Have been bossed too much for your own good," if as a child you were "Extremely disobedient," if you were "Expelled or nearly expelled from school," if you think you have "Often been punished unjustly," if you "Dislike to take your bath," and if you "can stand pain and blood."

The masculine person is fearless, dislikes school, and is bad; the feminine person is timid, obedient, and good. These items measured superiority and subordination rather than introversion-extroversion as it is now understood. They tell us a lot about training girls to know their place and about the boy's struggle to resist the socialization attempts of those good Victorian women, his teachers and his mother. His resistance was bolstered by the knowledge that ultimately men are better and "Miss Nancy" is inferior. The girls betrayed the strain involved in being a lady only by their desire for masculine occupations and by their tendency to get cross, but only, of course, over little things. Anger was unwomanly.

Validating the AIAS Against Outside Criteria

Terman and Miles discuss frankly their discovery that the ratings and observations that were to establish criterion validity for their test had miserably low reliability:

There remains the outside criterion of masculinity-femininity ratings of subjects by presumably competent judges, the difficulty here being that we have not been able to find two observers whose ratings of the same subjects agree to more than a trifling extent. . . . In fact, masculinity-femininity ratings, as we have shown by several experiments, seem to be less reliable than ratings of almost any other personality trait (Terman and Miles 1936:53, 64).

For example, the correlation between rated "sissiness" in boys and their MF scores was .03.

In a rather charming effort to test the Victorian stereotypes that real women are weak and real men are strong, Terman had 533 adults aged 25 to 65 rate their health from "robust" to "frail." Unhappily for the theory, the robust men scored slightly *less* masculine than the other men. Nor was the evidence compelling that "frail" women were more feminine. It is not clear how Terman reconciled the fact that his own mother bore 14 children and reared 10 to adulthood with the notion of feminine frailty.

A highly masculine husband and a highly feminine wife should prove to be the most compatible couple. Not so. For 126 "high happiness" couples, the husband–wife MF correlation is .02; for 215 "low happiness" couples the husband–wife MF correlation is .08 (Terman and Miles 1936:118).

Terman and Miles studied part orphans. Boys brought up "chiefly or only" by their mothers are somewhat *more* masculine than boys brought up by their fathers, or the average boy. Girls brought up "chiefly or only" by their fathers are slightly *more* feminine than girls reared by mothers only, or girls in general. So much for the necessity of a same-sex role model for learning cultural sex role norms!

Nothing worked very well. Ratings of a person's attractiveness to the other sex or of a person's interest in the other sex produced zero correlations with MF scores for men and for women.

Because of their confidence that differences between girls and boys, which served as the operational definitions of femininity and masculinity, "automatically validated" the test, Terman and Miles were not really disturbed by the failure of their test to correlate with outside criteria (Terman and Miles 1936:89). They concluded only that clarification of masculinity and femininity by professional psychologists was indeed badly needed. The average observer or rater was obviously in a fog. From our point of view, however, the defect is serious.

The second validity problem that Terman and Miles encountered was the discovery that MF scores are extraordinarily easy to fake:

subjects who know what the test is intended to measure are able to influence their scores so greatly as to invalidate them entirely (Terman and Miles 1936:4, 77).

A sample of men changed their scores to means of +208.8 and −140.5 when asked to answer in a masculine or in a feminine manner. (Except for the MMPI, the scoring of MF tests is perfectly correlated with the sex of the senior author. If he is male, then M is + and F is −.) Women were equally adept at faking MF scores, which they changed by seven or eight times the standard deviation of the test under suitable instructions (Terman and Miles 1936:78). Undaunted by this news, Terman and Miles claimed that no one guessed the purpose of the test, and so its validity was unlikely to be jeopardized!

Age. AIAS scores declined with age. Men reached the peak of AIAS masculinity in the eleventh grade. Women were most feminine in the eigthth grade. The average fifty-year-old man was less masculine than the average eighth-grade boy, who had barely reached puberty (1936:123)!

It is surprising that these age trends failed to disturb Terman and Miles. Virginal youngsters, unmarried and childless, could hardly have achieved the peak of developed femininity and masculinity of which they were capable! The AIAS's "face invalidity," to coin a phrase, would seem to be strong.

Who Are the Most Feminine and Masculine People?

Members of many occupational groups took the MF test. The most feminine women by far were "housewives, formerly domestic servants" who scored −107.8, or 33 points below the mean for women college graduates, which was −74.7.

In contrast, "high school and college teachers" (−48.1) and M.D.s and Ph.D.s (−34.) were among the least feminine women. The reason is probably that the AIAS gives femininity points for ignorance and for submissiveness.

The most masculine men were engineers, architects, bankers, lawyers, realtors, and salesman (+58 to +81); the least masculine men were office managers, artists, grocers, clergymen, editors, journalists, policemen, firemen, and men in the building trades (+8 to +32)! The relative femininity of the last three groups probably stems from lack of education. The grocers may know too much about food to be masculine (1936:159).

Nature or Nuture?

Were femininity and masculinity inborn or taught? Terman and Miles vacillated a bit but leaned toward heredity. The biological basis of sex was poorly understood. The X and Y chromosomes that determine genetic sex were discovered only in 1906 by Edmund Wilson and by Nettie Stevens of Bryn Mawr. (It would not become possible to measure human sex hormones—although only very crudely—until Rosalind S. Yalow and S. A. Berson developed the technique of radioimmunoassay in 1971.)

Margaret Mead's classic work *Sex and Temperament* was published shortly before Terman and Miles' book appeared (1935). Mead's thesis, that innate temperamental differences are in fact randomly distributed between the sexes by nature but are assigned to only one sex by society, was not congenial to Terman and Miles. They were politely unsympathetic to her book. When Terman referred to "the present day bias of the cultural anthropologists" he presumably had Mead's thesis in mind (Johnson and Terman 1940:331; see also Pleck, Chapter 9).

Inversion: Measuring Gays. Terman's student E. Lowell Kelly studied a group of 77 "passive" male homosexuals, many of them prostitutes, who called each other "the girls." Kelly used those AIAT items that discriminated between 98 eleventh-grade boys and the 77 homosexual men to construct his Inversion scale. Terman and Miles obtained profiles on 44 "active" male homosexuals convicted of sodomy (in Alcatraz prison) and on 18 women "inverts" (who were still a bit less "masculine" than 37 "superior women college athletes," who in turn showed an "absence of proneness to anger, disgust, and especially fear" (1936:570, 579).

Kelly's most interesting finding was that the completed "I" (for Invert) scale scores correlated .09 with the subject's original MF scores—that is, not at all (Terman and Miles 1936:263). This should have told not only Terman and Miles but also those who came after that there was no relationship between MF score and "inversion." Unfortunately these data were no match for the conviction that feminine women and homosexual men "must" have a lot in common, then or later. Terman and Miles made a brief but fairly strong plea for compassion and assistance for homosexuals but do not comment on the severe limitations of using prostitutes and convicts. Terman advised Kelly not to publish his dissertation until after he had made a name for himself with other publications. For a thorough discussion of tests of homosexuality, see Harrison 1975.

Terman's files contain a number of letters from men seeking reassurance of their heterosexuality. One man's psychiatrist had told him that he had latent homosexual tendencies. Terman reassured him. He wrote an artist that it was common for artists to be in the lowest quintile and it was no discredit. No matter how gently put, the potential negative impact of such information is considerable. A leading shaving cream company required its executives to take the AIAS. What were the prospects of the poor fellow who did not score high on M (Terman Archives)?

In my opinion, there is no evidence that the AIAS was ever a valid measure of the relative femininity of two women or of the relative masculinity of two men, and there is much evidence that it was not (Constantnople 1973, Pleck 1975). Terman and Miles' test construction was far superior to that of many later psychologists. They asked the important questions. Can the test be faked by those who know its purpose? (Yes.) How well does it correlate with outside behavioral criteria? (Very badly.) Does it measure homosexuality? (No.) Yet no amount of negative feedback—and there was much, faithfully reported—jolted their confidence in what they were doing.

The Eight Erroneous Assumptions About MF

Between 1925 and 1970, MF testers consistently made eight unwitting "innocent" (but mistaken) assumptions that blighted their attempts to measure MF:

1. None of the tests was validated as a measure to differentiate between more and less feminine women (or more and less masculine men), although that is the objective of an MF test. We do not need a questionnaire to simply distinguish women from men. The need for this fundamental validation was overlooked throughout 45 years of research. Differences between the scores of men and of women were mistakenly thought to be a substitute for *within-sex validity* studies. Because the tests have a large Social Desirability component, are highly subject to faking or "impression management," and are frequently uncorrelated with

behavioral criteria or observer ratings, we cannot forgo within-sex validity studies (see also Harrison 1975).

2. Any appealing items that showed *sex differences* were accepted as measures of femininity or masculinity (no matter how irrelevant these might be to cultural MF ideals). (As a result ignorance defined femininity; low moral standards defined masculinity.) This assumption can be rejected.

3. Femininity and masculinity were assumed to be *opposite* ends of a single dimension until about 1960 (see Pleck, Chapter 9) or 1975; Bem 1974; Spence, Helmreich, and Stapp 1974).

4. MF was conceptualized as a *static,* nondevelopmental, perhaps constitutional *trait* that existed from an *early age.* Therefore MF tests were developed by using school children as criterion groups. As a result virginal eighth-grade girls (and boys) scored as more feminine (or masculine) than the average adult woman (or man).

5. The responses of gay men and feminine women were treated as identical. The pre-1970 tests implicitly require the assumption *that homosexual men are identical to feminine women.* [Terman and Miles MF research was funded by the National Research Council's Committee for Research on the Problems of Sex (Terman Archives)]. The belief that the same measurement instrument could measure both heterosexual MF and a tendency toward "inversion" plagued all efforts to measure MF for many years and persists today. Sixty years of experience now argue against this belief.

6. Some test users assumed that substantial proportions (40% or 28%) of nonpatient general populations had an unconscious *other-sex gender identity.* As we shall see, this is unlikely.

7. The fact that *sex-role or gender (MF) norms are* intimately linked to the economic, political, and social conditions in society and change as those conditions change was ignored in practice. It was tacitly assumed that the MF ideals of nineteenth-century Victorian America were *universal* and *fixed.*

8. MF was conceptualized as a set of *personality traits and interests,* not as an aspect of the self concept. I believe this is a fundamental mistake. The "self-concept" or the "self-image" is conspicuously missing in Terman and Miles. Although William James and Mary Calkins emphasized the concept of the self, here it is ignored in favor of a trait approach.

These eight assumptions prevented MF tests from reaching their goal.

Terman and Miles were somewhat aware of the problem with measuring MF by means of sex differences, although they were unable to solve it. Sex differences may be incidental and irrelevant to masculinity or femininity:

Items . . . which . . . have a high discriminative index but which would have no psychological significance in the present study. . . . Items of this kind tell us nothing beyond the fact that the subject is male or female, which we already know. The principle involved here does, as a matter of fact, apply in greater or less degree to every item in the MF test. One may reasonably argue that the only way to avoid making the test too much a measure of accidental difference in experience is to take account only of the *number* of masculinity and femininity differences without regard to their size (i.e., without weighting some more than others, Terman and Miles 1936:53).

This is a remarkable paragraph. One could hardly ask for a finer statement of the fundamental difficulty than the first three sentences. Then suddenly the logic of the argument collapses: so long as we have a sufficient number of these suspect items, we can go forward!

What Did the AIAS Really Measure? If Terman and Miles were not measuring the relative MF of individuals, what were they measuring? The AIAS did accomplish something else. It revealed with great clarity the Victorian cultural MF schema, which was shared by the researchers and the youngsters who took the test. The Victorian MF schema was developed around 1840, and it lived on into the twentieth century in weakened form. As independently identified by historians, the Victorian MF schema defined men and women in terms of five basic ideological belief systems : (1) The Doctrine of the Two Spheres. Women's sphere was in most respects the opposite of men's sphere. Therefore femininity and masculinity were understood as opposite ends of one dimension, not as two independent (or similar) dimensions. (2) The Cult of True Womanhood. According to the Cult of True Womanhood (Welter 1978), femininity involves Purity, Piety, Submissiveness, and Domesticity. Women's interests and skills are domestic, religious, cultural and artistic, but not political, economic, or occupational. (3) The Moral Superiority of Women. Women's ethnical-

moral standards are higher than men's. (4) The Intellectual Inferiority of Women. Women know less than men: they express themselves more emotionally and less objectively than men. (5) The
Good Provider. The Victorian man's role was to be a Good Provider: to support his family financially (Bernard 1981). David and
Brannon (1976) suggest four components of masculinity: Don't
Be a Sissy (be different from women); the Sturdy Oak (be strong,
firm, and resolute); the Big Wheel (seek status, prestige, and fame);
and Give 'Em Hell (be aggressive, tough, and violent if pressed).
Men are interested in their occupations, economics, and politics.
They handle these cognitively but not emotionally, except for the
emotion of anger, which they express as a means to dominance,
status, and power. Women are passive, men are active. Neither
sex is very erotic, but men are more sexual than women. Very
briefly summarized, this is the traditional Victorian MF schema (see
Barbara Harris Chapter 1; and Lewin, Chapter 3).

It is remarkable how well Terman and Miles covered the Cult
of True Womanhood in the AIAS. Purity was measured by Emotional and Ethical Attitudes (subtest 4), Interests (5), and Introversion (7). Piety was measured by tests 4 and 5 and by Admired
Persons and Opinions (6). Domesticity was well covered by Word
Associations (2) and Ink Blot Associations (3) and by 5 (especially
Occupations). Submissiveness was assessed by 4, 5, and 7. Submissiveness, that is, female subordination and male dominance,
runs like a scarlet thread throughout all of the many MF tests produced between 1936 and 1974. Moral superiority was measured
by 4, 5, and 6. Ignorance is covered in Information (3). Apparently "housewives, formerly domestic servants" best exemplified
the ideals of Purity, Piety, Domesticity, Submissiveness, and Ignorance that the AIAS captured. The male role as the Good Provider, the Sturdy Oak, the Big Wheel, and Not a Sissy, who "gives
'em hell" is tapped by tests 1, 2, 4, 5, 6, and 7.

The AIAS measures masculinity and femininity as ideals only
insofar as the respondents in the mid-1930s saw themselves as
adhering to Victorian standards. As we have seen, older and better educated Americans of both sexes took the Victorian MF
schema less seriously than school children did.

In their conclusions, Terman and Miles show concern over
the rather unflattering portrait of males implicit in Victorian fe-

male moral superiority. They attempt to soften the blow to men.

The results support the view that the male has on the whole a more "objective" moral judgment than the female who tends to exaggerate minor offenses . . . the female judgments tend, on the whole to be more emotional and less objective than the male (Terman and Miles 1936:409).

I find no data to justify this conclusion.

[Masculine] aggressiveness need not imply selfishness or tyranny or unfair attack. The compassion and Sympathy of the female again appears from the evidence personal rather than abstract, less a principled humanitarianism than an active sympathy for palpable misfortune or distress. In disgust, in aesthetic judgment, and in moral censure, the evidence is rather for the influence of fashion and of feeling than of principle or reason. Our evidence need not imply the possession of a "truer" taste or a more discerning conscience [in women] (Terman and Miles 1936:448).

Feminine morality is mere fashion, not staunch principle. This tradition lingers on. Lawrence Kohlberg had similar views, at least before the work of Carol Gilligan (1977). The feminist consensus that supported Elizabeth Cady Stanton and Lucretia Mott in 1848 crumbled after 1920, undermined in part by the new scientific psychology (Rosenberg 1982). By 1936 the moral superiority of women was no longer unchallenged, although the data to support it were there.

The AIAS was clearly even more derogatory to women (especially to educated academic women) than to men, with its emphasis on subordination, timidity, and nervousness. What did Catherine Cox Miles make of it all? Did she believe that female Ph.D.s were unfeminine, or did she have secret doubts? A brief discussion with Anne Miles Jones (1981), the daughter of Catherine C. Miles, suggests that she understood femininity and masculinity in the framework of the then-popular theory of bisexuality. According to this view, cross-sex traits are desirable in both sexes — a view remarkably close to our present enthusiasm for androgyny. Her daughter recalls that Miles spoke with favor of the nurturing qualities of policemen and was eager to see sufficient feminine nurturing qualities developed in her grandsons. Like feminists today, she may well have taken pride in the academic woman's amalgam of MF attributes.

The Strong Vocational Interest Blank: MF Continued

The next major MF test was developed by Edward K. Strong as part of a study of occupational preferences, which Strong began soon after his arrival at Stanford in 1923 and continued throughout his professional life. Terman was his mentor.

Strong tried to do for occupational interests what Terman had done for MF. Strong's Vocational Interest Blank (SVIB) asks the subject to indicate that he likes, dislikes, or is indifferent to a given occupation, school subject, activity, type of person, etc. All of his scales, including the MF scale, are based on weighting responses proportionately to the weight given by criterion groups. Each subject received an interest score for each occupation, based on the degree to which her or his interests duplicate those of members of the occupation.

The SVIB includes a list of 40 traits. The subject must indicate whether or not he or she possesses the trait. The sexes differed on only three of these traits: the men "were quite sure of themselves," had "mechanical ingenuity," and "frequently made wagers" (Strong 1936:58). Dominance, real or feigned, was part of the masculine role.

Women also preferred art galleries, symphony concerts, dramatics, and the occupations of musician, sculptor, orchestra conductor, and landscape gardener more than men did, but not many women were actually in these preferred occupations (Strong 1936:60). Another of Strong's categories was "kinds of people; largely unfortunate and disagreeable." Women liked "women cleverer than you" and foreigners, nervous, sick, religious, very old, blind, crippled, or witty people better than men did (Strong 1936:62). (Subjects were not asked whether they liked "men cleverer than you.") Culture, tolerance, and sympathy were women's sphere.

In 1936 Strong believed that "one of the major factors in terms of which occupational interests of men are to be explained" was the relative masculinity or femininity of the given field (1936:66).

Farmers and engineers, for example, are essentially masculine in interest whereas writers, lawyers, and ministers are essentially feminine. . . . few women will ever wish to enter the first two (fields) . . . many women should be expected to enter the last three (1936:49).

Strong here ignores the fact that most women were farmers for fifty centuries. Strong wondered:

Are the differences in interests of engineers and lawyers to be found in differences in hormone secretions, or in early attachment to father instead of mother, or in the possession of certain abilities in which the sexes also differ? (1936:65).

By 1943, this tone was modified. The similarities between the sexes were now emphasized. We heard no more about hormones as determinants of occupational choices. Strong now wrote: "There is much more agreement than disagreement between . . . men and women" (Strong 1943:167–68). He urged psychologists to stop being surprised at these similarities between the sexes and to stop straining to explain them away (1943:72, 226). By 1943, the sex differences described above were no longer significant (1943:244). Strong reported that in 1940 E. B. Skaggs found the moral views of college men and women to be remarkably similar. The "one single outstanding exception" was their judgment on "Intimate Sex Relations Outside of Marriage." The double standard with regard to premarital and extramarital sex was strong.

The MF scale was based on only 13.5 percent of the items Strong used, because the two sexes agreed on 86.5 percent of the items. The adult norms used in Strong's 1943 book were based on 100 married couples. None of the various versions of the MF scale (there were six by 1943) was cross-validated on a second sample. The Strong MF scale was only slightly correlated with the Terman MF scale (1943:223). Lower social class was now *positively* correlated with masculinity ($r = +.41$), reversing Terman and Miles (Strong 1943:325).

Strong struggled for years to decide whether separate norms for women should be computed for each occupation. Is it more important that women be similar to the men or to the women in the field? Strong's student, M. A. Seder, in her doctoral dissertation, favored using the men's norms for women (Strong 1943:574). Strong disagreed. In 1973 Munley and Fretz finally concluded that the interests of women were more often similar to those of the men than to those of other women in the occupation and advised giving women both the forms, so that no important occupational possibilities would be overlooked. It is hard to estimate how much the vocational guidance of women suffered because of the structure of the SVIB. All we can say for certain is that very different occupational recommendations often resulted, depending on which form the female client took. At present the SVIB has been replaced by the Strong-Campbell Interest Inventory. One form is used for both sexes. No MF scale is included.

With respect to conceptualizing MF, Strong left Terman and Miles' ideas fundamentally unaltered. The similarity of the sexes was emphasized. An unmistakable note of skepticism entered between 1936 and 1943. Possibly the Second World War and "Rosie the Riveter" made a difference. By 1943 Strong was no longer convinced that MF was one of life's major determinants.

The Guilfords and Factors GAMIN

In 1936 J. P. and Ruth B. Guilford used the newly developed technique of factor analysis to analyze the responses of 1,745 students of both sexes to questions used to diagnose introversion-extroversion. One of the five factors they obtained was tentatively labeled M for masculinity. The Guilfords' were very cautious at first, suggesting that the factor could be dominance or ascendance-submission and noting that the sexes overlapped considerably. The correlation between M and emotionality was .01, which contradicted the belief that women were the emotional sex.

Further work was done in 1943 by J. P. Guilford and H. G. Martin and in 1956 by J. P. Guilford and Wayne Zimmerman, whose data came from 87 women and 126 men tested before 1945 by Lovell and Thurstone. The admirable caution about labeling the factor M had vanished by 1956. There was now "no doubt" about the identity of the MF factor (1956:11). The possibility that MF and sex differences might not be the same thing was mentioned in passing but then dropped.

M was now measured by 6 subtests, containing 40 items in all. The masculinity subtests were named Inhibition of Emotional Expression, Masculine Vocational Interests, Masculine Avocational Interests, Digustfulness (−), Fearfulness (−), and Sympathy (−). The last three tests were scored in the reverse direction. Masculinity and femininity were again operationally defined (scored) by differences in the responses of men and women. We recognize quite a few old friends from the Terman-Miles AIAT. "Do odors of perspiration disgust you?" (Disgustfulness). "Do you feel deeply sorry for a bird with a broken wing?" (Sympathy).

The Cult of True Womanhood lived on in the eyes of Guilford, Zimmerman, and their subjects. The masculine man remained a Sturdy Oak, ready to Give 'Em Hell without feeling too sorry for 'Em. Masculine people are "not emotionally excitable, or expressive; are not easily aroused to fear or disgust; (and are) somewhat lacking in sympathy" (Guilford and Zimmerman 1956:24). Feminine persons are less objective, are hypersensitive, and are inclined to take things personally, although "the correlation between M and Objectivity could be anywhere between zero and .52, depending upon where one prefers to draw the axes" (1956:11).

The woman who aspired to be feminine would not find a very appealing role model if she consulted Guilford. He could only suggest that she be easily frightened, easily disgusted, emotionally excitable, and avoid manly occupations and hobbies. The new technique of factor analysis made it possible to discover sex roles that proved to be quite similar to the sex roles that historians had already identified: disgustfulness was the new name for Purity, Sympathy is similar to Moral Superiority, and Fearfulness is linked to Submissiveness.

Strong and the Guilfords carried on the tradition initiated by Terman and Miles. Conceptually, a hodgepodge of sex differences was substituted for an effort to define the meaning of femininity and masculinity as psychological concepts. With very little discussion, these researchers assumed that personality traits and interests defined MF. Methodologically the necessity of determining whether the tests were actually valid measures of the relative femininity of two women, for example, was completely overlooked. On the positive side, these researchers left us a convincing if unanticipated empirical confirmation of the accuracy of the historians' analysis of the Victorian sex role schema. The saga of MF testing—from the MMPI to the instrumental-expressive distinction—is continued in the next article.

References

Allen, McGrigor. 1869. "On the Real Differences in the Minds of Men and Women." *Anthropological Review* 7. Cited in Duffin, *q.v.*, p. 65.

Bem, Sandra L. 1974. "The Measurement of Psychological Androgyny." *Journal of Consulting and Clinical Psychology* 42:155–62.

Bernard, Jessie. 1981. "The Good Provider Role: Its Rise and Fall." *American Psychologist* 36:(1):1–12.

Boring, Edward. 1929. *A History of Experimental Psychology*, vol. 1. New York: Appleton-Century.

Calkins, Mary W. 1895. "Wellesley College Psychological Studies." *Psychological Review* 363–60.

—— 1896. "Community of Ideas of Men and Women." *Psychological Review* 3:426–30.

—— 1930. Autobiography in Murchison (1930).

Constantinople, Anne. 1973. "Masculinity-Femininity: An Exception to a Famous Dictum?" *Psychological Bulletin* 80 (5):389–407. Reprinted in F. Denmark and R. Wesner, eds. *Women*, vol. 1. New York: Psychological Dimensions, 1976.

Cox, Catherine, assisted by Terman, Lewis. 1926. *Genetic Studies of Genius, II*. Palo Alto, Calif.: Stanford University Press.

David, Deborah and Robert Brannon. 1976. *The Forty-Nine Percent Majority: The Male Sex Role*. Philippines: Addison-Wesley Publishing Company.

Distant, W. L. 1874. "The Mental Differences Between the Sexes." Cited in Duffin, *q.v.*, p. 82.

Duffin, Lorna. 1978. "Prisoners of Progress: Women in Evolution." In Sara Delamont and Lorna Duffin. *The Nineteenth Century Woman*, pp. 57–91. New York: Barnes and Noble.

Finison, L. and L. Furumoto. 1980. "Status of Women in American Psychology, 1890–1940, or How To Win the Battles Yet Lose the War." Paper delivered at Chevron, Bowdoin, Maine.

Furumoto, L. 1979. "Mary Whiton Calkins (1863–1930), Fourteenth President of the American Psychological Association." *Journal of the History of Behavioral Sciences* 15:346–56.

Gilligan, Carol. 1977. "In a Different Voice: Women's Conceptions of Self and Morality." *Harvard Educational Review* 47(4):481–517.

Guilford, J. P. and R. B. Guilford. 1936. "Personality Factors S, E, and M and Their Measurement." *Journal of Psychology* 2:109–27.

Guilford, J. P. and H. G. Martin. 1943. "An Inventory of Factors GAMIN." Beverly Hills, Calif.: Sheridan Supply Co.

Guilford, J. P. and W. S. Zimmerman. 1956. "Fourteen Dimensions of Temperament." *Psychological Monographs* 70(10):11–24.

Harrison, James. 1975. "A Critical Evaluation of Research on Masculinity/Femininity and a Proposal for an Alternative Paradigm for Research on Psychological Differences and Similarities Between the Sexes." *Dissertation Abstracts International* 36(4), Series B, University Microfilms No. 75-22890.

Hollingworth, L. S. 1916. "Sex Differences in Mental Traits." *The Psychological Bulletin* 13:383.

—— 1922. "Differential Action upon the Sexes of Forces Which Tend to Segregate the Feebleminded." *Journal of Abnormal and Social Psychology*, pp. 35–37.

Hollingworth, L. S. and Helen Montague. 1914. "The Comparative Variability of the Sexes at Birth." *The American Journal of Sociology* 20:335–70.

James, William. 1890/1950. *The Principles of Psychology*, (2 vols.). New York: Dover.

Jastrow, J. 1896. "Note on Calkin's Community of Ideas of Men and Women." *Psychological Review* 3:430–31.

Johnson, W. and Lewis Terman. 1940. "Some Highlights in the Literature of Psychological Sex Differences Published Since 1920." *Journal of Psychology* 9:327–36.

Jones, Anna Miles. 1981. Daughter of Catherine Cox Miles, personal communication.

Lewin, Miriam. 1979. *Understanding Psychological Research.* New York: Wiley.

—— 1982a. "The Anatomy of Failure: Psychology's Struggle To Measure Femininity and Masculinity." Paper delivered at the Eastern Psychological Association meetings, Baltimore, Md., April 14–17.

—— 1982b. "Rather Worse than Folly?" Terman and Miles Measure Femininity and Masculinity." Paper presented at CHEIRON, International Society for the History of the Behavioral and Social Sciences, June, Newport, R.I.

Mead, Margaret. 1935. *Sex and Temperament in Three Primitive Societies.* New York: Morrow.

Murchison, Carl, ed. 1930. *The History of Psychology in Autobiography,* vol. 1. Worcester, Mass.: Clark University Press.

Pleck, Joseph. 1975. "Masculinity-Femininity: Current and Alternative Paradigms." *Sex Roles* 1(2):161–78.

Rosenberg, R. N. 1982. *Beyond Separate Spheres: Intellectual Origins of Modern Feminism.* New Haven: Yale University Press.

Seagoe, May. 1975. *Terman and the Gifted.* Palo Alto, Calif.: William Kaufmann.

Spence, Janet T., R. Helmreich, and J. Stapp. 1974. "The Personal Attributes Questionnaire: A Measure of Sex-Role Stereotypes and Masculinity-Femininity." *JSAS Catalog of Selected Documents in Psychology* 4:43–44.

Strong, E. K. 1936. "Interests of Men and Women." *Journal of Social Psychology* 7:49–67.

Strong, E. K. 1943. *Vocational Interests of Men and Women.* Stanford, Calif.: Stanford University Press.

Terman Archives, Stanford University, #SC38, container 14, folder 19, 13–33.

Terman, Lewis. 1906. "Genius and Stupidity: A Study of Some of the Intellectual Processes of Seven 'Bright' and Seven 'Stupid' Boys." *Pedagogical Seminars* 13:307–73.

—— 1923. "The Mental Test as a Psychological Method." Presidential address, American Psychological Association. *Psychological Review* 31:93–117. Reprinted in Ernest R. Hilgard, ed. 1978. *American Psychology in Historical Perspective.* Washington D.C.: American Psychological Association, p. 222.

—— 1936. "Autobiography Trails to Psychology." In Murchison, *q.v.*, 2:297–332.

Terman, L. and C. C. Miles. 1936. *Sex and Personality, Studies in Masculinity and Femininity.* New York: McGraw-Hill.

Welter, Barbara. 1978. "The Cult of True Womanhood, 1820–1860." In Michael Gordon, ed. 1978. *The American Family in Social Historical Perspective*, 2nd. ed., pp. 313–33. New York: St. Martin's Press.

Wooley, H. T. 1903. *The Mental Traits of Sex.* Chicago: University of Chicago Press, pp. 167–68.

—— 1910. "Psychological Literature: A Review of the Recent Literature on the Psychology of Sex." *Psychological Bulletin* 7:335–42.

—— 1914. "The Psychology of Sex." *Psychological Bulletin* 11:353–79.

8 Psychology Measures Femininity and Masculinity, 2

From "13 Gay Men" to the Instrumental-Expressive Distinction

T erman and Miles set the style for most of the subsequent tests of masculinity and femininity (or MF) (See Lewin, Chapter 7, 1982a,b). The next MF test was developed by Hathaway and McKinley.

Hathaway and McKinley: 13 Gay Men Define Femininity

The Minnesota Multiphasic Personality Inventory (Hathaway and McKinley 1940), known as the MMPI, has been called "the most widely-used and well-researched psychological test in existence"

The support of a 1979 summer stipend from the National Endowment for the Humanities for preliminary work on MF testing is gratefully acknowledged.

(Sobel 1980). It is the proud accomplishment of the psychometricians at the University of Minnesota. The MMPI was designed to measure psychopathology. It consists of 550 items worded in the first person, e.g.: "I would like to be a nurse." The client checks true, false, or cannot say for each item.

The MMPI MF scale was first published in 1943. Reviewer Albert Ellis, in the 1959 edition of Buros' *Mental Measurements Yearbook,* which already listed 779 references on the MMPI, wrote:

It can confidently be stated that in the whole history of modern psychology there has been no other personality inventory on which so much theoretical and practical work has been done (1959:166).

Still, he argued, its validity remained in doubt. Warren Norman, Buros' second reviewer, disagreed, calling the construct validity of the scales "impressive."

The initial desire to include a measure of "inversion" as one of nine measures of psychopathology was based on the Kraepelin system of classification. The 60 items were the same for men and for women except for about 5 items; 27 items dealt with liking for occupations, 24 with "altruism" and "personal and emotional sensitivity" (i.e., Moral Superiority). Six questions were straightforward sexual preference or gender identity items such as: "I am very strongly attracted by members of my own sex," "I have often wished I were a girl" (or if the subject is a girl: "I have never been sorry that I am a girl"), and "I have never indulged in any unusual sex practices" (false). Some of the items seem related to the social problems of homosexuals: "I have often felt that strangers were looking at me critically" (true), "I frequently find myself worrying about something" (true), and "I am entirely self-confident" (false) (Dahlstrom and Welsh 1960:65–66, 460).

Hathaway explains how the MF (inversion) scale was constructed:

At first it seemed reasonable to collect relatively large samples of homosexual invert males and homosexual females for more complete criterion evidence. The plan went awry because . . . the homosexual samples were too heterogeneous. . . . the groups were much more obviously divisible into several subtypes . . . a pseudo-homosexual type where neurotic features related to inferiority seem to be dominant; a psychopathic variety . . . a group in which a constitutional factor seems probable . . . and possibly other subgroups. . . . this project was never finished. In the meantime the MF scale has become widely used and although it was omitted from much of our experimental work, it contributes considerably to routine clinical interpretations" (Hathaway 1956:110).

The final sentence in this quotation is hardly reassuring.

What Hathaway and McKinley actually did was to use 13 homosexual males as a criterion group to identify those MMPI items (plus some of Kelly's "Invert scale" items from the AIAT) that differentiated the 13 gay men from a group of 54 heterosexual male soldiers. (67 women airline employees of unknown femininity were also used, but just how it is not explained [Dahlstrom and Welsh 1960:64].)

While the original MF scale was developed solely as an experimental measure, the scale soon got locked into the standard MMPI profile package, and it has never been revised (Hathaway 1956, cited by Goldberg 1971:326).

Hathaway goes on to explain that one attempt was made to develop a second MF (inversion) scale by using homosexual women as a criterion group:

the fact that cross-validation did not particularly favor the new scale, even for identification of homosexual females, indicated its abandonment (Hathaway 1956:110).

It is rather staggering to realize that the *femininity dimension of this popular test was "validated" on a criterion group of 13 male homosexuals!* When people are informed of this fact, they are incredulous. We assume that a femininity scale has somehow been validated on a sample of exceptionally feminine women. How many users of this test in psychological, pastoral, vocational, academic, medical, and occupational counseling centers understand what MF on the MMPI means?

How did psychology end up in a situation where the distinctive responses of 13 male homosexuals came to define the nature of femininity? If the scale was to measure homosexuality, why name it "MF"? Because of a fundamental conceptual confusion not limited to Hathaway and McKinley. If sex differences, femininity and masculinity, and sexual preference had not been confused with one another, the beliefs of gay men would not have become the measure of femininity in women. Given this conceptual confusion, what happened is not surprising.

Unfortunately by 1960 the description of scale 5 (MF) had become much bolder. In their second basic reference book on the MMPI, Dahlstrom and Welsh say of MF:

Scale 5 was designed to identify the personality features related to the disorder of male sexual inversion. This syndrome is another homogeneous subgroup in the general category of psychopathic personality. . . . This group shows considerably more uniformity than is found in the psychopathic personality catagory as a whole. Persons with this personality pattern often engage in homoerotic practices as part of their feminine emotional make-up; however, many of these men are too inhibited or full of conflicts to make any overt expression of their sexual preference. The feminism of these men appears in their values, attitudes, interests, and styles of expression and speech as well as in sexual relationships (1960:64).

As far as I can tell, these comments are still based on the original 13-man criterion group. Note that alleged inverts who are in fact heterosexual are nevertheless classified as gay but too "inhibited" to express their (true) sexual preference. (Overt male homosexuals and homophobic heterosexuals in fact "obtain very similar mean scores" on scale 5, Renaud 1950, cited by Sanford 1951/1967.)

The MMPI was soon used extensively with normal subjects; 206 undergraduate women at Stanford took the MMPI and also described themselves and their dormitory mates on an adjective list. Black reports that the expected "lack of femininity" among the "high 5" (scale 5 = MF) women is "implicit but subtle." Hathaway and Meehl had written "it is our clinical impression that low MF scores in females represent an almost masochistic passivity" (Black 1956:161). Black says tartly that his peer descriptions

certainly do not substantiate the suggestions in the literature. . . . There is no evidence, however, that the scale points to "abnormal sexual interest" (1956:161).

Black concludes that the high 5s are generally effective women who tend to underrate themselves.

There is no evidence that the MMPI provided a good measure, much less an improved measure, of general femininity or masculinity that overcame the deficiencies of the AIAT, the Strong, and the Guilford. The authors themselves took little satisfaction in its ability to accurately identify male homosexuals and even less satisfaction in its ability to identify female homosexuals. The number of persons incorrectly suspected of being unfeminine, unmasculine, or gay is unknown.

Gough and the California Psychological Inventory, "Fe" Scale

Back at the University of Minnesota there was yet another toiler in the vineyard of MF measurement. Harrison Gough got his Ph.D. at the University of Minnesota in 1949 and joined the faculty. He wanted to produce a test similar to the MMPI but less offensive or upsetting to normal subjects who were not psychiatric patients. Gough created the California Psychological Inventory (CPI) in 1952. It may well be the world's second most widely used personality measure. He wished to include a "simple, straightforward, and practical" device for identifying psychological femininity. Once again the objective was to combine the uncombinable and develop a single measure that would simultaneously differentiate the more from the less feminine (and masculine) and "sexual deviates" from normals (Gough 1952:427). Some of his items came from Terman and Miles. Others were MMPI items. Gough discovered that nine, or 38 percent, of the 24 MMPI MF items he used now had to be scored in the *reverse* direction (1952:436)! According to Gough, his 59-item Fe scale demonstrated that femininity consisted of feelings of "sensitivity," "response to the nuances of social interaction," "acquiescence," "compassion," "niceness," "clean white-collar work," and "lack of interest in the larger political and social world." I would add "male dominance and female submissiveness" to Gough's list:

Thus, females indicate that they would never feel right about shirking the hard work in a group, that they find it hard to chastise someone, that they are easily hurt, and that they get very nervous when blamed for a mistake, and that censure or disapproval makes them tense and anxious—all relative to males. . . . Related to this are feelings of social timidity and lack of confidence. . . . Males are given to "braggadocio" and "hyperbole" (the Big Wheel, Gough 1952:430).

The Victorian MF scheme remains evident. Gough thought he had validated his test when he found similar sex differences in the United States and cross-culturally. The conceptual distinction between sex differences and MF was overlooked again. Gough attempted to validate the FE scale as a measure of "inversion" by using 38 pairs of prisoners. Only 13 items discriminated, the means were rather close (1.3 S.D.), and the best cutting point produced 18 percent errors. Differences between prisoners and average gays were ignored (Gough 1952:434).

By 1957 the CPI included a 38-item Fe (femininity) scale. Mussen reported the surprising fact that high masculine adolescent boys on the Fe were poorly adjusted as adults, lacking leadership, dominance, self-confidence, and self-acceptance (1962: 440).

Low Fe women had more "poise, ascendency, and self-assurance" than high Fe women; high Fe men were more dominant and responsible than low Fe men. Both low Fe women and high Fe men were *better* adjusted (as measured by the full CPI itself) than their counterparts (N = 517, Vincent 1966: 198. See also Rosenberg and Sutton-Smith 1971).

Gough (1968:60, 73) provided interesting data that fraternity and sorority members admired men who scored high on the CPI Dominance scale ("ambitious, planful"), but not women who scored high on Dominance ("bossy, conceited").

Like its predecessors, the Fe scale included various sex differences, such as the item "Sometimes I feel that I am about to go to pieces" (true = feminine) (1952:429). That item may possibly reflect a genuine difference in depression rates, but it cannot be justified as a defining characteristic of femininity. But "dustbowl empiricists" such as Gough ignored conceptual issues.

The Terman-Miles Paradigm, 1956–71

Between 1956 and 1971 MF was the single most popular construct for inclusion in new personality inventories. Although most of the scales shared items, correlations between MF scales, computed separately for males and females, were low: usually around .2, .3, and .4 (Goldberg 1971:326, 328). Correlations between MF scales in mixed-sex groups were higher: .6, or .7 or in one case

.8. "Obvious" items such as "I like to wear pretty, frilly panties" worked best. It seems clear that MF tests did distinguish the two sexes but did not measure the relative femininity of two women or the relative masculinity of two men. No wonder Goldberg and other reviewers concluded that the item: "Female − −, Male − −, Check One" or "I am a homosexual, True − −, False − −" would do better than any MF scale.

How did a construct so frequently panned by reviewers and so gingerly handled by several of its intellectual fathers as MF prove to be so invulnerable and long-lived? For one thing it was just too easy to construct an MF scale. The other reason was faith that MF as conceived did exist and that it must be possible to measure it.

The Franck Test: Measuring
Unconscious Gender Identity

Terman, Miles, Strong, Hathaway, McKinley, Guilford, and Gough shared a common approach to measuring MF. In 1946 Kate Franck attempted to do something different: to measure unconscious MF in a culture-free way. She started with Freud's idea that symbolic representations of the sex organs represent sexual wishes or fears.

In her first study the subject selected the more attractive of two drawings designed to represent either male or female anatomy in an abstracted, unrecognizable way, but the results were poor. Therefore, Franck and Ephraim Rosen (1949) presented their subjects with new, simple, abstract drawings to complete as they liked. They found significant sex differences on 36 of 60 sketches ($N = 250$), which were cross-validated on a second sample ($N = 300$). Subsequently Strodtbeck and Creelan (1968) found that only 11 of the 36 drawings showed consistent sex differences.

Some proportion of women may handle spatial material distinctively. Psychologists have repeatedly discovered sex differences in the handling of visual-spatial stimuli since Helen Thompson Wooley first published her findings in 1903. The basis for these differences is still unknown. What did these sex differences mean to Franck and Rosen?

The subjects express something which might be called "body image" in a sense that includes both structures and impulses. This image, which is part of the individual's awareness of his identity and potentialities, corresponds to physiological reality if it is not surrounded and distorted by defensive measures. It follows that the MF test presented here is a measure of the degree of acceptance of the individual's sex role, conscious or unconscious (1949:255).

Franck and Rosen assume that the two completion styles unconsciously represent the male and female sex organs; second, that gender acceptance is operationally defined by the style of one's completion; third, that people who are troubled about their gender use the style of the other sex (1949:254–55); and fourth, that persons troubled about their gender are also homosexuals. (The last assumption was universal among MF researchers at that time. In fact, the majority of homosexuals do *not* draw an other-sex figure first on the Draw-A-Person test—Brown and Tolor 1957, cited by Jackaway 1972). Unfortunately Franck and Rosen made no effort to test these four hypotheses. Why must persons necessarily represent their own sex organs when they complete simple drawings even if their gender identity is firm? It is equally consistent with psychoanalytic theory for people to fantasize about the bodies of the *other* sex.

The same difficulty arises with regard to Hall and Van de Castle's (1965) frequently reprinted study of the dreams of college students. If men's dreams contained female symbolism (images interpreted as representing breasts, etc.) Hall and Van de Castle, following Freud, assumed that these represented erotic desire, not the man's own body image. However, when women's dreams contained images interpreted as male symbols, Hall and Van de Castle assumed that these did not represent erotic desires but rather the women's wished-for body image (penis envy). It is our Victorian heritage that leads us to arbitrarily classify women as asexual and men as lustful (see Lewin, article 3).

To the best of my knowledge no attempt was made to validate the popular Franck test. A suitable validation study would use subjects—perhaps people in therapy—who were seriously concerned about their femininity or masculinity. Do they complete drawings differently from control subjects? We do not know.

A second attempt to measure unconscious femininity by subliminal tachistoscope exposures of two T.A.T.-like pictures is unfortunately similarly unvalidated (Kraugh 1960). Ursin, Baade, and Levine (1978) found that Kraugh's "feminine" men did *better* on their first parachute jump.

The Franck and other MF test scores are uncorrelated (Shepler 1951; Lansky 1960; McCarthy, Anthony, and Domino 1970). Male subjects can fake the Franck test (produce feminine responses on demand—Bieliauskas, Miranda, and Lansky 1968). Franck scores were not correlated to self-concept measures (Bieliauskas and Mikesell 1972).

I have no quarrel with Franck's and Rosen's and Kraugh's objectives. Some people do more or less unconsciously doubt their adequacy as a person of their gender, but gender adequacy doubts are not the same as reversed masculinity or femininity. Most of these people do not think they are members of the other sex. They doubt their competence, attractiveness, etc., as a member of their *own* sex.

Unconscious and Conscious MF:
the Double Classification Paradigm

Because the Franck and the conventional MF measures were un-correlated, it now became possible to classify people on both their unconscious MF, defined as their Franck score, and their con-scious MF, often measured by their Gough CPI Fe scale score. Double classification produced four groups of male subjects: the MF or "unconsciously masculine-consciously feminine" men, the FM or "unconsciously feminine-consciously masculine" men, the MM men (masculine both ways) and the FF men (feminine both ways). Four parallel groups of women might have been studied but were not (Pleck, article 9).

Around 1950 Sanford studied graduate students using eight different measures of MF, including staff ratings and the depart-mental ratings (1951/1967). The results were bewildering. Staff MF ratings correlated .17 with departmental MF ratings. Neither of these correlated well with other measures. Sanford's most mas-culine students received the lowest departmental ratings on po-tential for future success. In mulling over his results, Sanford con-cluded:

A reasonable explanation would be that the Franck-Rosen Completion of Drawings Test provides an estimate of deeper-lying femininity—femininity at the level of body feeling—while preference for male symbols [the other Franck test] represents a striving for masculine identity. Men who obtain high feminine scores on both tests . . . accept their femininity and are flexible to the point of irresponsibility.

(No evidence of irresponsibility is presented.)

The men with underlying femininity who prefer male symbols . . . maintain their inhibition of passive impulses by concentrating upon manifestations of an opposite significance . . . which . . . favors rigidity. . . . It is not femininity pure and simple . . . in some basic sense of being passive or receptive, of feeling like a woman, or wanting to act as if one were a woman—that goes with intellectual or artistic achievement in men. It is rather *sublimated* femininity (italics in original).

Sublimated femininity is not defined. High FM scores may be obtained *either* by men with "genuine sublimated femininity" who have "enough masculine" identity to be "disciplined," "organized," and "productive," or by men who are

openly passive, loosely organized, impulsive, and easy-going individuals whose "feminine" interests and attitudes express a true lack of masculinity or a desire to display . . . their psychological inversion (Sanford 1951/1967:196–98).

That would seem to make the tests rather useless. Even outstanding psychologists like Sanford were seduced into meaningless discourse by the amorphous nature of the 1850–1950 MF concept (see Pleck, article 9 for a different view).

Sanford wrote eloquently in favor of equality of the sexes. He was disappointed when college women abandoned their education in the grip of an "overcompensating flight into femininity." But he did not abandon his MF concepts. Senior college women who scored more masculine on MF tests (as they tended to do) were "not in reality becoming less feminine," but the senior woman "is facing up to her inevitable masculine impulses. . . . our culture views the two sexes as unequal." But "the inequality of prestige is an even greater handicap for men than it is for women." She can develop fully as a person so long as she rejects her inferiority, whereas the man is prevented from becoming a whole per-

FEMININITY AND MASCULINITY, 2   189

son because he is "forced" to deny his own "biological and psychological feminine dispositions" (Sanford 1951/1967:200–202).

Sanford's views provide an excellent example of the way Victorian concepts of 1880, such as bisexuality, were reintroduced into American psychology in the 1950s, when psychoanalysis penetrated academic psychology. Sanford's ideas came straight from Freud: for example, that femininity consists of "passive" impulses. By passive Freud meant not taking the initiative, and accepting subordination. (Thus Sanford believed that effeminate men suppress impulses to be subordinate.)

Miller and Swanson and their student Lansky, using the Franck, classified 28.5 percent of a sample of 522 male ROTC, physical education, engineering, and business students at the University of Michigan as unconsciously feminine (Miller and Swanson 1960:94). Is it plausible that 28.5 percent of these men had an unconscious feminine identity? More than a tendency to draw canoes and sailboats rather than candles and kitchen knives is required to justify such a conclusion.

Miller, Swanson, and Lansky defined unconscious feminine identity in a man by interests, skills, and "expressive style" (gait, posture, physical strength, inflection of voice, and gestures such as bending the wrist) (Miller and Swanson 1960:88, 273). Expressive style is a particularly critical component of unconscious femininity. The feminine man is passive and prone to "emotional dilation" (shouting, yelling, weeping). It may be possible for a man "to behave passively with a person in authority and still think that he is being masculine" (1960:284, 286, 90). The psychological core of femininity is (1) obedience to authority, (2) not taking the initiative, and (3) being dependent on others.

Miller and Swanson made no effort to measure the homosexuality, expressive style, or childhood history they assumed to be characteristic of the FF men. They tested a milder, attenuated version of their theory. Could the researchers have hesitated to test the conventional wisdom about femininity in men because they might have discovered that it was a house of cards?

As late as 1967 American psychologists were still taking a strong stand in favor of male dominance and female submission:

When males and females come together in social relations they must bring . . . certain familiar patterned sequences of behavior or run the risk of upsetting the social structure (an "anomic," hence undesirable group out-come), thereby engendering interpersonal tensions, from which must ulti-mately stem personal maladjustments of various sorts. "Queer" males and "castrating" females are only the most extreme sample of this maladaptive pattern. . . . males in our society . . . are expected to take the more ascen-dent-dominant social role and vice versa for the females. This is the most viable pattern. . . . individuals who depart . . . will be more prone to per-sonal maladjustments. . . . Feminine men can do rather well in the world if they have the crucial ascendance-dominance to take the lead at PTA meetings or to speak up when the boss is present (Rychlack and Legerski 1967:32–34).

Women should not take the lead at PTA meetings or speak up when the boss is present.

The double classification paradigm was pursued by Lipsitt and Strodtbeck (1967) and by Strodtbeck and Creelan (1968). Their reasoning was delightfully Victorian. The home is a secure haven (although perhaps dull): "Within the tested and secure confines of the home, most possible and reasonable actions have already been performed . . . and their effects are known" Strodtbeck and Creelan 1968:304). Home requires mothers whose ego bounda-ries are not too firm, who are "intuitive," as Darwin and Spencer thought they were. Men, in contrast, need a strong, "persistent sense of self-other distinctions" and must pay close attention to whether or not their goals are realized. (Apparently whether or not mothers have a firm identity or actually realize their goals at home doesn't matter much.) Women but not men must be "personally sensitive." The hypothesis that the unconsciously feminine man would be more sensitive than his masculine peer was not con-firmed, but it is obvious that the Doctrine of the Two Spheres was alive and well in 1968 (see Lewin, article 3).

Women's cognitive style involves "conscience-driven think-ing" (Strodtbeck and Creelan 1968:304). The man asks "How can I gain an advantage?"; the woman, "If I gain an advantage over him, what sort of person will I become?" Feminine types tend to pursue "lost causes" (Strodtbeck, Bezdek, and Goldhammer 1970:306). Bezdek and Strodtbeck (1970:500) "make a *moral* dis-tinction" between the feminine and masculine styles (italics in the original). It is interesting that just at the beginning of the new women's movement, Strodtbeck and his colleagues returned to the Moral Superiority of women. Elizabeth Cady Stanton would have found this reasoning comfortable in 1850.

Bezdek and Strodtbeck compared persons with high and low Franck scores on numerous behavioral measures and found no behavioral distinctions except that the feminine boys were rated as the "most responsible" and as more "emotional." They used the Franck test to classify 40 percent of their normal subjects as unconsciously cross-gender identified (1970:499, 501). Again we must wonder whether it is plausible that such a large percentage of a sample could have a cross-gender identity.

What were their research results? Unconsciously masculine girls and boys said they would be more willing to try to solve "Solvable Non-Serious" community problems, whereas unconsciously feminine girls and boys said that they would be more willing to try to solve "Serious Non-Solvable" community problems (Bezdek and Strodtbeck 1970; see also Strodtbeck, Bezdek, and Goldhammer 1970).

With this discovery 1970 was, mercifully, the highwater mark of double-classification MF research. It is not surprising that a solid body of knowledge failed to develop from the unconscious-conscious MF paradigm. When "progress" in psychology consists of classifying subjects by two unvalidated and unconceptualized psychological measures instead of one, we cannot expect our research results to make much sense and they do not.

Parsons and Bales: Femininity and Masculinity as Instrumental and Expressive Roles

The last attempt to define MF that can be included in this essay is that of Talcott Parsons, at one time America's leading sociologist. Between 1946 and 1972 Parsons was a member of Harvard's Department of Social Relations. The man who gathered the data was his colleague R. Freed Bales, a social psychologist. The exposure of psychologists (e.g., Strodtbeck) and anthropologists (Zelditch) to the Social Relations program gave Parsons' "instrumental-expressive" definition of masculinity-femininity especially wide currency.

Parsons described Freud as "one of the few crucial intellectual experiences of my life" in his autobiography (Parsons 1970:835). Beginning in 1946 Parsons was psychoanalyzed by Greta Bibring, M.D., of the conservative Freudian Boston Psychoanalytic Institute (Wacker 1980). Parsons was thus exposed to people who stood in the direct line of succession to Victorian thinking.

Parsons was not unaware of what today we would call sexism. In 1942 he published an interesting analysis of sex role strain. Discrimination against women college graduates was noted. The fact that the husband "*alone*" determines the status and prestige of the family "deprives the wife of her role as a partner in a common enterprise" (1942:609). Housework is a kind of "pseudo-occupation." What options were open to women? The *Domestic* pattern had the lowest prestige. The more prestigeous and satisfying pattern was the *Glamour* pattern, but it forced the woman to separate her role from her total personality and was most feasible when she was very young. (Today we would say it forced her to become a sex object.) Only those who had the "strongest initiative and intelligence" found satisfaction in the *Good Companion and Community Service* pattern. Marriage was so important to women's status and yet so difficult to maintain on the level of human companionship because of the highly specialized occupational role of the husband (1942:610–13). In 1947, after starting his analysis, Parsons began to shift away from his sex role strain analysis and espoused male sex role identity theory (Pleck, article 9).

Bales, Parsons' collaborator, spent a summer at the National Training Laboratories in Bethel, Maine, soon after they were founded by a few of Kurt Lewin's students in 1947. Inspired by the study of small groups in actions, Bales continued to study group processes in his laboratory (Bales 1950a, b; Bales and Strodtbeck 1951). Groups of two to seven members discussed a topic, usually for four sessions. All of Bales' subjects were men (Parsons and Bales 1955:261). Bales recorded twelve categories of interaction, such as "gives suggestion," "asks for suggestion," and "gives opinion." If an act was goal directed, forward looking, and cognitively oriented toward some end to be accomplished, it was coded as instrumental. If it was "felt to be caused in a nonmeaningful manner by . . . emotion . . . tension . . . and not . . . anticipated by symbolic manipulation," it was coded as expressive (Bales 1950a:39, 51). This core meaning is very close to the Darwinian distinction between rational, cognitive male thought and irrational feminine feeling and emotion. As Bales recorded them on his Interaction Recorder, the components of the expressive leadership function were: *raises the status of others, agrees, concurs, complies, passively accepts, gives help, rewards, understands, shows tension releases and laughs, shows solidarity.* In 1950 the distinction had not yet been linked to gender.

Bales found that the best idea man in his all-male groups (as rated by the members) was not the best liked. The best idea man was also usually the instrumental leader; the best liked man was usually the group's expressive leader. (Stereotypes tend to grow as they pass from hand to hand. A current leading textbook on *Group Dynamics* reports "college men tend to be task-oriented and concerned with getting the task completed, whereas college women tend to be concerned with establishing harmonious relation with others" (Shaw 1981:186). Thus do findings from all-male laboratory groups turn into myths!

By 1955 Parsons' views had changed dramatically. The same male and female roles that Parsons called a "source of strain" in 1942 became universal, inevitable, and functional in 1955: the expressive and the instrumental patterns. The sources of this remarkable transformation are not clear. The instrumental-expressive distinction was characteristic of all social systems (Parsons and Bales 1955:22). In the family the instrumental leader was the husband-father. The expressive leader was the wife-mother (1955:77). Permissiveness, support, nurturance, and love defined the mother's expressive role; discipline and demands for achievement and autonomy defined the father's instrumental role. "This basic uniformity of family structure . . . insures that the mother-figure is always the *more permissive* and supportive, the father the *more denying* and demanding" (1955:80—italics in the original).

Parsons and Bales saw a close association between superior power and the instrumental role, and inferior power and the expressive role (1955:77). So have many others. The stroking function (pleasing and soothing) is the age-old weapon of the weak and their best hope for exerting influence. The strong do not need to please (Janeway 1971).

The only empirical data on families offered by Parsons and Bales (1955) to support their assertion was a study by their student Morris Zelditch Jr., who tested the theory cross-culturally by using anthropological data. The instrumental leader was also the "boss-manager," the "final judge," "executor of punishment, discipline, and control over the children." "Alter" (the other person) "shows respect to (instrumental) ego." Expressive behavior included "supportive behavior to others, the desire to please, and be liked. . . . the comforter, the consoler." (Zelditch in Parsons and Bales 1955:309–10, 318–19).

Zelditch concluded that 46 of 56 preliterate societies showed sex role differentiation (10 did not!), that the mother was the expressive leader in all 46, and that the father (or the mother's brother) was the instrumental leader in 38 societies. "Respect" (by the wife for the husband) vs. "affection" (by the husband for the wife) was critical to the definition of instrumental and expressive leadership "in at least half of the cases" (1955:338).

I suggest that Zelditch unwittingly conducted a study of male dominance and female submission. What he really discovered was the widespread character of sexism! In 38 of 56 preliterate societies women are subordinate to dominant husbands. In 1955 the conceptual climate within the social sciences did not help Zelditch, Parsons, or Bales to recognize what they had in fact learned.

The conservative social values that so often were attached to a Parsonian functional analysis are evident in the following passage:

Why after all, are *two* parents necessary? . . . a stable, secure attitude of members depends, it can be assumed, on a *clear* structure being given to the situation so that an *uncertain* responsibility for emotional warmth, for instance, raises significant problems for the stability of the system. And an uncertain managerial responsibility, an unclear definition of authority for decisions and for getting things done, is also clearly a threat to the stability of the system (Zelditch in Parsons and Bales 1955:312—italics in the original).

This comes pretty close to saying that a couple must have one boss, and he is the husband!

The cultural belief that masculinity is instrumental and femininity is expressive is much older than 1955. In 1818 women were already characterized by feeling, men by thought (Berg 1978:125). In 1889 Grant Allen proposed that women were good at relating to people, men to the world of things (Dubbert 1979:90). In 1905 President Grover Cleveland asked women who followed the "Divinely appointed path of true womanhood" to devote themselves to the expressive role and give their man boundless self-confidence (Dubbert 1979:90). William James was only one of many who observed that men did not understand the emotions, especially the tender emotions, as well as women did.

The instrumental traits of men were also widely recognized in the nineteenth century. Economic and social changes between 1750 and 1950 had removed many of the instrumental functions from the wife's role, leaving her less to offer her husband except the expressive or stroking function. Middle-class and upper class women no longer contributed to the so-called productive (cash) sectors of the economy. By the mid-twentieth century, if a woman was asked "What do you do?" a typical reply was "Oh, nothing. I'm just a housewife." On the lips of many justahousewife became one word.

These same economic changes undermined the value of children to their father. Increasingly men looked upon children as primarily for the wife's benefit. In terms of their social roles, women now needed to be wives and mothers far more than men now needed to be fathers or husbands. In a purely economic sense wives and children had become a luxury to men by 1950 — an economic liability instead of the economic asset they had once been. When children become an economic liability, then the economic value of the mother who raises them is also diminished.

What Parsons and Bales accomplished was to put the stamp of social science validation upon a midcentury historical and economic *fait accompli,* the linking of the instrumental to the male and the expressive to the female roles, which they mistook for a universal element of social structure. But they failed to recognize that a division of labor that had grown out of the Industrial Revolution was neither necessary nor particularly functional (as Parsons had perceived in 1942). The subordination that is inherent in the expressive role, and the dominance, status, and power that define the instrumental role are apparent to those who look closely at the definitions and the data. "Instrumental" and "expressive" were in fact euphemisms for "dominant" and "subordinate." Today Bales believes that minimizing I-E role differentiation in the family is desirable (1982).

Experimental Tests of the Parsons-Bales MF Paradigm

The next step was to use the instrumental-expressive distinction to define masculinity and femininity, in the hope that these concepts could finally be rescued from the theoretical and conceptual vacuum in which they had lodged so unhappily since 1925. In 1958 Brim did a further analysis of data on 384 young children collected by Helen Koch. Koch, using a heroic 24-cell factorial design, assessed five- and six-year-olds on 58 dependent variables, using personality trait ratings by teachers (1956). With three other judges Brim classified 31 of these behaviors as expressive or instrumental.

The instrumental (masculine) traits were tenacity, aggressiveness, curiosity, ambition, planfulness, not dawdling or procrastinating, responsibleness, originality, competitiveness, not wavering in decisions, and self-confidence. The expressive (feminine) traits were: not angry, not quarrelsome, not revengeful, not teasing, not extrapunitive (not angry at others), not insisting on rights, no exhibitionism, not uncooperative with group, affectionate, obedient, not upset by defeat, responds to sympathy and approval from adults, not jealous, speedy recovery from emotional disturbance, cheerful, kind, friendly to adults and to children, not negative, no tattling. Again a strong flavor of submissiveness and grooming for subordination is apparent in the feminine traits. What did Brim discover? "Girls with brothers appear to be masculine to a greater degree than do any of the males themselves." Brim commented on "the implausibility of any group of girls being more masculine than all boys," but he did not give up the new MF definition. In addition, "all the girls seem to be more feminine than the boys are masculine; indeed the major characteristics of the boys is to be anti-feminine, not masculine" (1958:13). He meant that the boys often expressed negative emotions. Although Brim demonstrated that allegedly masculine or feminine traits appeared in both sexes, the new MF definition was nevertheless widely adopted by psychologists.

The Androgyny Paradigm

A series of important challenges to traditional MF concepts appeared in the 1970s. In 1972 Sandra Bem published the first of several explorations of androgyny, which she proposed as a replacement for the existing MF paradigms (Bem 1972, 1974, 1975).

By 1973 Anne Constantinople, in a thoughtful review, concluded that if femininity and masculinity could not be measured then perhaps they did not exist. Several other psychologists proposed that the ultimate goal of sexual identity development was not MF but androgyny or sex role transcendence (Osofsky and Osofsky 1972; Block 1973; Mede, Hefner, and Oleshansky 1976). Janet Spence, Robert Helmreich, and Joy Stapp published a new MF scale in 1974 (see also Spence and Helmreich 1975, 1978). In 1975 Joseph Pleck published a deflating critique of MF paradigms and of the identification model of MF development, which he followed by further analysis of the male sex role (Pleck 1975, 1976, 1981). James Harrison conducted a thorough critical evaluation of research on homosexuality (1975).

Although these voices were raised to challenge MF conventions, the Parsonian instrumental-expressive role paradigm still thrived among the majority of MF researchers. Space does not permit me to examine the post-1970 MF tests in detail. The most widely used MF tests today are those of Bem (1974) and Spence, Helmreich, and Stapp (1974). Their authors wisely refer to them as measures of conformity to sex role stereotypes, although the labels Feminine and Masculine are applied to certain scores. Interestingly, Spence and Helmreich have themselves concluded that the instrumental-expressive dimension is the major defining characteristic of both tests and, most significantly, that this dimension has "no face validity and at best only minimal construct validity as a sex role measure" (1980:156, 161). This places Spence and Helmreich quite close to my position that the tests lack construct validity *as measures of femininity and masculinity.*

The present enthusiasm for androgyny is reminiscent of past reliance on the concept of bisexuality by Fleiss, Freud, and Jung, and other nineteenth-century thinkers. It seems that whenever specific personality *traits* are assigned to one sex—by the culture or by social scientists—then concepts such as bisexuality or androgyny must promptly be evoked in order to deal realistically with the complex human beings we actually see coping with a demanding world. As we have seen, nothing productive is accomplished when psychologists first classify traits as either masculine or feminine and then are forced to add hastily "but of course men are also feminine and women are also masculine." It would be better not to categorize in the first place. Psychological concepts such as androgyny and sex role transcendence represent the partial breakdown of the Two Spheres in society and the assignment of components of each to both sexes.

Conclusions

Are MF tests satisfactory? No. There is no evidence that the MF tests of the last sixty years provide a valid measure of the relative femininity of women or the relative masculinity of men. The failure is due primarily to the inadequate conceptualization of femininity and masculinity, a failure that led directly to methodological errors. In the preceding article I identified eight assumptions of MF testers that I believe to be erroneous. The most important of these was the mistaken assumption that femininity and masculinity consist of, and are conceptually defined by, a list of traits and interests (based on sex difference statistics). It was this conceptual confusion that led directly to the chief methodological error, the failure to recognize that validating the tests against within-sex behavioral criteria was absolutely critical (Lewin, 1979).

Instead, I argued in the preceding article that MF tests served as a "group projective test" or "cultural Rorschach card." The MF testers did very successfully identify and confirm the components of the Victorian sex role schema that have been proposed by historians. This gratifying cross-disciplinary accomplishment is no less valuable for having been an unintended serendipitous finding. The MF tests reviewed in this article continue to confirm the historians' analysis. Purity acquired a new name: Disgustfulness. Curiously, the Victorian belief in women's moral superiority was revived by psychologists around 1970 just as the new, second women's movement was about to develop.

Male dominance and female subordination, or what the Cult of True Womanhood called Submissiveness, may confidently be placed at the top of the list of core values in the Victorian MF schema and in all the self-report MF tests. The terms instrumental and expressive are in large part euphemisms for male dominance and female subordination. From Freud to Sanford, Miller, Swanson, and Lansky, femininity has been equated with passivity, which to these authors means (1) obedience to authority, (2) not taking the initiative, and (3) dependence on others; that is, accepting subordination. Dominance and submissiveness are what MF tests really measure, even the current androgyny tests.

What have psychologists discovered about those who conform more or less closely to the Victorian MF schema? In a recent review, Magnus, drawing on Bem (1972) among others, concludes:

> For males, high masculinity has been positively correlated with anxiety, guilt proneness, neuroticism, suspiciousness, low self-acceptance, and low self-assurance, while low masculinity has been correlated with warmth and emotional stability. . . . For females, high femininity has been associated with high anxiety, low self-esteem, and low social acceptance (1980:188–9).

Women with "masculine" interests show higher self-acceptance, well-being, self-control and tolerance. Less sex typing is associated with higher intelligence and greater creativity in both sexes (Magnus 1980:189). Those who conform most closely to the nineteenth-century Victorian MF schema do not seem to be the better for it.

The tests reviewed in this chapter strongly confirm the conclusion based on the earlier tests that the attempt to measure femininity, masculinity, and sexual preference (homosexuality) simultaneously in one test will only guarantee the failure to measure any of them adequately. Whether it be "13 gay men" or "130 gay men," sixty years of MF testing have demonstrated that it cannot be done. I find no justifiable basis for assuming that substantial proportions (40 percent) of general populations have an unconscious other-sex gender identity. We are forced to agree with Lewis Terman's suspicion, voiced in 1923, that to call "an unanalyzed complex of Heaven-knows-what contributing elements" MF is indeed "rather worse than folly."

What Then are Femininity and Masculinity?

If MF does not consist of a set of traits and interests, what is it? A fair question. I propose that MF be conceptualized as *the gender-relevant aspects of a person's self-concept* or self-image. This definition provides room for individual variation in the specific content of the self-image as related to gender. Some people internalize conventional sex role stereotypes at a given stage of their life and others do not.

For many adults sexual functioning and enjoyment is a critical aspect of their own gender self-image. In true Victorian fashion that topic has been omitted from MF tests (except for a very few items). Loving relationships and parenting may be important to the feminine or masculine self-image.

This definition conforms to ordinary usage better than the psychologist's MF definition. A person's sense of herself or himself as feminine or masculine is the critical dimension. In determining how we label other people, I believe that their perceived self-image will be more compelling than their perceived traits or interests.

The attempt to measure MF should begin by working only with heterosexual people. Psychologists are still so ignorant of gay psychology and so lacking in any satisfactory theory of sexual preference that the study of gay persons to clarify MF seems ill advised.

MF tests should assess gender self-confidence. The test should measure individuals' beliefs that they are, or are not, living up to various aspects of their personal gender-relevant self-concepts. Do they feel competent as members of their own sex? Are they meeting their own standards of femininity or masculinity? What doubts do they have about their own gender-relevant behavior? However psychologists should not confuse doubts about one's gender adequacy with an other-sex gender identity, a rare and different condition.

The stages of development of the gender-relevant self-concept should be studied over the life cycle. Core juvenile gender identity develops around the age of two or three. It may be followed by a stage of gender conservation and by other stages, such as sex role transcendence.

Sixty years of MF testing have primarily demonstrated what femininity and masculinity are not; they are not two sets of interests and traits.

References

Bales, R. F. 1950a. *Interaction Process Analysis.* Cambridge, Mass.: Addison Wesley.
—— 1950b. "A Set of Categories for the Analysis of Small Group Interactions." *American Sociological Review* 15(2):257–63.
—— Personal Communication, May 22, 1982.
Bales, R. F. and Fred Strodtbeck. 1951. "Phases in Group Problem Solving." *Journal of Abnormal and Social Psychology* 46(4):485–95.
Bem, Sandra, L. 1972. "Psychology Looks at Sex Roles: Where Have All The Androgynous People Gone?" Paper presented at UCLA symposium on women.
—— 1974. "The Measurement of Psychological Androgyny." *Journal of Consulting and Clinical Psychology* 42:155–62.
—— 1975. "Sex-Role Adaptability: One Consequence of Psychological Androgyny." *Journal of Personality and Social Psychology* 31:634–43.
Berg, Barbara. 1978. *The Remembered Gate: Origins of American Feminism.* New York: Oxford University Press.
Bezdek, W. and Fred Strodtbeck. 1970. "Sex Identity and Pragmatic Action." *American Sociological Review* 35:419–502.
Bieliauskas, V. J., S. B. Miranda, and Z. M. Lansky. 1968. "Obviousness of Two Masculinity-Femininity Tests." *Journal of Consulting and Clinical Psychology* 32:314–18.
Bieliauskas, V. J. and R. H. Mikesell. 1972. "Masculinity-Femininity and Self-Concept." *Perceptual and Motor Skills* 34:163–67.
Black, J. D. 1956. "Adjectives Associated with Various MMPI Codes." In Welsh and Dahlstrom (1956), *q.v.*
Block, Jean. 1973. "Conceptions of Sex-Role: Some Cross Cultural and Longitudinal Perspectives." *American Psychologist* 28:512–26.
Brim, Orville. 1958. "Family Structure and Sex-Role Learning by Children: A Further Analysis of Helen Koch's Data." *Sociometry* 21:1–16.
Brown, D. and A. Tolor. 1957. "Human Figure Drawings as Indicators of Sexual Identification and Inversion." *Perceptual and Motor Skills* 7:199–211.
Buros, Oscar. 1959. The Fifth Mental Measurements Yearbook. New Jersey: Gryphon Press, pp. 739–42.
Dubbert. Joe L. 1979. *A Man's Place.* Englewood Cliffs, N. J. Prentice-Hall.
Ellis, Albert. 1959. Cited in Buros (1959), *q.v.*
Franck, K. and E. Rosen. 1949. "A Projective Test of Masculinity-Femininity." *Journal of Consulting Psychology* 13:247–56.
Goldberg, Lewis. 1971. "A Historical Survey of Personality Scales and Inventories." In McReynolds (1971), *q.v.*, 2:293–381.
Gough, H. G. 1952. "Identifying Psychological Femininity." *Educational and Psychological Measurement* 12:427–39.
—— 1968. "An Interpreter's Syllabus for the California Psychological Inventory." In McReynolds (1971), *q.v.*, 1:55–79.
Hall, Calvin and R. Van de Castle. 1965. "An Empirical Investigation of the Castration Complex in Dreams." *Journal of Personality* 33:20–29.
Harrison, James. 1975. "A Critical Evaluation of Research on Masculinity-Femininity." *Dissertation Abstractions International* 36(4) series B. University Microfilms no. 75-22890.

Hathaway, S. R. 1956. "Scales 5 (Masculinity-Femininity), 6 (Paranoia) and 8 (Schiz-ophrenia)." In Welsh and Dahlstrom (1956) *q.v.*, pp. 104–11.

Hathaway, S. R. and J. C. McKinley. 1940. "A Multiphasic Personality Schedule (Minnesota); Construction of the Schedule. *Journal of Psychology* 10: 249–54.

—— Foreword to Dahlstrom and Welsh (1956), *q.v.*, pp. vii–xi.

Hollingworth, L. S. 1916. "Sex Differences in Mental Traits." *Psychological Bulletin* 13:383.

—— 1922. "Differential Action Upon the Sexes of Forces Which Tend to Segregate the Feebleminded." *Journal of Abnormal and Social Psychology,* 17:35–37.

Jackaway, Rita. 1972. "Assessment Techniques and the Masculine-Feminine Con-struct." Unpublished paper, pp. 1–21.

Janeway, E. 1971. *Man's World, Women's Place: A Study in Social Mythology.* New York: Dell.

Koch, H. L. 1956. "Sissiness and Tomboyishness in Relation to Sibling Characteris-tics." *Journal of Genetic Psychology* 8:231–44.

Kraugh, Ulf. 1960. "The Defense Mechanism Test: A New Method for Diagnosis and Personnel Selection." *Journal of Applied Psychology* 44(5):303–9.

Lansky, L. M. 1960. "Mechanisms of Defense: Sex Identity and Defense Against Aggres-sion." cited in Miller and Swanson (1960), *q.v.*, pp. 272–88.

Lewin, Miriam. 1979. *Understanding Psychological Research.* New York: Wiley.

—— 1982a. "The Anatomy of Failure: Psychology's Struggle To Measure Femininity and Masculinity." Paper delivered at the Eastern Psychological Association meetings, Baltimore, April 14–17.

—— 1982b. " 'Rather Worse Than Folly?' Terman and Miles Measure Femininity and Masculinity." Paper presented at Cheiron, International Society for the History of the Behavioral and Social Sciences, June, Newport, R.I.

Lipsitt, P. and F. Strodtbeck. 1967. "Defensiveness in Decision-making as a Function of Sex-Role Identification." *Journal of Personality and Social Psychology, 6,* (1):10–15.

Magnus, Elisabeth. "Sources of Maternal Stress in the Postpartum Period: A Review of the Literature and an Alternative View." In Jacquelynne Parsons, ed. *The Psy-chobiology of Sex Differences and Sex Roles.* 1980. Washington, D.C.: Hemi-sphere Publishing, McGraw-Hill.

McCarthy, D., R. J. Anthony, and G. Domino. 1970. "A Comparison of the CPI, Franck, MMPI and WAIS Masculinity-Femininity Indexes." *Journal of Consulting and Clinical Psychology,* 35:414–16.

Mede, Rebecca, Robert Hefner, and Barbara Oleshansky. 1976. "A Model of Sex Role Transcendence." *Journal of Social Issues 32* (3):197–206.

McReynolds, Paul, ed. 1971. *Advances in Psychological Assessment* (2 vols.). Palo Alto, Calif.: Science and Behavior Books.

Miller, D. R. and Guy E. Swanson, eds. 1960. *Inner Conflicts and Defense.* New York: Holt, Rinehart, Winston.

Miller, Jean Baker. 1976. *Toward a New Psychology of Women.* Boston: Beacon.

Mussen, Paul. 1962. "Long-term Consequences of Masculinity of Interests in Adoles-cence." *Journal of Consulting Psychology* 26(5):435–40.

Osofsky, J. and H. Osofsky. 1972. "Androgyny as a Lifestyle." *Family Coordinator* 21:411–19.

Parsons, Talcott. 1942. "Age and Sex in the Social Structure of the U.S. *American Sociological Review* (Oct.) 7(5):604–16.

—— 1970. "On Building Social Systems Theory: A Personal History." *Daedalus* (Fall) 99(4):826–81.

Parsons, T. and R. F. Bales. 1955. *Family, Socialization, and Interaction Process.* Glencoe, Ill.: Free Press.

Pleck, Joseph. 1975. "Masculinity–Femininity: Current and Alternative Paradigms." *Sex Roles* 1(2):161–78.

—— 1976. "The Male Sex-Role: Definitions, Problems, and Sources of Change." *Journal of Social Issues* 32(3):155–64.

—— 1981. *The Myth of Masculinity.* Cambridge, Mass.: MIT Press.

Rosenberg, B. G. and B. Sutton–Smith. 1971. "Sex Role Identity and Sibling Composition." *Journal of Genetic Psychology* (March) 118 (1):29–32.

Rosenberg, R. N. 1982. *Beyond Separate Spheres: Intellectual Origins of Modern Feminism,* New Haven: Yale University Press.

Rychlak, Joseph and Anne T. Legerski. 1967. "A Sociocultural Theory of Appropriate Sexual Role Identification and Level of Personal Adjustment." *Journal of Personality* 35:31–49.

Sanford, Nevitt. 1951, 1967. *Self and Society.* New York: Atherton.

Shaw, Marvin. 1981. *Group Dynamics.* New York: McGraw-Hill.

Shepler, B. 1951. "A Comparison of Masculinity-Femininity Measures." *Journal of Consulting Psychology* 15:484–86.

Sobel, D. 1980. "Testing the Psyche Can Strain Belief." *New York Times,* September 28, p. 22E.

Spence, J. T. and R. Helmreich. 1978. *Masculinity and Femininity: Their Psychological Dimensions, Correlates and Antecedents.* Austin: University of Texas Press.

—— 1980. "Masculine Instrumentality and Feminine Expressiveness." *Psychology of Women Quarterly* (Winter) 5(2):147–63.

Spence, Janet T., R. Helmreich, and J. Stapp. 1974. "The Personal Attributes Questionnaire: A Measure of Sex-Role Stereotypes and Masculinity-Femininity." *JSAS Catalog of Selected Documents in Psychology* 4:43–44.

—— 1975. "Ratings of Self and Peers on Sex-Role Attributes and Their Relation to Self-Esteem and Conceptions of Masculinity and Femininity." *Journal of Personality and Social Psychology* 32(1):29–39.

Strodtbeck, F. and P. Creelan. 1968. "The Interaction Linkage Between Family Size, Intelligence, and Sex-Role Identity." *Journal of Marriage and the Family* (May), pp. 301–7.

Strodtbeck, F., W. Bezdek, and D. Goldhammer. 1970. "Male Sex-Role and Response to a Community Problem." *Sociological Quarterly* (Summer), pp. 291–307.

Ursin, H., E. Baade, and Seymour Levine, eds. 1978. *The Psychobiology of Stress.* New York: Academic Press.

Vincent, Clark E. 1966. "Implications of Changes in Male-Female Role Expectation for Interpreting Masculinity-Femininity Scores." *Journal of Marriage and the Family* (May), pp. 196–99.

Wacker, Fred R. 1980. "Sociology at Harvard: Institutionalization and Ideas." Paper delivered at Cheiron meeting, Bowdoin College, Maine, June.

Welsh, G. S. and W. G. Dahlstrom. 1956. *Basic Readings on the MMPI.* Minneapolis: University of Minnesota Press.

Wooley, H. T. 1903. *The Mental Traits of Sex,* pp. 167–68. Chicago: University of Chicago Press.
Zelditch, Morris. 1955. "Role Differentiation in the Nuclear Family." in Parsons and Bales (1955) *q.v.* 307–51.

9 The Theory of Male Sex Role Identity

Its Rise and Fall, 1936 to the Present

JOSEPH H. PLECK

The theory of male sex role identity (MSRI) has been the dominant paradigm in American psychology for understanding male experience (Pleck 1981a). In brief, this theory holds that for individuals to become psychologically mature as members of their sex, they must acquire male or female "sex role identity," manifested by having the sex-appropriate traits, attitudes, and interests that psychologically "validate" or "affirm" their biological sex. However, many factors conspire to thwart the attainment of healthy sex role identity, especially for males (e.g., the actual or relative absence of male role models, and women's changing roles). The resulting problems for males include effeminacy and homosexuality (too little masculinity), as well as hypermasculinity (too much masculinity). This theory provides the underlying basis for many well-known lines of research and theory on diverse topics such as the effects of the absence of the father, male crime and violence, male attitudes toward women, boys' problems in elementary schools, adolescent initiation rites, and black males. Only recently, as we step back from the conventional social scientific wisdom of the 1950s and 1960s on sex roles, has it become clear how thoroughly dominated the social sciences have been by this highly explicit and detailed theory of the male role.

Background

From the 1930s to the recent present, the study of sex roles was preoccupied with, as much as with any other single question, "What makes men less masculine than they should be, and what can we do about it?" To understand why, it is necessary to place the theory of male sex role identity that psychologists began to construct in the 1930s in the context of the cultural concerns about masculinity that had developed earlier.

During the century before the explicit emergence of the theory, men were increasingly perceived as not measuring up to the new and more stringent demands placed on them by a changing society. Changes in women's role in the nineteenth and twentieth centuries seemed to threaten women's mental and physical well-being. Recent research brings to light how men seemed to face profound risk as well. To give only a few examples, Jessie Bernard (1981) reminds us of De Toqueville's observation in the 1830s that America's equality of opportunity imposed a subtle demand on men to not simply be family providers but also to be *good* family providers through success in a competitive economy. Demos (1974) notes the rise of the "tramp" in the nineteenth century, the large and growing number of men who gave up, often fled, the male provider role. Peter Filene (1975) recounts the cultural shock that occurred when nearly half of World War I recruits were physically or mentally disqualified for military service. In these and other ways, American men in the nineteenth and early twentieth centuries gave indications that they were having trouble meeting male role demands (see also Pleck and Pleck 1980).

Over the same period, women were seen as taking a larger role with children, particularly sons. In the early nineteenth century, the mother was considered to be a far less significant figure in the child rearing of sons (and to some extent daughters as well) than she is today. Examination of correspondence between parents and children suggests sons' relationships with their fathers were actually closer than those with their mothers (Demos 1982; Rotundo 1982). But during the mid- and late nineteenth century, mothers were encouraged to take the dominant emotional role in childrearing. Notions of women's moral "purity" arose, which elevated women above men and made them particularly suited for "rearing" the young. The increasing involvement of women in childrearing was also manifested in early education. Educational reformers like Horace Mann greatly increased the numbers of women teachers in the schools (Suggs 1978), departing from the earlier pattern of male elementary teachers.

Women's influence on boys' and men's difficulties in their role came to be formulated in terms of "feminization." Articles with titles like "The Effeminization of Men" appeared in popular magazines as early as 1893 (Dubbert 1974). In 1909, the prominent psychologist J. McKeen Cattell argued that the new confinement of the boy in elementary schools exposed him to the ministrations of a "vast horde of female teachers" who tended to "subvert both the school and the family" because of their spinsterish attitudes (quoted in O'Neill 1967). Concerns about feminization were a major factor in the rapid rise of the Boy Scouts, which received a federal charter in 1911. As Hantover (1978) emphasizes, scouting served to relieve the masculine anxieties of the scoutmasters at least as much as those of the boys they worked with. Altogether, such concerns set the stage for the emergence of the theory of male sex role identity.

Initial Formulation: 1936–1945

The first step in the explicit development of the theory of male sex role identity was taken by Lewis Terman and Catherine Miles in *Sex and Personality* (1936). They formulated a notion that gave previously existing cultural concerns about men's (and women's) roles more precise intellectual focus: for each sex, there is a psychologically normative or ideal configuration of traits, attitudes, and interests that members of that sex demonstrate to varying degrees. Men (and women) are psychologically normal to the extent that they possess these sex-appropriate characteristics and psychologically deficient or abnormal to the extent that they do not. Terman and Miles introduced the term "masculinity-femininity" (MF) for the personality dimension on which members of each sex varied, and the first of what soon became many psychological tests to assess it (see Lewin, "Measuring Femininity and Masculinity . . ." and "Rather Worse . . . ," this volume, for related discussions of Terman and Miles and of MF scales).

In Terman and Miles's (1936:1–2) words:

The belief is all but universal that men and women as contrasting groups display characteristic sex differences in their behavior, and that these differences are so deep and pervasive as to lend distinctive character to the entire personality. That masculine and feminine types are a reality in all our highly developed cultures can hardly be questioned. . . . But along with the acceptance of M-F types of the sort we have delineated, there is an explicit recognition of the existence of individual variants from type: the effeminate man and the masculine woman. Grades of deviates are recognized ranging from the slightly variant to the genuine invert who is capable of romantic attachment only to members of his or her own sex. . . . It is highly desirable that our concepts of the M-F types . . . be given a more factual basis. . . . A measure is needed which can be applied to the individual and scored so as to locate the subject, with a fair degree of approximation, in terms of deviation from the mean of either sex.

and again (1936:451):

Masculinity and femininity are important aspects of human personality. They are not to be thought of as lending to it merely a superficial coloring and flavor; rather they are one of a small number of cores around which the structure of personality gradually takes shape. . . . The M-F dichotomy, in various patterns, has existed throughout history, and is still firmly established in our mores. In a considerable fraction of the population it is the source of many acute difficulties in the individual's social and psychological adjustment.

Terman and Miles' notion of normative personality styles for each sex, whose presence (or absence) reflects psychological health (or deficit), was widely adopted in American psychology. Its popularity is attested by the many other MF tests that rapidly proliferated in the late 1930s and 1940s (see Lewin, articles 7 and 8). Particularly important were the MF measures included as component scales in a new kind of psychological instrument, the omnibus personality inventory. The MF scales of the Strong Vocational Interest Blank (Strong 1943), Guilford's Temperament Survey (Guilford and Guilford 1936), and the Minnesota Multiphasic Personality Inventory (Dahlstrom, Welsh, and Dahlstrom 1972) are among the most important examples, together with the slightly later California Psychological Inventory (Gough 1964). These machine-scorable tests met the growing needs of "people-processing" institutions of increasing social importance: the military, the modern firm, prisons, and mental hospitals.

Terman and Miles' idea of normative, sex-linked personality patterns that are essential for psychological health applied equally to both sexes and did not give any special attention to the male role. The conceptual developments necessary to elaborate this notion into a theory concerned primarily with the male role came only later. The work of Terman and Miles (and their successors) had as yet too simple a theoretical basis. Its immediate intellectual context was the successful scientific operationalization of intelligence in the early twentieth century, the event that, as much as any other, established psychology as a modern science. Terman himself had been senior author of the Americanized revision of Binet's classic children's intelligence scale, and a milestone in its own right, the Stanford-Binet Intelligence Scale (Terman 1916). After this triumph, psychologists began to look to other domains of personality that were socially important, the object of confusion and disagreement, but that might likewise yield up their true nature when subjected to the scientific psychological method. They first turned in the 1920s to moral behavior, which, like intelligence, was of great concern to a society that felt itself flooded by foreign immigrants of possibly deficient character. But here psychology faltered: Hartshorne and May's classic *Studies in the Nature of Character* (1928–30) failed to reveal any commonality of association between prosocial moral behaviors across a variety of settings and circumstances.

Led by Terman and Miles, the field of psychology turned next to sex typing, or within-sex variation in sex-role-related traits, attitudes, and interests. The study of intelligence provided a direct model. Binet and his successors had, in effect, defined intelligence as the capacity to answer correctly those items that older children answered correctly more often than younger children. In like fashion, masculinity-femininity was operationalized as having those characteristics that one sex said they had more often than the other sex did. Having sex-appropriate traits was, thus, like having intelligence. Terman and Miles included in their scale such then-contemporary psychometric methods as word associations and perceptions of inkblots but interpreted them in a strictly empirical way, not in the psychodynamic context in which they are seen today.

One respect in which Terman and Miles and their followers were theoretically bolder was their postulation of homosexuality as the extreme end of the continuum of the "grades of deviates" who depart from the normative male and female patterns. Homosexuality was of great concern to both the developers and users of MF tests. Nearly 20 percent of *Sex and Personality* is devoted to various studies of homosexuality. (There is a foretaste of the theory's later focus in males in that nearly all of these are studies of male homosexuals.) The MMPI MF test is based on comparisons of 54 male soldiers, 67 women airline employees, and 13 male homosexuals (Dahlstrom, Welsh, and Dahlstrom 1972:201–2). Harrison Gough (1952:427) writes that the goal of his MF scale (later integrated into the California Psychological Inventory) "has been to develop an instrument which is brief, easy to administer, relatively subtle and unthreatening in content, and which will, at the same time, differentiate men from women and sexual deviates from normals." The critical assumption: male homosexuals differ from male heterosexuals in the same respects as women differ from men (see also Lewin, article 8). These tests were in fact considered effective to screen male populations for homosexuals.

Giving homosexuality such central attention as a departure from the personality structure considered psychologically normative for each sex was an important conceptual step, and it was later to be elaborated much further. But even here, Terman and Miles' theoretical simplicity is evident. They interpret homosexuality not from the perspective of psychoanalysis, but rather from that of the early twentieth-century "sexology" which classified and described homosexuality and other sexual deviations in an elaborate taxonomy. If Terman and Miles have another intellectual forerunner besides Alfred Binet, it is Havelock Ellis, not Sigmund Freud.

There was some contemporary opposition to Terman and Miles' concept of psychologically normative personality styles that are inherently related to psychological health. The most notable was Margaret Mead's *Sex and Temperament in Three Primitive Societies* (1935). Mead's book is invariably cited only as providing disconfirming exceptions to Western stereotypes about cultural patterns of sex differences (i.e., Arapesh men are gentle and artistic, Mundugumor women are aggressive, etc.). In reality, Mead did not see her contribution primarily as showing that the *actual* characteristics of the sexes differed across the three cultures she studied. Rather, it was showing that the temperaments considered *ideal* for men and women, and therefore the characteristics of those who deviated from these ideals, varied. Since individuals differ in their personality characteristics within each sex, not everyone can conform to any particular ideal, and a subgroup of each sex in each society is perceived by both others and themselves as deviating from the prescribed temperament. But since societies vary in their ideals for the sexes, those viewed as deviant will be different subgroups in each one. The titles of the final chapters on each society convey Mead's focus on sex role deviants: "The Arapesh Ideal and Those Who Deviate from It," "Deviants from the Mundugumor Ideal," and "The Unplaced Tchambuli Man and Women." Mead's real point was that a man or woman perfectly adapted to the sex role norms of one culture could be a misfit (a term Mead used repeatedly) in another.

Mead's cultural relativism directly challenged Terman and Miles' interpretation of masculinity and femininity as universal psychological ideals or norms like intelligence. But Terman and Miles' view prevailed. It is perhaps not a coincidence that *Sex and Personality* was published in 1936, in the midst of the Great Depression, clearly the greatest single historical crisis in the institutional basis of the traditional male role: the breadwinning job. As the conventional social arrangements underlying traditional roles eroded so dramatically, the culture sought to reestablish them on a hypothetical inner psychological basis. In short, if holding a job could no longer be counted on to define masculinity, a masculinity-femininity test could.

Theoretical Maturation and Development: 1945–1970

In the postwar period, Terman and Miles' masculinity-femininity conception, which had equal application to both sexes, evolved into a theory primarily focusing on males. Several trends in men's experience and how it was socially perceived helped set the stage for this theoretical development.

In some respects, World War II caused a temporary reversal in the long-term historical decline of the traditional male role and of the shorter term, more specific crisis of the Depression. The economic boom that anticipated World War II put many men back to work. In the war itself, men lived by themselves, away from women, in a war perceived as brutal but morally justified, and emerged victorious. But these effects were short-lived, compared to other social anxieties and social changes the war stimulated. Repeating the experience of World War I, there was great concern about the large number of males who had been physically or mentally disqualified for the draft, and particularly about the high incidence of male emotional breakdowns in battle. Not everyone interpreted these as failings of masculinity (e.g., Grinker and Spiegel's *Men Under Stress* 1948, a milestone work in stress research). But others, like psychiatrist Edward Strecker in *Their Mothers' Sons* (1946), did.

During the war and after, male-female relationships underwent a transformation. During the wartime boom, women had been drawn into the labor force, and particularly in previously male blue-collar work. They also developed a new degree of psychological independence from men by virtue of having to live without them. When men returned, they found that their wives and girl friends had changed. Negotiating new relationships with women posed a real challenge to men; the spurt of postwar divorces provided testimony. Altered equally by the war was men's economic role. Wartime technological advances had transformed the economy. A good job now required levels of education and training previously unprecedented. Severe postwar inflation caused by war-deferred consumer demand undermined men's family provider role even more.

Social analysts noticed that the new occupational roles and associated life-styles emerging as dominant for men in the 1950s in response to these changes were discordant with what they saw as men's traditional self-image and might have negative effects on men's identities. This was actually one of the main themes in two major sociological studies not usually interpreted in this light, C. Wright Mills's *White Collar: The American Middle Classes* (1956) and W. F. Whyte's *The Organization Man* (1956). Ehrenberg (1960), extending Mills' views further, explicitly argued that the new, impulse-restraining male role was damaging to men's mental health. The title of Whyte's book became a widely used term for the bureaucratically domesticated male. Popular culture in the 1950s also expressed these concerns. As Ehrenreich and English (1979:240) note:

> In cartoons, the average male was shorter than his wife, who habitually entered the frame in curlers, wielding a rolling pin over her cowering husband. TV squeezed the American male's diminished sense of manhood for whatever laughs—or thrills—were left. The domesticated Dad, who was most hilarious when he tried to be manly and enterprising, was the butt of all the situation comedies. Danny Thomas, Ozzie Nelson, Robert Young, and (though not a father) Jackie Gleason in "The Honeymooners," were funny only as pint-sized cariacatures of the patriarchs, frontiersmen, and adventurers who once defined American manhood.

A particularly dramatic example occurs in still the most popular of James Dean's films, *Rebel Without a Cause*. In the film's psychologically most powerful scene, Dean seeks out his father for advice but recoils in disgust after finding him wearing an apron while washing dishes. World War II's respected returning war hero had been transformed into a henpecked husband whose son holds him in contempt.

New Theoretical Conceptions: Identification

The theoretical development that led to a special focus on males was the introduction of the psychodynamic concept of identification to the study of masculinity-femininity. The basic notion is that the developmental origin of MF is the individual's psychological identification with the mother or father. The acquisition of MF is, in fact, a process of "sex role identification." But since mothers are such central figures in the lives of children of both sexes, this means that boys initially identify with a female and therefore develop a feminine identity. Thus, males have far more difficulty than females in acquiring an appropriate sex role identity. In turn, overcoming their initial feminine identification is hypothesized to be the central problem in males' psychological development. This argument is the essence of the theory of male sex role identity.

The first clear statement of this view appears to be Talcott Parsons' (1942) essay, "Age and Sex in the Social Structure of the United States," and it was a major argument in Parsons and Bales' (1955) influential *Family Socialization and Interaction Process.* Franck and Rosen (1948) are apparently the first to conceptualize an MF measure as revealing sex role identification. This expression and its variants soon supplanted MF itself as the term for within-sex differences in sex-role-related traits, attitudes, and interests. Developmental psychologists began to study sex role development in children. Through the work of Brown (1956, 1958), Lynn (1961, 1969), Kagan (1964), and Biller (1972, 1974; Biller and Borstelmann 1967), the theory of male sex role identity became the reigning interpretation of sex role development in American psychology.

Although this core argument in the theory of male identity used the psychoanalytic concept of identification, it was never a mainstream view within psychoanalysis itself. To the early Freud, the father was the towering figure in the life of the son. He gave a role to the mother, but only as the object of the son's libidinous drives. To the early Freud at least, the mother was psychologically important primarily because the male child's love for her brought him into competition with his father in an Oedipal drama whose outcome—identification with the father and the resulting consolidation of the superego—would shape the boy's character structure. Freud saw the girl—not the boy—as facing special problems in psychosexual development.

Led by Freud himself, psychoanalysis in the 1920s began to focus on pre-Oedipal issues. "Pre-Oedipal" is, in fact, the psychoanalytic codeword denoting the mother. Within the variant formulations, the overall theme was: the Oedipal conflict is the key to the clinically less serious neurotic disorders, but the more severe forms of psychopathology (the psychoses and personality disorders) result from far earlier and more fundamental problems in the pre-Oedipal period. As developed by theorists like Bowlby, Mahler, Winnicott, Klein, and Benedek, the problem of the pre-Oedipal relationship is that the mother is rejecting or otherwise inadequate as an attachment figure, or at the other extreme, the mother facilitates the child's attachment but then refuses to permit the child to individuate. To these theorists, the idea that the male child might *identify with* the mother, leading to a cross-sex identification, would have seemed quite novel.

Hypermasculinity

The notions that an individual's sex typing derives from parental identification and that the boy's initial identification with his mother could therefore be a source of difficulty, combined with the psychoanalytic idea of the unconscious, stimulated another theoretical development of great importance: the concept of "hypermasculinity" (exaggerated, extreme masculine behavior) as a defense against the male's unconscious feminine identification. In Terman and Miles' earlier conception, the potential problem for males was only in not having enough masculinity. With this new concept, too *much* masculinity could be viewed as a psychological problem as well. Because of the many behaviors which could be interpreted as expressions of hypermasculinity, this conceptual advance considerably broadened the range of phenomena which the theory of male sex role identity addressed.

While this concept had been foreshadowed in such European psychodynamic writings as Adler's (1927) "masculine protest" and Boehm's "femininity complex in men" (1932), it caught on in the American social sciences only during and after World War II. We earlier noted cultural concerns about draft disqualifications and battle breakdowns as showing widespread masculine inadequacy during the war, and about the apparent domestication of masculinity in the 1950s. But the war and postwar period simultaneously seemed to reveal, perhaps more starkly than before, another side of masculinity that called out for explanation: first, wartime male aggression (and the blind obedience that could make it the tools of a fascist state), and later, male juvenile delinquency in the 1950s.

The wartime roots of the hypermasculinity concept are evident in its early history. In "Certain primary sources and patterns of aggression in the social structure of the Western world," Talcott Parsons (1947) interpreted male violence as due to the male's need to disengage himself from the inner feminine identification caused by the Western pattern of close mother–child relations. In what is now recognized as the pioneering work of "psychohistory," psychoanalyst Walter Langer prepared a case study of Adolf Hitler for the OSS (published in 1972 as *The Mind of Adolf Hitler*). Langer concluded that the dictator was a divided personality who masked a timid side with an exaggerated and sadistic version of masculinity.

In Adorno et al.'s (1950) *The Authoritarian Personality* (the first two of whose four authors were European refugees from Hitler) one of the study's principal interpretive hypotheses concerned defenses against unconscious cross-sex identity. As Adorno et al. (1950:428, 405) put it:

One might expect high-scoring [i.e., authoritarian] men to think of themselves as very masculine, and that this claim would be the more insistent the greater the underlying feelings of weakness. . . . There seems to be, in the high-scoring men, more of what may be called psuedo-masculinity—as defined by boastfulness about such traits as determination, energy, industry, independence, decisiveness, and will power—and less admission of passivity.

As Nevitt Sanford (1966:196), one of the study's investigators, recounted later, "The authors of *The Authoritarian Personality* became convinced that one of the sources of this personality syndrome was ego-alien femininity—that is to say, underlying femininity that had to be countered by whatever defenses the subject had at his disposal."

Sanford was the only one of *The Authoritarian Personality*'s investigators to follow up the hypermasculinity hypothesis. In an utterly intriguing article originally prepared in 1950, Sanford (1966) brilliantly perceived the opportunity provided by combining the older questionnaire MF scales with the newer, projective tests (then just starting to appear) aspiring to tap unconscious sex role identification. By interpreting the questionnaire scales as assessing superficial, conscious-level sex role identity and the projective tests as tapping the unconscious level, he could sort subjects into a fourfold classification representing the various combinations of conscious and unconscious masculine and feminine sex role identity. Sanford's study concerned the correlates of the various sex role identity patterns on intellectual productivity and creativity in a sample of postwar male Berkeley graduate students. He chose these dependent variables apparently because, in his ego-psychological   perspective,   he   expected   the   unconscious-feminine/conscious-masculine (FM) pattern in men to have a great potential cost in the cognitive rigidity necessitated by the repression of inner femininity. But the main conclusion of his study was, interestingly, not the problems of the FM males, but rather the unusual creativity and intellectual strength of the reverse male pattern: unconscious-masculine/conscious-feminine   (MF).   (Lewin questions these findings.)

Sandord's conclusion harked back to Jung's notion that the mature personality requires the integration of the unconscious cross-sex self, men's *anima* and women's *animus*. But such an idea could not be incorporated in 1950s thinking. Sanford dropped this research, not even publishing his results until 1966. However, Daniel Miller and Guy Swanson's *Inner Conflict and Defense* (1960), turned Sanford's methodological breakthrough into a line of research more consistent with the cultural concerns of the period. They adopted some of Sanford's measures (the Franck Drawing Completion Test as the unconscious measure and the Gough MF scale as the conscious one) and arranged his sex role identity categories as a series of stages in male development. Males start as FFs (unconscious and conscious feminine identity) totally identified with the mother, then progress to the FM stage acquiring superficial masculine traits but maintaining their deep feminine identity, and complete their maturation as MM's, developing inner masculine identification to match the surface behavior they earlier acquired. At the MM stage, argue Miller and Swanson, male development is complete. Miller and Swanson simply omitted Sanford's fourth type, the MF, whom he regarded as the most mature and creative.

The studies in *Inner Conflict and Defense* that used this revised, threefold typology of sex role identity examined arousal of guilt and defenses against agression, viewed as ego-psychological personality processes, as hypothetical correlates of the FM pattern. This line of research then passed to Fred Strodtbeck and his students at the University of Chicago (Strodtbeck and Creelan 1968; Strodtbeck, Bezdek, and Goldhammer 1970; Bezdek and Strodtbeck 1970; Lipsitt and Strodtbeck 1967; Cottle 1968; Cottle, Edwards, and Pleck 1970). Like Sanford, and Miller and Swanson, Strodtbeck and his students focused on cognitive, ego-psychological variables as dependent measures. One study in the series (Lipsitt and Strodtbeck 1967), however, got closer to sex role issues. In this study, subjects heard what was purported to be a naval court-martial about an event modeled loosely after Melville's *Billy Budd,* in which a handsome young sailor accidentally kills an officer. Under one experimental condition, evidence is included implying that the defendant is homosexual. The prediction was that in this condition, the FM males would more often find the defendant guilty and recommend the death sentence. (The prediction was not clearly supported; see Pleck 1981a:105–6.)

The unconscious feminine identity hypothesis became an extremely popular one, and began to extend in many directions. McClelland and Watt (1968) and others (see Pleck, 1981a) applied it to psychopathology more generally. Burton and Whiting (1961) applied it to male initiation rites, by establishing an association, in a sample of world cultures, between "exclusive mother-child sleeping arrangements" (the father sleeps in a different room, and often in a different building, than the mother and young child) and male initiation ceremonies. Robert and Ruth Munroe (1971, 1973a, 1973b) studied both the couvade (a practice in many cultures in which husbands of pregnant wives engage in symbolic birth ceremonies of their own) and psychosomatic symptoms in expectant fathers in the U.S. in light of the unconscious cross-sex identity hypothesis. But the topic studied by far most frequently in light of the hypermasculinity hypothesis was male juvenile delinquency. Walter Miller introduced hypermasculinity as a leading interpretation in his "Lower class culture as a generating milieu of gang delinquency" (1958).

Absent Fathers and Black Males

The consequences of the fathers' absence on sons and the sex role problems of black males each became important new substantive areas in which the theory of male sex role identity was applied in the 1950s and 1960s. To some degree, these substantive issues were theoretically linked to hypermasculinity: the model study of this period was an investigation of delinquency as a consequence of the sex role identity problems resulting from the father's absence in black males (e.g., Rohrer and Edmonson 1960; Silverman and Dinitz 1974). Studies of hypermasculinity, paternal absence, and black males all reinforced each other.

In many senses, the father's absence as a large-scale social problem had been created by World War II. The war had, of course, directly taken fathers away from their children (for many, permanently), and the earliest studies concern these wartime separations. But more indirectly, the changes in male–female relations resulting from war had led to a spurt of postwar divorces, creating more absent fathers. The war also greatly stimulated the migration of rural dwellers, particularly blacks, to cities, where many factors led to the breakdown of their traditional two-parent family structure. Male identity theory proved a convenient and convincing explanation of the delinquency and other social problems that resulted. The effects of paternal absence on sons quickly became one of the most frequently studied topics in the sex role field. The contrast with the earlier period is striking. In the psychological theories of Freud and Jung, the father is the towering figure in the psychological development of the child (Lewin 1980). In the 1950s and 1960s, he became a dominating figure not by his presence, but by his absence.

When social science began to pay serious attention to blacks in the 1960s, male identity theory was prominent among the conceptual perspectives it employed. On the basis of MF studies of a sample of Alabama convicts and working class veterans in Wisconsin, social psychologist Thomas Pettigrew in *A Profile of the Negro American* (1964) interpreted black males as suffering from sex role identity problems. To Pettigrew, common to all black males' problems—from the father-absent, mother-dominated home to their overrepresentation in low-paying service jobs occupied by females—is the underlying theme of threat to male sex role identity. As Pettigrew put it, "The sex-identity problems created by the fatherless home are perpetuated in adulthood" (1964:21). In the following year, Daniel Patrick Moynihan leaned heavily on this hypothesis in "The Negro Family: The Case for National Action" (1965/1967), the so-called "Moynihan Report." He argued that the humiliations suffered by blacks during Reconstruction had a particularly devastating effect on black males because "the very essence of the male animal, from the bantam rooster to the four-star general, is to strut" (1965:62). As American mobilization in Vietnam grew, he also praised military service as an almost ideal solution to black men's frustrated masculinity, which he saw as having such destructive consequences for them and the whole society: "Given the strains of the disorganized and matrifocal family life in which so many negro youth come of age, the Armed Forces are a dramatic and desperately needed change: a world away from women, a world run by strong men of unquestioned authority" (1965:42). In a somewhat later expression of liberal concern in the same vein, Biller and Meredith's (1975) *Father Power*, a popular guide for fathering, includes material on black fathers only in a chapter titled "Fathers with Special Problems," of which the other examples are the physically handicapped and elderly father.

Decline: 1970–Present

Starting in the 1970s, the dominance of the male role identity paradigm in sex role research began to wane. I have recounted in detail elsewhere (Pleck 1981a, 1981b) the theoretical and empirical problems accumulated in its component lines of research. For example, it became apparent that research failed to support the bipolar conception of masculinity-femininity so essential to interpreting MF tests as measures of sex role identity (Edwards and Abbott 1973; Tyler 1968; Constantinople, 1973). Measures of sex typing did not have the relationships predicted with psychological adjustment and well-being (see especially Mussen 1962). Father absence did not prove to have the effects it was so widely believed to have on boys' sex typing, school performance, and delinquency (Herzog and Sudia 1971–73).

Male identity theory declined, however, not so much because of a detailed critique of its internal problems as because of new conceptual and research developments and new social attitudes about sex roles. One such research development was Money and Ehrhardt's (1972) distinction between "gender identity" (the individual's awareness of and satisfaction with being a male or female) and "gender role" (the extent to which individuals have the traits, attitudes, and interests culturally expected for their sex— i.e., what is measured by MF scales). They argued that once gender identity is established (as it is without difficulty for all but the tiniest minority), variations in gender role do not cause psychological problems.

A second research development was Bem's (1972, 1974, 1978) and Spence and Helmreich's (1974, 1978) studies of psychological androgyny. Actually, mainstream sex role identity researchers (Biller and Borstelman 1967; Biller 1968; Gonen and Lansky 1968) had somewhat earlier first proposed assessing masculinity and femininity as separate dimensions as a way of solving the problems that had become evident in sex role identity research concerning the relationship between sex typing and psychological adjustment. But Bem, Spence, and Helmreich used this new conceptualization to challenge in a more fundamental way the then-dominant prediction that traditional sex typing was necessary for good adjustment. This research legitimated individuals' having traits associated with the other sex.

At a broader social level, feminism challenged the traditional patterns of sex roles for which the theory of male identity provided ideological justification. Initially, though, feminists appropriated certain arguments from the theory that superficially appeared to support change in sex roles. For example, Betty Friedan (1963:265) argued that one of the negative consequences of excluding women from employment is that the full-time housewife is too powerful a mother in the lives of her sons and that her overprotectiveness is responsible for "the homosexuality that is spreading like a murky smog over the American scene." Early feminist psychoanalysis (Chodorow 1971, 1974) also wholly incorporated male identity arguments about men's fear and hatred of women as the result of the male child's identification with the mother. Another example is Farrell's (1974:116) recommendation for greater paternal participation in childrearing because it will reduce male homosexuality. More recent feminist works, however, use such arguments increasingly less frequently (e.g., Chodorow 1978).

Because of these developments in both research and social attitudes, the theory of male sex role identity is no longer a dominant paradigm in psychology. Rather, it is now an event in psychology's history. Consideration of this history will help contribute to new paradigms in the study of sex roles that are more relevant to the need of contemporary society.

References

Adler, A. 1927. *The Practice and Theory of Individual Psychology.* New York: Harcourt.

Adorno, T. W., E. Frenkel-Brunswick, D. J. Levinson, and R. N. Sanford. 1950. *The Authoritarian Personality*, part 1. New York: Wiley.

Bem, S. 1972. "Psychology Looks at Sex Roles: Where Have All the Androgynous People Gone?" Paper presented at UCLA Symposium on Sex Differences.

—— 1974. "The Measurement of Psychological Androgyny." *Journal of Clinical and Consulting Psychology* 42:155–62.

—— 1976. "Probing the Promise of Androgyny." In A. Kaplan and J. Bean, eds. *Beyond Sex Role Stereotypes: Toward a Psychology of Androgyny*. Boston: Little Brown.

Bernard, J. 1981. "The Good-Provider Role: Its Rise and Fall." *American Psychologist* 36:1–12.

Bezdek, W. and F. Strodtbeck. 1970. "Sex Role Identity and Pragmatic Action." *American Sociological Review* 35:491–502.

Biller, H. 1968. "A Multiaspect Investigation of Masculine Development in Kindergarten Age Boys." *Genetic Psychology Monographs* 78:89–138.

—— 1972. *Father, Child, and Sex Role*. Lexington, MA: Heath Lexington.

—— 1974. *Paternal Deprivation: Schools, Sexuality, and Society*. Reading, MA: Heath Lexington.

Biller, H. and L. Borstelmann. 1967. "Masculine Development: An Integrative Review." *Merrill-Palmer Quarterly* 13:253–94.

Biller, H. and D. Meredith. 1975. *Father Power*. New York: Doubleday.

Boehm, F. 1932. "The Femininity-Complex in Men." *International Journal of Psychoanalysis* 11:444–69.

Brown, D. 1956. "Sex-Role Preference in Young Children." *Psychological Monographs* 70(14), Whole No. 421.

—— 1958. "Sex-Role Development in a Changing Culture." *Psychological Bulletin* 55:232–42.

Burton, R. and J. Whiting. 1961. "The Absent Father and Cross-Sex Identity." *Merrill-Palmer Quarterly* 7:85–95.

Chodorow, N. 1971. "Being and Doing: A Cross-Cultural Examination of the Socialization of Males and Females." In V. Gornick and B. K. Moran, eds. *Woman in Sexist Society*. New York: Basic Books.

—— 1974. "Family Structure and Feminine Personality." In M. Z. Rosaldo and L. Lamphere, eds. *Woman, Culture, and Society*. Stanford: Stanford University Press.

—— 1978. *The Reproduction of Mothering: Psychoanalysis and the Sociology of Gender*. Berkeley: University of California Press.

Constantinople, A. 1973. "Masculinity-Femininity: An Exception to a Famous Dictum?" *Psychological Bulletin* 80:389–407.

Cottle, T. 1968. "Family Perceptions, Sex Role Identity, and the Prediction of School Performance." *Educational and Psychological Measurement* 28:861–86.

Cottle, T., C. N. Edwards, and J. H. Pleck. 1970. "The Relationship of Sex Identity and Social and Political Attitudes." *Journal of Personality* 38:435–52.

Dahlstrom, W. G., G. S. Welsh, and L. E. Dahlstrom. 1972. *An MMPI Handbook*, vol. 1: *Clinical Interpretation*. Minneapolis: University of Minnesota Press.

Demos, J. 1974. "The American Family in Past Time." *American Scholar* 43:422–46.

—— 1982. "The Changing Faces of Fatherhood: A New Exploration in Family History." In S. Cath, A. Gurwitt, and J. Ross, eds. *Father and Child: Development and Clinical Perspectives*. Boston: Little, Brown.

Dubbert, J. 1974. "Progressivism and the Masculinity Crisis." *Psychoanalytic Review* 61:433–55.

Edwards, A. and R. Abbott. 1973. "Measurement of Personality Traits: Theory and Technique." *Annual Review of Psychology* 24:241–78.

Ehrenberg, O. 1960. "Concepts of Masculinity: A Study of Discrepancies Between Men's Self-Concepts and Their Relationship To Mental Health" (doctoral dissertation, New York University). *Dissertation Abstracts International,* 21(5). (University Microfilms No. 60–3740.)

Ehrenreich, B. and D. English. 1979. *For Her Own Good: 150 Years of the Experts' Advice to Women.* New York: Anchor.

Farrell, W. 1974. *The Liberated Man.* New York: Random House.

Filene, P. 1975. *Him/Her/Self: Sex Roles in Modern America.* New York: Harcourt Brace.

Franck, R. and E. Rosen. 1948. "A Projective Test of Masculinity-Femininity." *Journal of Consulting Psychology* 13:247–56.

Friedan, B. 1963. *The Feminine Mystique.* New York: Norton.

Gonen, J. and L. Lanksy. 1968. "Masculinity, Femininity, and Masculinity-Femininity: A Phenomenological Study of the MF scale of the MMPI." *Psychological Reports* 23:183–94.

Gough, H. 1952. "Identifying Psychological Femininity." *Educational and Psychological Measurement* 12:427–39.

—— 1964. "An Interpreter's Syllabus for the CPI." In P. McReynolds, ed. *Advances in Psychological Assessment* (Vol. 1). Palo Alto: Science and Behavior Publications.

Grinker, R. and J. Spiegel. 1948. *Men Under Stress.* Philadelphia: Blakiston.

Guilford, J. and R. Guilford. 1936. "Personality Factors S, E, and M and Their Measurement." *Journal of Psychology* 2:109–27.

Hantover, J. 1978. "The Boy Scouts and the Validation of Masculinity." *Journal of Social Issues* 34(1):184–95.

Hartshorne, H. and M. May. 1928–1930. *Studies in the Nature of Character:* vol. 1, *Studies in Deceit;* vol. 2, *Studies in Self-Control;* vol. 3, *Studies in the Organization of Character.* New York: Macmillan.

Herzog, E. and C. Sudia. 1971. *Boys in Fatherless Families.* U.S. Government Printing Office. DHEW Publication No. (OCD), pp. 72–33.

—— 1973. "Children in Fatherless Families." In B. Caldwell and P. Ricciuti, eds. *Review of Child Development and Research,* Vol. 3, Chicago: University of Chicago Press.

Kagan, J. 1964. "Acquisition and Significance of Sex Typing and Sex-Role Identity." In M. L. Hoffman and L. W. Hoffman, eds. *Review of Child Development Research,* Vol. 1. New York: Russell Sage Foundation.

Langer, W. 1972. *The Mind of Adolf Hitler.* New York: Basic Books.

Lewin, M. 1980. Personal communication.

Lipsitt, P. and F. Strodtbeck. 1967. "Defensiveness in Decision-Making as a Function of Sex-Role Identification." *Journal of Personality and Social Psychology* 6:10–15.

Lynn, D. 1961. "Sex Differences in Identification Development." *Sociometry* 24:373–83.

—— 1969. *Parental and Sex Role Identification: A Theoretical Formulation.* Berkeley: McCutchan.

McClelland, D. and N. Watt. 1968. "Sex-Role Alienation in Schizophrenia." *Journal of Abnormal Psychology* 73:226–39.

Mead, M. 1935. *Sex and Temperament in Three Primitive Societies.* New York: Morrow.

Miller, D. and G. Swanson. 1960. *Inner Conflict and Defense.* New York: Holt.

Miller, W. 1958. "Lower-Class Culture as a Generating Milieu for Gang Delinquency." *Journal of Social Issues* 14:5–19.

Mills, C. W. 1956. *White Collar: The American Middle Classes.* New York: Oxford University Press.

Money, J. and A. Ehrhardt. 1972. *Man and Woman, Boy and Girl.* Baltimore: Johns Hopkins University Press.

Moynihan, D. 1967. "The Negro Family: The Case for National Action" (1965). In L. Rainwater and W. Yancey, eds. *The Moynihan Report and the Politics of Controversy.* Cambridge: MIT Press.

Munroe, R. L. and R. H. Munroe. 1971. "Male Pregnancy Symptoms and Cross-Sex Identity Symptoms." *Journal of Social Psychology* 84:11–25.

Munroe, R. L. and R. H. Munroe. 1973. "Psychological Interpretation of Male Initiation Rites: The Case of Male Pregnancy Symptoms." *Ethos* 1:490–98.

Munroe, R. L., R. H. Munroe, and J. W. M. Whiting. 1973. "The Couvade: A Psychological Analysis." *Ethos* 1:30–74.

Mussen, P. 1962. "Long-Term Consequents of Masculinity of Interests in Adolescence." *Journal of Consulting Psychology* 26:435–40.

O'Neill, W. L. 1967. *Divorce in the Progressive Era.* New Haven: Yale University Press.

Parsons, T. 1942. "Age and Sex in the Social Structure of the United States." *American Sociological Review* 7:604–16.

—— 1947. "Certain Primary Sources and Patterns of Aggression in the Social Structure of the Western World." *Psychiatry* 10:167–81.

Parsons, T. and R. F. Bales. 1955. *Family Socialization and Interaction Process.* Glencoe, Ill.: Free Press.

Pettigrew, T. 1964. *A Profile of the Negro American.* Princeton, NJ: Van Nostrand.

Pleck, E. H. and J. H. Pleck, eds. 1980. *The American Man.* Englewood Cliffs, N.J.: Prentice-Hall (Spectrum Books).

Pleck, J. 1981a. *The Myth of Masculinity.* Cambridge: MIT Press.

—— 1981b. "Prisoners of Manliness." *Psychology Today* pp. 69–83.

Rohrer, J. and M. Edmonson. 1960. *The Eighth Generation Grows Up.* New York: Harper.

Rotundo, E. A. 1982. "Manhood in America, 1770–1910." Ph.D. dissertation, Brandeis University.

Sanford, R. 1966. "Masculinity-Femininity in the Structure of Personality." In R. Sanford, *Self and Society.* New York: Atherton.

Silverman, I. J. and S. Dinitz. 1974. "Compulsive Masculinity and Delinquency." *Criminology* 11:499–515.

Spence, J. and R. Helmreich. 1978. *Masculinity and Femininity: Their Psychological Dimensions, Correlates, and Antecedents.* Austin: University of Texas Press.

Spence, J. T., R. Helmreich, and J. Stapp. 1974. "The Personal Attributes Questionnaire: A Measure of Sex Role Stereotypes and Masculinity-Femininity." *JSAS Catalog of Selected Documents in Psychology* 4:43.

Strecker, E. 1946. *Their Mothers' Sons.* Philadelphia: Lippincott.

Strodtbeck, F., W. Bezdek, and W. Goldhammer. 1970. "Male Sex Role and Response to a Community Problem." *Sociological Quarterly* 11:291–306.

Strodtbeck, F. and P. Creelan. 1968. "Interaction Linkage Between Family Size, Intelligence, and Sex-Role Identity." *Journal of Marriage and the Family* 30:301–7.

Strong, E. K. 1943. *Vocational Interests of Men and Women*. Stanford, Calif.: Stanford University Press.

Suggs, R. 1978. *Motherteacher: The Femininization of American Education*. Charlottesville: University of Virginia Press.

Terman, L. 1916. *Stanford-Binet Intelligence Scale*. Boston: Houghton Miflin.

Terman, L. and C. Miles. 1936. *Sex and Personality*. New York: McGraw-Hill.

Tyler, L. 1968. "Individual Differences: Sex Differences." In D. Sills, ed. *International Encyclopedia of the Social Sciences*. New York: Macmillan.

Whyte, W. H. 1956. *The Organization Man*. New York: Simon and Schuster.

10 Mother

Social Sculptor and Trustee of the Faith

SUSAN CONTRATTO

There was a young man loved a maid
Who taunted him, "Are you afraid,"
She asked, "to bring me today
Your mother's heart upon a tray?"

He went and slew his mother dead,
Tore from her breast her heart so red,
Then towards his lady love he raced,
But tripped and fell in all his haste.

As the heart rolled on the ground
It gave forth a plaintive sound.
And it spoke, in accents mild:
"Did you hurt yourself, my child?"
(J. Echergaray 1904, quoted in Bernard 1975)

This article[1] examines psychological statements, from just before 1900 through the present time, about what mothering can do and ought to be.[2] Clothing their views in the scien-

tific method, writers have produced an array of conflicting directives: they have enjoined mothers to encourage or to repress, to
educate themselves or to trust their instincts, to control their
emotions or to control their babies, to be affectionate but avoid
overprotection, to take time out from constant care but avoid partial deprivation, to provide friends but screen bad company, to
avoid neurotic repression but encourage development (at the right
time and in appropriate ways), to be psychologically healthy
themselves, and to avoid the historically determined models that
they might unconsciously adopt.

As I present the different psychological views, overarching
themes, as well as differences, will emerge. I also describe a post-
World War II shift that includes reaffirmation of woman's role as
the socioemotional nexus of the family. I argue that psychological
advice givers are apologists, that they have provided the "scientific reasons" for women's affective function in the family and, until recently, for man's lack of function.

The most important woman's chore since the early nineteenth century has been the nurturing of young children. Psychological writers specified that the mother needs to be the primary
caretaker. They argued that dire consequences would follow if she
relinquished this role, and they 'documented' the noxious effects
of mothers, even good mothers. They tried to persuade, threaten,
and induce guilt, precisely because large numbers of women were
not shaping their work life to accommodate full-time motherhood
after the Second World War (Degler 1980).[3]

I begin with the nineteenth century and then describe the
association between G. Stanley Hall and the members of the National Congress of Mothers. After briefly looking at the pre-1940
setting in America, I discuss the three major theoretical thrusts of
this era — behaviorism, psychoanalysis, and cognitive-developmental theory. I look at some major shifts in women's experience
after the 1940s and relate these to psychological writings about
mothering. In the final section of the paper I try to account for
why we cling to certain ideas about mothering with such tenacity.

The Nineteenth-century Setting

From the eighteenth to the nineteenth century advice givers (primarily clergy, some physicians, and a few prominent women)

shifted their audience from both parents to the mother. The vocation of domesticity gave women power and control in the home. "Motherhood was proposed as the central lever with which women could budge the world" (Cott 1977:84). The success of the government depended on stability and self-control among the citizens (1977:95). Women, who were felt to be particularly pious, pure, gentle, and devout, were as mothers "to stabilize society by generating and regenerating moral character" (1977:97). With the spread of female literacy in the nineteenth century, there was a publication explosion, instructing women on their responsibility in their separate sphere and, in particular, their duties as mother.

Nineteenth-century arguments for the extension of higher education to women were enmeshed in concern for her special role. Proponents asserted that women needed to be well educated to assume their responsibility in the family as the principal childrearer. Opponents, led by Victorian scientists, argued "that it was an inappropriate pursuit for young women because their brains and their ovaries could not develop simultaneously" (Jacoby 1977:63).

Further evidence that large numbers of women took their special role seriously was their wholehearted participation, from the first decades of the nineteenth century, in a variety of organizations that either attacked vice in society or provided additional instruction in domestic virtues for themselves and their peers. Women were active in abolitionist organizations, religious associations, maternal associations, temperance groups, and moral reform societies. They engaged in social housekeeping (Ryan 1979). In the 1830s and 1840s more than 400 chapters of the American Female Moral Reform Society grew up in New England and the Middle Atlantic States (1979:67). The 1890s brought a flurry of new foundings. Among them was the National Congress of Mothers in 1897. The relationship between psychology and mothers began when G. Stanley Hall, the founder of child study, addressed the National Congress of Mothers in 1897.

The Nineteenth-Century Child

Industrialization and urbanization brought mobility for young people (Ryan 1979). Concurrent with this movement of young people out of the family, the literature on childrearing gradually shifted from a Calvinist emphasis on the child's natural depravity and the parent's responsibility to break his or her will (often through harsh physical punishment) to a concern with encouraging the internalization of cherished values (Sunley 1955:151). This latter attitude assumed that the child was a social being, motivated to please, comply, and internalize. The ideas underpinning this viewpoint came from Jean Jacques Rousseau's *Emile* (1762), in which the Genevan philosopher argued that education needed to be fitted to the special nature of children (or at least of boys), that childhood was natural, and that nature was good. (See Badinter 1981 for Rousseau's position and its effect on motherhood in France.) The Swiss educator Johann Pestalozzi echoed similar ideas. The writings of both were well known in the United States (Degler 1980). The Romantic poets emphasized the unspoiled, good nature of the child. Wordsworth's "Intimations of Immortality" became a favorite mid-nineteenth-century reference point about the child. Both of these notions, the Calvinistic and the Rousseau-Romantic one, argued that the child was particularly malleable before the age of six and that therefore early "proper" training was most important.

The birth rate fell sharply in the nineteenth century (see Lewin article 3). Children were cherished more, not only because they were perceived differently, but also because there were fewer of them.

The National Congress of Mothers and G. Stanley Hall

Alice Josephine McLellan Birney (1858–1907) (James 1971) was the founder and first president of the National Congress of Mothers. She was born in Marietta, Georgia, to a close-knit family. As a young adult, she was active in the church, taught school briefly, and attended Mount Holyoke Seminary in Massachusetts for a year (1875). She married in 1879 and was left a widow with an infant daughter a year later. She returned to her parents' home, abandoning her hopes for a medical career. In 1892 she married Theodore Birney, a Washington lawyer, and had two more daughters. Taking her vocation as mother with deep seriousness, she studied the works of G. Stanley Hall, the psychologist; Fredrich

Froebel, the kindergarten innovator; and Herbert Spencer, the philosopher. She became concerned with how all mothers could be educated and "the *nation* made to recognize the supreme importance of the child." She enlisted the aid and financial support of Phoebe Apperson Hearst (1842–1919) (James 1971).

Mrs. Hearst had been an active supporter and financial backer of the kindergarten movement in San Francisco before her husband George was appointed U.S. Senator in 1886. In Washington, she continued her kindergarten interest, helping to found the Columbian Kindergarten Association in 1893 and a training school for kindergarten teachers in 1897.

In Phoebe Hearst, Alice Birney found a conscientious social mother, whose husband had made a fortune in mining, to underwrite financially the early years of the National Congress of Mothers. Progressivism, women's special role, and the education they had won to perform it well came together with some small crumbs from the bounty of laissez-faire economics. The founding meeting was held in Washington, D.C., on February 17, 1897, and was attended by 2,000 delegates and many members of the press.

The program of this first meeting of the National Congress of Mothers (*The Work and Words of* . . . 1897) was adorned with "appropriate and beautiful quotations." At the top of the program was written: "A baby: A tiny feather from the wing of love dropped in the sacred lap of Motherhood." The following epigram appeared after the notice of the reception at the White House given by Mrs. Grover Cleveland: "The destiny of nations lies far more in the hands of women—the mothers—than in the possessors of power." "Let the very playthings of your children have a bearing upon the life and work of the coming man; it is early training that makes the master" was written before the session addressed by G. Stanley Hall. And finally, toward the end of the program appeared: "Mother is the name of God in the heart and lips of little children"; "Do you realize that many habits and much of your baby's character is formed in the cradle"; and "Nothing, perhaps, has been more misunderstood than childhood."

True to the spirit of the age, this group of primarily middle-class women were intent on learning about this most important of all professions, mothering, and putting into practice their knowledge for the good of others. As Mrs. Theodore Birney put it in her opening address: "It has therefore seemed to us good and fitting that the highest and holiest of all missions — motherhood — the family institution upon which rests the entire superstructure of human life — and the element which may indeed be designated as the foundation of the entire social fabric, should now be the subject of our earnest and reverent consideration" (1897:6–7). Kindergartens, public education, playgrounds, and juvenile probation work were to be some of the means of effecting change. In psychology, and more particularly in the field of child study, founded in 1891 by Hall, they would find the knowledge they needed.

G. Stanley Hall was delighted to participate in this First Congress and to share with those present some of what he had learned through his observations (1897:165–71). His theory of development was based on evolutionary theory à la Herbert Spencer, which rested heavily on the notion of recapitulation, e.g., that the developing child passed through proper ancestral stages of development, it was hoped, without interference. Adolescence was a critical period, for it was during this time that the child passed from preconscious animality to conscious humanity. He enlisted mothers' help as observers and data collectors in child study. He warned of the harm that schools could do to children by having curricula that ignored the child's developmental stage. He urged mothers to influence academic curricula and to watch carefully for signs that schools were injuring their children.

Professor Elmer Gates, who addressed the gathering on "The Art of Rearing Children," also spoke from research and in the name of science. While he admitted that his findings had not yet been replicated by others, he was confident that they would be in the near future "and the mothers of the civilized world would be in possession of the data that will enable them to scientifically regulate the most sacred of all human functions by the light of biological and psychological science. All hail to that time!" (1897:242). Gates held to the Lamarckian view that acquired characteristics could be inherited. Further, he believed that a mother's 'evil' emotions caused secretions that would retard and distort cellular production in the sperm, egg, and later the fetus. He advised that "parents should for at least six months or a year before creating a child avoid all evil emotions and dirigate [sic] all good emotions" (1897:247) and that pregnant women should be particularly careful to avoid feeling these noxious emotions. The task was formidable but the goal was certainly worthwhile: "According to your skill in doing this will you convey to your child the best and the noblest of all legacies—a capable and moral mind" (1897:251).

Gates set an impossible but momentous task, vaguely defined. These dimensions apparently did not trouble the conferees. Another speaker, Mrs. Helen H. Gardener, made the merger of real and ideal the goal: "If she had the wisdom of the fabled Gods and the self-poise of the Milo, she would not be too well equipped for bearing and educating the race within her keeping" (1897:146). With knowledge, training and good intentions, these mothers believed they could attain the ideal.

The Congress also met in Washington in 1905 and again was addressed by Hall, as well as by Theodore Roosevelt and many others. Membership had grown. There were nine state organizations. The congress had been politically active, being concerned, for example, with unseating Reed Smoot, a Mormon elected to the U.S. Senate, whose tolerance of polygamy, they believed, would undermine the family (*Report* 1905:225).

In spite of organizational growth and activity, Mrs. Frederic Schoff reminded the membership in her presidential address that the problems were enormous and the work nowhere near completed. The vast numbers of foreigners who had no conception of American laws or government posed a particular challenge: "To educate these children whose parents are unAmerican to become good American citizens is of the greatest importance if we are to hold the country up to the standards set by its founders" (1905:69). The divorce rate and growth of reformatories were indicators that the home was being undermined. She called for more education for boys and girls about marriage, the home and, in particular, for child study and suggested that parents and teachers work together in associations to introduce these curricular revisions.

While Mrs. Schoff believed that knowledge applied in a systematic public way could lead to individual enlightenment, Roosevelt's address to the congress suggested that the problems were not lack of information but selfishness. President Roosevelt's enthusiastically received speech was a stirring celebration of the sexual division of labor. Man was the breadwinner—woman "the helpmate, the housewife, the mother" (1905:79); therefore their training should be different. He called on the women to reproduce and concluded," and so the most important, most honorable, and desirable task which can beset any woman is to be a good and wise mother, in a home marked by self-respect and mutual forbearance, by willingness to perform duty and by refusal to sink into self-indulgence or avoid that which entails effort and sacrifice" (1905:80–81).

Hall's (1905:14–27) ambivalence about women's role was apparent in his address to the meeting. He was concerned about what education did to women. Influenced by Galton and his theory of eugenics, he expressed alarm that some significant proportion of women who went to college remained single and thereby removed themselves from the gene pool. He further believed that higher education might actually be harmful: "The danger is that she will overwork, overdraw her resources, and take out of her system a little more than it can bear" (1905:19). Her child's adolescence was the critical period when this poor heritage emerged: "Children whose parents did not bequeathe them a great deal of vitality, and who do very well until they gradually begin to fall behind in the race and become sort of pessimistic—not quite right" (1905:26). His evidence was that one-fifth of the asylum population was adolescent.

The pieces fit together; self-indulgence leads to a woman's involving herself in higher education, which overtaxes her, which leads to later permanent problems, which manifest themselves in adolescence in her yet unborn children. The *time bomb effect*—what you do now, however seemingly unconnected from your child, might have serious permanent effects later on, and even though things seem normal ("children who do very well"), there is that fatal, maternally produced flaw that will dominate under the right conditions (age, particular stress, and so forth)—is a familiar and untestable expert assertion that comes up over and over again throughout the next eighty years.

The answer for woman was not in education but rather in their instincts: "The body and soul of womanhood, which is larger and more typical, more generic, as I said, than that of man, is nearer the child and shares more of its divinity than does the far more highly specialized and narrowed organism of the man" (Hall 1905:27). Hall, remembering his audience, was talking opaquely. Like many neo-Lamarckian recapitulation theorists of his time, he believed that women were lower on the evolutionary rung than men. He was associating that belief, here, with the more palatable romantic belief in the natural divinity of the child. In fact, however, his theory argued that the lower stages were animalistic, e.g., less divine. In a later paper, he was clear about his concern with maternal interference:

In general, nearly every act, sensation, feeling, will and thought of the young child tends to be paleopsychic just in proportion as the child is let alone or isolated from the influence of grown-ups, whose presence always tends to the elimination of these archaic elements, and in all cases makes havoc with them, over-repressing some that should have their brief fling (1909:262).

Hall hoped, I believe, that trusting her instincts would lead to species-appropriate mothering and, therefore, less harmful interference.

1900–1940: Social and Political Background

By the beginning of the twentieth century, women were in many occupations but predominantly filled lower level jobs and received lower pay than men. There were relatively few women in professions. Most women worked "temporarily" before marriage. In 1900, fewer than 4 percent of married women in intact families worked outside the home. By 1940, almost 15 percent of married women were in the labor force. Still, most worked from economic necessity, and they were disproportionately black.

Combining work and children was a problem for these women. Labor leader Alice Henry, writing from the perspective of 1915, acknowledged the dilemma but was optimistic that there would be a solution, particularly for the professional woman: "so many have solved the difficulties and have made the adjustment that it seems only a question of time when every professional woman may accept the happiness of wifehood and motherhood when it is offered to her without feeling that she has to choose once and for all between a happy marriage and a successful professional career" (Degler 1980:411).

The 1920s brought some new ideas. Smith College set up an Institute to Coordinate Women's Interests in 1925 that took as its mandate the investigation of innovative solutions to the home/career decision. Barnard College in 1932 adopted an official policy of six months paid maternity leave for women faculty and staff (Degler 1980:413). The Depression of the 1930's not only brought an end to these programs but also provided a reason for not hiring or for firing women whose husbands worked.

1900–1940: Psychological Writings

From 1900 until the present, three distinct lines of thinking—behaviorism, psychoanalytic theory, and cognitive-developmental theory—have affected childrearing. They ran side by side, sometimes one in vogue, sometimes another, but all available for maternal consumption. I present these points of view, trying to point out similarities and continuities, though the advice itself might be quite different and even contradictory.

All of the writers believed in and claimed to use the scientific method (though the 'method' varied with the practitioner). Without evidence they accepted the malleability of the child, critical periods for certain kinds of development, the continuity of development; and they took as a given the importance of the mother, either because she is present early on or because she is naturally more capable in childrearing, or both.

The congress speakers used phrases such as "responsible for civilization" and "carries the destiny of the human race" when talking of the power of mothers. Beginning in 1905 they began to talk of the disintegration of institutions—marriage, the family, and community. These two themes, that familiar reliable institutions are changing precipitously and that mothers are therefore even more important, recur. While the language changes, the task remains crucial. Good mothering prevents social disintegration by creating adults who are socially and democratically connected with each other.

Behaviorism and John B. Watson

Mrs. Max West, author of the first edition of *Infant Care*, the Children's Bureau perennial best seller, told parents that the first two years of life were of greater consequence than any other two years because the nerve impulses made pathways which "deepen" through repetition (1914:64). "Habits are the result of repeated action. A properly trained baby is not allowed to learn bad habits which must be unlearned later at great cost of time and patience to both mother and babe" (1914:59). Mrs. West advised parents on playing with the baby (not to), how to avoid bad habits such as crying without a cause ("a spoiled, fussy baby, and a household tyrant whose continual demands make a slave of the mother") (1914:60), pacifiers (destroy), masturbation (eradicate), as well as on how to establish a system for care in all areas.

John B. Watson was not as sanguine as Mrs. West about undoing bad habits: "once a child's character has been spoiled by bad handling which can be done in a few days, who can say that the damage is ever repaired" (1928:3) (See Harris, Ben, and J. G. Morowski, this volume).

In all areas Watson stressed regularity, consistency, and keeping to a schedule; toilet training and self-care in general should begin as early as possible. For example, he suggested a schedule whereby the baby was up at 6:30, had orange juice, was "put on the toilet for the relief of the bladder (only)," and at 8 A.M. was put on the toilet for "twenty minutes or less" (until the bowel movement was completed). By eight months the child should be strapped on the toilet and left alone with the door shut for this activity (1928:121). In short, Watson advised parents from the beginning to "Treat them as though they were young adults," with behavior that is objective, firm, kindly, and consistent.

He felt that mothers were the problem. Watson shared with Freud and Hall a deep ambivalence about women. For Watson, the rearing of a happy child was the most important of all human responsibilities. But the agent, alas, was a woman who he seriously doubted was capable of the task. His book was sarcastically "dedicated to the first mother who brings up a happy child" (1928:frontispiece).

His misogyny, like Hall's and Freud's, was theoretically rationalized. As a strict behaviorist, he had a social explanation; women were not born lesser, they were made so. He believed that women were more 'adolescent' than men because society had denied them the growth-producing experience of absorbing work (1919:417). They were left with child care, not because they were especially suited, but because they were physically weaker than men and the political construction of the economic system was such that men got better paying jobs. He stated that men were not less fond of children than women "but they [men] cannot nurse them nor are they willing to be bored by looking after their hourly needs and since they are stronger, they in general, have their way" (1919:382–83). To sum up Watson's message to mothers: the task is vital and precarious — its daily execution boring; if you follow my scientific advice you shall be successful — but you will probably fail.

Freud and Psychoanalysis

Watson and his followers confidently provided very specific instructions. A major problem in the application of psychoanalytic theories has been the lack of specific instructions, as well as the possibility of hidden meanings in any given maternal or child action. Stone and Church's comparison of *Infant Care* (1938) and *Infant Care* (1942) suggests a dramatic, pervasive, and orthogonal change from habit training to concern with satisfaction of needs (1957:67–68). However, psychoanalytic theories first entered the arena some years earlier.

Sigmund Freud was invited to Clark University by G. Stanley Hall in 1909. He gave five lectures, a general account of psychoanalysis, with lecture four focusing on the highly controversial topic of infantile sexuality. According to his biographer Ernest Jones, "Their initial reception was very mixed" (1955:57). Jones quotes a pronouncement from the Dean of the University of Toronto: "An ordinary reader would gather that Freud advocates free love, removal of all restraints, and a relapse into savagery" (1955:57). Jones tells us that Freud was originally enthusiastic about his relationship with Hall but that Hall's interests in psychoanalysis did not last and after several years he became a follower of Adler, "the news of which hurt Freud very much" (1955:58). However, Freud, like Hall, was a devoted Lamarckian and recapitulationist.

Freud's theory was a stage theory, with the critical periods (oral, anal, and phallic) taking place before the age of five and culminating in the oedipal period. He posited a biologically determined sequence of eroticized zones which sought gratification. The response of the caretaker to this pleasure-seeking did not alter the sequence but might lead to a fixation point which would manifest itself in adult personality structure. Out of the particularly charged triangular relationships of the oedipal period nec-

essary repressions took place that led to the formation of the superego, the foundation of the moral sense, the ego ideal (what
one aspired to be like), and the beginning of mature ego defenses
and coping abilities, as well as a sense of one's masculinity or
femininity and attraction to individuals of the opposite sex.

The key to this development was infantile sexuality; the sexual impulses seeking gratification operated normally in infants and
young children in the absence of outside stimulation. Freud saw
the first five years as particularly important because these strong
sexual impulses were impinging on a weak ego. The first educational task of the child, then, was to learn to control these impulses, but in doing so, there was the risk of neurotic illness. "Thus
education has to find its way through the Scylla of non-interfer-
ence and the Charybdis of frustration" (Freud 1933:149). Freud
suggested that those who had been analyzed themselves were best
equipped for this difficult job. "Parents who have themselves experienced an analysis and owe much to it . . . will treat their children with better understanding and spare them much of what they
themselves were not spared" (1933:149). Note the similarity with
Hall; Freud's concern with fixation and neurotic illness is parallel
to Hall's preoccupation with overrepressing archaic elements.

But, paradoxically, the agent for this very tricky task was
often an unanalyzed woman, who, though "normal," might be
particularly ill equipped for this job. Women were *inherently* masochistic, passive, and narcissistic, had less of a sense of justice,
and were less ready to take on hardships than men (Freud
1925:257). As Freud said in *Civilization and Its Discontents:*
"Women represent the interests of the family and the sexual life;
the work of civilization has become more and more men's business; it confronts them with ever harder tasks, compels them to
sublimations of instinct which women are not easily able to
achieve. . . . Woman finds herself thus forced into the background by the claims of culture and she adopts an inimical attitude towards it" (1930:50–51). Woman, then, who not only was
less developed in personality than man but also was naturally
hostile to cultural aims, was left with the job of producing accul-
turated children. Within this paradox rest the seeds for the more
overtly hostile theorists (discussed later) who followed within the
psychoanalytic tradition.

Elizabeth Lomax (1978) suggests several problems with the

application of psychoanalytic theory to childrearing. She argues that the popular childrearing literature ignored the idea that the child's constitution set limits on the meaning of experience and the manifestation of behavior. She provides numerous question-and-answer examples from *Parents* magazine in the 1930s that gave mothers the impression that if they did right by their children, all would be well.

Two major groups who appropriated psychoanalytic theory were the child guidance movement and the parent education movement. Maud Watson, a psychiatric social worker who was the director of the child guidance division of the Children's Fund of Michigan, traced the beginning of intensive history taking based on the belief that the child could be understood only in the light of his particular family background to Dr. William Healy of the Juvenile Court of Chicago in 1909 (1932:15). She quoted Dr. Healy as writing in 1927: "1. Nothing not even behavior happens without a cause, hence the newer psychology devoted to the study of the motivation of conduct, 2. No two persons are altogether alike, hence the psychology of individual differences, 3. No treatment should be undertaken without diagnosis. . . . Hence therapy based on science" (1932:15). Child guidance clinics, established first in 1921, existed for a while side by side with habit clinics, the former influenced by psychoanalytic thinking, the latter by behaviorism. Maud Watson's study itself, carried out in the late twenties, used the "ego-libido scientific"[4] method of history taking and is a classic early example of the "inevitable" transmission of psychopathology from a mother who was poorly mothered to her child, who in turn will be a poor mother.

In 1928, the year John B. Watson published his child care manual, the National Council of Parent Education held its biennial conference.

Council members had no doubt about the need for parent education: "The recognition that the tasks of modern parenthood can no longer be left to the so-called 'parental instinct' or to the 'innate' wisdom of those who find themselves responsible for children, or to the 'folk-lore' of previous generations, seems well-nigh universal" (1931b:1). Gone for the moment are Hall's "generic" mothers, trusting their instincts.

Gone, too, are straightforward directives that are within the power of an individual to perform. Lawrence Frank argued that important attributes of parenting cannot be taught didactically but are "incorporated in the personality through emotional and aesthetic experiences" (1931a:46). The preparation for parenthood was equivalent to preparation for "sane, wholesome" adult living. Ergo—psychologically healthy adult parents rear children who grow up to be psychologically healthy adult parents. Affection, reassurance, and an opportunity to play with same sex peers are some especially important components of a healthy childhood (1931a:46–48). Two empirical studies, one a 2,000-subject questionnaire survey of adolescents (Burgess 1931a) and the other a study of 100 families (Stutsman 1931a) lent the support of science to Frank's pronouncements. The Burgess study, for example, found that there was a "medium" degree of association between frequency of mother's kissing and good adjustment (adjustment being measured by a sum score of 25 yes/no questions such as: "Have you always liked the nicknames you have been given?" with "no" falling in the poor adjustment category).

Gesell and Cognitive-Developmental Theory

The work of Arnold Gesell, a 1906 graduate of Clark University, and his colleagues at the Yale Clinic of Child Development constituted a third theoretical thrust. Gesell adhered to Hall's organismic concept of growth, that the genetic equipment determined the sequential phases of development, modified or accentuated by environmental factors that were most important in the early years before permanent structures had evolved (Lomax 1978: 36–38).

If Watson convinced the reader that he was scientific by telling him so, Gesell did so by presenting a wealth of precisely documented data, the observations of "the products and processes of mental growth" (Gesell and Thompson 1934:8) in infants and young children. Arguing that those before him had concentrated too heavily on superimposed acculturation, Gesell's goal was to uncover and document "the generic pattern characteristic of the species" as well as to look at the individual's "unique pattern" as it unfolds within the larger sequence (Gesell and Ilg 1943:256). In his 1927 study of infants from four weeks to six years, he had a sample of 107 infants—58 girls, 49 boys—at fifteen age levels up to fifty-six weeks, who were carefully observed and photographed in the laboratory on a lunar month basis for a full half day (Gesell and Thompson 1934). Few researchers today can boast of Gesell's detail and thoroughness.

The task of the mother was to facilitate development through knowledge of the generic stages, and the provision of an appropriately stimulating, encouraging, and reassuring environment that would maximize potential at each stage. After their description of "typical" 3½-year-old behavior, Ilg and Ames described the responsibility—the "privilege"—of the adult:

If the adult in charge knows in advance that all this uncertainty, insecurity, inco-ordination quite normally mark the three and a half age period, it can help considerably. First of all, it can keep you from blaming various aspects of the environment for any or all of the different inco-ordinations. It can stimulate you to improve the environment. And it can help give you patience to show the child extra affection, the extra understanding which he so desperately needs at this age (1964:40).

Recurring words are "encourage," "promote," "have patience," "help to curb," "help to spread out"—the Gesell mother was to be a marvelously sensitive, warm, innovative, and well-prepared teacher who at the moment the child was ready to take the next growth step had primed the emotional and physical environment so that the chances of his being successful were greatest.

By the mid-1930s there were at least three rather distinct models for mothers. One was the behaviorist mother for whom the infant was a tabula rasa waiting to learn important social habits taught through scheduled, rational care; regularity was the means to happiness, and displays of affection the undoing of it. Second was the psychoanalytically oriented mother who, being (it was hoped) the product of affectionate, sane parents herself, would respond in a "mature" affectionate way to her own children. Third was the Gesell mother who, knowing what to expect at each stage, responded cheerfully and patiently by organizing her child's environment. The first mother made the child fit the schedule; the third made the environment and herself fit the child's changing schedule; while the second engaged in a complex, dimly understood exchange—promoting growth through repression without creating neurosis through repression. Mothers who chose any of the models could believe they were backed by science, that what they did was enormously important, and that inadequate performance might have immediate and long-term individual and social consequences.

The Social and Political Background After 1940

During and after World War I, married women's participation in the labor force increased dramatically. In 1940, 10 percent of mothers with at least one child under six worked outside the home. By 1975, the number was more than three times as many, 36.6 percent (Degler 1980:418), and by 1979 this figure had risen to 43.2 percent (Hacker 1980:40). Simultaneously, the postwar years witnessed a baby boom that reached its peak in 1960, began to taper off, and has been precipitously falling since 1970. In the 1940s and 1950s there was a mounting public and political concern about who was caring for these children as mothers left home to work (Degler 1980:441).

In 1963 Betty Freidan published *The Feminine Mystique,* and in 1966, using profits from the sale of the book, she founded the National Organization for Women. As numerous feminist organizations have sprung up, so have organized antifeminist movements (Degler 1980:446ff). The "moral majority" aimed to "save the family" and has introduced legislation, through Senator Paul Laxalt, that would encourage women to stay home.

After 1940: American and British Psychological Trends

In 1943 the American psychiatrist David Levy published *Maternal Overprotection* and clarified a new theme: normal mothering could be psychopathogenic. "Magnified" normal mothering led to psychopathology. Levy speculated that the maternal instinct was biologically based since it was required for survival (a throwback to evolutionary theory and a preview of sociobiology). He argued that women who were overprotective were "constitutionally maternal to a high degree" (Levy 1943:159).

He began, of course, with the assumption that the mother was the most potent influence on the child and that what happened early in that experience affected the child's entire life. His evidence was consensus: "This belief is fairly common to investigators in human psychology regardless of their generally conflicting viewpoints" (1943:4). He 'proved' his conclusions about the impact of maternal overprotection, which frequently masked aggression, by using twenty carefully selected case files from a child guidance center. Levy's research meets neither clinical nor quantitative standards.

Levy provides a good example of certain kinds of psychological thinking. Overprotecting mothers, for example, were either too present or too permissive; the pathological behavior of their children ranged from overcompliance to rebellion. Protection itself, keeping safe and preserving, could actually be hostile and injurious. Such notions—where anything could be anything—created great self-doubts among women and were used freely against them and against particular ethnic groups (Ehrenreich and English 1978:210–11).

Levy speculated that "the maternal overprotective attitude is a very common one, very likely universal" (1943:15). Maternal instincts, biologically based, lead mothers who may think they are doing the right thing to create psychopathology for their children—and this is very likely universal.

The German-American ego psychologist Erik Erikson discussed mothering and mother blaming in his 1950 book *Childhood and Society*. He speculated that historical shifts lay at the root of "Mom," the pathogenetic mother who appeared in "case history after case history." "This will be sufficient to indicate that 'mom' is a woman in whose life cycle remnants of infantility join advanced senility to crowd out the middle range of mature womanhood, which thus become self-absorbed and stagnant" (1963:291). Erikson codified and gave a psychiatric label to this hateful person. He becomes another theorist of the "normal" mothering is noxious mothering school.

Erikson recognized the growing problem with mother blaming in the literature. He described the tone of "revengeful triumph, as if a villain had been cornered" (1963:289) that many psychiatric writers used when talking of mothers. He then went on to blame mothers for this, too: "No doubt both patients and psychiatric workers were blamed too much when they were children; now they blame all mothers, because all causality has become linked with blame" (1963:289).

Erikson followed the individual through the life cycle with special emphasis on the first stage, in which there should be "the firm establishment of enduring patterns for the solution of the nuclear conflict of basic trust versus basic mistrust" (1963:249), and adolescence, where the task was identity versus role confusion. His work was based on "therapeutic research," generalizations from clinical "specimens" (1963:38).

This theory became the basis of a 1952 government publication, "A Healthy Personality for Your Child," by James L. Hymes. He told parents that at each "stage of his growing" a child has "one big hunger" (1952:3). Each hunger corresponded to one of Erikson's developmental stages; for example, trust versus mistrust was "That sure feeling—everything is o.k.!" (1952:4). Hymes was optimistic: "Sometimes dreams of cash or health or jobs crack up, and no one is to blame. . . . One dream you can surely help come true: **That your child shall have a healthy personality"** (1952:1, emphasis in original). Presumably, if your child did not end up with a healthy personality, you had yourself to blame.

Joseph Rheingold (1964), research associate at the Harvard Medical School, extended the parameters of noxious mothering still further. His book *The Fear of Being a Woman: A Theory of Maternal Destructiveness* arose from clinical work. He proposed that fear (the fundamental horror of being female) led to maternal destructiveness, which had a harmful influence on individual early ego development and which, in turn, had enormous social consequences. Looking at the state of the world (wars, man's inhumanity to man, the breakdown of the family, famine, and so forth), he concluded that there was an "overwhelming dominance or prepotency of the forces of destructiveness" (1964:688) — destructiveness whose roots were in "the primary pathogenic influence of maternal destructiveness" (1964:688). In Rheingold's view maternal destructiveness, while not normal, was the norm.

René Spitz, an analyst who worked on the supposed impact of mother-infant separation (Spitz 1945), sharpened his focus on specific psychopathology in the mid-1960s. Anna Freud remarked in the preface to his book that "Dr. Spitz goes further than most in ascribing specific psychotoxic disorders of the infant to specific emotional disorders of the mother." (1965:viii). Spitz proposed, for example, that a mother who oscillated between pampering and hostility would cause her infant to suffer from hypermotility (rhythmic rocking), whereas "partial emotional deprivation" would cause an anaclitic depression (1965:209).

Concurrent with the American "normal mothering is noxious" trend, British psychoanalysts were active in reasserting woman's primary responsibility in the family. First among these was John Bowlby. In 1948, when he was director of the child guidance department of the psychoanalytically oriented Tavistock Clinic, he was enlisted by the social commission of the United Nations to make a study of the needs of homeless children. The resulting document, *Maternal Care and Mental Health*, was enormously influential. It had numerous printings and was translated into twelve different languages.

Bowlby's confidence was great: "There is a high level of agreement among child-guidance workers in Europe and America" that "what is essential for mental health is that the infant and young child should experience a warm, intimate, and continuous relationship with the mother (or permanent mother substitute)" (1952:11). He was sure of his scientific data: "direct studies . . . make it plain" and "the retrospective and follow-up studies make it clear" and the "sombre conclusion [that some children are gravely damaged for life when deprived of maternal care] must now be regarded as established" (1952:15; see also 1969).

While it has been enormously important to challenge and change the treatment of institutionalized children, as he did, Bowlby's conclusions extended beyond this group to a general theory of the nature of the mother-child bond and the long-term and permanent consequences of any disruptions in this attachment. These judgments have been called into question by a number of scholars. (Clarke and Clarke 1979; Lomax 1978; Kagan, Kearsley, and Zelazo 1978; and Rutter 1979 all provide summaries of these debates.)

The monograph was a deeply conservative reassertion of the importance of full-time mothering in the "natural home group," the family. According to Bowlby the family was the only structure that could provide the environment necessary for maternal devotion, "constant attention day and night, seven days a week and 365 in the year" (1952:67). Maternal devotion prevented permanent retarded development, depression, antisocial behavior, and in some cases, death. While Bowlby was imprecise about what constituted the range of behaviors that might be harmful, he was clear that full-time (40 hours a week) maternal employment was destructive to infants; he lumped it together with war, famine, death of a parent, and imprisonment of a parent as one of the reasons why the "natural home group" fails to care. To put it slightly differently, full-time (8-hour) maternal employment was unnatural, whereas constant maternal devotion (24-hour) was natural. All mothers must have wondered if they were providing the "constant attention" their infants apparently required. This unbounded and impossible task is reminiscent of what the experts and mothers themselves believed was possible and desirable in 1897. *Childhood and Adolescence* illustrates the tightrope that mothers felt they were walking. When presenting Bowlby's findings the authors attempted to be reassuring. A baby whose mother had to leave him with a grandmother for a week or two was not thereby doomed: "Young babies are quite elastic and can tolerate a fair amount of *mishandling*" (Stone and Church 1957:66, added).

D. W. Winnicott, a psychoanalyst who was once president of the British Psycho-analytic Association, wrote for mothers and talked to them over the BBC in the 1950s. His theoretical biases were similar to John Bowlby's: "good enough mothering" could be provided by the "ordinary devoted mother" who is present full time if she was in a setting that allowed her instincts to take over. "The mother is able to fulfill this role if she feels secure; if she feels loved in her relation to the infant's father and to her family; and also feels accepted in the widening circles around the family which constitute society" (Winnicott 1958:3). And when, as is common enough, her husband, her family, and her society do not love and accept her, presumably the consequences are dire.

Are We Doing Any Better?—the 1970s

Elizabeth Lomax (1978) argues that the empirical method is self-corrective; psychologists are rejecting grand theories and are inquiring more deeply into specific problems. Findings become public only when well established. I am not as sanguine as Lomax.

Influential works that appeared in the 1970s reiterate the familiar themes: the critical importance of full-time 24-hour mothering, its biological naturalness, and how easy it is to do the wrong thing.

The work of Anna Freud and her colleagues (Goldstein, Freud, and Solnit 1973) and that of Selma Fraiberg (1977) in the psychoanalytical framework are both deeply conservative and policy directed. Goldstein, Freud, and Solnit believe in the primary parent—the mother. The attachment to her heavily outweighs, for the child, any other relationships, including specifically the relationship to the father. Their recommendations on custody considerations reflect this view: children should be with their first "object," the mother. She should have total control over the child's contact with the father or other relatives, including the right to forbid any contact with the father or other kin. Again, she is the 'natural' parent.

Fraiberg (1977) also predicted dire consequences for infants deprived of full-time 24-hour maternal care before the age of three; some would subsequently pass on their experiences of lack of love to their own children, while others, who were more seriously harmed, would become the fringe of society, vagrants, prostitutes, or underworld figures (1977:45–62). See also my discussion, Weisskopf 1980). Interestingly, Fraiberg used fictitious primitive tribes to illustrate how removed we had become from "natural, instinctive" motherhood. Earlier psychologists argued that Western nations were more civilized, higher up the evolutionary ladder, than tribal peoples. Hall used evolutionary theory to argue that we could think our way to good mothering, whereas Fraiberg, Winnicott, and Bowlby argued that the theory tells us to feel our way to good mothering.

In a provocative essay, William Arney (1980) takes on the bonding research, theory building, and policy making of the 1970s. He concludes that much of it is methodologically flawed, but it is socially and politically useful. (The bonding theory and research of the 1970s forced hospitals to restructure practices that previously had been written in stone.) His work casts doubt on Lomax's belief that we are going to small theory making.

Burton White's work is an example from the cognitive developmental area. White's 1975 book *The First Three Years of Life* is a report of his research on how many young children learn. It is also a manual of proper maternal behavior that will "ensure that [the] child will develop the full range of social and intellectual skills" (White 1975:xi, quoted in Clarke-Stewart 1978). The mother should attend to the child's cognitive development all day long, especially during the first three years, when competence is established for life. White is as specific and opinionated as John Watson was 50 years earlier: "I firmly believe that most children will get off to a better start in life when they spend the majority of their waking hours being cared for by their parents than they would in any form of substitute care . . . , It's [home is] where we learn our humanity. . . . Babies belong in mothers' arms. . . . People learn to think by the time of their third birthday" (Boston *Globe* 1981). It is not surprising that these quotes appear in a newspaper, for White is a popularizer of his opinions. He developed a television series, *The First Three Years,* from his book, and he is the director of the Center for Parent Education in Newton, Massachusetts.

Why We Cling to Certain Ideas About Mothering

In the context of the recent debate over media psychologists and the ethics of advice giving on television, radio, and newspapers, we should remember that professional advice giving has been with us since G. Stanley Hall. John Watson publicized his views through regular columns in *Harpers* and *Colliers;* Frances Ilg and Louise Ames, Gesell co-workers, had a syndicated advice column and a weekly television show in the 1950s; and at the same time, Bruno Bettleheim offered psychoanalytically oriented advice through the columns of the *Ladies Home Journal.*

Psychologists took over the cultural function of instruction about how to raise good citizens from the ministers of the nineteenth century. Just as ministers were not concerned about the ethics of their profession, neither, apparently, were the psychological advice givers. By the time psychologists took over, mother was the only relevant person. She was to be the social sculptor who could create the good citizens of the future. Hers was a powerful role. Many professionals attribute delinquency, drug abuse, school failure, schizophrenia, depression, neurosis, and virtually all antisocial manifestations to bad mothering—without any clear evidence that a particular maternal behavior or pattern of behaviors is causally linked to these outcomes. We continually scan for these links, though all we know for sure is that gross neglect and abuse, and not even that in every instance, contributes to psychological difficulties.

In addition to creating good citizens, Mother as social sculptor was to provide a safe haven from frightening social change. Since the 1905 conference, psychologists have felt that familiar institutions were crumbling. Rapid social change was neutrally or negatively presented in all but one instance. John B. Watson's "problem solving" child would "work equally well in most types of civilizations" that would arise from "the top to bottom" changes taking place (1928:186). Maud Watson wrote of "world wide economic insecurity" (1932:v) that had brought about a universal need for mental hygiene. Lawrence Frank is the exception, the one delighted by the passing of the old: "The older traditionally sanctioned patterns are crumbling and to anyone seriously concerned with the problem of sane, wholesome living, their passing cannot be deplored" (1931:51). Gesell warned that the culture might not survive (1943:9–14). The loss of familiar patterns of patrician and agrarian identities was, Erikson argued, the major reason that questions of identity had become a problem (1963:279–82). René Spitz argued that Protestantism undermined patriarchal authority and industrialization disturbed the mother-child relationship that "set the stage for rapid disintegration of the traditional form of the family." The consequences were juvenile delinquency and growing numbers of neuroses and psychoses (1965:299–300). Rheingold (1964), and Fraiberg (1977) presented equally apocalyptic visions.

Wars were particularly important. Maud Watson (1932:4–14) and Erikson (1963:288) both described the psychiatrists' shock at having to send home or reject hundreds of thousands of young men who were unfit for service. Their explicit belief was that mothers created sons unfit for war rather than the possible alternative, that wars were psychologically destructive to large numbers of normal individuals. For Rheingold (1964) maternal destructiveness led to wars. Mothers simultaneously caused the event (through their politician sons) and provided many ill-equipped fighter sons for it. Mothers, in this view, are very powerful people, indeed.

These authors share the prevalent cultural notions about women. Prominent among these is a (sometimes) obvious misogyny. Women are simply less able than men in important areas involving power, prestige, and money. Women's sole important role is a familial one—the companionate wife and nurturing mother. As women have rebelled against this role (a mother of small children who works outside the home is, and is perceived to be, in rebellion against strong cultural norms), psychological writers on mothering reacted both by putting her back in her place with a vengeance and by being angry and disparaging of her. Greater numbers of mothers refusing to do nothing but mothering caused a reaction that is a piece of the mammoth cultural backlash to save the imagined nineteenth-century family.

But misogyny is only a piece of the picture and too simple an explanation. If the arguments were simply antiwoman, they would not carry the ring of truth. Psychological ideas about mothers are deeply and emotionally held by psychologists, as well as fathers, mothers themselves, and children. Nancy Chodorow and I (1982) propose that there is a dominant and shared cultural fantasy that is reinforced by our own childrearing experience. The fantasy is of that of the all-powerful mother, open to negative and positive idealization. We argue that because there has been such a powerful role prescription over the last 180 years, because so many women have tried to follow this prescription (or have been conscious that they were deviating from the norm), and because children have been raised in a system with these expectations, "Psyche and culture merge here and reflexively create one another." Infancy and early childhood are times of powerful feelings; we attribute both the cause and solution of these feelings to mother. To give up idealizations of others and ourselves is a painful and difficult process. But we are culturally encouraged to maintain maternal idealizations; as grownup children they give us a cause for our problems and as mothers they give us a double-edged sense of power and control. Beginning in the mid-nineteenth century, we seem to have exchanged a cultural belief in God the Father for an ideology of the all-powerful mother.

For mother, the human being, having such a fantasy as the

norm creates stress, anxiety, and guilt. There is evidence (Bernard 1975:69–89) that being the mother of young children produces increases in tension, violence, loneliness, and general inadequacy in women. The exclusivity and isolation of the mother-child dyad creates problems for both the child and the adult. Daily exchanges are frequently physically and emotionally exhausting in our 'ideal' mothering arrangement, made more so because the mother has been advised that her moves are so important and that the consequences may not be immediately apparent: the time bomb effect. Screaming at a three-year-old child today may cause a separation problem when kindergarten starts or a bad marriage in twenty years. Many mothers daily and anxiously assess their own and their child's behavior for indices of problems. In the absence of obvious problems, they remain anxious because they do not know how the child will 'turn out.'

A second consideration is the bind in which this places men. When good mothering is based on biological explanations that are sex specific, men are excluded from participation. For some men, excused father absence may be a welcome relief. It leaves many others feeling awkward, bumbling, and scared; they become the Dagwood Bumsteads of the nursery.

The child growing up with these idealized beliefs, and culturally encouraged to retain them, remains a potential mother blamer. Things go wrong in life. We frequently misattribute the original source as bad mothering. Psychiatric patients blame mothers, clinicians blame mothers, mothers vow not to be like their own mothers, and fathers cringe at resemblances between their wives' mothering and their mothers' mothering.

There is an additional explanation. Married women, the mothers of small children, moving into the paid labor force in great numbers, have confronted psychologists with a deeply ominous prospect—a world without mothers as they knew them (and as they believed they had to be). Science requires us to give up obviously irrational beliefs. What is apparent in the tenacious power of the ideology of Mother is that many people gave up one set of beliefs (in God the Father) for an equally irrational but deeply felt set of beliefs about the Mother. The assertion of the Mother's power and importance in the family is perhaps indicative of the existential panic we feel at not being able to have faith in anything.

Notes

1. The constructive response of The Family and Sex Roles Project at the Institute for Social Research and the Feminist Methodology Seminar, Ann Arbor, to an earlier version of this paper was enormously helpful. I am grateful for Miriam Lewin's detailed and incisive comments on a previous draft. In the early stages of this paper, I received support from NIMH training grant 5T32-MH14618.

2. In view of restrictions on space I am forced to omit many important works, including, unfortunately, many Freudians and neo-Freudians.

3. Degler (1980) proposes a functional view of the emergence of the modern family that I question and ignores recent criticism and questioning about family studies (see, for example, Breines, Cerullo, and Stacey 1978; Collier, Rosaldo, and Yanagisako 1982; and Thorne 1982). Further he accepts without question the contention that full-time early mothering is essential.

4. The "ego-libido scientific method" is a good example of the appropriation of psychoanalytic vocabulary common in the 1920s and 1930s. It was a system of history taking devised in 1924 by Marion Kenworth, M.D., a psychiatrist, who was director of the mental hygiene department, State of New York. According to this method, there are two broad trends (instincts) in a person, the ego "instincts of protection domination and self-maximizing" and the libido instinct, love values extending to friends, family, and "in the highest sense," a mate. Each experience has a plus or minus value according to whether it fulfills, or not, these trends. Looking at the pattern of pluses and minuses "brings understanding and objectivity to history taking" (Watson 1932:20–21).

References

Arney, William Ray. 1980. "Maternal-Infant Bonding: The Politics of Falling in Love With Your Child." *Feminist Studies* (Fall) 6(3): 547–70.

Badinter, Elizabeth. 1981. *Mother Love, Myth and Reality.* New York: MacMillan.

Bernard, Jessie. 1975. *The Future of Motherhood.* New York: Penguin Books.

Birney, Mrs. Theodore. 1897. "Address of Welcome." In *New Work and Words* (1897) *q.v.*, pp. 6–9.

Bowlby, John. 1952. *Maternal Care and Mental Health.* Geneva: World Health Organization.

—— 1969. *Attachment.* New York: Basic Books.

Breines, Wini, Margaret Cerullo, and Judith Stacey. 1978. "Social Biology, Family Studies, and Antifeminist Backlash." *Feminist Studies* (Spring) 4(1):43–67.

Burgess, Ernest W. 1931a. "Family Relationships and Personality Adjustment." In National Council of Parent Education (1912a), *q.v.*, pp. 21–43.

Chodorow, Nancy and Susan Contratto. 1982. "The Fantasy of the Perfect Mother." In Thorne, *q.v.*, pp. 54–75.

Clarke, Ann M. and A. D. B. Clarke. 1979. *Early Experience: Myth and Evidence.* New York: Free Press.

Clarke-Stewart, K. Alison. 1978. "Popular Primers for Parents." *American Psychologist* (April) 33(4):359–369.

Collier, Jane, Michelle Rosaldo, and Sylvia Yanagisako. 1982. "Is There a Family? New Anthropological Views." In Thorne, *q.v.*, pp. 25–39.

Cott, Nancy F. 1977. *The Bonds of Womanhood.* New Haven, Conn.: Yale University Press.

Degler, Carl. 1980. *At Odds: Women and the Family in America From the Revolution to the Present.* New York: Oxford University Press.

Ehrenriech, Barbara and Deirdre English. 1978. *For Her Own Good.* Garden City, N.Y.: Anchor.

Erikson, Erik H. 1950/1963. *Childhood and Society.* New York: Norton.

Fraiberg, Selma. 1977. *Every Child's Birthright: In Defense of Mothering.* New York: Basic Books.

Frank, Lawrence K. 1931a. "Some Aspects of Education for Home and Family Life." In National Council of Parent Education (1931a) *q.v.*, pp. 45–46.

Freud, Sigmund. 1925. "Some Physical Consequences of the Anatomical Distinction Between the Sexes." in James Strachey, ed. *The Standard Edition of the Complete Psychological Works of Sigmund Freud,* 21:248–58. London: Hogarth.

—— 1930. *Civilization and Its Discontents.* Translated by James Strachey. New York: Norton, 1961.

—— 1933. "Explanations, Applications and Orientations." In James Strachey, ed. *New Introductory Lectures on Psychoanalysis,* pp. 136–57. New York: Norton, 1964.

Gardener, Mrs. Helen H. 1897. "The Moral Responsibility of Women in Heredity." In *The Work and Words* (1897) *q.v.*, pp. 130–47.

Gates, Elmer. 1897. "The Art of Rearing Children." In *The Work and Words* (1897) *q.v.*, pp. 242–51.

Gesell, Arnold and Frances L. Ilg. 1943. *Infant and Child in the Culture of Today.* New York: Harper.

Gesell, Arnold and Helen Thompson. 1934. *Infant Behavior: Its Genesis and Growth.* New York: McGraw-Hill.

Goldstein, Joseph, Anna Freud, and Albert J. Solnit. 1973. *Beyond The Best Interests of the Child.* New York: Free Press.

Hacker, Andrew. 1982. "Farewell to the Family: Ten Recent Books." *New York Review of Books* (March 18) 29(4):37–44.

Hall, G. Stanley. 1897. "Some Practical Results of Child Study." In *The Work and Words* (1897) *q.v.*, pp. 165–71.

—— 1905. "New Ideals of Motherhood Suggested by Child Study." in *Report of the National Congress of Mothers, q.v.*, pp. 14–27.

—— 1909. "Evolution and Psychology." American Association for the Advancement of Science. *Fifty Years of Darwinism.* New York: Holt, pp. 251–61.

Hymes, James L., Jr. 1952. "A Healthy Personality for Your Child." Children's Bureau Publication, No. 337. Washington D.C.: U.S. Government Printing Office.

Ilg, Frances L. and Louise Bates Ames. 1964. *Child Behavior.* New York: Publishing, 1951.

Jacoby, Robin Miller. 1977. "Science and Sex Roles in the Victorian Era." In The Ann Arbor Science for the People Collective, eds. *Biology as a Social Weapon,* pp. 58–68. Minneapolis: Burgess.

James, Edward T, ed. 1971. *Notable American Woman 1607–1950.* Cambridge, Mass.: Harvard University Press.

Jones, Ernest. 1955. *The Life and Work of Sigmund Freud,* Vol. 2. New York: Basic Books.

Kagan, Jerome, Richard B. Kearsley, and Phillip R. Zelazo. 1978. *Infancy: Its Place in Human Development.* Cambridge, Mass.: Harvard University Press.

Levy, David M. 1943. *Maternal Overprotection.* New York: Columbia University Press.

Lomax, Elizabeth M. R. 1978. *Science and Patterns of Child Care.* San Francisco: W. H. Freeman.

National Council of Parent Education. 1931a. *Papers on Parent Education Presented at the Biennial Conference of the National Council of Parent Education,* Nov. 1930, Washington, D.C., New York.

—— 1931b. *Problems for Parent Educators, Vol. 2 Queries Based Upon Papers Presented at the Biennial Conference of the National Council of Parent Education,* Nov. 1930, Washington, D.C., New York.

Report of the National Congress of Mothers. 1905. Washington, D.C.

Rheingold, Joseph. 1964. *The Fear of Being a Woman: A Theory of Maternal Destructiveness.* New York: Grune & Stratton.

Rutter, Michael. 1979. "Maternal Deprivation, 1972–1978: New Findings, New Concepts, New Approaches." *Child Development* 50:283–305.

Ryan, Mary P. 1979. "The Power of Women's Networks: A Case Study of Female Moral Reform in Antebellum America." *Feminist Studies* (Spring) 5(1):66–85.

Schoff, Mrs. Frederic. 1905. "The Children of the Nation." In *Report of the National Congress of Mothers* (1905) *q.v.,* pp. 67–76.

—— 1905. "President's Report: February 24, 1902–March 10, 1905." In *Report of the National Congress of Mothers, q.v.,* pp. 224–29.

Spitz, René A. 1945. "Hospitalism." *Psychoanalytic Study of the Child* 1:53–74.

—— 1965. *The First Year of Life.* New York: International Universities Press.

Stone, L. Joseph and Joseph Church. 1957. *Childhood and Adolescence.* New York: Random House.

Stutsman, Rachel. 1931a. "Report of a Study of Home Atmosphere." In National Council of Parent Education (1931a) *q.v.,* pp. 5–19.

Sunley, Robert. 1955. "Early Nineteenth Century American Literature on Child Rearing." in Margaret Mead and Martha Wolfenstein, ed. *Childhood in Contemporary Cultures,* pp. 150–67. Chicago: University of Chicago Press.

The Work and Words of the National Congress of Women. 1897. New York: Appleton.

Thorne, Barrie. 1982. "Feminist Rethinking of the Family: An Overview." In Thorne, ed., *Rethinking the Family,* pp. 1–24. New York: Longmans.

Watson, John B. 1919. *Psychology From the Standpoint of a Behaviorist.* Philadephia and London: Lippincott.

—— 1928. *Psychological Care of Infant and Child.* New York: Norton. Reprint edition 1972, Arno Press.

Watson, Maud E. 1932. *Children and Their Parents.* New York: F. S. Crofts.

Weisskopf, Susan Contratto. 1980. "Substitute Childcare: Its Impact on Mothers and Children." *Harvard Educational Review (February) 50(1):92–97.*

West, Mrs. Max. 1914. *Infant Care.* U.S. Department of Labor, Children's Bureau, No. 8. Washington: U.S. Government Printing Office.

White, Burton L. 1975. *The First Three Years of Life.* Englewood Cliffs, N.J.: Prentice-Hall.

—— 1981. "Interview." Boston *Globe,* Saturday, Jan. 3.

Winnicott, D. W. 1958. "The First Year of Life: Modern Views on the Emotional Development." In Winnicott, ed. *The Family and Individual Development*, pp. 3–14. New York: Basic Books.

11 "To Pet, Coddle, and 'Do For'"

Caretaking and the Concept of Maternal Instinct

STEPHANIE A. SHIELDS

The quality of parenting has become a popular research topic within recent years. Fathering, responsiveness to the young, and other previously uninvestigated issues are now recognized as important variables in the study of caretaking (see, for example, Pleck, this volume; Parke 1979; Lynn 1974). The study of human caretaking behavior is, nevertheless, still in a formative stage. Many researchers, questioning the effectiveness of previous research strategies, have been making efforts toward developing new theoretical models that will more accurately reflect the complexity of parenting (e.g., Bell and Harper 1977, Bandura 1978, Baumrind 1980). New models must include some way of portraying the dynamic qualities of the infant's first relationship, but so far this research has had relatively little success. The task is difficult and far from complete.

What can account for the difficulty in creating models that capture the transactive nature of the parent–infant relationship?

Under any circumstances social scientists have difficulty in describing, defining, and empirically testing predictions about systems that have process rather than product as their central feature. In the case of human caretaking behavior, however, the development of adequate explanatory models has been further impeded by the cultural ideology surrounding motherhood that is expressed as the persistent, though often covert, belief in the existence of a distinct and special maternal instinct. Historically, the concept of human maternal instinct was a direct outgrowth of cultural conceptions of ideal female nature. The concept of maternal instinct has survived to influence scientific definitions of parental behavior, both as it is and as it ought to be. Even during the heyday of behaviorism, social science was visibly influenced by the belief that positive maternal behavior was a normal component of the female's innate behavioral repertoire and that deficiencies in caretaking were symptomatic of pathology rather than of unsuccessful learning.

This chapter reviews the history of the concept of maternal instinct and the effect it has had on the study of human caretaking behavior. The question of whether such an instinct or disposition actually exists is not of concern here; rather, the consequences of believing in its existence are examined. The chapter focuses on the scientific development of the concept during the latter half of the nineteenth century and the social and scientific implications of accepting the concept.

Within comparative psychology today there is no one acceptable formulation of the constituents of instinctive behavior. Dewsbury (1978:170), in summarizing the most widely accepted criteria of instinct, defines as instinctive those behavioral patterns "that appear essentially complete on first occurrence and that appear not to require specific learning for the development of their specific stimulus orientation or motor patterning." Dewsbury also cautions us to remember that the environment influences the ontogeny of all behavior. Even behaviors that meet the strict criteria for instinct exhibit great diversity and complexity in their expression. Some are more or less susceptible to disruption by early rearing experience, others to the configuration of the stimulus for the behavior, and so on. Such rigorous definition of instinct has not characterized application of the concept to human maternal behavior. Even in contemporary research literature it is not unusual to find assertions that mothering behavior and interest in infants is biologically programmed in the human female (e.g., Rossi 1977, Harlow 1971).

Throughout its history, the question of maternal instinct has ultimately been reducible to a question of gender difference. Do the sexes differ in their propensity to nurture younger and helpless beings? Propensity to nurture has been defined in two ways. The first pertains to the quality of the nurturing behavhior, specifically: are females more likely than males to render quicker and/or more effective responses to the young? The second pertains to the affective properties of caretaking behavior: is it more emotionally satisfying to females to behave nurturantly? That is, is it a unique property of female nature to find it pleasurable to "pet, coddle, and 'do for' others" (Thorndike 1914:293)? Although adequacy of response is separable from the affect associated with making a response, in the history of maternal instinct the two are treated as causally linked.

Even before the mid-nineteenth century, a scientific explanation of maternal instinct had been fairly well sketched out (Shields 1975a). Briefly, female physiology (brain size or composition, or reproductive organs, or "nervous constitution") was responsible for women's ability to exercise rational thought to the same degree as men. The lower mental processes (perception and emotion) were more prominent in women and, compared with men, apparently more highly developed. Perceptiveness made women sensitive to others' needs and caused them to focus on the immediate, concrete situation rather than on abstract ideas. Their emotional lability directed women to focus on the immediate and feeling-oriented. Female perceptiveness, focus on the immediate, and emotionality interacted to produce a predisposition in the female to be disgusted and repulsed by the ugly and brutal and attracted to the small and helpless. This tendency was considered a major constituent of women's gentility and strong moral sense. (An understanding of justice was believed beyond the reach of most women, however. A sense of justice, more cognitively than affectively based, would necessarily be a male attribute.) More important, the tendency was believed to prove the existence of distinct, innate, universal maternal sentiments. The concept of maternal instinct is an ideal example of the intellectual products of the scientific model of the biology of the time (Haraway 1982).

Furthermore, it epitomizes the world view and gender schema of the upper middle class nineteenth-century scientist. Throughout its history maternal instinct has served as both an adjunct to and an expression of male scholars' ambivalence about female sexuality.

A Historical Overview

The intellectual antecedents of the concept of instinct can be traced back to the first ancient considerations of a comparison between human beings and animals (Diamond 1974). The prescientific controversy over instinct did not, like contemporary disputes, focus on defining instinct. Prescientific models construed instinct as a set of complex, unlearned, adaptive behavioral patterns directed toward some goal. The mechanism accounting for instinct's operation was typically thought to be supernatural: as Dewsbury (1978:156) notes, "The hand of God was often invoked." Instead of definition, debate concerned the compatibility of innate, unreasoning behavior with human rationality and spirituality. Instinct was brutish and to allow the possibility of human instinct was to acknowledge the human being's animal constitution (Beach 1955, Diamond 1974).

Charles Darwin is credited with translating the instinct concept from philosophical-religious explanation to natural history construct. Others who followed Darwin (e.g., Herbert Spencer, George Romanes, C. Lloyd Morgan, and William McDougall) fell between the natural history approach of Darwin and the older telelological view. It was this group of scientists who most directly affected the social sciences' views on human maternal behavior and its unlearned biological bases. Darwin described the affective quality of instincts as occupying a continuum: anchoring one end were those instincts similar in expression and operation in animals and in human beings, and at the other end were those sentiments more complex and uniquely human. In *The Descent of Man* (1872), he distinguished "complex emotions," such as jealousy and love, from "simple emotions," which could be observed from the simplest organisms up to human beings. Darwin judged mother love clearly to be among the simple emotions. In discussing mother love's manifestation across species, Darwin (1872:70) concurred with the opinion of another scientist: "who that reads the touching instances of maternal affection, related so often of the women of all nations, and of the females of all animals, can doubt that the principle of action is the same in the two cases?" Darwin's emphasis on the emotional basis of instinct is echoed in later theories.

The premier Social Darwinist, Herbert Spencer, used maternal instinct to explain a whole set of female traits. Woman's reproductive physiology caused her intellect to focus on "the concrete and proximate rather than on the abstract and remote"; hence she was more responsive to "infantile helplessness" than to important social matters. She was, in short, the perfect instrument for nurturing the young. In contrast, the objectivity and reason of the male broadened his horizons as protector. Men were more inclined to extend their concern "to all the relatively weak who are dependent upon him" (1891:375), including the female, whose attention was wholly focused on the young. Spencer's attempt to describe the biological basis of relationships among women, men, and children is remarkably congruent with the ideal family of the late nineteenth century.

The scientific legitimization of maternal instinct in the nineteenth century is linked to Victorian concern for controlling female sexuality. Public discussion of sexual matters was couched in florid euphemisms, and sexuality was deemed a hygienic danger. Social concerns regarding female sexuality in particular were apparent in a number of social institutions (e.g., Cott 1979). Restrictions most often appeared in the guise of measures to protect the female's delicate moral sensibilities. For example, the maintenance of proper moral standards dictated that physicians only rarely examine female patients, that delivery be accomplished in darkened rooms with the mother fully draped to protect her modesty, and so on (Dye 1980). Concessions to female delicacy occasionally worked to women's benefit: female moral superiority gave women the right to refuse sexual intercourse in marriage (Lewin, "The Victorians . . .", article 3). An added impetus to preserve the image of female asexuality came from evolutionary theory itself. Sexual selection, which was construed as a driving force of evolution, is not a concept immediately compatible with the image of female passivity. Female sexuality was neutralized by emphasizing the female's maternal role over her conjugal role. Several scholars have also suggested that the idealization of up-

Several scholars have also suggested that the idealization of upper class womanhood in the latter part of the nineteenth century was also a reaction to the increased participation of women in worklife and other activities outside the home (Kerber 1974, Lerner 1979). The reality of mid-nineteenth-century women's life bore little resemblance to the sheltered and comfortable ideal portrayed in scientific publications and popular tracts. The ideal, the chaste angel of the household, if she existed at all, was to be found only in the upper claases (Rapp 1978).

Darwin considered the development of instinct to be governed by the same processes as the evolution of other behaviors, namely, a combination of natural selection and inheritance of acquired characters. George Romanes (1894) adopted this view and applied it to his assessment of mental evolution. Through the publication of Romanes' work the distinction between primary and secondary instincts became an accepted scientific principle. Primary instincts were those "which arise by way of natural selection, without the intervention of intelligence," secondary, those "which are formed by the lapsing of intelligence" (Romanes 1894:178). As would be expected, Romanes classified maternal tendencies with the nonrational primary instincts. In fact, all prebehavioristic theorists who distinguished between primary and secondary instinctive behaviors considered maternal instinct primary. In addition, the instinctive response was assumed to generalize beyond one's own offspring and not to be contingent upon biological motherhood. Many theorists, such as Hobhouse (1926), viewed maternal behavior as a specific form of the general innate emotional tendency of females.

The major proponent of human instincts in the first quarter of this century was William McDougall (1923), who viewed instinct as a disposition consisting of an innate readiness to perceive specific stimuli in specific ways. The readiness to perceive had a strong emotional component that was the major connection between the instinctive actions of animals and the emotional experience of human beings. Emotional energy was the essential feature of instinct, and therefore the identification of primary emotions could be used as a guide for distinguishing among the instincts (McCurdy 1968). In his view (McDougall 1913:68), parental instinct was one of the primary emotions, and the maternal instinct, "which impels the mother to protect and cherish her young, is common to almost all the higher species of animals." McDougall made very explicit the difference between "tender emotion" and "pairing." The former was "the root of all altruism" (1913:66), while the latter consisted merely of sexual attraction, "sometimes called love— an unfortunate and confusing usage" (1923:234). The two instincts operated jointly in producing heterosexual love. In the female, the pairing instinct "has specially intimate innate relations to the instincts of self-display and self-abasement so that the presence of the male excites these" (1913:83). For his part, the male's parental instinct is elicited at the sight of the coy and helpless female and moderates the more overpowering sexual impulses.

A certain physical weakness and delicacy (probably moral also) about the normal young woman or girl constitute in her a resemblance to a child. This resemblance . . . throws the man habitually into the protective attitude, evokes the impulse and emotion of the parental instinct. He feels that he wants to protect and shield and help her in every way (1923:425).

All of the proponents of human instinct included parental, or more frequently, maternal, instinct as one of the most powerful of innate behavioral tendencies. There was disagreement, however, regarding its relationship to other instincts. James (1890) proposed that a very heterogeneous group of behavioral tendencies comprised human instinct. These ranged from highly specific behaviors, such as sucking, to general modes of behavior, such as those prompted by curiosity and play. Parental love was, of course, included in his list of instincts, and he emphasized the special strength with which it is exhibited in women. Sutherland (1898) and Ribot (1897), like McDougall and James, considered maternal instinct primary, although both viewed it as a consequence of the general instinctual disposition toward sympathy and pity, rather than as ontogenetically independent of it. Shand (1920) equated parental instinct with maternal instinct, defining them as a system of instincts "inter-organised for the preservation of the offspring" (1920:40). Shand considered the maternal response as emotionally more complex than his contemporaries did, asserting that it included negative feelings such as anger and sorrow, as well as more positive tendencies. Nevertheless, this complex affective system was put in motion by the sight of the helpless offspring.

. . . mother's love becomes active with the first perception of her offspring and in the human mother often before birth, because there is an innate connection between it and the appropriate stimulus. And it seems to be partly for this reason that this most complex system is spoken of as an instinct, because it both instinctively responds to its stimulus and instinctively pursues its disinterested end (1920:42).

Sutherland (1898), too, emphasized the value of parental instinct for species survival. In his view, the parental instinct was the most rudimentary form of all other affects, ultimately serving as the basis for all moral feeling. The emotion that underlay parental behavior and mutual respect between the sexes, most especially as a "sympathetic regard for women's weakness" (p. 9), was not a function of sexual drive. In fact, Sutherland reported that sex, and its associated jealousies and strife, appeared to be waning in its capacity to motivate behavior. Men were becoming more chaste in their thoughts and deeds, indicating that "the sensuous side of man's nature is slowly passing under the control of sympathetic sentiments" and, as for women, "there is ample reason to believe that educated women now largely enter upon marriage out of purely sympathetic attractions" and "sexual desire enters not at all into the minds of a very large proportion of women when contemplating matrimony" (p. 288).

The male's paternal instinct was only infrequently considered, and then it was most often viewed as an expression of a general instinctive response to protect the helpless. The added element here, according to Hobhouse (1926) and others (e.g., Bain 1859, Ribot 1897), was the father's sense that the child was his own offspring. Men's protective tendencies could thus be partially accounted for by pride of ownership. Scientific belief about the difference between paternal and maternal instinct was consistent with beliefs about gender differences in general. That is, any given female trait was considered less advanced than the corresponding male trait but complementary to it nevertheless.

There is nowhere, perhaps, a more beautiful instance of complementary adjustment between the Male and the Female character, than that which consists in the predominance of the Intellect and Will, which is required to make a man successful in the 'battle of life,' and of the lively Sensibility, the quick Sympathy, the unselfish Kindliness, which give to woman the power of making the happiness of the home, and of promoting the purest pleasures of social existence (Carpenter 1894:417)

Expression of the paternal instinct in males was not confined to offspring but was extended to the helpless in general. Paternal instinct was most often manifested as a chivalrous impulse to protect the more vulnerable female, no matter what the cost to the male himself. Sutherland (1898:354), for example, romanticized the male's sympathetic tendency in a most Victorian fashion, stripping it of any sexual sentiment.

. . . [and] when, within the doomed vessel whose bulwarks are almost awash, he willingly helps to fill the last boat with the women, though fully realising that in a few minutes he himself will in consequence be a drifting corpse in the deep sea, in such cases he proclaims how, after a long story of slow development, that sympathy which was originally the finer side of mere sexual feeling has spread and spread till at last it extends to every one that bears the shape of a woman.

Even with the decline of the Victorian model of gender roles, social scientists continued to comment on the innate bases of caretaking behavior. The influence of the behavioristic paradigm is especially evident in distinctions made between primary and secondary instincts. For example, Pillsbury (1926), like McDougall, discriminated between primary and secondary instincts. However, he considered the primary instincts behaviors performed completely and adequately the first time emitted, whereas the secondary instincts, while directing action toward a specific goal object, required rehearsal for competence. Parental instinct, most notably manifested in females, was of the latter type. While the "satisfaction at the sight and feeling of the child impels the mother to remain in its presence as the pleasure from nursing would probably impel to that act, not necessarily wisely as to time or amount as measured by the results of pediatrics" (1926:65). Left to its own devices, maternal instinct could only by trial and error produce behavior to meet the chid's needs. Thus, "the end to which the instincts impel is attained more certainly by the rules of the child specialist than by compliance with the immediate instinctive tendencies" (pp. 65–66).

In the behaviorist era, the concept of instinct did not fare well. The putative father of behaviorism, John B. Watson, asserted that instinct could not play a significant role in the behavior of the new mother.

Certainly there are no new ready-made activities appearing except nursing. The mother is usually as awkward about that as well she can be. The instinctive factors are practically nil (Watson 1919:182).

Nevertheless, innate factors did appear to play a role in eliciting an emotional reaction of the mother to her infant, "We are not denying however that there are some instinctive factors here. It should be recalled that the nursing of the child and the fondling of it is not without a sex stimulating effect upon the mother" (p. 183). The mother's susceptibility to pleasurable feelings were probably partially due to the female's less differentiated and so less complex emotional repertoire (Watson 1926). Watson's conceptualization does represent an advancement over the earlier concept of the ready-made mother. Because the potential for mothering originated in sexual pleasure, only the emotional qualities associated with caretaking appeared to be innate. Unlike earlier scientists, Watson did not view women as behavioral automata genetically equipped to perform the duties of caretaker without rehearsal.

Watson's followers in behaviorism, though eschewing the notion of instinctive maternal behavior, were less adamant that only affective anlagen were innate (e.g., Fox 1932). Even textbooks that acknowledged the role of "differences in training" (Gast and Skinner 1929:126) as a source of gender differences in behavior hedged in favor of biology when caretaking behavior was considered: "The most striking difference in instinctive equipment consists in the strength of the fighting instinct in the male and the motherly instinct in the female" (p. 126). Likewise, parental feelings were not viewed as sequelae of sexual feelings as they had been by Watson (e.g., Colvin and Bagley 1918). Retreating from Watson's position, the dissociation between sexuality and maternity was maintained as it had been during the previous century.

Thus maternal instinct was not, for the scientist of the late nineteenth and early twentieth centuries, just one of a constellation of female personality attributes but was *the* attribute. It was the one female tendency necessary for survival of the species and a direct consequence of woman's reproductive role and its attendant intellect and temperament. The maternal, nurturant aspect of the female was consistently treated with reverence. Maternity was the *raison d'être* of all other female attributes, most of them precious and childlike, which constituted the Victorian scientists' conception of ideal female personality. Acceptable female sexuality was in the service of reproduction only; other expressions of sexuality were indicative of individual aberration or the lack of restraint characteristic of certain races and social strata. The mother, as constructed by social scientists, was remarkably similar in Britain and the United States. She was upper class, a bit frivolous, emotionally labile, and intellectually unremarkable. She was a paragon of morality and nurturance. The mother, who could become a mother only through sexual relations, was neutered by science. Her female attributes were not womanly but motherly. Her girlish enthusiasms and debilities were prologue to her real mission in life, the role of maintaining the continuity of the species and serving as its moral guardian. Science did not know what to make of women, so women were made into mothers. Of course, the real difficulties and challenges of motherhood remained unexamined. (See Shields 1975b for a summary of the response of one psychologist of the time, Leta Hollingworth, to such science.)

Woman as mother is epitomized in the writings of G. Stanley Hall, who, among his other accomplishments, was a founder of developmental psychology. For Hall, whose views were a bit extreme, the eternal womanly (*Das Ewig-Weibliche*) was a quality to admire and to pity. The eternal womanly is

a very definable reality, and means perennial youth. It means that woman at her best never outgrows adolescence as man does, but lingers in it, magnifies and glorifies this culminating stage of life with its all-sided interests, its convertibility of emotions, its enthusiasm, and zest for all that is good, beautiful, true, and heroic. This constitutes her freshness and charm, even in age, and makes her by nature more humanistic than man, more sympathetic and appreciative (1918:293–94).

Hall considered a virgin-mother image as the most descriptive of the natural woman: "To be a true woman means to be yet more mother than wife. The madonna conception expresses man's highest comprehension of woman's real nature" (1918:297). The major function and fulfillment of woman lay in childbearing. If a woman should choose self-fulfillment over devotion to maternal duties, she would cheat civilization of continuity and would ultimately lose her own womanliness.

Effects on Contemporary Research

Where do we find maternal instinct today? Historical influence is best illutrated in three assumptions regarding maternal behavior that recur in research and clinical literature.

1. The first assumption is that human females exhibit a greater readiness than males to respond positively and adequately to the needs of the young and that this gender difference is innate. If an individual woman does not exhibit these behaviors to an appropriate degree, the inadequacy is diagnosed as indicating pathology or personality aberration (Oakley 1979). And, of course, concomitant with the belief in instinctive maternal behavior, is the belief that defects in the mother–child interaction are the primary cause of later personality pathology in the offspring (Contratto, article 10). The concept of the schizophrenogenic mother, popular in the 1950s, is a good example of the extreme case of instinct gone afoul. Mother-blaming, as a clinical concept, appears not only in the psychoanalytic tradition but also in other developmental theories. (See Magnus 1980 for a discussion of the effects of the motherhood ideology on the study of postpartum stress.)

Scientific evidence of the female's readiness to respond appropriately to the young has relied heavily on cross-species comparisons of nurturant behavior. Authors who would shy away from the comparative approach to other issues without qualification accept the idea that nurturance is nurturance no matter what the species. Alice Rossi (1977), for example, asserts that sex differences in nurturance are "fundamental human characteristics rooted in our biological heritage" (1977:2) and that the limits to social change can be comprehended through modern biological theory. Focusing on the family structure itself, she argues that always and everywhere the primary care of infants has fallen to women, a simple result of the biological fact of maternity. No amount of social restructuring can change the destiny of the female to be the primary caretaker of the young: biology will triumph. In Rossi's model probabilities become inevitabilities. The implied "oughtness" of genetic influences adds an immoral cast to social attempts to alter the unfolding of genetic destiny. Such determinism has come under substantial criticism, particularly from feminist social scientists (e.g., Breines, Cerullo, and Stacey 1978; Gross et al. 1979).

2. A second assumption is not only that maternal instinct involves a predisposition to exhibit adequate caretaking behavior but also that women derive more pleasure than males from engaging in caretaking behavior. The affective basis of human instincts is an old theme and the consequent gender difference is assumed to be immutable. The female's supposedly limitless pleasure in mothering makes it possible to overlook the highly isolated and exhausting character of the mother's 24-hour days and to accept as "natural" the absence of the kin group and the village community, which shares the responsibility for child care in many societies. The belief further promises feelings of guilt for any mother who allows a lapse in her maternal feelings. And if males are predisposed neither to care for the young nor to enjoy it, then we should not expect to see men nurture, encourage men to nurture, or set up social supports for male nurturant behavior. Men's failures at good parenting are to be expected—they do not have the necessary dispositions. (See the current spate of popular books that idealize the traditional concept of mothering, such as Heffner 1980).

3. A third assumption links maternal instinct inextricably to other personality traits that are also presumed to have a biological basis, e.g., female emotionality. Sometimes it is asserted that the tendency to nurture is the source of additional sex differences, e.g., the Buffery-Gray hypothesis that sex differences in verbal fluency evolved from maternal contact with the young (Buffery and Gray 1972), at other times that nurturance is identified as an effect of these differences, e.g., purported gender differences in attraction to infants. Seldom are proximal social or situational conditions examined as possible causal agents for observed gender differences in caretaking or the preference to caretake.

Rather than ask whether sex differences in behavior exist— they do—it is probably a much more fruitful strategy to examine when and how these differences appear (Berman 1978). Likewise, there is little scientific value to be gained from denying the existence of unlearned behavioral responses to the young. However, we should not suppose that adult reactions to such stimuli have no significant learned component (Unger 1979). Our whole educational and childcare system requires females' extended contact with infants and children. Socialization is geared to enhance the female's and to minimize the male's attachment to the young. Indeed, in a brilliant review Berman (1980) has shown the powerful effect of social role in influencing responsiveness to the young.

Bonding: A New Version of Instinct Theory?

Ethological theory stimulated the bulk of the empirical research on the early mother-infant relationship (see, for example, Bowlby 1973, Ainsworth 1974), although learning theory has also produced models of attachment (see Rajecki, Lamb, and Obmascher 1978 for a summary). Bonding, a popular addition to the parent-infant interaction literature, shares instinct theory's reverence for biological determinism. Bonding is a positive emotional attachment that develops between mother and infant immediately after delivery or in the few days following delivery (Klaus and Kennell 1976). The father and infant or anyone present at the delivery and the infant may also "bond," but research has emphasized the maternal response. Proponents of the concept believe that there are lifelong consequences of the success or failure at bonding, most of which involve the child's later ability to form successful interpersonal relationships. The infant, by way of temperament or alertness, may resist the bonding process, and the structure of the birth and early social environment may likewise aid or impede it, but the ultimate responsibility for successful bonding rests directly on maternal behavior. As in the earlier maternal instinct literature, the individual woman is simultaneously relieved of individual initiative because the processes, innate and invariant, are assumed outside her direct control, yet she is held culpable as the single figure ultimately responsible for the infant's well-being.

Klaus and Kennell (1976), who stimulated the current surge of interest in human bonding, base their case for immediate postpartum mother-infant contact as the sine qua non of bonding on their study of maternal behavior in high-risk teenage mothers. Another popular expert on bonding has developed a birth environment designed to maximize the effects of mother-infant physical contact (Leboyer 1975). Despite the consistent failure of research to demonstrate any consistent or long-term behavioral effects of perinatal bonding (Svejda, Campos, and Emde 1980; Lamb 1982), the concept appears to be increasing in scientific and social popularity. One recent advice book on the subject (Verny and Kelly 1981) even suggests that the bonding process begins prenatally: the fetus may sense a mother's rejection of the pregnancy and so bond poorly after birth! On the positive side, a number of researchers are beginning to explore more fully a transactional approach to parent-offspring influence (e.g., Bell and Harper 1977, Lewis and Rosenblum 1974).

Because the concept of bonding grew from the work of practitioners rather than of theoreticians, research has focused primarily on questions of efficacy rather than of cause. The construct is nevertheless treated as if it had explanatory power, as if intuitively defining the optimal developmental environment obviates the search for other causes and processes. As the concept is currently used, "bonding" is the single label applied to a complex array of factors that guide and shape individual development and the parent-child relationship.

One critique of the bonding literature (Balk 1980) rejects the concept of bonding as a scientific ploy to mask the fact that racism and classism are the true delimiters of a child's developmental potential. That is, if one blames pathologies of bonding for a child's developmental failure, the eradication of economic and educational impediments to development is no longer necessary: the blame rests on maternal failure. Among the shortcomings of the bonding concept, Balk identifies maternal feelings of guilt, removal of the father from the role of caretaker, and lack of scientist's concern for the effects of bonding on the mother.

Another problematic, and broader-reaching, implication of the bonding concept is the unacknowledged equation of biological determination with an absolute standard of good (Lambert 1978) — that is, the view that there is an intrinsic rightness to innate behavioral patterns and that social tampering is inherently bad: the natural is the good. If the mother's role is to be studied effectively, closer examination must be made of the variables which reflect maternal concerns, particularly those over which she has some direct control. The mother-infant relationship, like the infant's relationship with other people, must be described as a process. Mother's expectations, baby's temperament, quality and quantity of social supports, and so on, interact in a dynamic fashion to constitute the relationship. The definition of maternal behavior by the proponents of bonding as a unitary, coherent, and predictable set of behaviors inadvertently circumscribes the domain of acceptable maternal behaviors and prevents us from identifying other effective caretaking styles. Perhaps even more damaging is its distortion of the study of the real challenges, joys, and burdens of that most intimate human relationship.

Why do women mother? It is a simple question that has garnered more than its share of simplistic answers over the years. Prescientific philosophers did not ask it: Women mother because they are female and females have the bodies and the instincts to perform maternal duties. Instead, their concern was with identification of the final cause, whether a diety or simple animal nature, of instinctive behavior (Diamond 1974). Final cause is not the concern of contemporary science, but the heritage of animal models suggests a simple model of maternal behavior that transcends species boundaries. Apparent simplicity is complicated, however, by the tangled web of nature-nurture interaction, and theoretical efforts to unravel that relationship are still far from wholly satisfying. Is it any wonder that the finality of deterministic biological models is so very appealing?

References

Ainsworth, M. D. S. 1974. "Infant-Mother Attachment and Social Development: Socialization as a Product of Reciprocal Responsiveness to Signals." In M. P. Richards, ed. *The Integration of the Child Into a Social World*. Cambridge, England: Cambridge University Press.

Bain, A. 1859. *The Emotions and the Will*. London: Longmans, Green (3rd ed., 1875).

Balk, S. 1980. "Parent-Child Bonding." In E. Tobach and B. Rosoff, eds. *Genes and Gender, III: Genetic Determinism and Children*. New York: Gordian Press.

Bandura, A. 1978. "The Self System in Reciprocal Determinism." *American Psychologist* 33:344–58.

Baumrind, D. 1980. "New Directions in Socialization Research." *American Psychologist* 35:639–52.

Bell, R. Q. and L. V. Harper. 1977. *Child Effects on Adults*. Hillsdale, N.J.: Lawrence Erlbaum.

Beach, F. A. 1955. "The Descent of Instinct." *Psychological Review* 62:401–10.
Berman, P. W. 1978. "Comment on Reesa Vaughter's 'Psychology: Review essay.' " (vol. 2 no. 1). *Signs* 3:515–16.
—— 1980. "Are Women More Responsive Than Men to the Young? A Review of Developmental and Situational Variables." *Psychological Bulletin* 88(3):668–95.
Bowlby, J. 1973. *Attachment and Loss* (2 vols). New York: Basic Books.
Breines, W., M. Cerullo, and J. Stacey. 1978. "Social Biology, Family Studies, and Antifeminist Backlash." *Feminist Studies* 4:43–68.
Buffery, A. W. H. and J. A. Gray. 1972. "Sex Differences in the Development of Spatial and Linguistic Skills." In C. Ounstead and D. C. Taylor, eds. *Gender Differences: Their Ontogeny and Significance*. Baltimore: Williams and Wilkins.
Carpenter, W. B. 1894 (4th ed.). *Principles of Mental Physiology*. New York: Appleton.
Colvin, S. S. and W. C. Bagley. 1918. *Human Behavior, A First Book in Psychology for Teachers*. New York: Macmillan.
Cott, N. F. 1979. "Passionlessness: An Interpretation of Victorian Sexual Ideology, 1790–1850." In N. F. Cott and E. H. Pleck, eds. *A Heritage of Her Own*. New York: Simon & Schuster.
Darwin, C. 1897 (2nd ed., 1st ed., 1872). *The Descent of Man and Selection in Relation to Sex*. New York: Appleton.
Dewsbury, D. A. 1978. *Comparative Animal Behavior*. New York: McGraw-Hill.
Diamond, S. 1974. "Four hundred years of instinct controversy." *Behavior Genetics* 4:237–52.
Dye, N. S. 1980. "History of Childbirth in America." *Signs* 6:97–108.
Fox, C. 1932. *The Mind and Its Body*. New York: Harcourt Brace.
Gast, I. M. and H. C. Skinner. 1929. *Fundamentals of Educational Psychology*. Chicago: Benjamin M. Sanborn.
Gross, H. E., J. Bernard, A. J. Dan, N. Glazer, J. Lorber, M. McClintock, N. Newton, and A. Rossi. 1979. "Considering 'A Biosocial Perspective on Parenting.' " *Signs* 4:695–717.
Hall, G. S. 1918. *Youth, Its Education, Regimen and Hygiene*. New York: Appleton.
Haraway, D. J. 1982. "The High Cost of Information in Post World War II Evolutionary Biology: Ergonomics, Semiotics, and the Sociobiology of Communication Systems." *Philosophical Forum*, in press.
Harlow, H. F. 1971. *Learning to Love*. San Francisco: Albion.
Heffner, E. 1980. *Mothering*. New York: Doubleday/Anchor.
Hobhouse, L. T. 1926. *Mind in Evolution*. London: Macmillan.
James, W. 1890. *The Principles of Psychology*. New York: Holt.
Kerber, L. K. 1974. "Daughters of Columbia: Educating Women for the Republic, 1787–1805." In S. Elkins and E. McKitrick, eds. *The Hofstader Aegis, a Memorial*. New York: Knopf.
Klaus, M. H. and J. H. Kennell. 1976. *Maternal-Infant Bonding*. St. Louis: Mosby.
Lamb, M. 1982. "Second Thoughts on First Touch." *Psychology Today* 16(4):9–11.
Lambert, H. H. 1978. "Biology and Equality: A Perspective on Sex Differences." *Signs* 4:97–117.
Leboyer, F. 1975. *Birth Without Violence*. New York: Knopf.
Lerner, G. 1979. *The Majority Finds Its Past*. New York: Oxford University Press.
Lewis, M. and L. A. Rosenblum, eds. 1974. *The Effect of the Infant on Its Caregiver*. New York: Wiley.

Lynn, D. B. 1974. *The Father: His Role in Child Development.* Monterey, Calif.: Brooks/Cole.

Magnus, E. M. 1980. "Sources of Maternal Stress in the Postpartum Period: A Review of the Literature and an Alternative View." In J. E. Parsons, ed. *The Psychobiology of Sex Differences and Sex Roles.* Washington, D.C.: Hemisphere.

McCurdy, H. G. 1968. "William McDougall." In B. B. Wolman, ed. *Historical Roots of Contemporary Psychology.* New York: Harper and Row.

McDougall, W. 1913. *An Introduction to Social Psychology* (7th ed.). London: Methuen.

—— 1923. *Outline of Psychology.* New York: Scribner's.

Oakley, A. 1979. "A Case of Maternity: Paradigms of Women as Maternity Cases." *Signs* 4:607–31.

Parke, R. D. 1979. "Perspectives on Father-Infant Interaction." In J. D. Osofsky, ed. *The Handbook of Infant Development.* New York: Wiley.

Pillsbury, W. B. 1926. *Education as the Psychologist Sees It.* New York: Macmillan.

Rajecki, D. W., M. E. Lamb, and P. Obmascher. 1978. "Toward a General Theory of Infantile Attachment: A Comparative Review of Aspects of the Social Bond." *The Behavioral and Brain Sciences* 3:417–36.

Rapp, R. R. 1978. "Family and Class in Contemporary America." *Science and Society* 42(3):278–300.

Ribot, T. 1897. *The Psychology of the Emotions.* New York: Scribner's.

Romanes, G. J. 1894. *Mental Evolution in Animals.* New York: Appleton.

Rossi, A. J. 1977. "A Biosocial Perspective on Parenting." *Daedalus* 106:1–31.

Shand, A. S. F. 1920. *The Foundations of Character.* London: Macmillan.

Shields, S. A. 1975a. "Functionalism, Darwinism, and the Psychology of Women: A Study in Social Myth." *American Psychologist* 30:739–54.

—— 1975b. "Ms. Pilgrim's Progress: The Contributions of Leta Stetter Hollingworth to the Psychology of Women." *American Psychologist* 30:852–57.

Spencer, H. 1891. *The Study of Sociology.* New York: Appleton.

Sutherland, A. 1898. *The Origin and Growth of the Moral Instinct,* vol. 1, London: Longmans, Green.

Svejda, M. J., J. J. Campos, and R. N. Emde. 1980. "Mother-Infant 'bonding': Failure to Generalize." *Child Development* 51:775–79.

Thorndike, E. L. 1914. *Educational Psychology,* vol. 3. New York: Teacher's College, Columbia University.

Unger, R. K. 1979. *Female and Male: Psychological Perspectives.* New York: Harper and Row.

Verny, T. R. & Kelly, J. 1981. *The Secret Life of the Unborn Child.* New York: Summit Books.

Watson, J. B. 1919. *Psychology From the Standpoint of a Behaviorist.* New York: Lippincott.

—— 1926. *Psychologies of 1925 (Powell Lectures in Psychological Theory).* Worcester, Mass.: Clark University Press.

12 Metatheoretical Influences on Conceptions of Human Development

KENNETH J. GERGEN AND SUZANNE BENACK

It has long been recognized within the philosophy of science that observation cannot serve as the impetus to theoretical understanding. One cannot derive theory from sense data. Thus, in scanning the horizon, one's visual experience would permit one to distinguish simply between "figure" and "ground" or to make as many conceptual distinctions as there are possible sensory discriminations (along with all possible permutations and combinations of such discriminations). Nature does not itself dictate one's choice in such matters (Hanson 1958). Although a satisfactory account of how theoretical conceptions do spring to life has yet to be fashioned within either philosophy or psychology, the fact that theories are observationally underdetermined does invite close attention to the extrascientific sources for such accounts. If nature does not prescribe theory, in what degree can such accounts be traced to the existing Weltanschauung, to dominant institutions, or prevailing ideologies?

Preparation of this chapter was facilitated by a grant from the National Science Foundation (#7809393) to the senior author.

Such inquiry is particularly important in the behavioral sciences as theoretical accounts, once propounded, come to serve as symbolic surrogates for nature. In effect, behavioral theories take on the character of objective description, reflections of "what there is." And, once this process of objectification has occurred, it is often this symbolic account that feeds the process of decision making. Action becomes grounded in the meaning that nature has acquired rather than in nature itself. To bring the matter closer to home, existing theories of human development do not appear to be generated or required by the nature of human activity itself; however, once such theories are elaborated and disseminated by the profession, they become the grounds for wide-ranging decisions within the society, including parent's about childrearing, legal decisions regarding children's rights, and governmental legislation concerning the family unit, day-care centers, and special education. Given the insinuation of developmental theory into the culture, it is thus of special importance to examine the nonobjective or extrascientific influences that fashion the contours of developmental theory.

Between 1920 and 1940 the dominating force in American psychology was clearly that of behaviorist psychology. Its environmentalist orientation, promising that all human activity was subject to modification and control, was optimistically compelling. Its arguments for a flourishing science based on the observation of reliable contingencies between stimuli and responses were both powerful and attractive. The works of J. B. Watson (1924), B. F. Skinner (1957, 1969), E. L. Thorndike (1911), E. C. Tolman (1932), and C. L. Hull (1943) furnished impressive support for an immense array of developmental studies. Largely under the aegis of social learning theory (Bandura 1977, Bandura and Walters 1963), along with research on the shaping of children's actions through situational manipulation, research concerned with the impact of environment on development continues into the present.

Many would be willing to argue that, regardless of its limitations in dealing with the full range of human activity, the behaviorist emphasis on learning and on early experience is necessary to account for certain important aspects of development. Such reservations seem reasonable enough until three important factors are considered. First is the emergence of alternative theoretical perspectives. Behaviorist theory is largely *mechanistic* in form;

it posits stationary mechanisms (connections, associations, habits, etc.), dependent for their functioning on exogenous influences. This orientation may be contrasted with that of *organismic* theory (Overton and Reese 1973), which emphasizes the intrinsic capability of the organism for self-directed growth. Thus, for theorists such as Werner (1948), Piaget (1952), and Kohlberg (1969), developmental trajectories are viewed as forms of epigenetic unfolding. Environmental influences are quite secondary. Both of these views may be contrasted with the *aleatory* orientation (Gergen 1980), an approach emerging primarily in contemporary life-span study. From this perspective human action is dependent on voluntary choice. The individual confronts historically contingent rules and decides upon courses of action with respect to such rules and as his or her skills permit. Human nature, on this account, demands that one do very little. One is fundamentally free to alter the character of the life-course at any point. As argued elsewhere (Gergen and Gergen 1982), each of these explanatory orientations may successfully interpret or explain most of the evidence used to substantiate the behaviorist position. In effect, there are viable theoretical alternatives to the behaviorist perspective.

A second reservation with the behaviorist program must be voiced over its corollary assumption that early experience has profound effects on adult character. Very little in the way of convincing support for this "early impact" supposition has emerged over the years (Brim and Kagan 1980, Clarke and Clarke 1976, Rutter 1972). As reviewed elsewhere (Gergen 1977), the evidence is mostly derived from clinical case studies. These case materials are sufficiently rich that virtually any theoretical view may be sustained. More rigorous, longitudinal research offers little more in the way of support. Robust correlations between early and later periods have generally failed to appear. Other sources of evidence have also yielded equivocal results, are subject to serious methodological difficulties, and/or are open to a variety of alternative interpretations. In effect, the behaviorist view that early treatment of the child has substantial long-term effects simply does not possess compelling empirical support.

A third major reservation with the behaviorist perspective stems from its social and value implications. The orientation informs the parent that he or she is the manager or creator of the child's character. The child is thus denied rights of self-determination and reduced to the status of a pawn. Behaviorist theory also informs parents that they should judge their capacities as parents in terms of the success and/or failure of the offspring. Because the parents are the creators of the child, the child's failures impugn the character of the parents, and the child's success comes to substitute for the successes the parents might otherwise seek through their own actions.

The belief that the early years "bend the twig" also lends support to the traditional dichotomy in sex roles. If the child's future is crystallized during the early years, only the irresponsible parent would entrust caretaking to a day-care center or a surrogate family. The female would be chiefly at fault. By securing the mother to the home and forcing the male into the role of economic provider, the traditional family is maintained. Alternative social arrangements (e.g., communal living) are discouraged, and people in nontraditional roles are rendered suspect. The tax structure in many Western nations penalizes the single parent, the homosexual, the bachelor, and the unmarried woman. Again we find reason for assessing behaviorist theory and its assumptions.

The Metatheoretical Context of Theory Construction

Most analyses of extrascientific influences on theory construction have centered on the ideological, economic, and sociostructural conditions impinging on the theorist (Buss 1979a, Riegel 1972, Apfelbaum and Lubek 1976, Sampson 1981, Buck-Morss 1975, Morawski 1979). Such analyses have been particularly useful in destroying the shibboleth of descriptive neutrality. Scientific knowledge frequently reflects prevailing value commitments. The long sacrosanct distinction between an impersonal *fact* and a personal *value* fades. Factual accounts, it would appear, invariably reflect human interest (Habermas 1971, Putnam 1978).

The present analysis attempts to expand the arena of relevant inputs into theory by considering the relationship between prevailing theories of science (metatheory) and scientific theories of behavior. Such consideration is based on the assumption that requisite for participating in the process of science is a conception of that process, its functions, products, and criteria for evaluation. The scientist commences inquiry, then, committed to certain suppositions about the character of his or her own activity. At the same time, such conceptions of science also habor wide-ranging ontological and epistemological assumptions. They themselves are premised on beliefs about the character of the world, the capacities of the human being, the nature of human functioning (including sensory, intellectual, and motivational domains), and the relationship between the world and the apprehending individual. Thus, for example, empiricist theories of science are typically premised on a belief in nature independent of the knower. They endow the knower with sensory capacities for apprehending nature, capacities for the execution of logic, and evaluative processes that may motivate the scientific endeavor but interfere with its validity if allowed free reign. In effect, to accept a given metatheoretical perspective is simultaneously to incorporate a rudimentary view of nature, human functioning, and their relationship. In this light we find that when the task of theory construction commences, the scientist is already committed to certain views of human functioning. To the extent that intellectual coherence is maintained, such views must be consistent with the scientist's subsequent descriptions of the world. There is a vital relationship between scientific metatheory and theoretical description in the sociobehavioral sciences. Metatheoretical commitments have important fashioning effects on theories of human conduct (Gergen 1982).

In the pages that follow, our initial task is to demonstrate that the conception of science prevailing during the period 1920–40 largely fashioned the contours of the behaviorist orientation in general and learning theory in particular. The behaviorist orientation toward the developing child receives special attention. We then take up the intimate connection between the behaviorist perspective and the early impact assumption. Finally, we consider the development of alternative conceptions of human development and their implications for the future of the science.

Logical Empiricist Metatheory and the Behaviorist Perspective

During the present century one of the most optimistic movements in Western philosophy took form, a movement committed to the view that inhering in the scientific process is a method of acquiring certain knowledge of the world. By following certain rules, it was argued, psychology could also anticipate the same productivity as physics; ultimately the two disciplines might become unified. This movement became known as logical positivism. The various participants in the Vienna Circle, namely, Ayers, Carnap, Feigl, Neurath, and Schlick, were optimistic in their hopes for establishing a unified science. Although philosophers were hardly in complete agreement concerning proper methods of establishing "proof through science," psychologists succeeded in distilling a general rationale for guiding scientific conduct within psychology (Marx and Hellix 1963, Koch 1959, Mandler and Kessen 1975). This "received account" appears to have laid the foundation for the behaviorist view of the developing child.

The received view first makes an essential distinction between the natural world and the observer; the former is granted an ontological status independent of the scientist attempting to understand this world. It is thus the task of the scientist to develop a theory that maps with fidelity the contours of the world as given. As it is said, "the essential task of the scientist is to identify facts with the highest possible precision, for they form the stock in trade of all his work" (Brown and Ghiselli 1955:7). The received view also endows the scientist with several major capacities through which objective knowledge may be acquired. Among the most important of these are the capacities for accurate observation and logic. Initial observation is said to furnish the scientist with a rudimentary acquaintance with the phenomenon of interest. Such observation, when combined with the canons of inductive logic, enables the scientist to formulate a series of tentative hypotheses concerning the conditions under which various phenomena occur. Essentially, the scientist derives a set of propositions (normally of the variety "if X antecedent . . . then Y consequence") to account for observed regularities in the relationship among observed events. In the case of psychology the focus of interest is the behavior of the individual. Such behavior thus enters as the *consequence* for which real world conditions serve as antecedents. Given various general propositions and a hypothesized explanation for their relationship, the scientist may then employ deductive logic to move "beyond the data given." The scientist moves from statements about existing nature to predictions about its future character.

On the basis of these deductively derived hypotheses the scientist again enters into the world of nature. Controlled observation is used to test the validity of the initial set of "if . . . then" propositions. The experiment is typically viewed as the optimal methodology for such inquiry. The results of this new set of observations, like the first "behavioral entities," serve as informative indicators regarding the world of nature. However, in this case, they serve the additional function of sustaining or correcting the propositions initially propounded by the scientist. Thus, through experimentation, scientists amend or discard their initial propositions.

This skeletal account of what is typically termed the hypothetico-deductive process is diagrammed in the upper half of figure 12.1. Ideally the process of observation-proposition-test-refine should be sustained indefinitely, and the result is an increasingly precise, differentiated, and well-validated network of interrelated propositions. It is the latter that is considered "objective knowledge" and that should facilitate the prediction and control of human activity. In Brown and Ghiselli's terms, "The object of the scientist is to understand the phenomenon with which he is working. He considers that he understands it when he can successfully predict its expressions . . . or when his knowledge enables him to control its expressions to achieve certain ends" (1955:35).

Yet it is essential at this point to note the way temporal and causal sequences are coordinated within the received view. As one moves temporally through the various stages of the system, one is also following a causal path in which the events at any given stage are (or should be) determined by events at the preceding stage. The world of nature is the initial given. Its characteristics limit and drive the scientist. The scientist's observations and logic must prove adequate to nature rather than the other way around. Observation and logic determine the form of subsequent testing; and the results of such testing should determine the conclusions. Each step of the process, then, is dependent upon that which precedes it. The "first cause" lies within the realm of environmental givens.

Given this brief sketch of the hypothetico-deductive orientation to science we may now scan the behaviorist conception of human functioning. As will be demonstrated, the essential form

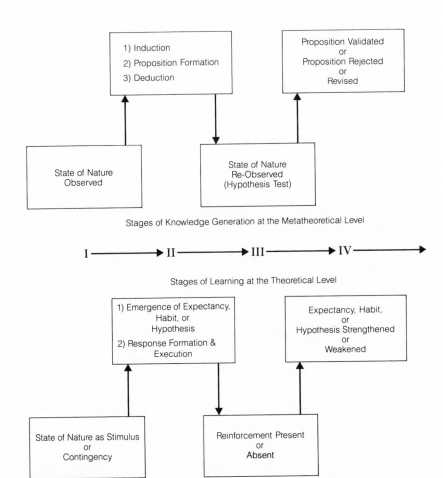

FIGURE 12.1. Hypothetico-Deductive Metatheory as paralleled by Behaviorist Theory

of the metatheoretical orientation becomes reincarnated as a theory of human activity. When theorists set out to "observe," and "discover" the nature of human activity, unencumbered so they believed by previous conceptions, they only reproduced the intellectual form to which they adhered—that of the hypothetico-deductive theory of science.

At the outset behaviorist theory possesses a strong environmentalist bias. From the behaviorist perspective human activity is viewed as a series of responses guided, controlled, or stimulated by environmental inputs. Thus, at the outset we find "stimulus inputs" at the theoretical level serving as a substitute for "behavioral units" at the level of metatheory. Their status as preeminent determinants of human activity is virtually identical with that of the world of nature within the metatheory. Figure 1 may again be consulted for a full illustration of the parallels.

With respect to the processes of observation and logic, we must distinguish between the two prominent paradigms within the behaviorist movement. Theorists such as Watson and Skinner had so thoroughly assimilated the "lore of science" and its concern with observables that statements about the hypothetical realm of psychological states were assiduously avoided. Within radical behaviorism, the reinstigation of the second stage of the hypothetico-deductive process is not readily apparent. Equivalencies to psychological processes such as "observation" and "logic" are difficult to locate. However, the second stage does manifest itself, not in statements about the internal workings of organisms, but as descriptions of the ends served by behavior. Although nothing is said about internal processes of rational thought, the human species acts so as to maximize its adaptiveness—that is, in a rational manner. As Watson (1924) described it, "although born more helpless than almost any other mammal, [man] very quickly learns to outstrip other animals by reason of the . . . habits he acquires" (p. 224). And as Skinner (1974) put it: "The process of operant conditioning . . . supplements natural selection. Important consequences of behavior which could not play a role in evolution because they were not sufficiently stable features of the environment are made effective through operant conditioning during the lifetime of the individual whose power in dealing with his world is thus vastly increased" (p. 46). In effect, although no specific mental processes are identified, radical behaviorists describe the human as a rational, problem-solving creature. The second step of the hypothetico-deductive process is thus achieved covertly.

Owing in large measure to the liberalization of positivist metatheory (Koch 1959), radical behaviorism has been largely supplanted by neobehaviorist (S-O-R) theory. The early positivist tenets, which laid great importance on the precise correspondence between theoretical terms and real-world observables, were found too rigidly constricting. As it was argued, mature sciences do have a place for theoretical terms that do not directly refer to observables. Terms such as "gravity," "force field," and "magnetism" are all highly serviceable within the natural sciences, and yet without immediately observable referents. This liberalization on the metatheoretical level enabled psychologists to develop the concept of "hypothetical constructs" (MacCorquodale and Meehl 1948), terms that referred to hypothetical psychological states intervening between stimulus and response. With the door thus open to introduce talk about "the mind," the behaviorist was free to develop terms that stood in functional correspondence to the processes of observation and logic so central to the metatheory. Thus, for Clark Hull (1943), such terms as "habit strength," "incentive strength," and "inhibitory potential" operated in concert to produce adaptive responses to given circumstances. Within expectancy-value formulations (Hoppe 1930, Lewin et al 1944, Rotter 1954, Ajzen and Fishbein 1980), the term "expectancy" furnishes a parallel at the theoretical level for "hypothesis" at the metatheoretical level. Social learning theorist Albert Bandura (1977) employs the concept of expectancy in the same way but adds additional processes of "covert problem solving" and "verification through thought" to the psychological arsenal.

As featured in figure 12.1, the third stage of the metatheoretical system is most clearly recapitualted at the theoretical level by the concept of reinforcement. For theorists such as Skinner (1974), Thorndike (1911), and Bandura (1977), reinforcement sustains certain patterns of activity while discouraging others. Patterns of the former variety are often termed "adaptive" while the latter are "maladaptive." In this sense, the results of the hypothesis test serve the same function as reinforcement: they are nature's means of informing one of the adequacy of one's actions. It follows from this analysis that the fourth stage of the hypothetico-deductive model, theory extension and/or revision, is but

a later stage in the process of "behavior shaping" for the Skinner-
ian or a single step in a process of "expectancy confirmation" for
the more cognitively oriented learning theorist. The entire hypothetico-deductive system finds its coordinates in various forms of
behaviorist learning theory. The entire hypo-
Perhaps there is no more fitting conclusion to the present
demonstration than a pair of quotes from Clark Hull's *Principles
of Behavior*. Speaking first of the nature of science, Hull recites
the hypothetico-deductive litany:

> Empirical observation, supplemented by shrewd conjecture, is the main
> source of the primary principles or postulates of a science. Such formula-
> tions, when taken in various combinations together with relevant antecedent
> conditions, yield inferences or theorems, of which some may agree with the
> empirical outcome of the conditions in question, and some may not. Primary
> propositions yielding logical deductions which consistently agree with the
> observed empirical outcome are retained, whereas those which disagree are
> rejected or modified. As the sifting of this trial-and-error process continues,
> there gradually emerges a limited series of primary principles whose joint
> implications are progressively more likely to agree with relevant observations.
> Deductions made from these surviving postulates, while never absolutely cer-
> tain, do at length become highly trustworthy (Hull 1943:382).

The similarities between this account of science and Hull's theory
of learning are striking. With regard to the latter, Hull summarizes
his views as follows,

> The substance of the elementary learning process as revealed by much
> experimentation seems to be this: A condition of need exists . . . initiated
> by the action of environmental stimulus energies. This . . . activates numer-
> ous vaguely adaptive reaction potentials . . . laid down by organic evolution.
> In case one of these random responses, or a sequence of them, results in the
> reduction of a need dominant at the time, there follows as an indirect effect
> that is known as reinforcement. This consists in (1) a strengthening of the
> particular receptor-effector connections which originally mediated the reac-
> tion and (2) a tendency for all receptor discharges (s) occurring at about the
> same time to acquire new connections with the effectors mediating the re-
> sponse in question. The first effect is known as primitive trial-and-error learn-
> ing; the second is known as conditioned-reflex learning. As a result, when the
> same need again arises in this or a similar situation, the stimuli will activate
> the same effectors more certainly, more promptly, and more vigorously than
> on the first occasion. Such action, while by no means adaptively infallible, in

the long run will reduce the need more surely than would a chance sampling of the unlearned response tendencies. . . . Thus the acquisition of such receptor-effector connections will, as a rule, make for survival; i.e., it will be adaptive (Hull 1943:386–87).

Both science and human learning processes thus work in analogous manner toward similar ends.

Empiricism Enters the Nursery

Thus far we have glimpsed the manner in which logical metatheory is reproduced within behaviorist theories of human functioning. Theorists within this camp, in turn, speak directly to issues in the developmental sphere. Watson's classic work *Behaviorism* is almost singlemindedly devoted to descriptions of the impact of environmental events on the developing infant and to a diatribe against the nativist view of development. (Ben Harris, this volume) As Lomax, Kagan, and Rosenkrantz (1978) summarize Watson's view, "reward the behavior that you want your child to maintain and punish him for the behavior that you do not want him to maintain; apply that principle consistently for 10 years and you will have produced your 'dream child' " (p. 109). This view is echoed in Skinner's *Walden Two,* where the means by which "behavioral engineering" is used to shape the child to the specifications of the utopia is elaborately described.

The theories of professional psychologists have also informed the public. In Watson's volume *Psychological Care of Infant and Child,* a systematic attempt was made to furnish rules for the psychological management of the infant that would equal existing treatments of physical care. The flavor of this treatment is nicely conveyed in Watson's comments about the development of children's emotions in infancy:

It is especially easy to shape the emotional life at this early age. I might make this simple comparison: the fabricator of metal takes his heated mass, places it upon the anvil and begins to shape it according to patterns of his own. Sometimes he uses a heavy hammer, sometimes a light one; sometimes he strikes the yielding mass a mighty blow, sometimes he gives it just a touch. So inevitably do we begin at birth to shape the emotional life of our children. The blacksmith has all the advantage. If his strokes have been heavy and awkward and he spoils his work, he can put the metal back on the fire and start the process over. There is no way of starting over again with the child. Every stroke, be it true or false, has its effect. The best we can do is to conceal, skillfully as we may, the defects of our shaping" (pp. 46–47). (See also articles 6, 10, and 11.)

The behaviorist orientation continues to find expression in today's childrearing manuals. In one notable case, Azerrad's (1980) volume, *Anyone Can Have a Happy Child*, we find a bald recapitulation of the "law of effect":

Children's behavior, good or bad, is directly related to the consequences of that behavior. . . . It doesn't matter to children whether they're being rewarded for behavior adults think is 'bad or good.' In either case, the rewarded behavior is likely to continue. It's up to the parents to be selective about the kind of behavior that receives attention (1980:18).

Metatheoretical Base for the Early Impact Assumption

As earlier maintained, the logical empiricist metatheory furnishes not only the guiding suppositions for behaviorist theory of child development but also grounds for the correlated belief that the early years of life are deeply formative. The rationale for this linkage must now be explored.

As we have seen, the metatheory grants to the real-world environment a preeminent causal status. Knowledge is ultimately a pawn to nature. Human conduct is produced or constrained by the realities of the external world. Such suppositions demand that close attention be paid to parental practices during the early years. However, the magnified importance attached to the early learning experiences of the child derives from two different emphases within the metatheory. The first is the coordination of temporality and causality. As we have shown, any given action is a consequence of preceding environmental inputs. The individual's behavior is the result of immediately preceding stimulus-response sequences. However, the immediately preceding sequence must in turn be understood in terms of its antecedents. When the course of explanation is fully traced, it is the initial experiences of the individual to which all subsequent activity must logically be derived. Infant learning experience must, by virtue of metatheoretical logic, lay the foundation for later response sequences. The metatheory places the "first cause" in the environment of the newborn infant, and all effects of subsequent environments must be constrained or altered by these early precedents. The environment of the adult is thus limited in its potency, as the adult confronts that environment with a history that constrains the magnitude of its impact. From the behaviorist perspective, human development is characterized by the progressive inflexibility of the organism to environmental inputs.

The second metatheoretical underpinning of the early impact assumption is closely related to the first. As we see, the prevailing metatheory is premised on the empiricist belief that human knowledge is constructed from inputs from the environment. The classic view of this process was that of mind as a tabula rasa progressively articulated through mental association. Although twentieth-century empiricism has not exclusively adopted the associationist view of mind, it has retained the mechanistic image of human knowledge. That is, knowledge has no intrinsic capacities for growth and change; it essentially remains intact until disturbed by environmental inputs. It is not a process in continuous and spontaneous transformation; rather, it is a structure that endures across time. Imagery of the stable and enduring structure of the human mind furnishes the second significant thrust for the doctrine of early impact. The early environment establishes the basic structure of the mind, the "foundation." This structure is not subject to processes of intrinsic change. Unless special efforts are made at alteration, it endures. Given the imagery of structure rather than process, of an obdurate mass rather than an evanescent force field, that which is established tends to remain.

The clearest exposition of the arrogation of the early impact assumption to the status of universal behavioral principle is contained in Watson's works. To cite but one of many examples, Watson informs his readers:

If you take a young plant and put it near a lighted window, it bends toward the light. You slant the plant by putting it in a certain environment. If you grow an oak seedling out in the open and tie a weight to its tip, the shoot will begin to curve and grow downward. Just as surely do parents slant their children from the very moment of birth, nor does the slanting process ever end. The old, threadbare adage, "As the twig is bent, so is the tree inclined," takes on a fresh meaning. You daily slant your children; you continue the process until they leave you. Even after they leave the home and your immediate influence, your slanting does not cease to exert its effect. It has become so fixed in their modes of behavior and even in their very thoughts that nothing can ever wholly eradicate it. Truly do we inevitably create our young in our own image (1928:38–39).

In light of the paucity of evidence at Watson's disposal, such a statement must be viewed as little more than a cavalier expression of faith. Perhaps the most substantial evidence available had been generated by Watson himself. This took the form of his and Raynor's classic case study of little Albert. (See article 6.) This simple study became widely celebrated. As Murphy and Kovach comment in their historical account of modern psychology, "Despite its crudeness, this experiment immediately had a profound effect . . . for it appeared to support the whole conception that . . . important enduring traits of personality . . . may be 'built into' the child by conditioning" (1972:246).

Although child psychology of the past two decades has shifted strongly in the organismic direction, and thus in a direction antithetical to the early impact assumption, the assumption continues even today to demand broad credence. For example, in Kimble and Garmezey's introduction to psychology, we find, "It is the lack of mothering (i.e., handling, fondling, rocking, caressing) that produces profound effects on later adjustment" (1963:263). From another major text in the field, *Developmental Psychology Today*, we learn, "During early childhood certain areas of personality outweigh most others in importance. These elements include aggression, shame and guilt, dependence and independence, and proper sexual roles. These areas are important because experience in each of them fixes a certain portion of the personality" (p. 318). Such statements are also echoed in more advanced writings. For example, in Robert LeVine's contribution to *The Handbook of Socialization Theory and Research* (1969), we find, "The personality genotype . . . refers to a set of enduring individual behavior dispositions that may or may not find socially acceptable expression in the customary (or institutionalized) behavior of a population. Its major characteristics are early acquisition and resistance to elimination in subsequent experience" (p. 461).

These same views are also reechoed in a variety of influential treatises on childrearing. For example, as Benjamin Spock (1968:562) wrote, "It does irreperable harm to leave a child in the care of a person who does not give him security." Haim Ginnot, whose broad popularity almost equaled that of Spock, also advised, "Both sons and daughters are affected by the example of a weak father and a dominant mother. The boys may try to overcompensate. . . . Girls often . . . continue the reversal of roles for another generation" (1969:208). Finally, in Azerrad's (1980) more recent account, we find, "The foundation for (the adult) years is laid in the first years, when the group of behaviors that we might call the personality of the individual is learned with the guidance of the parents. . . . Raising happy children means creating the conditions for happy adults, who find the satisfaction of life within their grasp instead of always eluding them" (pgs. 197–98). The empirical support for such views is no less equivocal today than it was fifty years ago.

Toward Mindful Choice

The central focus of this chapter has been on the guiding influence of scientific metatheory on theorizing about human conduct. We have argued that in accepting the logical empiricist conception of the nature of science, psychologists have unwittingly adopted a behaviorist orientation toward human activity in general and the development of the child in particular. This view of the child and its malleability and of the potency of the environment to influence both immediate and enduring behavior patterns can scarcely be derived from observation. Rather, it justifies a preexistent faith. It remains now to deal with one major criticism of the present line of thought and to explore briefly some implications for the future.

Perhaps the most potent source of criticism of the present thesis might be furnished by neobehaviorist researchers. There are countless studies that seem to demonstrate unequivocally that reinforcement can and does shape the activity of the child (Fischer 1963; Gelfand et al. 1975; Midlarsky and Bryan 1967; Serbin, Tonnick, and Sternglanz 1977; Hallenberg and Sperry 1951; Deur and

Parke 1970). And from this standpoint it might be argued, that although the long-term effects of early learning may be problematic, research leaves no doubt about the potential power of environmental reinforcement on the conduct of the child.

Yet, when the assumptions underlying such studies are more closely examined, we find these conclusions insubstantial. In particular, they are based on the unwarranted conflation of sequence and causality. The investigator in such research is exposed only to sequences of the following variety: (1) child's action, (2) environmental event (in the form of reward or punishment), and (3) a modified form of the child's action. The sequence of events is all that one may be permitted to describe on the basis of observation alone. Yet the behaviorist investigator adds to this account a second-order assumption, to whit, the environmental event is the *cause* of the modification in the child's conduct. The reinforcement "causes" the alteration in pattern. This particular conclusion cannot be justified by reference to observables; it is a theoretically derived preference and it could be otherwise. One could, for example, view the child as an active agent in search of particular environmental events. When such events are discovered, the child makes a *voluntary* decision to adjust his or her activities to acquire them. In this case it is not the experimenter who is controlling the child but the child who is selecting out certain events made available by the experimenter. From this perspective, the only reason that studies of the traditional sort are successful is that they capitalize on what is already known about the child's autonomous search patterns.

To illustrate more fully, let us alter the content of the sequence and reexamine the premise that reinforcement shapes human activity. Let us suppose that an individual is experiencing difficulties in sleeping. He tries to put the cares of the day behind him, but to no avail. He continues restlessly to toss and turn. One day a friend suggests that he drink a double jigger of Glenfiddich before retiring. Indeed, it is found that when this option is selected, he sleeps quite readily. Thereafter, on days when work has been particularly stressful, the individual indulges himself before retiring. In effect, behavior at t_1 is followed by the presence of an environmental event, which is followed by a modified form of behavior at t_2. Yet in this case most people would not be prepared to argue that the alcohol consumption "caused" the subsequent modification in activity. Rather, one might say the individual was seeking a solution to a problem and when he found it he decided that it would often be useful to him. In this case we are willing to grant to the individual the causal power for his own actions. This is not to say that such an account is any more justified by observation than the behaviorist account is. However, it is to point out that sequence does not determine the allocation of causality and that the manner in which such allocations are made largely derives from malleable and historically located rules for rendering human activity intelligible.

What do these arguments suggest for the future science of child development? At the outset, it seems clear that whether one views the child as the pawn of environmental reinforcement must be decided on grounds other than empirical ones. There are significant competitors extant. The organismic view of human development, which holds the individual's life trajectory to be largely autonomous and predetermined, is one such possibility and its supporters are numerous. This account, too, has begun to find expression in the parental guidance literature. For example, as Ames and Ilg (1955) have advised in their volume on child behavior, "Gone are the days when psychologists likened the child's body to a lump of clay which you the parent could mold in any direction you chose. Nowadays most of us recognize the fact that though the child's behavior can be strongly influenced by the kind of home and other surroundings in which he grows up, many of the changes which will take place in his behavior are determined from within" (1955:1). The aleatory account, supported primarily by investigators in lifespan study, is another strong competitor. From this perspective, human development largely depends on the individual's choices over time as he or she interacts within malleable systems of social interdependence. Although this view is amply represented in advisory volumes for adults (Sheehy 1974), it has yet to find significant expression in sources for parental guidance. Perhaps parents of the present era are unprepared to grant the infant powers of voluntary choice.

What is required, then, is a more determined inquiry into the broader social consequences or ramifications of adopting one or another of these particular viewpoints. What forms of parental conduct are sustained or created by these various theoretical departures? What social institutions are favored and which are threatened?

Certain outcomes of adopting the behaviorist perspectives have been touched upon. Certain consequences of the organismic and the aleatory perspectives have been treated elsewhere (Gergen 1982:147–172). However, a thorough exploration of these matters has yet to be undertaken. At least one additional implication, outside the developmental arena might also be considered in such an undertaking, and that is the effects of theory on the dominant conception of science. If the behaviorist perspective is derived from the logical empiricist metatheory, and behaviorism is found both empirically arbitrary and valuationally unsuitable, then what are the repercussions for the prevailing theory of science? Both the organismic and the aleatory perspectives imply a radically different conception of science, its products, and its methods. Thus, to develop an alternative theory of child development is simultaneously to establish the basis for a new theory of knowledge.

References

Ajzen, I. and M. Fishbein. 1980. *Understanding Attitudes and Predicting Social Behavior.* Englewood Cliffs, N.J.: Prentice-Hall.

Ames, L. B. and F. L. Ilg. 1955. *The Gesell Institute's Child Behavior From Birth to Ten.* New York: Harper and Row.

Apfelbaum, E. and I. Lubek. 1976. "Resolution Vs. Revolution? The Theory of Conflicts in Question." In L. Strickland, F. Aboud, and K. J. Gergen, eds. *Social Psychology in Transition.* New York: Plenum Press.

Azerrad, J. 1980. *Anyone Can Have a Happy Child.* New York: Warner.

Bandura, A. 1977. *Social Learning Theory.* Englewood Cliffs, N.J.: Prentice-Hall.

Bandura, A. and R. H. Walters. 1963. *Social Learning and Personality Development.* New York: Holt, Rinehart & Winston.

Brim, O. G. and J. Kagan. 1980. *Constancy and Change in Human Development.* Cambridge, Mass.: Harvard University Press.

Brown, C. W. and E. E. Ghiselli. 1955. *Scientific Method in Psychology.* New York: McGraw-Hill.

Buck-Morss, S. 1975. "Socio-economic Bias in Piaget's Theory and Its Implications for the Cultural Controversy." *Human Development* 18:35–49.

Buss, A. R. 1979a. "The Emerging Field of the Sociology of Psychological Knowledge." In Buss, ed. *Psychology in Social Context.* N.Y.: Irvington.

—— 1979b. *A Dialectical Psychology.* New York: Halsted Press.

Clarke, A. M. and A. D. B. Clarke. 1976. *Early Experience: Myth and Evidence*. London: Open Books.

Developmental Psychology Today. 1972. Delmar, Calif.: CRM Books.

Duer, J. D. and R. P. Parke. 1970. "Effects of Inconsistent Punishment on Agression in Children." *Developmental Psychology* 2:403–11.

Fischer, W. F. 1963. "Sharing in Pre-school Children as a Function of Amount and Type of Reinforcement." *Genetic Psychology Monographs* 26:409–14.

Gelfand, D. M., D. F. Hartman, C. C. Cromer, C. L. Smith, and B. C. Page. 1975. "The Effects of Institutional Prompts and Praise on Children's Donation Rates." *Child Development* 46:980–83.

Gergen, K. J. 1977. "Stability, Change and Chance in Understanding Human Development." In N. Datan and H. Reese, eds. *Life-span Developmental Psychology: Dialectic Perspectives*. New York: Academic Press.

—— 1980. "The Emerging Crisis in Life-span Developmental Theory." In P. Baltes and O. Brim, eds. *Life-span Development and Behavior*, vol. 3. New York: Academic Press.

—— 1982. *Toward Transformation in Social Knowledge*. New York: Springer.

Gergen, K. J. and M. M. Gergen. 1982. "Explaining Human Conduct: Form and Function." In P. E. Secord, ed. *Explaining Human Behavior, Consciousness, Human Action and Social Structure*. Beverly Hills, Calif.: Sage.

Ginott, H. 1969. *Between Parent and Child: New Solutions to Old Problems*. New York: Avon.

Goslin, D.A., ed. 1969. *Handbook of Socialization Theory and Research*. Chicago, Ill.: Rand McNally.

Habermas, J. 1971. *Knowledge and Human Interest*. Boston: Beacon.

Hallenberg, E. and M. Sperry. 1951. "Some Antecedents of Aggression and Effects of Frustration in Doll Play." *Personality: Topical Symposia* 1:32–43.

Hanson, N. R. 1958. *Patterns of Discovery*. Cambridge: Cambridge University Press.

Hoppe, F. 1930. "Erfolg und Misserfolg (Success and Failure)." Doctoral Dissertation directed by Kurt Lewin. *Psychologische Forschung* 14:1–62. Translated in Joseph De Rivera. 1976. *Field Theory as Human Science: Contributions of Lewin's Berlin Group*, pp. 455–93. New York: Gardner Press.

Hull, C. L. 1943. *Principles of Behavior*. New York: Appleton-Century-Crofts.

Kimble, G. A. and N. Garmezey. 1963. *Principles of General Psychology*. New York: Ronald Press.

Koch, S. 1959. "Epilogue." In S. Koch, ed. *Psychology: A Study of a Science*, vol. 3, pp. 729–783. New York: McGraw-Hill.

Kohlberg, L. 1969. "Stages and Sequences: The Cognitive-Developmental Approach to Socialization." In Goslin, *q.v.*, pgs. 347–380.

LeVine, R. 1969. "The Child in Cross-cultural Perspective." In Goslin, *q.v.*, pp. 503–542.

Lewin, K. T. Dembo, L. Festinger, and P. Sears. 1944. "Level of Aspiration." In J. McV. Hunt, ed. *Personality and the Behavior Disorders*, 1:333–78. New York: Ronald.

Lomax, E. J. Kagan, and B. G. Rosenkrantz. 1978. *Science and Patterns of Child Care*. San Francisco: W. H. Freeman.

MacCorquodale, K. and P. E. Meehl. 1948. "On a Distinction Between Hypothetical Constructs and Intervening Variables." *Psychological Review* 55:95–107.

Mandler, G. and W. Kessen. 1975. *The Language of Psychology.* Melbourne, Fla.: Krieger.

Marx, M. H. and W. A. Hellix. 1963. *Systems and Theories in Psychology.* New York: McGraw-Hill.

Midlarsky, E. and J. H. Bryan. 1967. "Training Charity in Children." *Journal of Personality and Social Psychology* 5:408–15.

Morawski, J. G. 1979. "The Structure of Psychological Communities: A Framework for Examining the Sociology of Social Psychology. In L. H. Strickland, ed. *Soviet and Western Perspectives on Social Psychology.* Oxford: Pergamon Press.

Murphy, G. and J. R. Kovach. 1972. *Historical Introduction to Modern Psychology,* 3rd ed. New York: Harcourt Brace & Jovanovich.

Overton, W. F. and H. W. Reese. 1973. "Models of Development: Methodological Implications." In J. R. Nesselroade and H. W. Reese, eds. *Life-span Developmental Psychology: Methodological Issues.* New York: Academic Press.

Piaget, J. 1952. *The Origins of Intelligence in Children.* New York: Norton.

Putnam, H. 1978. *Meaning and the Moral Sciences.* London: Routledge & Kegan Paul.

Riegel, K. F. 1972. "Time and Change in the Development of the Individual and Society." In H. Reese, ed. *Advances in Child Development and Behavior.* New York: Academic Press.

Rutter, J. B. 1954. *Social Learning and Clinical Psychology.* Englewood Cliffs, N.J.: Prentice Hall.

Rutter, M. 1972. *Maternal Deprivation Reassessed.* Hardmondsworth: Penguin.

Sampson, E. E. 1981. "Cognitive Psychology as Ideology." *American Psychologist* 36:730–43.

Serbin, L. A., I. J. Tonnick, and S. H. Sternglanz. 1977. "Shaping Cooperative Cross-sex Play." *Child Development* 48:924–29.

Sheehy, G. 1974. *Passages: Predictable Crises of Adult Life.* New York: Dutton.

Skinner, B. F. 1957. *Verbal Behavior.* Englewood Cliffs, N.J.: Prentice-Hall.

—— 1969. *Contingencies of Reinforcement.* New York: Appleton-Century-Crofts.

—— 1974. *About Behaviorism.* New York: Knopf.

Spock, B. 1968. *Baby and Child Care.* New York: Simon & Schuster.

Thorndike, E. L. 1911. *Animal Intelligence.* New York: Macmillan.

Tolman, E. C. 1932. *Purposive Behavior in Animals and Men.* New York: Appleton-Century-Crofts.

Watson, J. B. 1924. *Psychology From the Standpoint of a Behaviorist,* 2nd ed. Philadelphia: Lippincott.

—— 1928. *Psychological Care of the Infant and the Child.* New York: Norton.

Watson, J. B. and R. Raynor. 1920. "Conditioned Emotional Reactions." *Journal of Experimental Psychology* 3:1–14.

Werner, H. 1948. *Comparative Psychology of Mental Development.* New York: International Universities Press.

13 The Study of Employed Mothers Over Half a Century

LOIS WLADIS HOFFMAN

R esearch on the effects of maternal employment on families and children began to appear during the mid-1930s. This work was begun in a climate of disapproval; maternal employment was widely considered undesirable and a source of social and psychological maladjustment in children, as well as the cause of a wide variety of social malfunctions. It has often been assumed that the research of this period reflected this judgment but that modern research has achieved objectivity. Neither of these assumptions is entirely correct. It is true that the well-known correlational studies of juvenile delinquency (Gleuck & Gleuck 1934) suggested a relationship to maternal employment because they failed to control on extraneous variables, but this was an error not reserved for the study of maternal employment. Absence of controls was a common fault in the early correlational studies whatever the topic. The interview studies (Mathews 1934, LaFollette 1934), on the other hand, presented a more complex picture and a more honest glimpse into the family life of the employed mother. The early research was limited because of inadequate theory and research skills, overattention to evaluative outcomes, and insufficient criticism from the researcher himself and his professional colleagues when the results matched expectations. In this sense, however, the present-day research is also limited. How these influences changed over the years, and how they remained the same, is the focus of this chapter.

The Changed Society

In considering how the research on maternal employment might have shifted over the years, it would be reasonable to assume that the major source of change would be in the social phenomenon itself, for during this period maternal employment has gone from an uncommon pattern to the modal family form. The rapidity with which maternal employment rates have increased can be seen in table 13.1. At present, for intact families, 63 percent of the mothers with school-aged children are employed; 48 percent of the

TABLE 13.1. Labor Force Participation Rates of Mothers With Children Under 18, 1940–80

Year	% of Mothers
1980	56.6
1978	53.0
1976	48.8
1974	45.7
1972	42.9
1970	42.0
1968	39.4
1966	35.8
1964	34.5
1962	32.9
1960	30.4
1958	29.5
1956	27.5
1954	25.6
1952	23.8
1950	21.6
1948	20.2
1946	18.2
1940	8.6

SOURCE: U.S. Department of Labor, 1977;
U.S. Department of Commerce, 1979;
U.S. Department of Labor, 1981.

mothers of preschoolers. For mothers in single-parent families, the comparable figures are 77 percent and 58 percent.[1] The effects of maternal employment on families and children obtained when this pattern was atypical cannot be generalized to the present situation when it is modal. Even if there were no other change, the sheer shift in prevalence might be expected to alter the effects. If, for example, the employed mothers of the past responded with guilt and overmothering, as one study in the 1950s showed (Hoffman 1961), guilt is less likely to be the response now that the pattern is so widespread. In fact, at the present time, it may be nonemployed mothers who are on the defensive and who, to justify their nonemployment, are overmothering (Hoffman 1980).

Furthermore, it is not only maternal employment rates that have changed. Family size is down, the amount of necessary housework has diminished, divorce rates are up, the educational levels of women have increased, and there has been a transformation in attitudes about women's roles (Hoffman 1979, Thornton and Freedman 1980). All of these are factors that influence and mediate the impact of maternal employment on the child and the family (Hoffman 1974). It is to be expected, then, that maternal employment status would have a different impact on the child at present than in previous generations.

In addition, because prevailing attitudes have changed, the pressures on the scientist, if not the biases of the scientist herself, might be expected to be different. Early research was often funded with the expectation, and the hope, that the data would demonstrate the social problems brought about by the employment of mothers, whereas present research is as likely to be funded and undertaken by the researcher to indicate its advantages or to show that it does not have ill effects. In much of the scientific community, there used to be an expectation that negative effects of maternal employment should be demonstrable, and the failure to show them suggested faulty measures or inadequate design. A close critical scrutiny was more likely to be forthcoming in peer review when the data failed to conform to the evaluator's expectations. Today peer review also varies in severity depending on whether or not the results conform to the reviewer's expectation, but it may be findings suggesting negative effects that bring close scrutiny today. Such criticism is not necessarily inappropriate or invalid, but critical acumen increases when the empirical results go counter to the prevailing view.

In view of these changes, it would not be surprising if the present empirical research on maternal employment showed very different effects than earlier work. What is surprising is that the empirical results have actually been remarkably stable over the years. The negative effects expected during the earlier years were not demonstrated except by inadequate research that was subsequently exposed for the failure to control on extraneous variables such as social class and father absence. Then, as now, maternal employment was not so robust a variable that a well-executed study could show differences of any kind except for specified subgroups or very homogeneous samples. Many of the patterns revealed in the data have remained the same. For example, in one of the earliest studies, published in 1934, Mathews found that sons of employed women expressed less positive attitudes toward home-life situations than sons of full-time homemakers, whereas daughters showed the opposite trend; this pattern of positive correlates of maternal employment for daughters but occasional negative ones for sons occurs also in the most recent studies. Around 1960, four major reviews of the literature on the effects of maternal employment on children were published (Maccoby 1958, Stolz 1960, Hoffman 1963, Siegel and Haas 1963). It is informative to reread them; they seem remarkably up-to-date.[2]

What has more clearly changed over the years, however, is the quality of the research, particularly during the late 1950s, and the quantity, particularly in very recent years.

Quality of the Research

In general, the quality of the research has improved over the years with a major advance in the 1950s and more modest subsequent changes. There are a number of events that might improve quality: an increase in funds available; more skilled researchers; advances in techniques of measurement, research design, or theory; or improvement in objectivity. Each of these will be considered as possible influences on the quality of research on maternal employment.

Funds

Availability of funds is probably only a minor factor in this case. Although the attitude of the funding agencies changed over the years, there is no evidence of a real increase in the amount of funds available for maternal employment research relative to the amount of funds available to social science generally. There has never been a great deal of money earmarked for maternal employment studies. Most of the research over the years has been carried out with small single grants or has been piggybacked onto a larger project.

It may be that the availability of large grants to investigate the effects of maternal employment might have enriched and facilitated the understanding of this pattern, but there is no evidence that fluctuations in the actual availability of funds has played a very noticeable role to date. There are, however, two possible exceptions. The first is that the Canada Council is the only funding agency that has shown a consistent interest during the last decade in the investigation of maternal employment effects on the child, and one of the results is that much of the better recent work has been done in Canada by Canadians (Kappel and Lambert 1972; Gold and Andres 1978a, 1978b, 1978c; Gold, Andres, and Glorieux 1979).

The other possible influence of funding sources on the quality of maternal employment research is an indirect one. Although there was no outpouring of funds for this particular topic, there was an increase in funds for research having social policy implications. This money went more toward the effort to improve the intellectual competence of children, and particularly toward the research associated with the Head Start programs, but the effects may have been broader in that research that seemed oriented toward understanding social issues became more accpetable in scientific circles.

Skilled Researchers

Research on maternal employment, until the middle of the 1950s, was carried out mainly by persons who were not trained in the social sciences (e.g., Mathews 1934, LaFolette 1934, Cummings 1944, Essig and Morgan 1946, Kasmar 1945). The study of social issues was not considered "real" science. Status-oriented researchers in psychology and, to a lesser extent, in sociology looked with disdain on such efforts. They were considered the province of social workers, home economists, and social reformers.

It was probably not until the late seventies that issue-oriented concerns became a truly accepted and integral part of these disciplines, but the change began in the mid-fifties. During that time, there were several studies of the effects of maternal employment on the husband-wife relationship, particularly on the division of labor and power (Nye 1958, 1961; Heer 1958; Hoffman 1960; Wolfe 1959; Blood and Hamblin 1958; Blood and Wolfe 1960). It was also during the 1950s that the first well-controlled studies of the effects of maternal employment on the child appeared. Nye (1952, 1958a, 1959) conducted such investigations of mother's employment status and the adjustment of adolescent children and reconceptualized the concept of juvenile delinquency by using self-reports rather than police records. Burchinal (1963) performed one of the few studies that examined not only current maternal employment status but also the period in the child's life when the mother had been employed, relating these to personality and cognitive measures obtained from adolescent children. Hartley (1959) interviewed elementary school children to compare the sex-role perceptions of children with employed and nonemployed mothers. Siegel and her colleagues (1959) conducted an outstanding study of independence and dependence exhibited by kindergarten children with employed and nonemployed mothers. The comparison groups were well-matched, employment status was clearly defined, the dependent variables were measured by behavioral observations, and data were reported separately for each sex. Hoffman's study (1961), also conducted during the fifties, compared the elementary-school-aged children of employed mothers to a group of nonemployed mothers' children who were pair-matched on age, sex, ordinal position in the family, and the father's occupation. Data were obtained from parents, children, teachers, and school records. The study was unusual in two respects: data were obtained to measure both parent-child relationships and child characteristics, and the data were analyzed separately for mothers who liked work and those who did not, revealing a different effect of employment, depending on the mother's attitude. Finally, the study by Yarrow and her colleagues (1962), much cited in subsequent years, indicated that full-time homemakers who preferred to work had the lowest score on an adequacy of mothering scale—lower than employed women whichever their preference and lower than satisfied homemakers. This same study, incidentally, also found that satisfied homemakers had the highest scores, though this finding has not been picked up as often in later discussions of the work.

There are several things to note about these studies. For one thing, they were all done by experienced, competent researchers. To some extent, this reflected the increased acceptability of conducting research on practical issues. The psychology studies were also conducted disproportionately by women. This may reflect in part the greater interest in the topic by women because it has a more direct relevance to their own lives. It might also reflect a lesser involvement of women professionals at that time in the conventional professional status system. In either case, it is possible that the increased interest in maternal employment by well-trained research psychologists reflected an increase in the number of women in the field.

The gender of the researchers may also be relevant to the fact that this group of studies looking at child effects analyzed the data separately for sons and daughters. This was extremely important in unraveling the effects of maternal employment, for its influence is very different for boys and girls, and combining them obscured relationships entirely because of the counterpatterns. The women psychologists may have been more sensitive to the gender-based differences in socialization processes. It is so commonplace now to analyze data separately for boys and girls that it is difficult to realize that this was not the usual practice even ten years ago. In the 1950s, many research projects eliminated girls because they did not conform to predictions, a few studies used only female subjects, but most studies that included children of each sex combined them into one group, children.

This body of research, together with the several literature reviews that provided summaries and integrations of the work (Maccoby 1958, Stolz 1960, Siegel and Haas 1963, Hoffman 1963, Blood 1963, Nye 1963, Nye and Hoffman 1963), changed the quality of the maternal employment research and provided the major framework within which the studies that followed were done. Maternal employment was established as a legitimate area for scientific investigation. Surprisingly, the research in the succeeding decade was sparse and not of remarkably superior quality. The shift of the 1950s set a new standard, and subsequent work has built on this, but there were not further major advances until quite recently.

Measurement, Design, Theory

In the subsequent research there have not been notable improvements in design, but there has been a decrease in the number of poorly designed studies. Thus, few studies since then have failed to control on social class and presence of father, and combining sons and daughters has become increasingly rare. The child development studies almost always control on the child's age at the time of measurement, and the recent series of Canadian studies have also considered the duration of the mother's employment. Family size is also more often matched than during earlier periods. On the other hand, neither family size nor the age of the children is consistently controlled in some of the more recent time-use studies that examine the effects of maternal employment on the time allocation of the parents and the division of labor by having subjects keep diaries specifying their ongoing daily activities. This constitutes a very serious problem in the interpretation of the time-use data that counterbalances the advantage otherwise offered by the more objective measurement of the dependent variables (Hoffman 1983a).

In addition to the general improvement in controls on extraneous variables, several studies in the last decade have examined maternal employment effects in specific subgroups of the population. For example, during the seventies, the professionally employed mother was a popular subject (Birnbaum 1975, Garland 1972, Holmstrom 1972, Rapoport and Rapoport 1971). Previously neglected populations, such as blacks, single-parent families, and poverty groups, were also studied (Cherry and Eaton 1977, Kreisberg 1970, Woods 1972). Most recently the age-specific studies have also turned to a previously understudied group: there has been burgeoning research on the effects of maternal employment on infants (Cohen 1978; Hock 1980; Vaughn, Gove, and Egeland 1980; Chase-Lansdale 1981; Pederson et al. 1981; Stuckey, McGhee, and Bell 1982).

There have been other improvements in study design since the 1950s but only modest ones. The point was made in the Hoffman study (1961) and in the various reviews (Hoffman 1963) that it was necessary to measure the steps in between and not simply link maternal employment status to a child characteristic. Theory development and social action require that one understand the process by which an effect occurs. A few studies have done this, such as the recent research of Gold and her colleagues (1979) and the investigations of Woods (1972), Cherry and Eaton (1977), and Goldberg (1977), but by and large most studies still consider only the two levels.

The need for longitudinal investigations has also been pointed out, yet there are only a few studies of this kind. One of the most ambitious was undertaken by Moore (1975) in England during the fifties. Children who received "noncontinuous mothering" (maternal employment in almost all cases) during their early years were compared with children whose mothers were home full time and were retested at various points up through adolescence. The early results of this study suggested negative effects of maternal employment (Moore 1963), whereas later results reporting the comparison at adolescence (1975) indicated positive effects. Over the years, as the data accumulated, Moore came to focus on the vulnerabilities and strengths of each pattern and to caution against judgmental outcome measurement. The study also indicated the importance of considering effects developmentally. Long-range effects of maternal employment may be quite different from short-term effects (Hoffman 1980, Dizard 1968). A few of the recent infancy studies have used short-term longitudinal designs (Vaughn, Gove, and Egeland 1980; Chase-Lansdale 1981), a pattern particularly desirable in infancy research since questions have been raised about the stability and reliability of the measures used in these studies. Cherry and Eaton (1977) also used a short-term longitudinal design to show the effects of early maternal employment on physical and intellectual growth. In general, developmental factors have become more salient in maternal employment studies, as well as in psychology as a whole.

The specific design introduced by Yarrow (1962), in which the comparison groups were based on a combination of employment status and role satisfaction, has been improved over the years. In the first study all the data came from maternal interviews and there were serious problems of contamination between the independent and dependent variables (Hoffman 1974). In subsequent research, the investigators have measured role satisfaction so as to differentiate this more clearly from feelings about mothering per se, and they have obtained independent measures of the dependent variables (Farel 1980; Schubert, Bradley-Johnson, and Nuttal 1980). The conclusions of the original study have been, by and large, substantiated, but the new evidence is more solid.

Measurement in maternal employment research has also shown minor improvements. With respect to the independent variable, it is easier to use more specific criteria in measuring employment status simply because of its increased prevalence. In the 1950s, for example, if one were studying all the fourth graders in a middle-sized community, the total number of children with "currently employed" mothers might not yield an adequate sample once it was restricted to intact families or families of a certain size. Today, maternal employment is so common that it is quite possible to secure an adequate sample even if that variable is specified to "maternal employment continuous over the last three years" or "maternal employment of over thirty hours per week." Increasingly employment status is being defined more specifically with attention to such aspects as the hours of employment, the skill level, or its timing with respect to other family and developmental events (Piotrkowski and Katz, 1982; Hetherington 1979; Hoffman, in press).

Dependent variables have largely followed the patterns of the field, used because they were available, with few measures developed for the specific subject matter or to test a particular theory. Thus, some research directions have been dropped because the measures lost credibility over the years—juvenile delinquency as measured by police contact, for example. There have also been fewer studies of the effects of maternal employment on the husband-wife power relationship—probably because the measures have been so severely criticized (Safilios-Rothschild 1970, Bahr 1974, Quarm 1977). The most common dependent variables that have been used, on the other hand, are the standard measures of cognitive ability such as the Stanford Binet, various other measures of achievement, and standard measures of personality and social adjustment.

The last decade has seen the development of a variety of

sex-role measures, and these have been widely used in the maternal employment research. In fact the new orientation toward women's roles has reshaped both measures and concepts about female mental health and thus opened the way for demonstrating some of the positive effects of maternal employment on daughters. For example, in one of the first of this new wave of research, Baruch (1972) used the recently developed technique of having women college students judge the competence of articles to which the names of male and female authors had been arbitrarily assigned. Her research indicated that the daughters of employed mothers were not affected in their judgments by the sex of the author, but the daughters of nonemployed mothers judged as less competent the articles attributed to women authors. The implications of this simple study for the development of self-esteem, achievement motivation, and social attitudes are considerable. Subsequent work has shown that having an employed mother, without even specifying the nature of her employment, diminishes sex-role stereotypes in both sons and daughters and seems to increase in daughters their independence and academic-occupational motivation (Hoffman 1979).

The increased evidence for a positive impact of maternal employment on daughters that has emerged in recent years may be in part a response to the various changes in society discussed above. However, there is evidence that some of these effects were there even thirty years ago but were more obscure and not always labeled as positive. The picture of the daughters of employed mothers as more active, outgoing, independent, career oriented, and admiring of their mothers was there even then if one considered the data from the various studies carefully, as was done in the reviews by Stolz (1960) and Hoffman (1963). These effects were not so clear that they provided the major conclusions of any particular study, but rather they emerged when one examined the reoccurring patterns of results across studies. Over the years an increased respect for these qualities in women developed and new personality and sex-role inventories replaced the previous ones, which had assumed that femininity and mental health in women included fearfulness, dependency, and a preference for baths over showers (Bem 1975, Herzog and Sundia 1973, Hoffman 1982b). Thus the sharper emergence of the positive effects of maternal employment on daughters in the recent studies may reflect these improvements in measurement even more than actual changes over time.

There are other examples of measurement improvement. For one, the time-use studies already mentioned formerly classified as "childcare time" all activities that stemmed from the presence of a child whether or not they involved actual interaction with the child. Robinson (1978), Goldberg (1977), and Hill and Stafford (1978) have, however, introduced important differentiations. That the specificity of the measure affects the conclusions about maternal employment is clear from the fact that Goldberg found in her study of nursery school children no difference between the employed- and nonemployed-mother families in the amount of one-to-one mother-child contact but a significant difference in the amount of indirect contact such as when the two were in the same room engaged in separate activities. A very different example of measurement advance is provided by the work of Birnbaum (1975). She revealed a sharp picture of the psychological meaning of professional employment and the full-time homemaker role among a group of educated mothers by using a set of projective measures developed for the study. And, as a final example, behavioral observation techniques have been more fully employed in several recent studies, reflecting probably the increased interest in research on preschool children and infants.

Theory development has not been impressive over the years. A theoretical basis for some of the results has been provided post hoc by Hoffman (1974, 1980) and by Bronfenbrenner and Crouter (1982), and some of the studies have been guided by theoretical orientations (e.g., Farel 1980; Gold et al. 1978b, c, 1979), but the theoretical contribution of this research on the whole has been disappointing.

Objectivity

Critical peer review keeps science "honest." Conscious falsification of data is very rare. The exposure of Cyril Burt, who falsified data to support the idea of the genetic basis of intelligence and to further his own career, is both horrifying, because it shows that deliberately fabricated data can be added to the body of supposed scientific knowledge, and also reassuring, for its failure to fit with the results of other studies very quickly marked it as suspect and eventually led to its total disrepute. This process of peer evaluation and integration with other results also corrects errors in research that come from inept work or unconscious bias.

In the short run, however, both the original research and the criticism may reflect some bias of which neither researcher nor reviewer is aware. It is interesting, for example, that the earlier research that did not institute adequate controls came to negative conclusions about maternal employment, a view that was consistent with the times. Later research, on the other hand, seemed to prematurely conclude that maternal employment had no effects. In fact, finding no differences between employed and nonemployed mother groups can result from inadequate measurement or faulty design, such as the use of heterogeneous samples that include counterpatterns, as discussed earlier in connection with the failure to analyze data separately for each sex. Selected subgroup analyses can reveal differences otherwise obscured. In both time periods, the flaws in the research may have escaped earlier detection because the researchers and the reviewers were satisfied with the results.

It is also possible that the social relevance of maternal employment influenced the course of the research through topic selection. In the reviews of the early sixties for example, particularly those by Stolz (1960) and Hoffman (1963), there were many suggestions for future research, but the ones that were followed were more consistent with the new tenor of the times. In the Hoffman review, for example, data from several studies of juvenile delinquency were reanalyzed. The results seemed to show no relationship between maternal employment and juvenile delinquency for lower class boys but a positive one for boys in the middle class. No one has picked up on the latter observation to explore it further or to see if the results could be replicated in a new study. Is it possible that this hypothesis was not explored further because the social climate had so changed that there was no longer interest in data that linked maternal employment to juvenile delinquency in any class?

As a researcher, then, bias can affect one's work by the persistence with which one pursues differences and the choice of topic; it can also affect the conclusions one draws from the results. As an example of the last, one can say "In eight independent comparisons there were no significant differences" or "Although there were no significant differences, in seven of the eight independent comparisons the direction of the difference was the same and in no case did the direction go the other way." Each statement may be accurate, but the implications drawn from them might be quite different.

Bias can also affect criticism. If the results of a particular study are inconsistent with accumulated findings, do not fit one's own theory, or are ideologically disturbing, motivation for detecting flaws is increased. This can influence what articles are accepted for publication, and if there is a general consensus among the experts who serve as reviewers, critical scrutiny can be unequally applied so that the published works disproportionately support the prevailing view. Because very few empirical studies are immune from criticism, the reviewer's predisposition may be important. Aware of this, however, some reviewers err in the opposite direction—to avoid the contamination of their own orientation they may too easily approve for publication articles on the opposite side. It is very difficult to avoid completely the influence of one's theoretical or personal position. It is hoped that objectivity is obtained through evaluation, criticism, and related work, but this process is slowed when there is widespread consensus.

Fortunately for the objectivity of the research on maternal employment, there is not at present total agreement. Before the mid-fifties, the bias was toward showing negative correlates of maternal employment. The new era in the late fifties, besides introducing methodological advances, was primarily countering the previous period. For more than a decade the prevailing view, noted in previous reviews (Hoffman 1963, 1974), seems to have been that maternal employment had no effect at all. At present, the position seems somewhat more sophisticated. Although it has taken almost twenty years, some of the new approaches are those suggested in the reviews of the early sixties. There seems to be new attention to the conditioning variables such as attitudes, social class, and family structure with an awareness that results might be positive under some conditions but negative under others. There is still an overemphasis on the evaluative dependent variables but more flexibility in considering the conditions under which one effect, rather than another, occurs.

Perhaps most notable on the current scene, however, is the interest and controversy surrounding the issue of maternal employment and the preschool child. If there is general consensus among researchers today that maternal employment does not have a negative effect on children, it does not extend to the preschool years. This controversy should keep the field honest and the research interesting.

Quantity

The quantity of research on maternal employment waned over the years, but attention to the topic revived again during the early 1970s. One incentive for this research was the new interest in women's roles and particularly in the factors that influence high achievement in women. Much of the accumulated data on maternal employment effects has come from studies during this period of the backgrounds of high achieving or professionally innovative women (Ginsberg 1971, Almquist and Angrist 1971, Tangri 1975). The interest in maternal employment was only incidental in this research, but among the predictive background factors, it persistently reoccurred. As already mentioned, there were also several investigations of that period that demonstrated a relationship between maternal employment and diminished sex-role stereotyping (Broverman et al. 1972, Baruch 1972, Miller 1975, Marantz and Mansfield 1977).

As part of the interest in elite women, research was undertaken to explore the lives of dual-career couples (Rapoport and Rapoport 1971, Holmstrom 1972, Poloma 1972, Garland 1972, Birnbaum 1975). Though none of these investigations focused on the parenting role, they all provided some data on the professional woman's role as mother (Hoffman 1973). Furthermore, they provided useful data on some of the intermediary processes by describing the adjustments in household routines, the marital relationship, and the psychological state of the couple, all of which are crucial in unraveling the process by means of which maternal employment affects the child.

It has already been mentioned that the 1970s also witnessed an increase in the number of studies of maternal employment among lower class blacks and single-parent families. Some of these studies, such as the ones by Woods (1972) and Cherry and Eaton (1977), were particularly valuable because they operationalized not only the child outcome dependent variables but also various intervening steps such as supervision patterns, maternal attitudes, and the financial advantage.

Most recently the boost in the number of maternal employment studies has come from the new attention to studying the effects on the preschool child. The major reason for this interest is the increased prevalence of employment among mothers of preschoolers. Though all maternal employment rates have increased steadily, this group has shown the most rapid rate changes in recent years. For example, 48 percent of the currently married mothers of preschoolers were employed in 1981, as already indicated, but that figure was only 19 percent in 1960. Employment rates for mothers with children under three have not lagged much behind. Among married mothers of children under three, 44 percent were employed in 1981; among separated or divorced mothers of children under three, 52 percent were employed.

This increase in employment rates has stimulated research in two ways. First, whereas opposition to maternal employment when children were school aged had pretty much quieted down, there was still widespread belief that the young child needed the full-time presence of the mother. Thus, maternal employment reemerged as a prominent social issue. Second, suddenly there were subjects available. Previously researchers interested in studying maternal employment and the preschooler had a very difficult time locating an appropriate sample of adequate size and often resorted to recruitment procedures, such as advertisements, which introduced a selection bias in the design. Samples of infants with employed mothers used to involve such atypical situations that effects were more likely to result from these factors than employment per se (Hoffman 1974). The change in maternal employment patterns brought new concerns and new subjects.

This new wave of research has also been stimulated by a general increase in interest in infancy among developmental psychologists. New techniques in studying parent-infant interaction, attachment, and developmental level have facilitated this work. There are still problems because measurement procedures with infants are cumbersome and expensive and thus sample sizes are small, making it difficult to do subgroup analysis or pursue serendipitous results. Nevertheless, this is an exciting new area of research with sufficient activity that each new study builds somewhat on the previous. Thus, Pederson et al (1983) and Stuckey, McGhee, and Bell (1982) have described interesting differences between employed- and nonemployed-mother families is the parent-infant interaction patterns for both mothers and fathers, while Chase-Lansdale (1981) has explored the mother-infant and father-infant attachment patterns associated with maternal employment.

The older preschool child has also been a popular subject in recent maternal employment research (Schachter 1981, Gold and Andres 1978c). It is important to distinguish this work from the studies of day care effects that are also currently prevalent because not all children in day care have employed mothers and most employed mothers use other kinds of child care arrangements. Furthermore, studies of preschool children that compare employed and nonemployed mothers' children in a particular child care or nursery school setting often run into methodological problems in interpreting their results. If the setting is a full-time day care center, selective factors might favor the employed mothers' children. They are in full-time day care because their mothers are employed, but the nonemployed mothers children may be there because of some disturbance in the family or an incapacity on the part of the mother. If then the employed mothers' children have higher scores on various social or cognitive measures, as they often do, it may reflect these selective factors. On the other hand, if the setting is a preschool regarded as a cognitively enriching experience, the selective factors might work the other way: nonemployed mothers' children may have been sent there because of a particular involvement by the parents in providing a cognitively stimulating setting, while the employed mothers' children may have been sent there simply to provide child care while the mother is at work. In this case, selective factors might favor the nonemployed mothers' children (Schachter 1981). Since samples of preschool children are most easily obtained in the group setting, and behavioral observations of peer group interaction are popular dependent variables, these problems frequently come up in the new research.

Other methodological problems have emerged along with the new wave of research on preschoolers. For example, it has already been noted that there is uncertainty about the long-range stability of some of the measurable characteristics of young children. Nevertheless, the new research is in many ways more promising than what has preceded it.

Communication of the Research Results

A particular problem that has vexed the researcher investigating the effects of maternal employment over the years involves the interpretation of the findings for public dissemination. This is actually part of a general problem of communicating social science research to persons outside the field. To the scientist, accuracy requires specifying the conditions under which the results were obtained and indicating precisely what outcomes were observed. From the layperson's standpoint, the need to make personal or policy decisions is often urgent, and it is difficult to extract the information desired from the researcher's cautions, qualifications, and jargon. This problem is, however, particularly troubling in the case of maternal employment research. There is considerable interest and concern about the effects on children of mothers' working and sometimes strong commitment to a particular position. Often writers are not seeking full information but only backup materials for already-formed opinions. The direction of the distortion has shifted over the years, but it has not disappeared. At present it is as likely to be toward minimizing the significance of maternal employment, or of saying it has no effects on the child unless the employed mother feels guilty, as it is to be in the traditional direction of maximizing its dangers. The former position is often presented in the popular "women's" magazines; the latter, by writers such as Burton White (1980), who are dealing only with the first three years. Neither position can be supported by data although both claim such support.

The findings are actually more complex. For one thing, it is not always possible to translate the effects observed into evaluative labels. If, for example, the preschool children of employed mothers are more assertive with their peers (Schachter 1981), is this a positive or a negative indication? Are the higher school performance scores sometimes obtained by sons of nonemployed mothers in the middle class a sign of superior cognitive ability or of overconformity (Hoffman 1980)? In addition, even where evaluation is easier, such as in the relative absence of a stereotype that females are incompetent noted in employed mothers' daughters, the effects usually depend on other aspects of the situation.

Thus, under the best of circumstances, it is very difficult to summarize empirical findings for communication outside the research world. The readers are likely to be impatient with all the qualifications necessary for accurate reporting. In addition, however, the writer usually has his own views and orientations and a particular audience that he wants to please. Because of the complications and ambiguities in the research findings, it is easy to formulate results selectively so that they conform to one's preconceived position.

Additional problems arise when the writeup is intended to influence individual or general policy decisions. In some cases, the data can be used to draw action conclusions that are not really warranted. For example, Cherry and Eaton (1977), in a study of lower class, largely single-parent, black families, found that when the mother had been employed during the first three years of the child's life, the child's Wechsler scores at four, seven, and eight years of age were higher than when the mother had not been employed. Comparable findings of positive correlations between full-time maternal employment and cognitive measures in similar samples have been reported in other studies (Woods 1972). These data might be used to infer that maternal employment had a positive effect on the child in this social class and therefore that the receivers of AFDC money should be encouraged to seek employment. In fact, however, these correlations might result from selective factors. It is possible that the fully employed mothers were better educated, more stable, and better organized. If such selective factors explain the correlations, forcing the nonemployed mothers into employment might exacerbate an already difficult situation. For the motivated policymaker, however, such subtleties can easily be overlooked.

In other cases, broad conclusions about maternal employment are drawn that are inappropriate for individual decisions. White (1980), for example, concludes that no mother of a child under three should seek employment, though in fact that is not at all what the data indicate. Some women are better mothers when they are employed (Schubert, Bradley-Johnson, and Nuttal 1980). In some cases, the nonmaternal environment can be an enriching experience for the preschool child (Belsky and Stern-berg 1978, Etaugh 1978). The individual decision depends on specific aspects of the situation. The data may indicate vulnera-bilities and strengths of the employed- and nonemployed-mother patterns, point out what aspects of the situation need to be con-sidered, and even suggest adjustments that might be made, but they cannot lead to blanket prescriptions.

Summary

Although the pattern of maternal employment has changed over the years—moving from an unusual event to the modal family style—and social attitudes have shifted profoundly, there is a great deal that has remained the same for the researcher. Many of the findings of the present-day studies could be discerned in the re-search of thirty years ago when the first solid investigations were undertaken. The quality of the research has improved over the last half-century, the quantity has fluctuated in response to professional trends and public concerns, but many of the prob-lems have endured. Science is not immune to bias whether it stems from the commitment to a particular scientific theory or to a social view. And the public communication of research results introduces yet another source of distortion. It is hoped that truth comes through in the critical process and in the commitment to empirical evidence, but unfortunately objectivity seems to be greater when one's own view prevails.

Notes

1. These figures are for March 1981 and are provided by the United States Department of Labor, Bureau of Labor Statistics, personal communication with Eliz-abeth Waldman.

2. This chapter is not intended as a review of the research findings. Several such reviews have recently been published (Bronfenbrenner and Crouter 1982, Hoff-man, 1979, 1980, in press). The Bronfenbrenner and Crouter survey (1982) is partic-ularly relevant to this chapter because it reviews the substantive findings from a his-torical perspective.

References

Almquist, E. M. and S. S. Angrist. 1971. "Role Model Influences on College Women's Career Aspirations." *Merrill-Palmer Quarterly* 17:263–79.

Bahr, S. J. 1974. "Effects on Power and Division of Labor in the Family." In Hoffman and Nye (1974), *q.v.*, pp. 167–85.

Baruch, G. K. 1972. "Maternal Influences Upon College Women's Attitudes Toward Women and Work." *Developmental Psychology* 6:32–37.

Belsky, J. and L. D. Sternberg. 1978. "The Effects of Day Care: A Critical Review." *Child Development* 49:920–49.

Bem, S. I. 1975. "Sex-Role Adaptability: One Consequence of Psychological Androgyny." *Journal of Personality and Social Psychology* 31:634–43.

Birnbaum, J. A. 1975. "Life Patterns and Self-Esteem in Gifted Family Oriented and Career Committed Women." In Mednick et al. (1975), *q.v.*, pp. 396–419.

Blood, R. O. Jr. 1963. "The Husband-Wife Relationship." In Nye and Hoffman (1963), *q.v.*, pp. 282–308.

Blood, R. O. Jr. and R. L. Hamblin 1958. "The Effect of the Wife's Employment on the Family Structure." *Social Forces* 36:347–52.

Blood, R. O. Jr. and D. M. Wolfe. 1960. *Husbands and Wives*. Glencoe, Ill.: Free Press.

Bronfenbrenner, U. and A. Crouter. 1982. "Work and Family Through Time and Space." In S. B. Kamerman and C. D. Hayes, eds. 1982. *Families That Work: Children in a Changing World*, pp. 39–83. Washington: National Academy Press.

Broverman, I. K., S. R. Vogel, D. M. Broverman, F. E. Clarkson, and P. S. Rosenkrantz. 1972. "Sex-Role Sterotypes: A Current Appraisal." *Journal of Social Issues*. 28(2):59–78.

Burchinal, L. G. 1963. "Personality Characteristics of Children." In Nye and Hoffman, (1963) *q.v.*, pp. 106–21.

Chase-Lansdale, P. L. 1981. "Effects of Maternal Employment on Mother-Infant and Father-Infant Attachment." Unpublished doctoral dissertation, University of Michigan.

Cherry, F. F. and E. L. Eaton. 1977. "Physical and Cognitive Development in Children of Low-Income Mothers Working in the Child's Early Years." *Child Development* 48:158–66.

Cohen, S. E. 1978. "Maternal Employment and Mother-Child Interaction." *Merrill-Palmer Quarterly* 24:189–97.

Cummings, J. D. 1944. "The Incidence of Emotional Symptoms in School Children." *British Journal of Educational Psychology* 14:151–61.

Dizard, J. 1968. *Social Change in the Family*. Chicago: Community and Family Study Center, University of Chicago.

Essig, M. and D. H. Morgan. 1946. "Adjustment of Adolescent Daughters of Employed Mothers to Family Life." *Journal of Educational Psychology* 37:219–33.

Etaugh, C. 1978. "Effects of Nonmaternal Care on Children: Research Evidence and Popular Views." Paper presented at the meeting of the *American Psychological Association*, Toronto (Aug.).

Farel, A. N. 1980. "Effects of Preferred Maternal Roles, Maternal Employment, and Sociolographic Status on School Adjustment and Competence." *Child Development* 50:1179–86.

Garland, T. N. 1972. "The Better Half? The male in the Dual Profession Family." In C. Safilios-Rothschild, ed., (1972) *q.v.*, pp. 199–215.

Ginsberg, E. 1971. *Educated American Women: Life Styles and Self-Portraits.* New York: Columbia University Press.

Glueck, S. and Glueck, E. 1934. *One Thousand Juvenile Delinquents.* Cambridge, Mass.: Harvard University Press.

Gold, D. and D. Andres. 1978a. "Developmental Comparisons Between Adolescent Children With Employed and Nonemployed Mothers." *Merrill-Palmer Quarterly* 24:243–54.

—— 1978b. "Developmental Comparisons Between 10-Year-Old Children With Employed and Nonemployed Mothers." *Child Development* 49:75–84.

—— 1978c. "Relations Between Maternal Employment and Development of Nursery School Children." *Canadian Journal of Behavioral Science* 10:116–129.

Gold, D., D. Andres, and J. Glorieux. 1979. "The Development of Francophone Nursery-School Children With Employed and Nonemployed Mothers." *Canadian Journal of Behavioral Science* 11:169–73.

Goldberg, R. J. 1977. "Maternal Time Use and Preschool Performance." Paper presented at the meeting of the Society for Research in Child Development, New Orleans (March).

Hartley, R. E. 1959. "Children's Concepts of Male and Female Roles." *Merrill-Palmer Quarterly* 6:83–91.

Heer, D. M. 1958. "Dominance and the Working Wife." *Social Forces* 36:341–47.

Herzog, E. and C. Sudia. 1973. "Children in Fatherless Families." In B. M. Caldwell and H. N. Ricciuti, eds. *Review of Child Development Research*, vol. 3, pp. 141–232. Chicago: University of Chicago Press.

Hetherington, E. M. 1979. "Divorce: A Child's Perspective." *American Psychologist* 34:851–58.

Hill, C. R. and F. P. Stafford. 1978. "Parental Care of Children: Time Diary Estimates of Quantity Predictability and Variety." Working Paper Series, Institute for Social Research, University of Michigan, Ann Arbor.

Hock, E. 1980. "Working and Nonworking Mothers and Their Infants: A Comparative Study of Maternal Caregiving Characteristics and Infant Social Behavior." *Merrill-Palmer Quarterly* 46:79–101.

Hoffman, L. W. 1960. "Effects of the Employment of Mothers on Parental Power Relations and the Division of Household Tasks." *Marriage and Family Living* 22:127–35.

—— 1961. "Effects of Maternal Employment on the Child." *Child Development* 32:187–97.

—— 1963. "Effects on Children: Summary and Discussion." In Nye and Hoffman (1963), *q.v.*, pp. 190–214.

—— 1973. "The Professional Woman as Mother." In R. B. Kundsin, ed. *A Conference on Successful Women in the Sciences.* New York: New York Academy of Sciences.

—— 1974. "Effects of Maternal Employment on the Child—A Review of the Research." *Developmental Psychology* 10:204–28.

—— 1979. "Maternal Employment: 1979." *American Psychologist* 34:859–65.

—— 1980. "The Effects of Maternal Employment on the Academic Attitudes and Performance of School-Aged Children." *School Psychology Review* 9:319–36.

—— 1982. "Social Change and Its Effects on Parents and Children: Limitations to Knowledge." In P. Berman and E. Ramey, eds. *Women: A Developmental Perspective.* Washington: U.S. Government Printing Office.

—— 1983. Increased Fathering: Effects on the Mother. In M. E. Lamb and A. Sagi, eds. *Fatherhood and Family Policy;* pp. 167–90. Hillside, N.J.: Lawrence Erlbaum Associates.

—— In Press. "Work, Family and the Socialization of the Child." In R. D. Parke, ed. *Review of Child Development Research.* Vol 7.

Hoffman, L. W. and F. I. Nye, eds. 1974. *Working Mothers.* San Francisco: Jossey-Bass.

Holmstron, L. 1972. *The Two-Career Family.* Cambridge, Mass. Schenkman.

Kappel, B. E. and R. D. Lambert. 1972. "Self-Worth Among the Children of Working Mothers." Unpublished manuscript. University of Waterloo, Ontario, Canada.

Kasmar, R. A. 1945. "Employed Mothers of Children in the ADC Program; Cook County Bureau of Public Welfare." *Social Service Review* 19:96–110.

Kreisberg, L. 1970. *Mothers in Poverty: A Study of Fatherless Families.* Chicago: Aldine.

LaFollette, C. T. 1934. *A Study of the Problems of 652 Gainfully Employed Married Women Homemakers.* New York: Teacher's College, Columbia University Press.

Maccoby, E. E. 1958. "Children and Working Mothers" *Children* 5:83–89.

Marantz, S. A. and A. F. Mansfield. 1977. "Maternal Employment and the Development of Sex Role Stereotyping in 5 to 11 Year Old Girls." *Child Development* 48:668–73.

Mathews, S. M. 1934. "The Effects of Mothers' Out-of-Home Employment Upon Children's Ideas and Attitudes." *Journal of Applied Psychology* 18:116–36.

Mednick, M. S., S. S. Tangri, and L. W. Hoffman, eds. 1975. *Women and Achievement.* Washington, D.C.: Hemisphere.

Miller, S. M. 1975. "Effects of Maternal Employment on Sex Role Perception, Interests and Self-Esteem in Kindergarten Girls." *Developmental Psychology* 11:405–6.

Moore, T. W. 1963. "Children of Working Mothers. In S. Yudkin and H. Holme, eds. *Working Mothers and Their Children.* London: Michael Joseph.

—— 1975. "Exclusive Early Mothering and Its Alternatives." *Scandinavian Journal of Psychology* 16:256–72.

Nye, F. I. 1952. "Adolescent-Parent Adjustment: Age, Sex, Sibling Number, Broken Homes, and Employed Mothers as Variables." *Marriage and Family Living* 14:327–32.

—— 1958a. *Family Relationships and Delinquent Behavior.* New York: Wiley.

—— 1958b. "Employment Status of Mothers and Marital Conflict, Permanence, and Happiness." *Social Problems* 6:260–67.

—— 1959. "Employment Status of Mothers and Adjustment of Adolescent Children." *Marriage and Family Living* 21:240–44.

—— 1961. "Maternal Employment and Marital Interaction: Some Contingent Conditions." *Social Forces* 40:113–19.

—— 1963. "Adjustment of the Mother: Summary and a Frame of Reference." In Nye and Hoffman (1963), *q.v.,* pp. 384–99.

Nye, F. I. and L. W. Hoffman. 1963. *The Employed Mother in America.* Chicago: Rand McNally.

Pederson, F. A., R. Cain, M. Zaslow, and B. Anderson. 1983. "Variation in Infant Experience Associated With Alternative Family Role Organization." In L. Laosa and I. Sigel, eds. *Families as Learning Environment for Children,* pp. 94–106. New York: Plenum.

Piotrkowski, C. and S. Katz. 1982. "Indirect Socialization of Children: The Effects of the Mother's Job on Academic Behaviors." *Child Development,* 53:1520–1529.

Poloma, M. M. 1972. "Role Conflict and the Married Professional Woman." In C. Safilios-Rothschild, ed., (1972), *q.v.*

Quarm, D. E. A. 1977. "The Measurement of Marital Powers." Unpublished doctoral dissertation, University of Michigan. University microfilm #7726339

Rapoport, R. and R. Rapoport. 1971. *Dual-Career Families.* Baltimore: Penguin.

Robinson, J. P. 1978. *How Americans Use Time: A Sociological Perspective.* New York: Praeger.

Safilios-Rothschild, C. 1970. "The Study of Family Power Structure: A Review 1960–1969." *Journal of Marriage and the Family* 32:539–52.

Safilius-Rothschild, ed. 1972. *Toward a Sociology of Women* Lexington, Mass.: Xerox Publishing.

Schachter, F. F. 1981. "Toddlers With Employed Mothers." *Child Development* 52(3):958–64.

Schubert, J. B., S. Bradley-Johnson, and J. Nuttal. 1980. "Mother-Infant Communication and Maternal Employment." *Child Development* 51(1):246–49.

Siegel, A. E. and M. B. Haas. 1963. "The Working Mother: A Review of Research." *Child Development* 34:513–42.

Siegel, A. E., L. M. Stolz, E. A. Hitchcock, and J. M. Adamson. 1959. "Dependence and Independence in the Children of Working Mothers." *Child Development* 30:533–46.

Stuckey, M. F., P. E. McGhee, and N. J. Bell. 1982. "Parent-Child Interaction: The Influence of Maternal Employment." *Developmental Psychology,* 18:635–650.

Stolz, L. M. 1960. "Effects of Maternal Employment on Children: Evidence From Research." *Child Development* 31:749–83.

Tangri, S. S. 1975. "Determinants of Occupational Role Innovation Among College Women." In Mednick, et al. (1975), *q.v.,* pp. 255–73.

Thornton, A. and D. Freedman. 1980. "Changes in the Sex Role Attitudes of Women, 1962–1977: Evidence From a Panel Study." In D. G. McGuigan, ed. *Changing Family, Changing Workplace,* pp. 39–44.

U.S. Department of Commerce, Bureau of the Census. 1979. "Population Profile of the United States: 1978, Population Characteristics" (Current Population Reports, Series P-20, No. 336). Washington, D.C.: U.S. Government Printing Office (April).

U.S. Department of Labor, Bureau of Labor Statistics. 1981. "Marital and Family Characteristics of Workers, March 1980." ASI 6748–58 (news release on microfiche).

U.S. Department of Labor, Women's Bureau. 1977. *Working Mothers and Their Children.* Washington, D.C.: U.S. Government Printing Office.

Vaughn, B. E., F. L. Gove, and B. Egeland. 1980. "The Relationship Between Out-of-Home Care and the Quality of Infant-Mother Attachment in an Economically Disadvantaged Population." *Child Development* 51:1203–14.

White, B. L. 1980. *A Parent's Guide to the First Three Years.* Englewood Cliffs, N.J.: Prentice-Hall.

Wolfe, D. M. 1959. "Power and Authority in the Family." In D. Cartwright, ed. *Studies in Social Power.* Ann Arbor, Mich.: Institute for Social Research.

Woods, M. B. 1972. "The Unsupervised Child of the Working Mother." *Developmental Psychology* 6:14–25.

Yarrow, M. R., P. Scott, L. DeLeeuw, and C. Heinig. 1962. "Childrearing in Families of Working and Non-Working Mothers." *Sociometry* 25:122–40.

Index

Abolitionism, effect on women's movement, 21

Abstinence, sexual, in Victorian marriage, 59

Achievement, female, and maternal instinct, 93

Admired Persons and Opinions Test, 162

Adolescence, 103

Affection, family, Watson on, 134

Age and AIAS scores, 165

AIAS: description, 161; Cult of True Womanhood in, 169, 170; and males, 170; measurement, significance of, 169; scores and age, 165; validity of, 163, 167; and women, 171

Alcatory orientation development, theory of, 276

Allen, Grant, MF ideas of, 194

Allen, McGrigor, sex differences ideas of, 156

Allport, Floyd: social psychology theory of, 117; work of, 116

America: demographic revolution in Victorian, 58; Cult of True Womanhood in, 42; sex roles in Victorian, 41; Victorian, psychic birth control in, 57

American: men, morality role of, 46; middle-class rise and family tradition, 60; women, de Tocqueville on, 43

American Female Moral Reform Society, 228

Androgyny: model, current, 119; paradigm, rise of, 196

Animal intelligence, Thorndike on, 85

Antifeminist conservative doctrine, Darwinism as example, 52

Antihereditarianism as Watson characteristic, 136, 137

"Aristotle," sex writings of, 58

Arney, William, mothering theories of, 247

Atlantis: family relations in, 102; Hall's vision of, 100, 101; male-female relationships in, 103; women, descrip-

Atlantis (Continued)
  tion of, 102; see also G. Stanley Hall
Attitude Interest Survey, see AIAS
Authoritarian Personality, The, 216

Bales, R. Freed: MF studies by, 191, 192;
  and Parsons, fallacy of ideas of, 195
Beecher, Henry, as behaviorist, 137
Behavior, instinctive: definition of, 257;
  Watson on, 111; see also Behaviorism; Parenthood; John B. Watson
Behavioral science in Utopia, 109
Behaviorism, 136; and childrearing,
  235; and development, 275; doctrine
  of Henry Beecher, 137; and instinct,
  conflict between, 264; and mothering, 277; remedial approaches of,
  130; validation lack for, 276; Watson
  stress on, 134, 135; see also Behaviorist; John B. Watson
Behaviorist: mother, 241; theory of child
  development, bases for, 286; theory
  and hypothetico-deductive metatheory, 280; Watson view of, 128, 140;
  see also Behaviorism; John B. Watson
Behaviorist's Utopia, The, 109
Bell, Mary Ann, Terman's research with,
  161
Bem, Sandra, androgyny studies by,
  196
Bezdek, W., MF classification by, 190
Biological differences among sexes and
  gender hierarchy, 3; see also Darwinism
Birney, Alice Josephine McLellan, and
  National Congress of Mothers, 229
Birth control, psychic: and Conservation of Force, 64; decline of, 70;
  emotional cost of, 68; and family limitation, 59; and fragile masculinity, 68;
  and Freud, 72; and sexual frustration, 69; and social class, 67; and risk
  of venereal disease, 69
Birth rate, nineteenth-century decline in,
  58
Bixsexuality, and Freud, 71

Blacks: sex-role problems of male, 218,
  219; Watson on racial inferiority of,
  136
Blackwell, Antoinette Brown, anti-Dar-
  win critique of, 52
Body-mind links, research on, 91
Bonding and maternal instinct, 269
Bowlby, John, on mothering, 245
Brigham, Arimiah, Conservation of
  Force and, 56
Brim, Orville, and studies of instrumen-
  tal-expressive traits, 196
Bruni, Leonardo, on female education,
  10

California Psychological Inventory, see
  CPI
Calkins, Mary Whiton, career of, 157;
  controversy with Jastrow, 157; mas-
  culinity and femininity study by, 158
Capitalism, effect of on family limita-
  tion, 63
Caretaking, child, see Childrearing;
  Mothering; Parenting
Castration: anxiety of males, impact on
  women of, 63; medical, in Victorian
  era, 63
Cattell, James McKeen: at Columbia
  University, 78; and female education,
  82; on male genius, 93; on social
  problems, 115
Chambers: evolutionary theory of, 49
Child: development of, 239; environ-
  ment reinforcement's impact on, 289;
  Freudian theory of, 238; future of,
  291; in nineteenth century, 228; see
  also, Childhood; Childrearing; Chil-
  dren; Mothering; Parenting
Child Care in Utopia, 110
Child Guidance movement, develop-
  ment of, 239
Childhood, Freudian theories of, 237
Childhood and Adolescence, 246
Childhood and Society, 65, 243
Child Psychology, Watson's influence on,
  127

Childrearing: and behaviorism, 235; changes in, 18; Lomax on psychoanalytic theory of, 238; twentieth-century theories about, 235; Watson views on, 128; *see also* Mothering; Parenting

Children: in America, increasing importance of, 133; family attitudes toward, 18; Hall's ideas on, 104; retarded, in clinical psychology, 91; Watson's ideas on, 127; Watson's study of, 132; *see also* Child; Childhood

Chodorow, Nancy, on mother fantasy, 250

Christianity, attitude toward women of, 4, 7

Civilization and Its Discontents, 238

Classes, social, Watson on separate spheres for, 149

Classicism, German, women in, 34

Clearing House for Mental Defectives, Hollingworth at, 91

Clinical psychology, retarded children in, 91

Clitorectomy, practice of, 63, 67

College student dreams, interpretation of, 186

Columbia University Psychology Department, advances of, 84; women graduate students in, 81, 82

Community, moral role for women in, 228

Comstock laws and contraception, 62

Comte, Auguste: antifeminist views of, 54; influence on Darwin of, 53

Concerning Famous Women, 6

Conscious and unconscious MF, classification using, 187

Conservation of Force: Newtonian Theory of, 56; and psychic birth control, 64; and Victorian sex roles, 57

Conservation of wages, theory of, 56

Constantinople, Anne, androgyny studies by, 197

Contraception: and Catholicism, 62; and Comstock laws, 62; and eugenics movement, 62; increase in, 70; and male fears, 62; nineteenth-century nonuse of, 61; Victorian female fear of, 63; and WASP community, 62

Contratto, Susan, on mother fantasy, 250

Courts, Watson on, 145

Couvade, Munroe studies of, 218

Cox, Catherine, *see* Catherine Cox Miles

CPI: description of, 183; evolution of, 184; MF classification by, 190; as MF test, 183; Victorian influence on, 184

Cult of True Womanhood, 1, 17; in AIAS, 169, 170; and factor analysis, 175; in nineteenth-century America, 42

Cultural evolution, Watson's faith in, 141

Darwin, Antoinette Brown, Blackwell's critique of, 52

Darwin, Charles: ideas about women of, 5; and instinct concept, 259, 261; intellectual abilities ranking by, 51; precursors of, 49; various influences on, 53; on women's education and heredity, 51; *see also* Darwinism; Evolution

Darwin, Erasmus, evolutionary theory of, 49

Darwinism: as antifeminist conservative doctrine, 52; and biological inferiority of women, 49, 50; Karl Marx on, 54; John Stuart Mill on, 55; misogyny of, 48, 50; and psychology, interaction of, 39; social importance of, 55; among social scientists, 49, 50; and women's suffrage, 52; *see also* Charles Darwin; Evolution

Daughters: and fathers in *Emilia Galotti*, 31; and fathers in Germany, relationship of, 29; effect of maternal employment on, 298, 305

"Declaration of Sentiments and Resolutions," 45

De Claris Mulieribus, 6

de Pisan, Christine: writings of, 6

Descent of Man, The, 259

Determinism, Watson's developmental, 132

Deutsch, Helene, views of, 65

Development: alcatory orientation, theory of, 276; and behavior, 275; theories, bases for, 275

Developmental determinism (Watson's), 137

Developmental Psychology Today, 288

Developmentalism, Watson behaviorism and, 135

Discrimination against education for women, 7, 11

Disease, sexuality considered as, 66

Distant, W. L., on sex differences, 156

Divorce, laws affecting, 13

Doctrine of the Two Spheres, 42; and double MF classification, 190

Double classification, MF: and Doctrine of Two Spheres, 190; paradigm, 187

Douglas, G. Archibald: sex writings of, 57

Draw-a-Person MF test, 186

Dreams, college student: interpretation of, 186

Early impact assumption: metatheoretical base for, 286; and Watson, 287

Economic changes, family interrelationships and, 195

Education, female: Cattell on, 82; and Church misogyny, 7; deprivation of and subordination, 40; discrimination in, 7, 11; in England, 9; in Europe, 8; Hall on, 233; and heredity (Darwin on), 51; in the home, 9; and humanism, 10; in the Middle Ages, 9; and race suicide theory, 82; during Renaissance, 9; Thorndike on, 83, 84; Watson on, 145

Egalitarian feminism, birth of, 20

Eighteenth century: male thought in, 40, 41; sexuality in, 57

Ellis, Havelock: teachings of, 70; utopia of, 100

Emilia Gallotti: analysis of, 31; father-daughter fixation in, 31

Emotional and Ethical Attitudes Test, 162

Employment, maternal: research on, 285, 297

England: female education in, 9; female moral superiority belief in, 45

Enlightenment: egalitarian aspects of, 27; women in, 26; political theory and women, 21

Environment: effect on instinct of, 257; effect on intellect of, 158; primacy, Watson belief in, 136; reinforcement, impact on child of, 289

Environmentalism, development in psychology of, 95

Environmentalist aspect of Watson behaviorism, 135

Erikson, Erik: ideas of, 65; on mother blaming, 243

Eugenia: family life on, 106; McDougall and, 105; science's importance on, 106; story of, 105

Eugenics: McDougall's espousal of, 107, 108; movement and contraception, 62

Europe: Enlightenment in, egalitarian aspects of, 27; female education in, 8; literary debates about women in, 6

Evolution: cultural, Watson's faith in, 141; Hall's use in psychology of, 103; Theory of, and nature of men and women, 48; various theories of, 49; *see also* Charles Darwin; Darwinism

Evolutionary theory and social science, link between, 54

Experimental psychology, Hollingworth's introduction to, 88; Hollingworth on women in, 84

Expressive traits, 196

Extroversion: and factor analysis, 174; and introversion test, 183

Factor analysis: and Cult of True Womanhood, 175; and Guilford, 174; and introversion-extroversion, 174; and MF traits, 174

Fall of Atlantis, The, 101

Family: affection, Watson on, 134; attitudes toward children, 18; changes in twentieth century, 297; ideal of 1920s, 97; interrelationships and economic changes, 195; life on Eugenia, 106; life ideals of National Congress of Mothers, 232; limitation and capitalism reform, 63; limitation through psychic birth control, 59; limitation and rise of American middle class, 60; middle class, Watson's view of, 144; nuclear, importance of, 117, 118; nuclear, predictions about, 119; problems of the 1920s; relations in Atlantis, 102; role in social psychology, 117; social relations, recommendations for, 98; studies by Zelditch and MF, 193; Watson ideas on, 127, 129; as Watson subject study, 133

Family Socialization and Interaction Process, 214

Fathering, *see* Childrearing; Mothering; Parenting

Father Power, 220

Fathers and daughters: fixation in *Emilia Galotti,* 31; in Germany, relationship of, 29

Fatigue, mental experiments on, 86

Fear of Being a Woman, The, 244

Fechner: psychophysics and, 57

Female: achievement and maternal instinct, 93; earnings scales, 16; education, basis of exclusion and discrimination in, 11; education, Cattell on, 82; education in England, 9; education in medieval Europe, 8; education and race suicide theory, 82; education during Renaissance, 9; education, Thorndike on, 83, 84; in egalitarian societies, privileges of, 3; emotionality and maternal instinct, 268; equality, Comte's views on, 54; exclusion from Society of Experimental Psychology, 65; fear of contraception, Victorian, 63; functions and private domain, 13; Hall on, 233; in the home, 9; and humanism, 10; idealization and male authors, 30; illiteracy, rates of, 12; inferiority, and Christianity, 4; inferiority, effect of concept of, 15; inferiority, Galton "proof" of, 53; inferiority and scientists and philosophers, 5; inferiority, traditions of, 2; intelligence, Hall on, 87; intelligence, Ward on, 87; liberation and social activism, 64; and male relationships in Atlantis, 103; and male relationships in Utopia, 110, 111; and male relationships, World War II effect on, 212; monasticism and intellectualism, 7; Oedipus complex, Freud's theories of, 36; penis envy, Freud on, 37; psychology, basis of, 22; reproductive system, psychological theories about link to intellect of, 64; role, British psychologists on, 245; roles in German literature, 29; sexuality, attacks on, 60; sexuality, ideas on, 17, 20; sexuality and maternal instinct, 260; skull capacity studies of Alice Lee, 54; stereotypes of Freud, 35; subordination and educational deprivation, 40; subordination and MF traits, 198; subordination, religious background of, 4; subordination and gender division of labor, 13; subordination and Western law, 12; variability, Hollingworth's research on, 93; vocational guidance and SVIB, 174; *see also* Feminine; Feminity; Woman; Womanhood; Women

Feminine: conception by Freud, 34; identity in men, unconscious, 189; identity in men, hypothesis of unconscious, 218; mental traits, 157

Feminine Mystique, The, 242

Feminism: as challenge to MSRI theory, 221; egalitarian, birth of, 20; and Enlightenment political theory, 21; and Freidan, 242; relative weakness of, 22; as social reform movement, 64; University of Chicago contributions to, 77; *see also* Feminist

Femininity: measurement attempts, 156; mental, Terman on, 160; unconscious, Kraugh measurement of, 186; *see also* Female; MF

Feminist movement, emergence of stimuli for, 21; opposition to, 242

Feminist tactics, nineteenth century, 21; see also Feminism

Force, Conservation of: and psychic birth control, 64; and Victorian sex roles, 57; Newtonian Theory of, 56; see also Life Force

Fraiberg, Selma, on motherhood, 247

Franck, Kate: gender identity test and, 185; see also Franck Test

Franck Test: assumptions of, 186; faking, 187; and MF scores, correlation of, 187; purpose of, 185; validation omission for, 186

Frank, Lawrence, on parenthood, 239

Freidan, Betty, and feminist movement, 242

Freud, Anna, on motherhood, 247

Freud, Sigmund: attitude toward women of, 1, 5, 238; conception of the feminine by, 34; female Oedipal complex theories of, 36; female penis-envy theory of, 37; ideas, bases of, 26; ideas, clarification of, 71, 72; influences on, 71; and Lamarckian pangenesis, 55; and libido, 57, 65; major theories of, 72; and MSRI, 214; patriarchal orientation of, 34; phallocentricity orientation of, 37; psychoanalytic theories of childhood, 237; sexual ideas of, 58; on sexuality and child development, 238; stereotypes of, 35

Froebel, Fredrich, kindergarten work of, 230

Galton, Francis: influence on Darwin of, 53; "proof" of female inferiority, 53; on sex differences, 156; utopia of, 100

Gardener, Helen H., motherhood ideal and, 232

Gates, Elmer, National Congress of Mothers and, 231

Gender: difference and maternal instinct, 258; division of labor, 2, 16; division of labor and female subjugation, 13; hierarchy and biological differences among sexes, 3; hierarchy as universal condition, 2; identity, measurement of unconscious, 185; variability, studies of, 92; see also Sex

Genetic Studies of Genius, 160

Genius, male, Cattell and Thorndike on, 93

German: Classicism, women in, 34; Enlightenment, women in, 26; fathers and daughters, relationship of, 29; literature, female roles in, 29; literature, Oedipal-bond treatment in, 33; literature, Richardson influence on, 29; middle-class family attitudes, 28; middle-class political impotence, 28; middle-class values, 27, 28, 32; tradition's influence on Freud, 26

Gesell, Arnold: on motherhood, 241; work of, 240

Gilbreth, Frank, ideas of, 141

Gilman, Charlotte Perkins, emotional repression and, 68

Ginnot, Haim, on parenting, 289

Goal orientation theory of McDougall, 107

Goldhammer: MF Classification by, 190; and sex role identity, 217

Gough, Harrison, CPI and, 183

Guildford, J. P. and Ruth B., and factor analysis, 174

Habit, primacy of, 137

Hall, G. Stanley: and Atlantis, 100; career of, 100; children and, 104; and college student dreams, 186; evolution and psychology of, 103; family utopian scheme of, 98; and female education, 233; on female intelligence, 87; influence of, 65; Life Force Theory of, 65; McDougall and Watson, comparison of, 112; on motherhood, 233, 266; and National Congress of Mothers, 229, 231; race suicide theory of, 62; social reform proposals of, 105; on women, 104; see also Atlantis

Handbook of Socialization Theory and Research, The, 288

Harrison, James: homosexuality and, 197

Hathaway, S. R.: MF test of, 179; *see also* MMPI

Health, MF correlation with, 164

"Healthy Personality for Your Child, A," 244

Hearst, Phoebe Appleton, and National Congress of Mothers, 230

Hedonism, rise of, 70

Helmholtz, Hermann: and Conservation of Force in psychiatry and physiology, 56; energy experiments of, 57

Helmreich, Robert, MF scale of, 197

Heredity: Darwin on, 51; Terman on, 159

History: as psychological tool, 119; and the psychology of women, 1

Hollingworth, Henry, as female advocate, 78

Hollingworth, Leta, at Bellevue Hospital, 91; career of, 77; career struggles of, 95; childlessness of, 80; doctoral thesis of, 89; early married life of, 79; graduate work start by, 80; introduction to experimental psychology, 88; on male researchers, studies of, 94; menstruation research of, 88; and mental testing, 91; on sex differences, 156; sex of retardates research, 92; variability of females research, 93; on women in experimental psychology, 94

Homosexuality: Harrison research on, 197; study in *Sex and Personality*, 210; Terman and Miles theory of, 210; *see also* Homosexuals; Inversion

Homosexuals: Kelly study of, 166; MMPI and identification of, 183; *see also* Homosexuality; Inversion; MF

Humanism and female education, 10

Hunter, John, sexual knowledge of, 58

Husband: supremacy over wife, 12; maternal employment's effect on, 300

Hymes, James L., and parenting, 244

Hypermasculinity: concept of, 215; and male juvenile delinquency, 215, 218

Hypothetico-Deductive Metatheory, 280

Idealization of women, male authors and, 30

Ideal state, various ideas on, 112

Identification: concept and MF study, 213; sex role and MF, 214

Illiteracy, female, rates of, 12

Immorality interests, attacks on women of, 47

Incapacity, periodic, *see* Menstruation

Individualism, Watson's faith in, 141

Industrial Revolution, effect on women of, 14, 16, 41

Infant Care, 235, 237

Inferiority, female: biological and Darwinism, 49, 50; and Christianity, 4; effect of concept of, 15; Galton "proof" of, 53; and scientists and philosophers, 5; traditions of, 2

Ink Blot Association Test, 161

Inner Conflict and Defense, 217

Insanity and sexuality, 67

Instinct: conflict with behaviorism, 264; Darwin and concept of, 259, 261; definition of, 257; environmental effect on, 257; as an evolutionary process, 261; and William James, 262; maternal, and female achievement, 93; McDougall theory of, 261; prescientific models of, 259; primary and secondary, 261, 264; *see also* Maternal instinct; Parental instinct

Instinctive behavior, definition of, 257

Institute to Coordinate Women's Interests, 234

Instrumental expressive distinction, 195, 196

Intellect: environmental effect on, 158; psychological theories about link between and female reproductive system, 64; *see also* Intelligence

Intellectual abilities, Darwin's ranking of, 51

Intellectualism, female monasticism and, 7

Intelligence: animal, Thorndike on, 85; female, Ward on, 87; Hall on, 87; human, Thorndike on, 86; testing and psychology, 209

Interests Test, 162

Inversion: classification, Kraepelin system of, 180; and factor analysis, 174; as measure of psychopathology, 180; and MF scores, 166, 168; scale in MMPI, 180; scale, Terman, 166; *see also* Homosexuals; Homosexuality; MF Inversion-Extroversion Test, 183
Island of Eugenia, The: 105

Jacobi, Mary Putnam, menstruation research of, 90
James, William: and instinct, 262; on psychological concept of habit, 137; on sex differences, 156
Jastrow, Joseph: Calkins' controversy with, 157; masculinity and femininity study by, 157; and psychologist's responsibility, 116
Juvenile delinquency: male, and hypermasculinity, 218; and maternal employment, 295

Kelly, E. Lowell, and homosexual study, 166
Koch, Helen, instrumental-expressive classification by, 196
Kraepelin system of inversion classification, 180
Kraugh measurement of unconscious femininity, 186

Labor: in America, gender-based division of, 2, 16; gender-based division of and female subjugation, 3, 13
Lamarck, Jean Baptiste, evolutionary theories of, 49, 51; and Freud's ideas, 55, 71
Langer, Walter, and hypermasculinity study, 216
Lee, Alice, female skull capacity studies of, 54
Lessing, Gotthold Ephraim, and father-daughter fixations in, *Emilia Galotti,* 31
LeVine, Robert, on behaviorism, 288
Lévi-Strauss, Claude, and division of labor by sex, 2
Levy, David, on motherhood, 242

Liberation, female, and social activism, 64
Libido: Freudian meaning of, 57; as life force, 64
Life Force: Theory of Hall, 65; Theory of Spencer, 64
Lippmann, W., on social reform, 115
Literature: European, debate about women in, 6; German, female roles in, 29; German, Oedipal-bond treatment in, 33; German, Richardson's influence on, 29
Logical positivism: description of, 279
Lomax, Elizabeth: on psychoanalytic theory of childrearing, 238; views of, 246

McDougall, William: career of, 105; and Eugenia, 105; eugenics espousal by, 107, 108; family utopian scheme of, 98; goal orientation theory of, 107; Hall and Watson comparison with, 112; instinct theories of, 261; social concerns of, 108; writings of, 107
McKinley: MF test of, 179; *see also* MMPI
Male(s): AIAS and, 170; American, morality role of, 46; anti-uterus prejudice of, 89; authors and female idealization, 30; black, sex role problems of, 218, 219; castration anxiety, impact on women of, 63; contraception fears of, 62; dominance and MF traits, 198; functions and public domain, 13; genius, prominent psychologists on, 93; juvenile delinquency and hypermasculinity, 215, 218; Mills and Whyte study of, 212; psychological needs of, 42; researchers, Hollingworth studies of, 94; sex-role identity, *see* MSRI; sexuality, Victorian ideas on, 66; stereotypes of Freud, 35; thought, eighteenth century, 40, 41; Victorian spermatic economy of, 66; violence, interpretation of, 215; *see also* masculinity; MF; Men; MSRI; Patriarchal
Male-Female Relationships: in Atlantis, 103; in Utopia, 110-11; World War II's effect on, 212

Malthus' influence on social science, 53

Marriage: and sexuality, 20; Watson on, 111, 130, 131

Married Women's Property Acts, 22

Martin, H. G., factor analysis and, 174

Marx, Karl, on Darwinism, 54

Masculinity: failings and Strecker, 212; -femininity research by Terman, 158; fragile, and psychic birth control, 68; measurement attempts, 156; mental traits specific to, 157; Terman on, 160; see also Male; Masculine; Men; MF; MSRI

Masturbation, Victorian ideas on, 66

Maternal behavior, influences on, 276

Maternal Care and Mental Health, 245

Maternal employment: changes in patterns of, 296; effect on child of, 298, 300, 305; effect on husband-wife relationship of, 300; and juvenile delinquency, 295; research on, 295, 297, 298, 305, 307, 309, 312; research, measurement, design theory, 302

Maternal instinct: and bonding, 269; concept, history of, 257, 259; current views of, 267; Darwin on, 258; early scientific explanation for, 258; and female achievement, 93; and female emotionality, 268; and female sexuality, 260; and gender difference, 258; and Romanes, 261; social science stress on, 265; theories of, 261, 262, 263; see also Instinct; Mother; Motherhood; Mothering

Maternal overprotection theory, 242

Maternal Overprotection, 242

Mead, Margaret: opposition to personality styles theory by, 211; on temperament, 167

Mechanistic development, *see* Behaviorism

Men: motherhood's effect on, 251; sex as domain of, 58; unconscious feminine identity in, 189

Menstruation: Hollingworth research on, 88; Mosher and Jacobi research on, 90

Mental: fatigue, experiments on, 86; femininity, Terman on, 160; masculinity, Terman on, 160; testing, Hollingworth and, 91; traits, masculine and feminine, 157, 158

Mental Traits of Sex, The, 78

Men Under Stress, 212

Metatheoretical: base for early impact assumption, 286; context of theory construction, 277

MF: classification using conscious and unconscious scores, 187; concept and self-image, 168; conceptualization recommendations for, 199; correlation with health, 164; correlation, Terman problems with, 164; cultural beliefs, typical, 194; double classification of, 187; erroneous assumptions about, 167; measurement and sex differences, 169; norms and society, 168; in personality inventories, 184; research, decline of double classification in, 191; scales, critiques of, 197, 198; score, arriving at, 161; scores, faking, 164; scores and Franck test, correlation of, 187; scores and inversion, 166, 168; scores and occupation, 165; scores and sex differences, 168; scores, within-sex validity study of, 167; and sex-role identification, 214; studies of Miller and Swanson, 189; studies by Parsons and Bales, 191; studies by Sanford, 187; study and identification concept, 213; test, CPI as, 183; test, Draw-A-Person, 186; test, Strong Vocational Interest Blank as, 172; test, Terman as, 160; tests, current, 187; tests, recommendations for, 200; tests, uselessness of, 188; traits and college students' dreams, 186; traits and core values, 198; traits, development fallacies of, 168; traits and factor analysis, 174; traits and instrumental-expressive distinction, 195; see also Femininity; Male; Masculinity

Middle Ages, education of aristocrats in, 9

Middle class: German family attitudes of,

Middle class (*Continued*)
28; German, political impotence of, 28; German, values of, 27, 28, 32; reaction to Watson, 148; rise of American and family limitation, 60; Watson view of families of, 144

Miles, Catherine Cox: androgynous ideas of, 171; and MSRI theory, 207; Terman work with, 160; *see also* Lewis Terman

Mill, John Stuart, on Darwinism, 55

Miller, Daniel, and sex role identity, 217; MF studies by, 189

Mills, C. Wright: sociological study of men by, 212

Mind-body links: research on, 91

Minnesota Multiple Personality Inventory, *see* MMPI

Misogyny: of Darwinism, 48, 50; and motherhood, 250

MMPI: description of, 180; femininity scale basis of, 181; and homosexual identification, 183; importance of, 179, 180; inversion scale in, 180; and psychopathology, 180; use of, 182; validity for women of, 181

Moral superiority of women: as American doctrine, 43; as British doctrine, 45; bases for doctrine of, 46; theory of, 66; and community, 228

Morality role of American men, 46

Mosher, Clelia Duel: menstruation research by, 90

Mother(s): Blaming, 45 (history), 157, 243 (Erikson on); love, Watson on, 129; nineteenth-century focus on, 227; role, psychological theories of, 248; role, writings on, 226; and social change, 249; and socialization, 117; working, implications of, 251; *see also* Female; Maternal; Motherhood; Mothering; Parenting

Motherhood: and career, combining, 234; effect on men, 251; effect on women, 251; Gesell on, 241; glorification of, 41; Hall on, 233; ideal, 231, 232; Levy on, 242; and misogyny, 250; models of the 1930's, 241; Mys-

tification of, 157; pleasure theory of, 268; Rossi theory of, 267; Voluntary, movement for, 59; and war, 249; Watson solutions for problems of, 139; Winnicott on, 246; *see also* Childrearing; Mother(s); Mothering; Parenting

Mothering: advice giving on, 248; and behaviorism, 277; British psychoanalysts on, 245; current theories of, 247; noxious, 243, 244; theories, attachment to various, 248; *see also* Childrearing, Mother(s); Motherhood; Parenting

Mott, Lucretia: and Seneca Falls resolution, 45

Moynihan Report and black males: 219

MSRI: and Freud, 214; and hypermasculinity, 215; and identification concept, 212; paradigm, decline, 220; and Parsons, 214; and paternal absences, 218; Terman and Miles and, 207; theory, background of, 206; theory, evolution of, 211; theory, feminism as challenge to, 221; and understanding male experience, 205; *see also* Males; Masculinity; MF; Men

Müller, Johannes, vitalist theories of, 56

Munroe, Robert and Ruth, couvade studies by, 218

Mystification of Motherhood, 157

National Congress of Mothers: family life ideals of, 232; and Hall, 229; program of, 230

National Council of Parent Education, program of, 239

Neobehaviorists: research of, 289; theories of, 283

Nevers, Cordelia, in Calkins study, 158

Newton and Theory of Conservation of Force, 56; influence on psychology of, 39

Nineteenth century: America, Cult of True Womanhood in, 42; attitudes toward women, 1, 17; decline of birth rate in, 59; child, 228; conflict between science and religion, 49; nonuse of contraception in, 61; focus on mothers, 227; position of sexes, 40; sexual distinctions in, 42; sexual repression in, 57

Normative personality styles: and sex, 207; theory, Mead's opposition to, 211

Norsworthy, Naomi, at Teachers College, 83

Noxious mothering, 243, 244; see also Mother Blaming

Nuclear family, importance of, 117, 118

Nurturing propensity, definition of, 258

Occupations: and MF scores, 165; SVIB and sex correlation of, 173

Oedipal: bond treatment in German literature, 33; complex, female, Freud theories of, 36

Omnibus personality inventory: components of, 209

"On Sex Differences in Non-Intellectual Mental Traits," 161

Organismic development theory, 276

Organization Man, The, 213

Ortner, Sherry, and division of labor by sex, 3

Overprotection, maternal, theory of, 242

Pangenesis: Lamarckian and Freudian thinking, 55; theory of, 51

Parent: education movement, growth of, 239; see also Childrearing; Mothering; Parental; Parenthood

Parental evaluation (Watson), 129

Parental instinct, theories of, 263

Parenthood: behavior, sex differences in, 268; Ginott on, 289; Hymes and, 244; ideal, 239; models, search for, 256; as research topic, 256; Spock on, 289; see also Childrearing; Mothering

Parenting, see Childrearing; Fathering; Mothering; Parenthood

Parsons, Talcott: fallacy of ideas of, 195; -Bales Paradigm, experimental tests of, 195; conservative social values of, 194; MF studies by, 191; and MSRI,

214; sexism awareness of, 192; sex-role strain study by, 192, 193

Paternal absences: and MSRI, 218; and World War II, 219

Patriarchal orientation of Freud, 34; see also Male; Men

Pearson, Karl: correlation coefficient, 54; ideological changes of, 54; Quetelet's influence on, 53; writings of, 54

Penis envy, Freud's theory of, 37

Periodic incapacity, see Menstruation

Personality inventories: MF in, 184; omnibus components of, 209

Personality styles, normative, Mead opposition to theory of, 211; normative, and sex, 207

Pestalozzi, Johann: and childhood, 229

Pettigrew, Thomas, studies of black males by, 219

Phallocentricity orientation (Freud), 37

Philosophers and female inferiority, 5

Pleck, Joseph, MF paradigm critique by, 197

Pre-Oedipal issues in psychoanalysis, 214

Principles on Psychology, The, 156

Profile of the Negro American, A, 219

Psychic Birth Control: and Conservation of Force, 64; decline of, 70; emotional costs of, 68; and family limitation, 59; and fragile masculinity, 68; and Freud, 72; influence on psychology by, 39; neurosis as result of, 69; and sexual frustration, 69; and social class, 67; and venereal disease risk, 69; in Victorian America, 57

Psychological: methodology, Watson on, 140; repression and Psychic Birth Control, 68; testing, innovation of, 159; see also Psychologists; Psychology

Psychological Care, 147

Psychological Care of Infant and Child, 127

Psychologists: changes in work of, 84; education of, vii; as experts on life, 113; misogynist ideas of, 79; and mother-role theories, 248; of 1920's,

Psychologists (*Continued*)
ideal family of, 97; of 1920s, social conditions and work of, 99; responsibilities of, Jastrow's ideas on, 116; and social welfare, 113; updating for, viii; and utopian thinking, 100; women, impact on Psychology of, 95; *see also* Psychological; Psychology

Psychology: in Atlantis society, 101; child, Watson's influence on, 127; clinical, retarded children in, 91; Department of Columbia University, 84; environmentalism development in, 85; experimental, Hollingworth introduction to, 88; experimental, Hollingworth on women in, 94; and guiding everyday life, 116; history's use in, 119; as humor subject, 113; and intelligence testing, 209; of men, necessity for thinking in, 119; needs of, 42; public appeal of, 114; as a science, influences on, 39; and science interrelationship, vii, 108; and sex typing, 209; social, Allport theory of, 117; social benefits of, 115; social, family role in, 117; as social influence, 39; and social work, relationship of, 116; suppositions of, vii; twenties role of, 113; of women, basis of, 22; women blaming in, 45; of women and history, 1; women psychologists' impact on, 95; *see also* Psychologists

Psychoanalysis, pre-Oedipal issues in, 214

Psychoanalytic theory of childrearing, Lomax on, 238

Psychoanalytically oriented mother, 241

"Psychology of Women, The," 35

Psychopathology, inversion as measure of, 180

Psychophysics and Fechner, 57

Quetelet, Adolphe, influence on Darwin and others of, 53

Race suicide: and female education, theory of, 82; theory of Hall, 62

Racial inequality: Terman on, 159; Watson on, 136

Recapitulation theory: Freud and, 71

Reinforcement, environmental: impact on child of, 289

Religion: background of gender hierarchy in, 4; nineteenth-century conflict with science, 49

Reproductive system, female, psychological theories about link to intellect of, 64

Retarded children: in clinical psychology, 91; Hollingworth studies of sex of, 92

Rheingold, Joseph: on mothers and war, 249; on noxious mothering, 244

Ricardo's iron law of wages, 53

Richardson, influence on German literature of, 29

Romanes, George, and maternal instinct, 261

Rosaldo, Michelle, and division of labor by sex, 3

Rosen, Ephraim, and gender identity, 185

Rossi, Alice: motherhood theory of, 267; on sex differences, 157

Rousseau, Jean Jacques: and influence of his views of childhood, 229; misogyny of, 65

Rush, Dr. Benjamin, and Conservation of Force, 56

Russell, Bertrand, Watson's influence on, 126

Sanford, Nevitt: hypermasculinity theory and, 216; MF studies by, 187; sexuality concepts of, 189; study of sex-role identity, 216

Schneider, G. H., on maternal instinct, 157

Schoff, Mrs. Frederic, on family life, 232

Schreiber, Olive, influence on Karl Pearson, 54

Science: importance on Eugenia of, 106; McDougall on, 108; and religion, 49; and social and political change, 114

Scientists and female inferiority, 5

Seder, M. A., and SVIB, 174

Seneca Falls "Declaration of Sentiment and Resolutions," 20, 45

Separate Spheres Doctrine of (Watson), 146, 149

Sex: correlation of occupations and SVIB, 173; differences and MF scores, 168, 169; differences, nineteenth-century measurements of, 156; differences in parenting behavior, 268; labor division by and subordination of women, 3; Lévi-Strauss and division of labor by, 2; as masculine domain, 58; mental traits of, 158; and normative personality styles, 207; of retardates, Hollingworth study of, 92; typing and psychology, 209; *see also* Gender; Sexes; Sex Roles; Sexual; Sexuality

Sex and Personality: 207; homosexual studies in, 210

Sex and Temperament in Three Primitive Societies, 211; Terman reaction to, 166

Sexes: nineteenth-century position of, 40; variability studies of, 92; Victorian dichotomy of, 45

Sex role: concepts, prevalence of, 67; identification and MF, 214; identity, Sanford study of, 217; measures in maternal employment research, 305; Parsons' study of strain, 192, 193; problems of black males, 218, 219

Sex roles, Victorian: American, 41; and Conservation of Force, 57; influence on psychology of, 39

Sexual: abstinence in Victorian marriage, 59; distinctions in nineteenth century, 42; division, Watson, 146; frustration and psychic birth control, 69; ideas of Freud, 58; nature of temperament, 166; repression in nineteenth century, 57; segregation in American labor force, 16; *see also* Sex; Sexuality

Sexuality: and child development, concepts, Sanford, 188; as disease, 66; in eighteenth century, 57; female, attacks on, 60; female, ideas about, 17, 20; female, and maternal instinct, 260; Freud and, 71, 238; and insanity, 62; male, Victorian ideas about, 66; and marriage, 20; and sublimation, 66; Victorian ideas about, 58; *see also* Sex; Sexual

"Should a Child Have More Than One Mother?", 109

Skinner, B. F., ideas of, 97

Skull capacity, Alice Lee studies of female, 54

Social: activism and female liberation, 64; benefits of psychology, 115; change, mothers and, 249; change and science, 114; change and social scientists, 115; class and psychic birth control, 67; classes, Watson on separate spheres for, 149; conditions and work of 1920s psychologists, 99; control, Watson theories of, 142, 143; Darwinism, importance of, 55; engineer, role of, 115; influence, psychology as, 39; life, controlling and adjusting through psychology, 116; problems, Cattell on, 115; productivity, Watson's faith in, 141; psychology, Allport's theory of, 117; psychology, family in, 117; reform, Lippmann on, 115; reform movement, feminism as, 64; reform proposals of Hall, 105; reform/welfare system and Watson, 145; relations, recommendations for family, 98; science and evolutionary theory, link between, 54; science, Malthus' influence on, 53; scientists, Darwinism among, 49, 50; scientists and social change, 115; values, of Parsons, 194; welfare and psychologists, 113; work and psychology, relationship of, 116

Social Psychology, 116

Socialization and mothers, 117

Society: egalitarian, female privileges in, 3; and MF norms, 168; pragmatic, Watson on, 147, 148; twentieth-century changes in, 296

Society for Experimental Psychology, female exclusion from, 65

Sons, maternal employment effect on, 298, 305

Spence, Janet, MF scale of, 197

Spencer, Herbert: ideas about women of, 51; Life Force theory of, 64; maternal instinct and, 359, 360

Spermatic economy, Victorian male, 66

Spitz, Réné, on noxious mothering and infants, 244

Spock, Benjamin, on parenting, 289

Stanford-Binet test, Terman's creation of, 159

Stanton, Elizabeth Cady, Seneca Falls Resolution and, 45

Stapp, Joy, MF scale of, 197

Stecher, Edward, masculinity feelings and, 212

Stodtbeck, Fred, MF classification by, 190; sex-role identity and, 217

Strong-Campbell Interest Inventory, 174

Strong, Edward K., MF studies by, 172

Strong Vocational Interest Block, see SVIB

Studies in the Nature of Character, 209

"Subjugation of Women, The," 55

Sublimation and sexuality, 66

Subordination of women: and division of labor by sex, 2, 3, 13, 16; and educational deprivation, 40; religious basis for, 4; and Western law, 12

Suffrage, female: Darwinism and, 52; liquor industry attacks on, 47

"Survival of the fittest," implications of, 50

SVIB: description of, 172; and female vocational guidance, 174; as MF test, 172; and sex correlation of occupations, 173

Swanson, Guy: MF studies by, 189; and sex-role identity, 217

Tarde, Gabriel, work of, 100

Tavistock Clinic, 245

Taylor, Frederick: ideas of, 141; and Watson, similarities between, 141

Temperament, sexual nature of, 166

Terman, Lewis: career of, 159; on heredity, 159; inversion scale of, 166; MF correlation problems of, 164; MF evaluation by, 199; MF research by, 158; MF test, 160; and Miles, homosexuality theory of, 210; -Miles Paradigm, 184; and MSRI theory, 207; on racial equality, 159; Stanford-Binet test creation by, 159

Testing: mental, Hollingsworth and, 91; psychological, innovation of, 159

Theory: construction, metatheoretical context of, 277; of Evolution and nature of men and women, 48; see also Charles Darwin; Darwinism

Their Mothers' Sons, 212

Thinking, critical necessity in psychology for, 119

Thompson, Helen: career of, 77; see also Helen Thompson Woolley

Thorndike, Edward: on animal intelligence, 85; on female education, 83, 84; on human intelligence, 86; on male genius, 93

Titchener misogyny of, 65

Tocqueville, Alexis de, on American women, 43

True Woman, virtues of, 43

True Womanhood, Cult of, 1, 17

Twenties: family problems during, 118; psychologists' ideal family of, 97; psychologists, social conditions and work of, 99; role of psychologists during, 113

Twentieth century: childrearing theories during, 235; occupational problems of women during, 234; social changes during, 296

Unconscious: and conscious MF, classification using, 187; feminine identity hypothesis, 218; feminine identity in men, description of, 189; feminity, Kraugh measurement of, 186

United States, gender-based division of labor in, 16

University of Chicago contributions to feminism, 77

Urbanization, effect on women of, 16, 41

Uterus, male prejudice against, 89

Utopia, Watson's view of, 109, 110, 111, 146

Utopian: family schemes of 1920s, 98; thinking and psychologists, 100

Van de Castle, and college students' dreams, 186

Variability, female, Hollingworth's research on, 93; among sexes, studies of, 92

Venereal disease, psychic birth control and risk of, 69

Victorian: America, demographic revolution in, 58; America, psychic birth control in, 57; America, sex roles in, 41; dichotomy of sexes, 45; era, ideas about women in, 2; era, medical castration in, 63; female, fear of contraception of, 63; ideas on male sexuality, 66; ideas on masturbation, 66; ideas on sexuality, 58; influence on CPI, 184; male, spermatic economy of, 66; marriage, abstinence in, 59; sex-role ideology, influence on psychology of, 39; sex roles and Conservation of Force, 57

Vienna Circle and logical positivism, 279

"Vindication of the Rights of Women," 41

Violence: male, interpretation of, 215

Visual-spatial stimuli and women, 185

Vocational guidance of females and SVIB, 174

Voluntary Motherhood movement, 59

Wages: Conservation of, Theory of, 56; Ricardo's iron law of, 53

War and motherhood, 249

Ward, Lester Frank, on female intelligence, 87

WASP community and contraception, 62

Watson, John B: antihereditarianism of, 136, 137; attitude to women of, 236; on behavior, 111; and behaviorism, 109, 128, 134, 135; career of, 109; childrearing views of, 128, 236; conflicting roles of, 144; on courts, 145; developmental determinism of, 137; distrust of moralists, 140; and early impact assumption, 287; on education, 145; elitist role of, 142; espousal of individualism and social productivity, 141; as experimentalist and expert, 139; faith in cultural evolution, 141; on family, 129, 134; family utopian scheme of, 98; guidance to women by, 133, 134; influence on Bertrand Russell, 126; influence on child psychology, 127; McDougall and Hall, comparison of, 112; marriage ideas of, 11, 130, 131; motherhood solutions of, 139; parental evaluation by, 129; poor people's reaction to, 148; popularity of, 127, 133, 136, 138; on pragmatic society, 147, 148; on psychological methodology, 140; psychological theory of, 135; on racial inferiority of blacks, 136; self-promotion by, 138; separate spheres doctrine of, 146; on sexual division, 146; social context of views of, 127; on social control, 142, 143; and social reform/welfare system, 145; solutions proposed by, 130; study of views of, 127; subject matter of studies of, 132; and Taylor, similarities between, 141; training recommendations of, 146; utopian community of, 146; variation in interpretations of, 148; view of behaviorist, 140; view of middle-class family, 144; on women, 129; working-class reaction to, 148; writings of, 128, 131, 135; see also Behavior; Behaviorism; Behaviorist

Watson, Maud: and child guidance movement, 239

"Weakness of Women, The," 147

Welfare system and Watson, 145

Western: law and female subordination, 12; society and women, characteristics of, 4; tradition of female inferiority, 2

"What About Your Child?", 129, 148

White, Burton, on motherhood, 247

White Collar: The American Middle Classes, 212

Whyte, W. F., sociological study of men by, 213

Wife, husband's supremacy over, 12

Wife beating, legalisms of, 48

Wilson, Edmund, work of, 87

Winnicott, D. W., on motherhood, 246

Wissler, Clark, work of, 84, 85, 87

Wollstonecraft, Mary, writing of, 41

Womanhood: Cult of True, 1, 17; *see also* Female, Mother, Women

Women: AIAS and, 171; American, de Tocqueville on, 43; in Atlantis, description of, 102; biological inferiority of and Darwinism, 49, 50; blaming in psychology, 45; and characteristics of Western society, 4; current cultural notions about, 250; Darwin's ideas about, 5; educated, and social activism, 64; in experimental psychology, Hollingworth on, 94; doctoral students at Columbia University, 81, 82; Freud's attitude toward, 1, 5, 238; in German Classicism, 34; in German Enlightenment, 26; Goethe's treatment of, 34; Hall on, 104; and heredity, Darwin on education of, 51; history and the psychology of, 1; immorality interests' attacks on suffrage for, 47; Industrial Revolution's effect on, 14, 16, 41; influence of nineteenth-century ideas about, 1; masculine, theory of, 66; MMPI validity for, 181; moral role in community of, 228; moral superiority theory, 43, 45, 46, 65; motherhood effect on, 251; nineteenth-century attitudes toward, 17; occupational problems in twentieth century of, 234; as patrons of learning, 9, 10; psychologists, impact on psychology of, 95; Spencer's ideas about, 51; subordination of and division of labor by sex, 3; suffrage for, Darwinism and, 52; in Utopia, 110; and visual-spatial stimuli, 185; Watson's guidance to, 133, 134; Watson's ideas on, 127, 129, 236; as Watson study subject, 133; *see also* Female; Mother; Womanhood

"Women's Mission," 45

Woodworth, Robert, work of: 84, 86

Woolley, Helen Thompson, impact of work of, 79; on sex differences, 156; and visual-spatial stimuli, 185; *see also* Helen Thompson

Word Association Test, 161

Working mothers, implications of, 251; *see also* Mother(s)

World War II: effect on male-female relationships, 212; effect on motherhood, 242; and paternal absences, 219

Yale Clinic of Child Development, work at, 240

Zeditch, Morris Jr., family and MF studies by, 193

Zimmerman, Wayne, and factor analysis, 174

ABOUT THE CONTRIBUTORS

Suzanne Benack is Assistant Professor of Psychology, Union College, Schenectady, New York.

Susan Contratto is in private practice in clinical psychology, Ann Arbor, Michigan.

Kenneth J. Gergen is Professor of Psychology, Swarthmore College, Swarthmore, Pennsylvania.

Barbara J. Harris is Professor of History, Pace University, New York City.

Ben Harris is Assistant Professor of Psychology, Vassar College, Poughkeepsie, New York.

Lois Wladis Hoffman is Professor of Psychology, University of Michigan, Ann Arbor.

Miriam Lewin is Professor of Psychology, Manhattanville College, Purchase, New York.

Jill G. Morawski is Assistant Professor of Psychology at Wesleyan University, Middletown, Connecticut.

Joseph H. Pleck is Program Director, Center for Research on Women, Wellesley College, Wellesley, Massachusetts.

Rosalind Rosenberg is Assistant Professor of History, Wesleyan University, Middletown, Connecticut.

Stephanie A. Shields is Assistant Professor of Psychology, University of California, Davis.

Gabriele M. Wickert is Assistant Professor of German Language and Literature, Manhattanville College, Purchase, New York.